PEARSON

We work with leading authors to develop the strongest
educational materials in study skills, bringing cutting-edge
thinking and best learning practice to a global market.

Under a range of well-known imprints, including Prentice Hall,
we craft high-quality print and electronic publications that
help readers to understand and apply their content, whether
studying or at work.

To find out more about the complete range of our
publishing, please visit us on the World Wide Web at:
www.pearsoned.co.uk

STUDY SKILLS FOR
INTERNATIONAL STUDENTS

Kathleen McMillan and
Jonathan Weyers

Prentice Hall
is an Imprint of

Harlow, England • London • New York • Boston • San Francisco • Toronto
Sydney • Tokyo • Singapore • Hong Kong • Seoul • Taipei • New Delhi
Cape Town • Madrid • Mexico City • Amsterdam • Munich • Paris • Milan

Pearson Education Limited

Edinburgh Gate
Harlow
Essex CM20 2JE
England

and Associated Companies throughout the world

Visit us on the World Wide Web at:
www.pearsoned.co.uk

First published 2011

© Pearson Education Limited 2011

ISBN 978-0-273-73115-3

British Library Cataloguing-in-Publication Data
A catalogue record for this book is available from the British Library

Library of Congress Cataloging-in-Publication Data
McMillan, Kathleen.
  Study skills for international students / Kathleen McMillan and Jonathan Weyers.
    p. cm.
  Includes bibliographical references and index.
  ISBN 978-0-273-73115-3 (pbk.)
  1. Study skills. 2. Students, Foreign – Great Britain. 3. College student orientation –
Great Britain. I. Weyers, Jonathan. II. Title.
  LB2395.M4443 2011
  378.1'70281—dc22

                                                            2010026567

10 9 8 7 6 5 4 3 2 1
15 14 13 12 11

Typeset in 9/12pt ITC Interstate Light by 35
Printed and bound in Great Britain by Henry Ling Ltd. at the Dorset Press, Dorchester, Dorset

Contents

About the authors

Kathleen McMillan is Academic Skills Advisor and Senior Lecturer, University of Dundee.

Jonathan Weyers is Director of Quality Assurance, University of Dundee.

This book represents a synthesis based on over 60 years of combined teaching experience. Between us, we've taught at all levels – including middle school, upper school, further education, undergraduate, postgraduate and within academic staff development. We've supported students in a wide range of topics – from biology to dentistry; architecture to orthopaedic surgery; history to social work, information and communication technology to English as a foreign language.

We've taken a special interest in the needs of international students and have tutored many individual students on a one-to-one basis and led classes for groups from many countries. One of us (KMM) has carried out research on the academic needs of students of different ethnic origins and has extensive experience organising and delivering academic induction activities for both international and home-based undergraduate and postgraduate students.

Over the years, we've presented hundreds of tutorials and lectures and run many workshops and practicals using a range of techniques, including team-teaching alongside colleagues and one-to-one tuition. Above all, we've spoken to countless students, both individually and in focus groups, consulted with fellow academics about core skills that underpin a wide range of disciplines, and have observed at close quarters our own children going through the university system. We have read widely and tested many ideas. This book is a distillation of all the best tips and techniques we've come across or have developed ourselves.

Preface

Welcome to *Study Skills for International Students*. We're delighted that you've chosen this book and we'd like to think it's because it promises insight into the UK university experience and gives you plenty of useful tips to help you settle into the rhythms of university life and learning in a new country.

Whatever your age, experience and background, learning at a UK university marks an exciting new phase in your life – a time of anticipation and of new challenges. Very quickly you'll be faced with sorting out your life as a student, attending your first lectures or seminars, getting logged on to the university computer system, email and e-learning tools. There will be a lot of information to gather, filter and make into some sort of sense. Meantime you'll be meeting new people of different ages and outlooks who are in exactly the same position. It's a stimulating but demanding time. For many, there will be a need to become immersed in another language community and understand the jargon of UK higher education. Learning at university in the UK builds on one basic notion: that students, regardless of age or experience, are good at organising themselves and so will quickly conform to the standards that the university community expects. As professional academics we know that this is not achieved quite as quickly as everyone – staff, students (and their families) – might wish, partly because there is so much to learn how to do.

This book is about helping you as an international student gain and develop the skills, attributes and knowledge that universities require. Of course, you will already have some of these skills – from school, from college, from employment and even just from life in general – but this book takes you further. In Toolkits A and B, we begin with some tips and insights about what coming to university in the UK involves and then take you through the very first days when you're coming to terms with your new environment and deciding how you're going to organise your new life.

Then we move into the kinds of things that you'll need to be able to do as your course gets underway. This all comes into Toolkit C: 'Developing your learning skills for the UK context' – useful tips on practical things such as listening and taking notes in lectures, using the library, engaging with e-learning and thinking critically. As your course gathers pace, you'll find that you're having to tackle all sorts of writing assignments and in Toolkit D, 'Improving your academic writing', you'll find valuable suggestions to guide you from planning to submission, so that your writing is well-developed and meets the expected academic requirements.

As you work your way through your first semester, you'll find that you encounter all sorts of different kinds of assessment – in lab practicals, in debates, in tests and other written submissions. Toolkit E, 'Performing well in course assessments', gives you some insights as to how these assessments work and how you can gain the best marks possible. Finally, we come to Toolkit F, 'Succeeding in exams', which gives you tried-and-tested tips from revision technique to coping with exam nerves.

We had many kinds of students in mind when we decided to write this text, both undergraduates and postgraduates, experienced English speakers and novices, those with knowledge of European educational traditions and those for whom this is an unfamiliar notion. We hope that it will meet your personal needs – regardless of your experience and background. We've tried to remain faithful to the idea that this book is one that you can dip into in time of need. We've tried to evolve a layout that makes information easy to find – the 'Guided tour' in Chapter 1 illustrates how the design works.

We wish you the best of times at university in the UK and hope that the tips we have collated will help you succeed in all you do, academically and socially, tackle assignments with confidence and produce better results. Despite all the advice given here, we acknowledge that there is always an element of luck in any good performance, and we hope you get this when and if required. We'd be delighted to hear your opinion of the book, any suggestions you have for additions and improvements, and especially if you feel that it has made a positive difference to the way you study and approach university life.

Kathleen McMillan and Jonathan Weyers
University of Dundee

Acknowledgements

We would like to offer sincere thanks to the many people who have influenced us and contributed in one way or another to the production of this book.

Countless students over the years have helped us to test our ideas. As we produced drafts of chapters, the following students made specific comments either as individuals or as members of focus groups: Scott Allardice, Mariam Azhar, Eleanor Dempsey, Sandie Ferrens, Daniel Harper, Wai Lee, Kara McAuley, Katherine McBay, Leanne Murphy and David Wallace. Our PREP resit summer school students also provided valuable feedback on the revision and exam tips.

We are grateful to the following University of Dundee colleagues and others who collaborated directly or indirectly: Margaret Adamson, Michael Allardice, John Berridge, Richard Campbell, Kate Christie, Neil Fleming, Margaret Forrest, Anne-Marie Greenhill, Jane Illés, Andy Jackson, Allan Jones, Lorna Jones, Neale Laker, Angela McDonald, Christine Milburn, Kirsty Millar, Eric Monaghan, Dave Murie, Julie Naismith, Fiona O'Donnell, Richard Parsons, Neil Paterson, Jane Prior, Mhairi Robb, Anne Scott, Dorothy Smith, Eric Smith, Gordon Spark, Karen Stulka, David Walker, Lorraine Walsh, Amanda Whitehead, Will Whitfield, David Wishart, Hilary-Kay Young and the late Neil Glen. We are indebted to the support and interest of the Royal Literary Fund and particularly the RLF Writing Fellows in our university, distinguished authors in their own right, who have given wise words of counsel – Bill Kirton, Brian Callison, Jonathan Falla, Tracey Herd and Gordon Meade. Also, we acknowledge those at other universities who have helped frame our thoughts, especially our good friends Rob Reed, Nicki Hedge and Esther Daborn, as well as the membership of the Scottish Effective Learning Advisors who work so energetically to help students to develop the key skills that are addressed in this book.

We owe a special debt to the senior colleagues who encouraged various projects that contributed to this book, and who allowed us the freedom to pursue this avenue of scholarship, especially Robin Adamson, James Calderhead, Chris Carter, Alan Davidson, Ian Francis, Rod Herbert, Eric Monaghan and David Swinfen.

At Pearson Education, we have had excellent support and advice, especially from Katy Robinson, Steve Temblett, Simon Lake, Elizabeth Wright, Joan Dale Lace and Alex Seabrook.

Finally, we would like to say thanks to our long-suffering but nevertheless enthusiastic families: Derek, Keith, Fiona and Tom; and Mary, Paul and James, all of whom helped in various capacities.

1 Using this book

How to get the most from *Study Skills for International Students*

This text is targeted at international students visiting the UK to study within the higher education system. You will gain more from the book if you understand the text's structure and what each component part aims to achieve. This chapter provides this information and it is strongly recommended that you read this material before looking at the rest of the book.

Key topics:
→ The book's layout
→ Guided tour

Essential vocabulary
Commentary   Glossary   Guidance   Jargon   Navigation   Planner   Practical tip

Understanding the way this book is constructed will help you get the most from it. First, take a look at the contents listing (pp. v–vii). This will show you that the book has 57 chapters arranged within six 'toolkits'. Each chapter will provide you with guidance and tips for a specific event or skill. The toolkits cover student life from entry into university until final exams. The aim is to provide bite-sized discussions of each topic that allow you to find and digest relevant material as easily as possible.

→ The book's layout

At the start of each chapter, there is a panel giving information about what you can learn and how the content is structured. The *Essential vocabulary* listing here notes specific educational terms used in the chapter and a selection of potentially unfamiliar words which might need definition. A full explanation of the meaning of each term is provided in the *Glossary of key terms* at the end of the book.

The main text starts with a brief introduction to the topics covered, then the core material, divided into appropriate sections. Additional tips, definitions, examples and illustrations are provided in three different types of tip boxes shown on p. 3. Some of these points are repeated in different chapters where this is justified on grounds of relevance, bearing in mind that the book is likely to be consulted on a chapter-by-chapter basis.

The core material in each chapter is as concise and straightforward as possible. It is laid out in numbered lists and bullet points wherever appropriate. Figures and tables are used to provide examples and to explore into 'deeper' or more detailed issues separately from the main text. Blank versions of some tables are included in the Appendix, in case you may wish to use these. Copyright on these forms is waived, so you can copy them for personal use as required.

Many cross-references to other chapters (**Ch**) have been included to avoid duplication of material and thereby save space. Near to the end of each chapter there is a set of practical tips that supplements the advice mentioned within the text. There follows a 'Useful phrases' section which includes a selection of spoken and written English expressions used in specific situations. The text references within chapters are collated on pp. 462–3.

You should treat all these elements as items on a menu from which you can select suitable ideas and approaches. Our advice is to adopt those you feel will fit with your needs and personality, but at the same time we would encourage you to experiment. If you are already using some of the tips successfully, take confidence from the fact that you are probably doing the right thing. If ideas are new, please keep an open mind. Confronted with lack of success, many students simply try harder with a set of failed techniques, when a complete overhaul of their approach to learning may be required.

Within the 'And now . . .' section, a set of further activities is suggested if you wish to take the content further in your day-to-day activities. Many of these are designed to promote reflection and deeper thinking about the issues covered, whereas others invite you to test out some of the techniques and ideas that have been discussed.

Many of the tips and ideas that you will find in *Study Skills for International Students* are integrated, albeit in slightly different formats, into *The Smarter Student Planner* which has been designed to help you to develop the key skills of problem-solving, action planning, reflection and lateral thinking by providing an easy to follow monthly planner along with week-at-a-glance space for all your appointments and assignments. It includes additional weekly and monthly tips that relate to the rhythms of the university year and supports your learning with a number of copyright-free templates for exam revision. The planner also provides information on grammar, spelling and punctuation as well as notes on basic maths and numeracy. These all provide quick access to reassuring information that you may need as you complete assessed work.

The following icons are used to help you to find your way around the tips and suggestions:

 Smart tip boxes emphasise key advice to ensure you adopt a successful approach.

 Information boxes like this provide additional information, such as useful definitions or examples.

 Query boxes raise questions for you to consider about your personal approach to the topic.

 Cultural awareness tips highlight areas where you should be aware of aspects of study in the UK that are especially important to understand as an international student.

 At the end of each chapter, there's a **Practical tips** section with additional tips. You should regard this as a menu from which to select the ideas that appeal to you and your learning personality.

 Useful language for . . . provides helpful language structures relating to the context of each chapter.

 Finally, the **And now . . .** section provides three suggestions that you could consider as ideas to take further.

TOOLKIT B
MANAGING YOURSELF IN THE UK

8 **Graduate skills and attributes:** how to communicate what you will gain from being at university

9 **Time management:** how to organise your activities effectively

10 **Budgeting and banking:** how to organise your finances in the UK

11 **Social life at university:** how to develop and maintain personal connections

12 **Keeping a good work–life balance:** how non-study activities can contribute to your well-being

Navigation and setting the scene
The book is divided into six toolkits, each with a contents list to help you navigate around the book.

Chapter opening pages provide an introduction to what you can learn, how the chapter is structured, and an introduction to key terms introduced in the chapter.

Additional tips, definitions, examples and illustrations are provided in 'Tips' boxes, allowing you to absorb supplementary information as directly as possible.

---

7 | **Getting organised**

How to interact with the university and prepare for study
Universities are large organisations, frequently with long traditions that have evolved over many generations. As an international student, you may not be aware of relevant customs and expectations. This chapter outlines ways in which you can prepare yourself so that you have a good start to your studies.

Key topics:
→ Communicating with the institution
→ Organising yourself
→ Developing your academic skills
→ Organising yourself for study
→ Looking after yourself

Essential vocabulary
Arts subjects   College   Counselling   Drop-in facility   Ethical   Faculty
Matriculation   PowerPoint   Reflect   Research postgraduate   School
Science subjects   Taught postgraduate   Virtual learning environment (VLE)

The academic community of a university consists not only of the lecturing staff who teach you, but also administrators, cleaners, janitors, secretaries, technicians, and a range of specialist staff who work behind the scenes. You will interact with many of these people as you study, maintain yourself and socialise. They will provide services for you but will expect you to do certain things to keep the system running smoothly. It will help you to understand their expectations and to try your best to meet these.

→ Communicating with the institution
The university machinery of administration is not really as complex as it sometimes seems. Your main role is to communicate with it effectively, for example by:

● matriculating (registering/enrolling) on the date and at the time given in your letter of acceptance;

● accessing your university email account regularly and responding to communications from staff members. Some departments will only communicate on coursework and routine matters through your university email account;

Email accounts `smart tip`
It makes sense to transfer all your emails to the account assigned to you at university. This will make it easier for you to check for messages from staff since much of the ongoing course information will be distributed via email.

54   TOOLKIT A   Adapting to a new educational experience

The time limitation in exams means you will need to work quickly when planning – either use a spider diagram/mind map or linear notes to generate ideas relevant to the question (**Ch 16**). From this, decide on a structure, for example, by numbering the order in which you intend to follow in your answer. This approach will help you to think laterally as well as in a linear manner – important, so that you generate all the points relevant to your answer. As discussed in **Ch 29**, you should probably think in terms of three basic components:

- **The introduction**: states briefly what your answer will say, sets the context and gives an insight as to how you intend to approach the topic.
- **The main body**: presents the information, the argument or key points of your response.
- **The conclusion**: sums up the answer as stated, reinforces the position outlined in the introduction, and puts the whole answer into a wider context.

? Can I make notes and plans in exam books?

It is perfectly acceptable practice to make notes in the exam answer booklet; however, you should always score through them before you submit the answer paper. A single diagonal line will suffice. Sometimes your plan may be used by the examiner to cross-check details of your answer (but do not count on this).

Tips for writing these elements are provided in **Ch 29**, while potential ways of organising the main body of essay-style assignments are considered in **Ch 30**. It is also important to consider the marking criteria in relation to your potential answer. It may be worth reviewing these before you start to write a coursework essay or as you prepare for exams. These criteria should be published in the module handbook. Table 38.2 provides a useful checklist in relation to presentation (**Ch 34**), structure (**Ch 30**) and content (**Chs 21, 23** and **28**).

Approaching essay-style assessments when English is not your first language

This can be a difficult area for some international students; you may be anxious and feel under time pressure.

- **Do your preparation** – when revising, think about ways you could phrase parts of answers that include concepts, ideas or fact. Write these key phrases down and practise using them. Learn all the specialist vocabulary you expect to use.
- **Keep things simple** – use short, uncomplicated sentence structures, and build your answer from these elements. You will not lose marks for simplicity, but you will probably lose marks if you attempt lengthy complex sentences that are more likely to contain errors.
- **Focus on understanding your topic fully** – especially in exams this will allow you to answer any type of question and will prove a far better strategy than memorising a 'prepared' answer ('question spotting', p. 433) which is unlikely to be relevant to the actual question on the exam paper.

318   TOOLKIT E Performing well in course assessments

Chapter cross-referencing is highlighted in the main text to avoid duplication and guide you to key material common to several subjects.

Examples and self-assessment activities allow you to delve deeper into particular issues separately from the main text.

Cultural awareness tips provide information and explanation to assist you to settle into your UK university environment.

---

schedules. If you will have to undertake such trips regularly, make sure that you know the timetable as well as the pick-up and drop-off points.

✔ Practical tips for getting to know your campus and university town

Plan your days ahead. Before you get to know your routine and the tracks you'll need to make between teaching venues, use your street map and the campus map to work out the shortest routes in advance.

Always carry your matriculation (ID) card when you are on campus. This is usually required for access to buildings and facilities, such as the library and students' union.

Take care over personal safety. Exploring a new town or city is interesting, but it is better to do this in company, particularly at night. Students' unions often run late-night bus services so that it should not be necessary to walk alone at night. If you feel a personal alarm would make you feel safer, these are normally sold in campus shops such as those run by students' unions.

💬 Useful language for . . . finding your way around campus

Most fellow students will be happy to help you. Look for people who seem at ease or to know where they are going. However, avoid those obviously in a rush to a lecture, tutorial or lab. At night, take care who you select to approach.

Context: asking for directions

Excuse me. I wonder if you could help me? I'm trying to find [name of place]. I'm not sure where I am on this map. Could you show me how to get there on the map, please?

Hi! Do you know where matriculation is?

Hi! I need to get to [name of building or lecture theatre]. Do you know where it is from here?

GO And now . . .

6.1 Visit university websites, including international student and Freshers' Welcome Week areas, and watch online video tours of the campus. These will help you feel more at home when you eventually move there.

6.2 Ask someone you know who is already a student to show you around when you arrive. They'll know all the shortcuts on the campus and be able to offer useful advice.

6.3 During Freshers' Welcome Week, time your journeys. This will allow you to work out, for example, when you'll need to set your alarm and get up, when you need to leave home, or whether you have time for a snack or coffee between venues.

6 Campus orientation   53

Practical tips sections at the end of each chapter supplement the information given in the chapter, and reinforce your understanding.

Useful language for . . . sections give you some sample sentences that will help you to speak about things in particular contexts.

'And now . . .' sections at the end of each chapter suggest a set of activities that will allow you to take what you have learnt further in your day-to-day activities.

Useful language for . . . asking for guidance

Context: it is acceptable to approach academic staff and tutors with questions like these, having first made sure that the person is available to speak with you. The politeness signified by the use of the words 'please' and 'thank you' is important in the UK when requesting help, even if you feel you should expect this support as part of your tuition.

'I don't understand the tip given on this page – please could you explain it to me?'

'This way of working is very different to what we do in [your home country]. I think I will need to adapt my approach. Please can you help me with the main points I will need to consider?'

'Thank you very much for your help. It will be very useful.'

(GO) And now . . .

Enjoy the rest of the book!

ADAPTING TO A NEW EDUCATIONAL EXPERIENCE

2 Understanding the UK educational system

How to adjust to the education system you are about to enter

If you understand some of the basic aspects of the UK educational system, this will allow you to compare the patterns of learning in your own country with those of the British system. It will also ensure that you are aware of the learning history of the UK students who might study alongside you and what staff will expect of all students. This awareness will help you make the most of your studies in the UK.

Key topics:
→ Early learning experiences in the UK
→ Secondary school and assessment in later school years in the UK
→ The UK university system
→ Recognising your new learning challenges

Essential vocabulary
**Ancient universities   Articulation   Further Education (FE) college
Higher education   Peer pressure   Polytechnic   Post-'92 universities
Primary school   Red-brick universities   Reflect   Russell Group universities
Secondary school**

If you are to study effectively in the UK, or indeed any other country apart from your own, then it is helpful to understand a little of how 'home' students have acquired their learning before they enter university. This will help you to recognise the qualities staff will expect all new students to demonstrate.

Table 2.1 provides a simple outline of the different stages and types of learning provision in the UK. There are fundamental differences across the UK – education in England and Wales is administered in one way, with Northern Ireland following similar patterns, and Scotland operates under a separate system. Nevertheless, there are some shared features and this table gives you an overview of the whole picture.

→ Early learning experiences in the UK

Schooling approaches in pupils' earlier years differ across the country but generally primary school learning is based on group work and learning by doing. This means that practical activities are based on a common theme or context. Pupils apply a range of skills and learning disciplines to the topic under study – for example, a study on 'Foods of the World' would include aspects of geography, history, mathematics, language, and the specific sciences of chemistry, biology, zoology and botany. The aim is to

Table 2.1 Summary of the educational systems operating in the UK. Note that there are fundamental differences within the UK, that is, between Scotland and the broadly similar systems in England, Wales and Northern Ireland.

The State System – School levels				
Stage of schooling	Age range	Status	Terminology	Assessment
Nursery	3–5 years	Optional (free)	Nursery School	None
Primary – entry generally based on catchment area	5–11/12 years	Compulsory (free)	Lower School Primary School	Continuous assessment
Secondary – entry generally based on catchment area	11/12–16 years	Compulsory (free)	Comprehensive Middle/Upper School	State examinations
		Compulsory (ability tested)	Grammar School	State examinations
Sixth Year/ Sixth-form college	16–18/19 years	Voluntary post-compulsory	Upper School/ Sixth-form College	State examinations/ International Baccalaureate (IB)
Independent Private School System – sometimes called 'Public Schools' (for historical reasons)				
Stage of schooling	Age range	Status	Terminology	Assessment
Nursery	3 months– 5 years	Fee-paying (Parental choice)	Nursery/ kindergarten	None
Preparatory – entry by examination from waiting list	5/7–11/12 years	Fee-paying (Parental choice)	Prep School	Internal qualifying examinations
Secondary – entry by examination	11/12–18/19 years	Fee-paying (Parental choice)	Public School (entry by examination and/or waiting list)	State examinations/ International Baccalaureate (IB)
		Fee-paying (Parental choice)	Grammar School	State examinations/ International Baccalaureate (IB)
Post-school education				
Stage of schooling	Age range	Status	Terminology/ features	Assessment
Further Education College	Post-16 years no age limit (undergraduate courses) Open admission	Various funding models depending on location – courses tend to be vocational and practical	FE College. State-funded through Funding Council	National examinations at Certificate, Diploma or Degree level
University – admission depends on meeting entry requirements	Post-16 years no age limit (undergraduate and postgraduate courses)	State-funded; fees applicable but levels vary across UK for home and international students	Higher Education Institution or University. State-funded, but aided by research income various sources.	Modular study assessed by examination or course-work
Open University – admission depends on meeting entry requirements	Generally post-18 years (undergraduate/ postgraduate courses)	Fee-paying distance learning students	Open University or OU	Examinations preferred to continuous assessment
University of Buckingham	Generally post-18 years (undergraduate/ postgraduate courses)	Fee-paying – only private university in the UK	Private University	Examinations

encourage pupils to transfer skills they learn in one area to new studies and topics. In addition, there are compulsory elements of learning in numeracy and literacy. Increasingly, there is an emphasis on social and communication skills, and most primary school pupils will use computers while studying.

→ Secondary school and assessment in later school years in the UK

At secondary school, learning is subject-based, with a general curriculum for the first two years or so, then successive specialisation, which for 'academic' pupils often focuses on either the arts or sciences. Subjects like English, Mathematics and a second language are compulsory for three or more years. The emphasis shifts through the teaching levels to assessment by public examination (for example, 'A-levels'). Pupils follow a prescribed syllabus in preparation for a standard national examination. At this stage, learning tends to focus on intensive knowledge on a limited knowledge base rather than on a broader education. In some areas of the UK, academic pupils will enter a 'sixth-form college' to prepare for later education, either at university or at a Further Education (FE) college (Table 2.1).

Exam results for each school subject are graded on a scale A (top), B, C, D and so on, and pupils with a good grouping of passes will be eligible for admission to university if they wish. To obtain good grades in school exams, pupils tend to depend on 'cramming' for the examination. There is considerable time given to revision and to doing practice examination papers; most schools run a series of 'mock' exams before the formal

How school teaching methods in the UK influence later approaches to learning

If you come from a different tradition, your natural approach to learning may differ from that of your fellow students; importantly, your tutors will expect all students to adopt this 'home' approach. Hence, you should recognise that:

- British school classrooms are less formal than those in many other countries, but more formal than in others.
- Many aspects of learning in the UK educational system are based on problem-solving, so that school pupils are required to respond to questions based on their understanding rather than simply repeating facts.
- Pupils are expected to ask questions of their teachers to confirm their understanding.
- Pupils are also encouraged to express their own opinions.
- Originality is valued and, to a certain extent, eccentricity is tolerated.

However,

- in schools, some pupils may have been influenced by the perceptions of their peers and consequently some may not wish to express opinions or contribute to discussions because they are shy, do not wish to be shown to make errors, or be identified as a 'swot'. This sort of 'peer pressure' may be something that you have experienced or noticed in your own country.

examinations. This gives pupils and their teachers the opportunity to identify weaknesses in knowledge, understanding and technique. Increasingly, coursework is included in assessment at this level, and there are usually opportunities for resubmission to take account of feedback.

Considerable support is given to pupils by teaching staff, but some parents pay for additional tutoring by private tutors outside school to help their children achieve higher grades. British school pupils are used to being monitored and directed as to what they need to learn, when and how. Generally, emphasis is on read-write approaches to learning (see **Ch 13**).

→ The UK university system

There are over 110 universities in the UK and they differ according to their age, origins and approach to teaching. Generally, students enter to study ('read') a particular degree but they are often allowed to keep their options open and change their declared course after years one or two. For most of the UK, the norm is a three-year honours degree, while the Scottish tradition is for a four-year undergraduate degree. This relates to the different ages of pupils at end-points of the secondary school systems. Note also that the undergraduate qualification in non-science subjects in England and Wales is a Bachelor of Arts (BA) while the equivalent Scottish undergraduate degree is called a Master of Arts (MA). This latter should not be confused with a Master's degree at postgraduate level.

University groupings

There are a wide range of terms that people use when categorising universities in the UK. The selected terms below are commonly used and you may see them in articles and publicity materials.

- **The 'Ancient' universities** include those created in the twelfth to sixteenth centuries. These are the Universities of Oxford, Cambridge, St Andrews, Glasgow, Aberdeen, Edinburgh, Trinity College Dublin. Dundee, because of its origins as an offshoot of St Andrews, also considers itself to be in this grouping.

- **The 'Russell Group'** - this group of 20 UK universities includes some of the Ancient universities. They formed a coalition in 1994 to represent their collective interests to Government. The 20 are the Universities of Birmingham, Bristol, Cambridge, Cardiff, Edinburgh, Glasgow, Leeds, Liverpool, Manchester, Newcastle, Nottingham, Oxford, Sheffield, Southampton and Warwick along with Imperial College London, King's College London, University College London, London School of Economics (LSE), and Queen's College Belfast.

- **The 'Red brick' universities** - six universities based in the old industrial towns of England - Universities of Birmingham, Bristol, Leeds, Liverpool, Manchester and Sheffield.

- **The 'Post-'92 institutions'** - these are institutions that were raised to university status in legislation dating from 1992. Their origins lie in the traditions of Further Education Colleges or Polytechnic Colleges. They have formed a think tank known as Million+.

Universities state minimum requirements for admission and these may vary from one subject to another and from one university to another. It is possible to enter university via the FE system, and some students may enter by routes that involve work experience, 'wider access' summer schools, student exchanges (such as the ERASMUS system within the EU/EEA) and 'articulations' with other universities and further education colleges. Nationally, over 45 per cent of UK school pupils enter university, and it is not a system intended to be based on privilege. All this means that your fellow students may come from diverse backgrounds.

The UK university learning and teaching culture (covered in Toolkits C and D) is one where a mature approach is expected and everyone is expected to contribute their ideas to discussions and play their part in all aspects of group activities – this is particularly important as many of these activities are assessed by the tutors, demonstrators and lecturers. Each student's ideas are valued, but it is important that they can support their points with sound argument and supporting evidence. In general, staff–student relationships are relatively informal and you may be surprised

Making choices – courses and universities

This book does not provide comprehensive guidance on courses and universities in the UK, but we provide here some pointers to decision-making in that area.

1. Deciding on the course of study you wish to follow
Your interest in a particular subject may relate to earlier experience, or qualifications you have obtained at school, college or university. In addition, your own career goals will contribute to your decision-making. However, as an international student, you should make sure that the course you select will allow you to follow your chosen career path. For example, if you come from outside the European Union, is a UK qualification recognised in your own country? You might need to do a supplementary course to be accepted for a post in your field in another country.

2. Choosing a UK university
Your choice of university might be dictated by a number of factors. These could include:

- the kind of course or subject you wish to study, which might narrow the choice;
- the status of the university you wish to attend and subsequently the status of the degree you hope to gain (see p. 12);
- your familiarity with a particular location or your desire to study in a particular place;
- reputation for teaching or research – of the university as a whole, a department/school, a specific group or a respected professor;
- the match between your qualifications and the entry requirements for a particular university;
- the recommendation of another person whom you know – for example, an academic or graduate who has studied in the UK.

You may find it possible to attend local university recruitment fairs in your own country. These fairs give you the opportunity to speak directly with recruitment officials from different universities. University websites will provide you with online information and web-based discussions and possibly other routes to *YouTube*-style visual presentations. It's a good idea to research a number of possible places before arriving at a decision (you may find the 'Unistats' website useful: **www.unistats.com/**).

Day-to-day etiquette when speaking to staff

You may come from an educational tradition where the role of teaching staff is based on a more formal and less interactive style of teaching. Thus, you may find it useful to be aware of certain practices that may seem strange to you. For example:

- In some disciplines, university teaching staff may introduce themselves using their first name and may expect students to call them by that name rather than by the more formal family names. This may not be the practice in your country.

- In other disciplines, there is a strict code of forms of address, thus, Professor Smith, Dr Green, Mr Brown, Mrs Black or Miss Gray or Ms White depending on their role and status within their discipline, especially so in Medicine, Sciences and Law.

Note that teaching staff usually have 'office hours' when you can speak with your lecturer or supervisor on a one-to-one basis. You may find information about staff availability in the course handbook or pinned to the tutor's office door.

by the approachability of senior staff; however, if you do not grasp something or have a problem, they will expect you to come to them: the assumption is that if you do not ask a question, then you do understand.

Assessment in UK universities (covered in detail in Toolkits E and F) is by a mix of coursework and invigilated exams. Assessments may include a formative element through tutor feedback but, in general, there is no resubmission opportunity.

→ Recognising your new learning challenges

Your academic goals will vary depending on the stage you have reached in your studies. If you are entering a UK university as an undergraduate you will not necessarily have any previous experience of university education in your own country so you will have a limited frame of reference. However, if you are intending to study in the UK as a postgraduate student you will probably have had at least one other experience of university study and a different perspective from undergraduate students.

Arriving in a new country and taking part in a different educational system necessarily presents challenges for all international students. These commonly include: speaking and writing in another language; understanding 'the system' and its jargon; and coping with new assessment methods. However, as an individual learner, there are further academic challenges you will need to acknowledge.

As an international undergraduate student, these may include learning to:

- voice your opinions within a discussion;
- respond to questions in a class learning situation;
- challenge the view of the person teaching you;
- be more critical of what you read and hear and;
- be able to present a structured argument and counter-argument defending your opinion.

In addition, you will be expected to take responsibility for organising your own learning and study time.

It will be assumed that all students, regardless of origin, will find out about and follow the administrative rules that apply to their course. Although this may seem daunting, your university will provide you with information about where to seek assistance if you are unsure of anything, often in a module, course or university handbook.

As an international postgraduate student your supervisor or course director will assume that as an undergraduate you developed the skills of analysis and critical thinking. This means that they will expect you to:

- voice your opinions within a discussion and take the initiative in such discussions;
- ask and respond to questions in a class learning situation or in individual supervision meetings;
- be more critical of what you read and hear. This means that you need to be able to select information that is relevant and contributes to your own understanding and project;
- challenge the view of the person teaching you or supervising your research;
- be able to present a structured argument and counter-argument defending your opinion.

This book contains guidance on many of the above issues, and aims to help you follow a path through UK higher education and so assist you to take full advantage of the opportunities that this learning experience can provide. One way to start this process is to reflect on your past education in the context of learning in the UK. Table 2.2 presents 14 aspects of education for you to consider.

✔ Practical tips to help you understand the UK educational system

Examine the way you were assessed during your school years. To do this you need to think about the kinds of things that were assessed and valued. For example, were pupils rewarded for learning and then reproducing facts, or were pupils rewarded for thinking through problems based on their understanding?

Consider the way that you interacted with teaching staff in your own education system. Recall how you and your peers communicated with those who taught you. For example, identify whether that relationship was informal or formal. Review how this relationship might have influenced your performance at school. Consider how the nature of your relationship with staff might be important to your new study situation in a UK university.

Think about the extent to which you received individual attention from teaching staff at earlier stages in your educational journey. The amount of special personal guidance you did or did not receive at earlier stages in your educational journey may have been a factor in your ability to think independently.

Table 2.2 What makes a UK university education different? People come to Britain from many backgrounds and with different ideas of what they might encounter. Their thoughts will be influenced by their earlier learning experiences and environments. This table outlines 14 key aspects of school, college and university learning environments in the UK, which should assist you to reflect on your own experience and expectations and gain an insight into that of your fellow UK-based students. In column 5 of the table you can note things that strike you as different and which might require you to adapt your approach while studying in the UK.

Aspect	Secondary school (UK)	Further education college (UK)	University 'higher education' (UK)	Notes related to your education in your home country
Control	• Directed by teaching staff	• Directed by lecturers and course leaders	• Directed by each college, faculty/school/department	
Attendance	• Mandatory and monitored	• By choice and monitored	• By choice and selection, with varying degrees of monitoring dependent on discipline	
Classes	• 40+ minutes per lesson	• 60+ minutes per lesson	• Multiples of one hour per lesson (typical lecture 50 minutes)	
Communication	• Daily bulletins and announcements • Noticeboards • Some electronic	• Handbooks • Classroom announcements • Noticeboards • Some electronic	• Largely electronic (email) • Web pages • Virtual learning environments (VLEs) • Electronic newsletters • Subject handbooks	
Learner's position in the class	• One of a few • Small classes • Pupils generally known by name	• One of a few • Smallish classes • Students generally known by name	• One of many • Large classes, maybe in hundreds • Students generally not known by name until later years	

TOOLKIT A Adapting to a new educational experience

Preparation required by student	• Regular homework for submission; finishing off class-work	• Regular homework for submission; finishing off class-work	• Preliminary reading, researching around topic • Largely self-directed
Teaching input	• Teacher-controlled • Feedback provided in class	• Lecturer-controlled • Feedback provided in class	• Lecturer-controlled in lectures • Less controlled in tutorials, practicals and labs • Less feedback
Teaching strategies	• New learning presented, checked, revised and reinforced • Consolidated in subsequent lessons	• Interactive dialogue in lectures	• Traditionally, little dialogue in lectures • Little time to ask/answer questions • In tutorials and labs, less formality and more interaction
Learning requirements	• Pace slow • Memorising information • One-word/short-response answers • Teacher confirms correct response	• Medium pace • Dialogue in lecture • Mainly information transfer • Opportunities for questions	• Pace very rapid • Students need to think for themselves
Writing requirements	• Repeat what has been taught in class • Little need for original thinking	• Repeat what has been taught in class • Interpret questions and respond with syllabus content	• Evidence required of syllabus knowledge and understanding • Independent analytical thinking expected, especially at higher levels • Originality expected

Table 2.2 (cont'd)

Aspect	Secondary school (UK)	Further education college (UK)	University 'higher education' (UK)	Notes related to your education in your home country
Presentational requirements	• Expressive • Often less emphasis on spelling, punctuation and grammar	• Presentation expected to be neat and correct in the main • Less monitoring of grammatical errors	• May be penalties for poor spelling, grammar and punctuation • Word-processed document may be mandatory	
Materials	• Colourful, visually explicit • Less text • Encouragement to use text word for word • Limited library facility	• Visually explicit, low on dense text • Class notes • Some use of more complex texts • Modest library facility	• Recommended textbooks • Journal resources • Web-based resources • PowerPoint slides/class notes • Extensive on-site library facilities	
Assessment procedures	• One-word/short responses • Teacher feedback expected and given	• Extensive feedback • Opportunities for multiple submissions before final assessment • strong emphasis on building confidence	• Little preliminary review at undergraduate level • One-time-only submission • Mark not negotiable • Checked electronically for plagiarism	
Examination strategy	• National level: repeat what has been taught in class in response to syllabus • Little need for original thinking • Externally moderated • Coursework forms part of assessment • No resit in same year	• Generally follow national exam format(s) • Local/national level: internally and externally moderated • Coursework forms part of assessment • Resit possibilities	• Internal examination: may contribute to final degree award • Moderated internally with oversight of external examiner • Continuous assessment may be included • Resit possibilities at early levels of study	

Recall the extent to which 'peer pressure' might have influenced your earlier learning experiences - both positively and negatively. Become aware of whether your previous learning experience dictated a strong competitive aspect or placed more emphasis on collaboration with others. Reflect on how these traits might influence your approach to learning in the UK university system.

Try to find someone from your own country who has studied abroad recently. Discuss their experiences and ask them for their recommendations and tips about studying in another country. However, remember that each individual will have a different perspective on how they met this new experience, so you need to be prepared to adopt an open mind to the personal academic journey you will begin in the UK.

 Useful language for . . . talking formally and informally

Context: you may be unsure about the level of formality that is appropriate when speaking or writing to academic and administrative staff. Generally, spoken language tends to be less formal and written communication is more formal. If in doubt, then it is best to start off using formal models of speech.

Speech - less formal register

'Professor Smith, could you please give me a further example of the application of that theory?'

'Mrs White, I would like to make an appointment to speak with Professor Smith.'

Writing (perhaps by email) - more formal register

Dear Professor Smith,

I would be grateful if you could suggest a further example of the application of [xxxx]. I would find it helpful if you could offer some recommendations of relevant references as you mentioned in your lecture. Please could I arrange an appointment to discuss these with you?

Thank you for your assistance.

Yours sincerely,

[your name]

2.1 Reflect on the education system you have experienced in your home country. Think about how classes were organised over the period of your compulsory education and consider how this has shaped the way you learn. Use Table 2.2 to help formulate your thoughts.

2.2 For further information, consult the prospectus and website for the UK university that has accepted you as a student. These sources often include quotations and anecdotes from other international students as well as guidance tips on studying as an international student. Reading this information may help you to prepare for your new experiences and answer some of your questions.

2.3 Participate in 'web chats' with other prospective students and staff from the university where you intend to study. Technology offers a range of ways of interacting with staff and other prospective students. For example, discussion boards and 'live' online conversations with staff can provide you with opportunities to obtain answers to questions that may be unique to you. If you cannot be given an immediate answer, the staff involved will be able to communicate with you directly to give you an answer offline when they have obtained the necessary information.

3 | Preparing for university in the United Kingdom

How to address the key issues that you may encounter

If you want to begin well at university in the UK, then there are several aspects of student life that you should think about first. This chapter will help you to consider some of the practical implications of moving to live and study in Britain.

Key topics:
→ Applying for a course
→ The admissions process
→ Financial matters
→ Accommodation
→ Health issues
→ Your family

Essential vocabulary
Campus   EEA   English for Academic Purposes (EAP)   EU   Frame of reference
Higher education   Pharmacy   Prospectus   Reality check   Services   Utilities

Attending university in another country is an exciting challenge. It will be exhilarating and mind-expanding, but there are many practical aspects that you need to consider so that you can study effectively. This chapter outlines some of the fundamental issues once you have decided which university is suitable for you. These include:

- the application process
- the particular admissions process that applies to international students including visa, passport and other documentary processes
- your competence in using English for academic purposes and requirements that apply for the university you have identified (if English is not your first language)
- the financial implications of studying abroad and the need to provide evidence of financial support
- accommodation
- health care
- whether it is realistic and permitted for your family to accompany you

The following sections deal with each of these areas in more detail.

Useful websites

Education UK This is the British Council site which gives useful information about study in the UK and provides useful signposts to different types of study opportunities: www.educationuk.org/pls/hot_bc/page_pls_all_homepage.

University and Colleges Admissions Service (UCAS) This site provides a step-by-step guide on how to apply to a UK university for an undergraduate course: www.ucas.com/students/wheretostart/nonukstudents/.

Unistats UCAS also organises this website which can help you make an informed choice when deciding on a university or college: **www.unistats.com/**.

UK Postgraduate Application and Statistical Service (UKPASS). This site gives information about applying for postgraduate courses, taught and research: www.ukpass.ac.uk/.

Detailed information relevant to the application process

- UK Borders Agency website for studying in the UK: **www.ind.homeoffice.gov.uk/studyingintheuk/**

- How to apply for a visa: **www.ukvisas.gov.uk/en/howtoapply/infs/inf29pbsstudent**

- Guidance leaflet on the entire process of visa application: **www.ukba.homeoffice. gov.uk/sitecontent/applicationforms/pbs/Tier4migrantguidance.pdf**

- Video on student visa application process: **www.youtube.com/watch?v=keBOZ9rFuuk**

- Visa online application form: **www.visa4uk.fco.gov.uk/**

- Register of sponsors: **www.ukba.homeoffice.gov.uk/sitecontent/documents/ employersandsponsors/pointsbasedsystem/registerofsponsorseducation/**

- Visa offer letter from sponsor (required by adult students): **www.ukba.homeoffice.gov.uk/employers/points/whatisthepointsbasedsystem/ visaletterforadultsudent/**

- Biometric Card/ID Foreign Nationals Information: **www.ukba.homeoffice.gov.uk/studyingintheuk/quickguideforstudent/ adultstudents/id-card-and-biometrics/**

- Home Office video on how biometric information is obtained: **www.youtube.com/watch?v=KTmZmk73RPY**

- Tuberculosis (TB) screening (required by students from certain countries): **www.ukvisas.gov.uk/en/howtoapply/tbscreening**

- Information about countries having reciprocal health care arrangements with the UK: **www.dh.gov.uk/prod_consum_dh/groups/dh_digitalassets/documents/digitalasset/ dh_107244.pdf**

- Information on making visa applications from your home country is available from the UKCISA site at: **www.ukcisa.org.uk/student/info_sheets/ applying_home_country.php**

- Information for students who require a Schengen visa can be found at: **http://www.theschengenoffice.com/explained/schengen_visa.html**

- Immigration Advisory Service: **www.iasuk.org/non-profit-fee-paying-service.aspx** and the Immigration Advisory Service Glasgow **www.iasuk.org/contact-us/ glasgow.aspx**

→ Applying for a course

All universities publish prospectuses which advertise their courses - available in paper form and online - and there may be different publications for undergraduate, taught postgraduate and research degrees. These will give information on application routes and the entry qualifications required. There will normally be details of an international office, with the function of helping you at every step of the application and arrival process. You should contact them at an early stage. Some universities employ local agents to facilitate applications and you may be expected to work with these people in the first instance.

For taught degrees, the application processes are centrally managed via the bodies UCAS (University Central Admission Service), for undergraduate degrees, and UKPASS (UK Postgraduate Application and Statistical Service). Postgraduate research degree applications are normally handled by each university's admissions office.

Your career plans and studying in a UK university – a reality check

The answers to the following questions should help you to define what you hope to achieve by studying abroad:

❑ What will you gain from this university learning experience?

❑ How will this contribute to your personal life and career goals?

❑ What skills will you enhance through this experience?

❑ How will the qualification you intend to achieve complement your current profile?

❑ What currency will this qualification have within your own country when you return?

❑ How much time will you need to make all the necessary arrangements to obtain an unconditional or conditional offer?

❑ How will you finance this venture?

Entry qualification requirements may vary according to courses and institutions, and specialist advisers within the admissions office will help. For some students, the existence of an articulation arrangement may assist this process. As part of your application, you will need to present certification, sometimes a portfolio of work and an indication of proficiency in English language if English is not your first language (see p. 24).

The admissions process

Specific admissions processes that apply to international students

These processes differ fundamentally depending on whether a student's home country is within the European Union (EU), the European Economic Area (EEA) or outside those areas. EU/EEA students have rights to study in the UK and essentially are treated in the same way as home students.

For those students from outside the EU/EEA, a new visa application process was put in place in early 2010 in which special procedures are administered through the UK Border Agency (UKBA). At the time of going to press, this process is known as the Points Based Immigration System (or 'Tier 4'). Since the regulations are subject to change it is advisable to obtain the most up-to-date information regarding studying in the UK from relevant areas of the UKBA website (**www.ukba.homeoffice.gov.uk/ studyingintheuk**). Similar information about immigration and visa requirements can be obtained from the Foreign and Commonwealth Office (FCO) website at **www.ukvisas.gov.uk/en**.

Providing evidence of your competence in English

As international students are often not native speakers of English, each UK university sets a scale of English language qualifications to the standard required for study at undergraduate and postgraduate levels. Note that these may not be the same; specific subjects at both levels may set particular requirements from international applicants. Achieving as high a standard as possible in English language is important to the success of your application and to your successful graduation.

Several English language testing systems are recognised by UK universities. These include the International English Language Testing System (IELTS) and the Test of English as a Foreign Language (TOEFL); the Cambridge Proficiency in English and Cambridge Advanced English. Note that some tests have particular elements related to academic English. Generally, tests gauge proficiency in the four communicative skills of listening, speaking, reading and writing. Many UK universities stipulate a score in these tests that requires a minimum level across all four skills. Test certificates, for example IELTS, are generally valid for two years, after which applicants are required to re-take the test. Some institutions and programmes offer pre-sessional English courses. However, these do not guarantee a place at that university.

Matriculation and induction

Each year, all students must register (enrol) for their course of study in a process called matriculation. You will be provided with details of where to attend and what to do with your acceptance letter. You may need to present documentary evidence as detailed above. The week before formal teaching begins there is usually a programme of activities designed to welcome new students – local, international, undergraduate and postgraduate – to their new university community. This may be known as Freshers' or Welcome Week. Universities are cosmopolitan places and this is an opportunity to meet people from all disciplines, interests and ages. There is time to explore your new 'home' and to deal with practicalities of registering with doctors, finding your own faith centre, organising your financial arrangements and personalising your accommodation. Often there are opportunities to meet informally with teaching and other key staff. This makes it additionally important that you try to organise your travel arrangements so that you arrive in time for Freshers' Week in your university. You will be able to find out more about all of these events on your university's Freshers' website. Further guidance on getting the most from these activities is provided in **Ch 5**.

Terms used at the start of your course

The following words have special meaning in relation to starting your course.

Enrolment - similar to matriculation (see below), but may also apply to individual modules.

Freshers' (Welcome) Week - a week devoted to events arranged to help new students settle in academically and socially, and fulfil certain administrative duties. In the UK, the expression 'Freshers' includes *all* new students - not just first-year undergraduates (as in the US model).

Induction - in a narrow sense, being introduced to something with guidance; in relation to starting at a university, an introduction to the campus, the staff, the teaching and assessment, the resources, the social environment and more.

Matriculation - a specific administrative event, where you 'sign up' for your programme or course.

Orientation - in a narrow sense, 'finding your way around', but often used in a wider sense more akin to induction (see above).

Registration - similar to matriculation (see above).

You may also be guided in your studies by one or more of the following, depending on the way your department/school organises these matters: Advisor of Studies, Director of Studies, Personal Tutor.

→ Financial matters

Figure 3.1 shows some of the major costs to include in your budget, and Table 3.1 provides a more detailed listing to help you predict and manage your costs. You will need to plan carefully in relation to course fees and living costs, as the amounts of money involved are large and some may need to be paid as lump sums, in advance. As course fees vary depending on the academic programme, and accommodation costs on your selection of residence or house, the best source of information is your prospective university's admissions website, or the relevant prospectus. The level of tuition fees you will need to pay will also depend on your origin - there are different levels for UK/EU(EEA) students and 'overseas students'. The distinctions are not always clear-cut and your university international office will assist you in determining your fee status.

Financial requirements for study in the UK

For non-EU/EEA students, UK immigration procedures require you to provide evidence that you have funds to support yourself (and your family, if you are accompanied) for the period of study and that you have proof of your ability to pay the tuition fees. Information about evidence of financial support can be obtained from the UK Council for International Student Affairs (UKCISA) website: **www.ukcisa.org.uk/student/index.php**

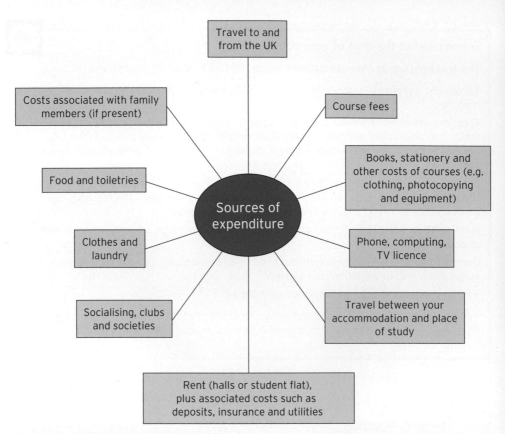

Figure 3.1 The main sources of expenditure associated with study in the UK. Use this 'mind map' (p. 205) and the more detailed listing in Table 3.1 when setting up a budget (**Ch 9**). Your university's International Office may provide estimates of some of these 'local' costs on its websites or in handbooks.

You need to be sure that you take into account costs that apply to living in a temperate climate – especially important if you come from a warm country. Thus, you may need to take into account a bigger proportion of your budget for heating and lighting than would be the norm in your own country.

Chapter 10 provides guidance on budgeting and banking matters. Most universities also have advisory services that offer advice on personal money matters. However, it is important to note that hardship funds are usually not available to international students, since one of the visa requirements is to show evidence of financial self-sufficiency. Once you have adjusted to the cost of living in the UK – that is, when you stop translating prices back into your own currency – then you will become aware of how much your allowance (stipend) will cover each week. Some universities have discount card arrangements with local and national retailers which will help you to live more economically.

Table 3.1 Expected and potentially unexpected costs of being a student in the UK.
This list is not intended to be exhaustive, but is designed to help you anticipate detailed categories of expenditure (see also Figure 3.1). Table Z.1 (p. 459) is a spreadsheet to help you manage your budget as a student.

Category of expenditure	Examples	Comments
Fees	• Tuition fees	These vary according to where you come from and where you are studying (see text)
Accommodation costs	• University residences/Hall fees • Rent/mortgage • Insurance • Utilities (gas, electricity, phone, internet)	At the present time, students do not have to pay council tax (a local tax). Insurance and utility costs are inclusive in some types of accommodation
Living and social costs	• Food • Drink • Entertainment • Clubs and societies	Even if living in catered accommodation, you will incur additional food costs, e.g. at lunchtime or in the evening
Local travel costs	• Fares or season tickets • Car maintenance and fuel • Parking • Tolls • Visits home	These are greatly dependent on the distance between your accommodation and the campus site(s) you need to visit
Study costs	• Books, stationery • Equipment • Lab deposits • Field trips • Computing • Photocopying and printing	Equipment costs, lab deposits and costs of field trips will only apply in certain subjects
Personal costs	• Mobile phone • Laundry • Toiletries • Haircuts • Clothing • Presents	These are dependent on lifestyle and how fashion-conscious you may be
Other	• Childminding/babysitting • Holidays • TV licence	A TV licence is required for all televisions in shared accommodation unless it is a group rental

→ Accommodation

Student accommodation is a real concern for all visiting students and is an issue that you should try to resolve before you travel to the UK. In most university towns and cities there is high demand for student accommodation that is reasonably priced. You are advised *not* to wait until you arrive on your university campus before you organise your accommodation. Factors to take into account when deciding on accommodation are shown in Table 3.2.

Table 3.2 Factors to consider when selecting accommodation for your period of study in the UK

	Living in university accommodation (student residences and flats)	Living in rented accommodation (private sector)
Potential advantages and benefits	• Costs reasonable • Facilities clean, warm and safe • Ready-made social network • Residences may have a good social calendar • Meals provided (at a cost) • Rent inclusive of some services* • Facilities like kitchen and laundry on hand • Support of hall warden(s) • Good complaints procedures	• Wide range of choice • More privacy • Less disturbance and noise (but not always) • Freedom to select those you live with • Your choice of food and meal times • Fewer restrictions
Potential disadvantages and problems	• Facilities possibly basic • Lengthy contract period • Can be noisy and lacking in privacy • No or little choice of neighbours or flatmates • You might not like the food • Restricted opening/curfews • Financial penalties for damage caused by others • You may have to share a room • Less easy to escape from campus confines	• Can be a costly option • Need to pay a refundable deposit • Additional costs of services* • Potential to be isolated and lonely • Conditions and furnishing may not be ideal • May need to sign up for a lengthy period • Shopping, cooking and cleaning required • Extra travel costs and loss of time commuting

* 'Services' normally include cleaning, heating, lighting, electricity and/or gas, telephone and internet connections.

University residences

It is recommended that you apply for a place at an early stage in your planning period. Most universities have a cut-off point for applying for accommodation with a guarantee of being allocated a room. You will normally be expected to sign a contract for a minimum of one term or semester.

Facilities in university student accommodation vary from one campus to another, but, if you are living in a large communal residence, the regulations require that you have your own toilet facilities (*en suite* facilities). If your residence is divided into flats, then you may have to share these facilities. It is best to check out what the format is in your university's residences before you apply.

Rented accommodation

In many towns and cities that have universities many private landlords rent accommodation to students. However, the population of a university is continuously changing so it may be difficult to find property that is readily available, is a reasonable distance from the university and with a rent that suits your budget.

You should also be aware that, if you decide to arrange accommodation privately, you may have to pay a deposit, for example, the equivalent of one month's rent in advance.

You may also have to pay standing charges for water, gas and electricity. When you leave, you may be charged for breakages or damage, hence it is important that you check through an inventory of the property with the landlord at the beginning of your lease (you and your landlord should each keep a signed copy noting any existing damage).

Note that some universities provide advice on rental arrangements and leases in particular. As an international student, it may be wise to check out any proposed lease agreement with your university advisory service – sometimes available through your university student union – so that you do not find that you face difficulties at the end of the lease. If your university does not provide that advice, then consult the local Citizens' Advice Bureau (**www.citizensadvice.org.uk/index/aboutus.htm** or, for Scotland, **www.cas.org.uk**).

→ Health issues

Before you leave your country

Note that students from some countries are required to show evidence that they are free from infectious pulmonary tuberculosis (TB). Screening programmes are in place so that, if this applies to your situation, then you can be screened and obtain the necessary clearance before you leave your own country.

Health care in the UK

In general terms, if your stay in the UK for study purposes is longer than six months, you (and your immediate family members accompanying you) may be eligible for free or subsidised treatment within the UK National Health Service (NHS). There is no time limitation on your residence in order to receive free treatment in Scotland. Note that you may need to pay for dental care or for services from an optician if you require these while you are studying in the UK.

If you are not eligible for free health treatment, then you should be advised by the health authorities in your own country about the need to take out personal health insurance to cover your health care costs while studying in the UK.

→ Your family

If you are single, and hence travelling to and living in the UK alone, you will need to think about how you will remain in contact with your family back home. You will miss them and they will miss you, so it is important to establish means of contact beforehand. For example, if family members have access to the internet, then web-based communication tools like *Skype* can be a low-cost option.

If you have a family, and intend to bring them to the UK with you, this has implications that you should think about carefully. Your decision may depend on the length of your course. Practical aspects to consider include:

● whether you can afford to spend more on accommodation at UK prices or, conversely, afford to maintain two homes – one in the UK and one in your own country;

- whether your spouse is able to cope independently with living in a new society perhaps with different ways of living from your own;
- whether your family have the necessary language skills to cope on a day-to-day basis with life in the UK;
- whether there will be a place available in a local school for your school-age children and whether your children will be able to adjust to a different school environment including learning in English;
- whether your family will be homesick;
- whether you can afford the expense of clothing your family suitably for the UK climate and to meet the uniform requirements of some UK schools.

✔ Practical tips for preparing to study in the UK

Check your official documentation - check all the letters and literature that have been sent to you by your university. Make sure that you send off all necessary forms in good time. Look at the university's website to check that you have all essential documents and that these are up-to-date, for example, your passport and visa.

Develop your English language skills - before you leave your own country, take every opportunity that you can to listen to, read, speak or write English. New technologies allow global access to many sources of spoken English and you should exploit these as far as you can so that your understanding of colloquial and formal English develops.

Invest in communication systems - as part of your preparations, explore realistic ways of keeping in touch with friends and family by using online facilities such as email, *Instant Messenger*, *Skype* and social networking sites (such as *Facebook*). This means that if your family remain in your own country, then you can keep in touch cheaply and frequently. Note that your university computing facilities may not support some of these systems and so you should check this before you leave your own country.

Learn to cook and care for your clothing before you leave home - if you are not accustomed to cooking or doing your laundry for yourself, then it would be worthwhile learning some basic strategies before you leave home. Cooking brings students together and is a very sociable activity. You'll want to be able to produce some of your national dishes for your new friends to taste. Similarly, if you have no experience of doing laundry, then some practice before you arrive might be helpful.

Context: these expressions focus on your need to arrange suitable university accommodation.

Can you tell me if heating charges are included in the residence fees?

Do I need to pay a deposit for my university accommodation?

How often will my room be cleaned?

Can I share my university residence room with my wife/husband?

I'd like to report that the shower/washing machine/cooker/heating in my flat is not working. Could you please arrange for it to be fixed?

I've lost the key to my room. Is it possible to obtain a replacement?

GO **And now . . .**

3.1 Check out the availability of English Language courses. Most universities provide on-going English language tuition as part of their support service and this is often free of charge. University is not the place to be learning fundamental grammar, although grammar revision may be part of the support programme, but you should look particularly to see whether the programmes include language tuition for your specific subject. Look especially for terms such as 'English for Academic Purposes' or 'English for Specific Purposes' in the prospectus.

3.2 Identify your university's discount card arrangements. Some universities offer generous discounts arranged with national as well as local companies which means that you can afford to eat out or buy some 'extra' items without creating a hole in your budget. Note that some retailers offer loyalty card schemes that allow you to accrue credit points related to the amount of money you spend in their stores or discounts on goods provided by other companies.

3.3 Visit the Freshers' website for your university well before you travel. These websites often contain useful checklists, travel tips and information about arrangements for meeting new students at stations and airports. There is often more detailed information about specific university amenities and local facilities that will be useful in helping you to settle in on your arrival.

4 Adjusting to another culture

How to adapt to life in a different country

Coming to university in the UK will involve changes in many aspects of your life. It is important that you are aware of cross-cultural issues that may be involved as these will influence how settled you feel, how much you gain from living in Britain and, indirectly, how well you succeed in your studies.

Key topics:
→ Cross-cultural awareness
→ Interpersonal awareness
→ Practical awareness

Essential vocabulary
Academics   Accent   Acculturation   Assimilation   Chaplaincy   Culture shift
Dialect   Preservation   Values

Studying abroad is not simply a matter of entering a new learning environment (**Ch 2**), it involves entering another culture – as well as the obvious changes in climate and language. Even if you come from another English-speaking country, you will find that the way of life, the codes and behaviour patterns that you meet will be different from those in your own country. This is true for everyone – undergraduate or postgraduate, single or accompanied. There will be things that you will see, hear and experience that may seem strange and even puzzling. This chapter explains some of the factors that will provide the background for your experience and your studies.

Cross-cultural awareness

As a student intending to study in the UK you will have some ideas and expectations of the society and culture you will find on arrival. These expectations will have been shaped by all sorts of influences – film, television, the internet, books, personal encounters and much more. Similarly, the reality of what you will experience will depend on many variables – the town or city where you live in the UK, whether you live on or off campus, whether you live with your family, whether you mix with students from all sorts of backgrounds and nationalities and the extent to which you explore the country beyond your university.

Culture shift and the impact on learning

Living in another culture is rather like beginning a new job. At first everything is novel, strange and exciting. As you settle into the new job, you may begin to wonder why things are organised in a particular way and you may even wish at some stage that you had not taken this new job. Similarly, when you arrive in another country, similar thoughts and feelings may occur to you. However, this is a normal human reaction to change and to new experiences. As with a new job, it is important to keep a sense of perspective and give yourself some time to adjust to your new living and learning environment.

This is a well-acknowledged process that many international students experience – as do national students who are living away from home for the first time. This experience is sometimes called 'culture shock', but that term seems to make a crisis out of a process that is actually very common and quite natural. Of course, most students will respond in some way to their new situation but this is more of a 'culture shift' taking place over time rather than the jolting blow that the term 'culture shock' implies.

As visitors, international students are observers of a different way of life and typically there are three broad reactions they can have towards life in a new culture. The case studies in Table 4.1 show how international students typically relate to the host community, but this does not happen instantly. Many stages can be identified in the process, each of which affects most students to some extent and these can relate closely to a student's academic progress. Figure 4.1 shows the potential pattern over time. At any given time in your studies, it may be useful to recognise where you might be in this process and to anticipate and think about your feelings and reactions. Different people will go through these stages at different times, and will be affected to a greater or lesser extent.

Table 4.1 Three case studies illustrating different reactions of students to culture shift

Case study 1 – preservation model
Ong is a student who comes from a culture which is family-centred. He has brought his wife and baby son with him but he does not like the idea of his wife going out alone. He prefers that she waits until he can accompany her. He is prepared to travel considerable distances to obtain food that is sourced from his own country and he insists that his wife wears traditional clothing although the climate in the UK is much colder than in their own country. His wife is becoming increasingly isolated and home-sick, which is making him spend more time at home with her than in his laboratory. They both miss the support of their families and have few people from the same culture with whom they can share their concerns and activities. However, Ong's wife has reasonably good English and she would be able to cope with routine chores such as shopping.
Ong is following 'the preservation model'. Such students reject almost everything about the 'host' culture that surrounds them. That means that he preserves as far as possible all the familiar behaviours and norms of his home culture and makes no concession to living in the 'host' community. He narrows the family's social interactions to those with others in the same cultural/nationality grouping and so has a relatively small circle of contacts. This reduces opportunities to learn about other approaches to attitudes and to studying. People who take this approach may not recognise or may not acknowledge different behaviours that are expected in the host social culture. The danger of this reaction is that such people do not adjust well to the new academic culture either. This could mean that their academic performance is not as good as it might be if they adopted a more receptive approach.

Table 4.1 (*cont'd*)

Case study 2 – acculturation model

Samu has come from a country that has strong links with the UK. He'd like to know more about the British way of life from first-hand experience. He finds the weather quite cold but understands that British people regard the weather as a 'safe subject' for conversation, so he has watched and learnt how to take part in this kind of conversation. He finds British food rather 'heavy' but has discovered that he can obtain many 'ethnic' foods in the supermarkets and so can cook the kind of food he likes, although he has become quite fond of fish and chips! He accepts that there are times when it is more appropriate for him to follow his own cultural norms, for example, by attending weekly prayers, and he has asked his course director if he can be allocated to a tutorial group which does not meet on Fridays, his prayer day. Samu has made some friends among the people on his course and has joined the Ski Club with them so that he can learn a new sport that he would never have the chance to follow in his own country.

Samu is following the 'acculturation model'. He has taken on the role of observer of UK culture. He's noticed some different practices that he thinks are good and others which he dislikes. For example, he likes the way that UK people offer help to strangers but at the same time, he prefers the more respectful ways towards the elderly and to teaching staff that are normal in his own culture. In particular, he finds the way that many younger British women act to be immodest. He misses the longer, brighter daylight, the noise and bustle of his own home town. Samu faces both cultures simultaneously. This approach is probably the most common for students who mix within a cosmopolitan student community. By adopting an approach that shows some adjustments and understanding of cultural variation, such students show that they are sensitive to difference and this will help them to identify crucially different approaches to learning in the UK university environment.

Case study 3 – assimilation model

Alexia is an international student who wants to remain in the UK to work. She is very proud of her own culture but has decided that the way to make the most of the opportunity to study in another country is to take part in as many things as possible, speak to as many people as possible and to learn more about the country in which she is studying. Before arriving on campus, she has already visited Land's End (the most southerly point on mainland Britain) and John O'Groats (the most northerly point). She reads British newspapers and watches television so that she can discuss topical subjects in English. She is keen to learn how to cook British food and has enrolled for a cookery class in the local community centre where she meets people from outside the university community. She has a wide circle of friends including some people from her own country but she insists on always talking English even with these friends.

Alexia is following the 'assimilation model' where the reaction is to adopt a high proportion of the habits and norms of the host community. For many students, it would be difficult to achieve this fully within the time span of their period of study. Nevertheless, many students do enter wholeheartedly into the value system of the host society. That does not mean that they take an extreme approach by suddenly changing their style of dressing, eating and religious habits and the values that are at the core of their lives. They simply absorb a parallel set of norms that recognise other ways that apply in the host culture. This breadth of intercultural understanding has the potential to enhance their learning within their course or research study.

Religious observance and value systems

The UK is a country which is nominally Christian but which also has a number of other faith communities. Details of where you can worship locally within your own faith community will be available from your university chaplaincy. Where there are special religious festivals that fall outside the Christian calendar, it may be possible to arrange for some time out of your classes for religious observance.

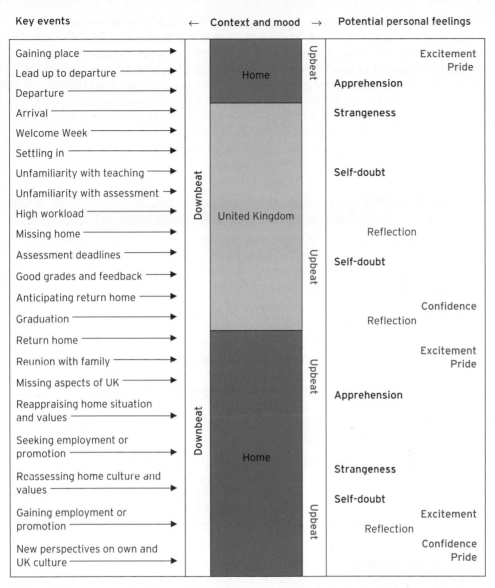

Figure 4.1 Processes of culture shift. This figure illustrates the typical events and feelings that a students experiences as they move from their home country and back again.

Many world religions follow daily rituals. It may be you will find that many people in the UK do not follow similar routines in relation to their religion. This lack of daily engagement with religion may seem strange. You may find that it is helpful to discuss your religious requirements with those teaching you so that they can be aware when you may not be available to participate in some learning activities. In practice, many students are permitted to perform their religious duties in such a way that does not intrude on their university day.

The UK is a liberal, multicultural country where an individual's values are generally a matter of free personal choice. At times the behaviour of people in British society may seem inconsistent. For example, there is tolerance of what might seem like extremely immodest behaviour in some countries, particularly in relation to drinking alcohol and sexual morality. On the other hand, there is a general expectation of honesty and observance of law. This 'value system' includes unwritten conventions associated with respect of others such as queuing, and saying 'please' and 'thank you' (p. 6 and 37). In relation to education, this respect includes acceptance that different viewpoints deserve a hearing and extends to open-mindedness towards radical and original ideas.

→ Interpersonal awareness

Many of the differences between your home country and the UK will be evident in the interactions between individuals.

Language

- **Accents and dialects.** To study in the UK, you will find you need various 'Englishes' – English for study and learning situations ('academic English'), English for daily interactions with non-students, English for official business, English for speaking with your peers, and many more besides. You will have to cope with accents (alterations in the intonation), dialect (some words and expressions that are particular to specific geographical areas) and some slang and idiomatic language also. However, all of this is manageable because it is generally the case that people will modify their language to 'proper English' when they realise that you are using English as an additional language.

- **Register and etiquette.** Using language appropriately is not just a matter of word choice, it is closely related to the way words are used. Sometimes the intonation patterns of a person's first language can influence their spoken English. Especially in your early days in the UK, listen carefully to how people ask politely for information, services or items. If you observe these conventions, then you will not unwittingly offend anyone.

- **Taboos and language.** Sometimes visitors pick up inappropriate language – slang expressions, swearing and vulgar language. This 'taboo' language is not recommended and should be avoided. As in any country, while it may be 'acceptable' for people from that country to break the taboo conventions, if someone from another culture does so, this is regarded as a violation of custom.

- **Television and other media.** Generally, television and other media provide international students with good models of language. However, that is not true of all programmes. There are several 'soap operas', for example, that would not generally provide good models of spoken English. By contrast, news, discussion and documentary programmes would generally provide you with examples of good standard English. If you then read about the same topics in a British newspaper, this will help you by giving you a printed version of the vocabulary that you might have heard on television or radio.

Language use in informal and formal (academic) situations

Greetings – 'Hi', 'Hello', 'Hey' and 'Hiya' are informal, and while suitable for informal situations, they are not appropriate when speaking to a member of academic staff or other professional (say 'Good morning'/'Good afternoon'/'Good evening'). Always choose the more formal options until you have worked out the style that is used in your particular circle of contacts. A formal style is recommended in emails to staff. 'Hey' or 'Hi' are not appropriate.

Farewells – The commonly used informal send-off 'See you later' does not mean that you will actually see that person later. 'Cheers' is often used informally, but would not be appropriate in formal and semi-formal situations. If in doubt, use an expression such as 'Goodbye' or 'Good morning/afternoon/evening'. Note that the expression 'Bye' is generally informal.

Requests and showing appreciation – 'Please' and 'Thank you' are important code words in the UK which are expected by everyone for every kind of action – even if someone is being paid to provide the service or action, for example, thanking the bus driver at the end of your journey, asking the library staff for assistance, thanking the departmental secretary for arranging an appointment for you. Not saying 'please' and 'thank you' is regarded as bad-mannered and uncultured.

Apologies – 'Sorry' is appropriate and widely used in the UK (even when someone has bumped into you, both people will say 'sorry'). Although 'Excuse me' can also be used for making an apology, it is often used when you need to gain someone's attention. If you wish to speak with someone who is already speaking to another person, then you should wait until there is a pause in their conversation rather than interrupt immediately. Note that British people sometimes use 'sorry' and 'excuse me' as 'softeners', that is, an expression indicating that you are needing assistance or wish to assert yourself politely.

Body language and related conventions

Body language (see p. 38) is acknowledged as a key factor in cross-cultural communication. Importantly, if you are unaware of some of the simpler points about body language and related conventions, you could remain puzzled about the reactions of others to your perfectly correct English sentences when others misinterpret your physical actions.

Living with neighbours

In the setting of student residences you will find that you will be sharing facilities with other students and each university will have special arrangements for ensuring that people conform to a set of rules so that everyone feels comfortable. However, communal living can have some disadvantages and the general convention is that people respect each other's privacy and do not behave in ways that might be regarded as disruptive or antisocial.

If you live in private accommodation, then you need to be aware of any conventions that might be observed, for example, disposing of rubbish, cleaning common areas such as hallways or stairways, or parking. Being a good neighbour usually means being a polite neighbour. British reserve (shyness) can sometimes seem unfriendly; on the whole your neighbours will be helpful if you need information.

Body language and related conventions

Eye contact: British people expect the people to whom they are speaking to make eye contact with them.

*If someone does not make eye contact, then they are regarded as suspicious and possibly dishonest. If your culture dictates that you do **not** make eye contact with superiors (for example, lecturers), then you may find that you need to train yourself to make eye contact, even if you think that this seems rather rude. However, you need to identify the balance between maintaining eye contact and staring at people, which would be regarded as rude.*

Greeting people in the street: this is one of the exceptions to the above rule. Where people meet in the street, their body language will tell you whether they have time to stop and chat.

If the person has no time to stop, they will look you in the eye as they draw level, but quickly look at the ground after they have greeted you and keep walking. If they do have time to chat, they will keep looking at you, usually with a smile.

Hand-shaking: this is something that British people tend to do on meeting someone new for the first time or if they have not met for a very long time. At subsequent meetings no hand-shaking would take place. The 'British' handshake is firm but without squeezing the fingers too much.

If you come from a culture where people shake hands every time they meet, then you may have to make a conscious effort not to do so in the UK, although it would not usually be considered rude or strange if you did do this. Note that British women would expect to shake hands with male and female acquaintances.

Kissing as a greeting: the British tend not to use cheek kissing as a greeting (as on the European mainland) although some sectors of society are gradually adopting it. In the main, it is used by family members and people who have a long-standing friendly relationship. There are gender differences in behaviour: two women friends might kiss as a greeting, while two men friends would shake hands. A son, however, might kiss his mother, but shake hands with his father.

If you sense that someone intends to kiss you, it would be considered rude to decline. However, there are difficulties because there is no consensus on the 'normal' number of kisses – offer one cheek initially and if it is clear that a second kiss is expected, offer the other.

Personal space: this is important to British people, who will feel threatened and may even retreat if their personal space is invaded. You may observe this in commuter trains where people stare straight ahead and do not speak to people who are too close to them.

You will soon know if you have invaded a British person's personal space because they will move away from you or shift position to one side.

Queuing: the British have quite strict conventions in relation to queuing and expect everyone to wait patiently in line, taking their place as they arrive. When someone steps out of the order, then this is called 'jumping the queue' and is regarded as very bad manners and may result in indignant comments.

Think about queuing conventions in your own country, then watch to see how British people deal with the queue situation in bus stops, banks, doctors' surgeries, libraries and even matriculation.

Smiling: British people tend to smile when greeting or leaving others, when offering or asking for a service and when passing acquaintances in the street, among many other situations. They may also add a short greeting like 'Hi' and/or hold a hand up, palm forward to acknowledge you.

If you do not respond to a smile or verbal acknowledgement, then this may be regarded as rude. Some people perceive the way the British smile as insincere while others find it welcoming and genuine. Your perception will depend on your own cultural norms and how you perceive the smile. British people often cite as a fact that more muscles are needed to frown than to smile!

This section deals with a number of practical matters where you may need to adopt approaches different to those in your home country.

Medical matters

The British National Health Service (often referred to simply as 'the NHS') has an ethos of providing free care, although there may be some charges. The main elements are general practitioners (or GPs), who are effectively community doctors, a system of local dental surgeries, and hospital services, for example accident and emergency (A&E) and ward-based care. On arrival in the UK, you should register with both a local GP practice and an NHS dental practice. Information on how to do this will be provided in Freshers' packs or at matriculation.

How to register with a general practice surgery/clinic

Choose the practice you wish and then visit it to register – you can usually find a list at the university health service or centre or via **www.nhs.uk** (for England) or **www.nhs24.com** (for Scotland). Take with you three forms of identification, for example:

1 your passport;
2 matriculation card/letter of acceptance to the university;
3 documents that show your local address.

Note that when you visit a GP surgery, you may be seen first of all by a 'nurse practitioner' who will be able to treat minor problems or refer you to be seen by the GP.

How to register with a dentist

In the UK at present there is a shortage of NHS dentists and many people have difficulty registering with a dentist. This means that they have to pay for private treatment. However, you are entitled to register as an NHS patient and you will be able to find a list of local dentists from the Yellow Pages (phone directory on yell.com). It is advisable to make a list of dentists located close to your university or accommodation and then phone or visit to find out whether the dentist is currently accepting National Health Service (NHS) patients. Although some of the costs are covered, you will normally have to pay for a percentage of the treatment. Check what these costs will be before you undergo treatment.

Universities usually have their own health service and this may be more convenient to use than the GP surgery. However, the nurse or doctor will only be willing to treat certain conditions and will refer you to other public services as necessary. The university service can be useful for monitoring early symptoms or dealing with minor cuts, bruises and joint injuries. University health services can also assist with advice on contraception and mental heath matters.

Before your appointment with the nurse, doctor or dentist, write down important information about yourself including your full name, date of birth and passport number, your symptoms, how long you have been having these symptoms and questions you would like to ask. You may need to show your university matriculation/

How to obtain medical help

- **Non-emergency illnesses** (examples might be influenza ['flu] or persistent migraines), you can receive some initial advice through NHS Direct in England and Wales (via **www.nhsdirect.nhs.uk**) or NHS24 in Scotland (via **www.nhs24.com/content**). Note that both these websites offer printed information in languages other than English. You can also call for advice by phone. However, the GP practice should be your main point of contact. You will need to telephone to make an appointment, which may not be on the same day. At night-time there may be an out-of-hours service operating by telephone, with rare home visits. If you haven't kept a note of the phone numbers they will be in the Yellow Pages telephone book or at **www.yell.com**.

- **For accidents** (examples might be a deep cut or a suspected broken arm), you may present yourself at the accident and emergency (A&E) department of a hospital. If you don't have access to transport, use a taxi – the hospital will only send an ambulance in rare cases. You will be assessed by an experienced nurse and may have to wait some time for treatment by a doctor, depending on how busy the service is.

- **For emergencies** (involving extreme conditions, such as unconsciousness or injuries resulting from a severe motor accident), you should telephone using the code '999'. This will connect you to call-centre staff who will ask you questions about the situation, including who you are, where you are, and what has happened (be prepared with answers). He or she will then advise you what to do and will contact the ambulance, police or fire service(s) as appropriate.

ID card on your first visit. If you are unsure of what the nurse/doctor/dentist has told you or has instructed you to do, then ask them to write the important points down for you so that there is no risk of misunderstanding about the treatment.

You can buy some 'over the counter' remedies such as pain killers and cold and 'flu treatments in supermarkets and chemist shops. However, if you need more complex medicine, then your GP will give you a prescription that you need to take to the local pharmacy or chemist shop. There is a small fixed charge for each item the GP has prescribed and you pay this charge when you collect the medicine from the pharmacy.

Weather and clothing

The weather in the UK is changeable and it can seem drab and grey at some times in the year; conversely, at other times, it can be bright and beautiful. In the course of year, you may experience high winds, mist, fog, persistent rain and lying snow as well as heatwaves, thunderstorms and lengthy dry periods. Temperatures can, in extreme weather, fall as low as –10°C in winter, and be as high as 35°C in summer. While this variety in weather conditions may seem negative, one of the upsides of the British weather is that it is never the same for very long and each season brings its own weather highlights.

The British take a keen interest in weather forecasts and use this information to decide on clothing for the day. If you are accustomed to warmer temperatures, then it is important that you factor heating into your budget and add warm clothing to your list of items to bring with you or to buy as required. Clothing in Britain need not be expensive if you shop in the 'high-street' stores. Many students – UK and international – buy 'retro' clothing or special items that may not be needed very often (for example, a winter coat) from the many 'charity shops' that are found in most towns. These sell second-hand clothing at low prices to help support charities that fund research into conditions such as cancer or meningitis.

Food, diet and shopping

Love it or hate it, British food is a response to climate and to the availability of fresh produce. The multicultural nature of modern Britain means that in cities you can find many familiar items if you know where to look. However, foods from your own country may be sold at much higher prices than you would expect at home. Your university will often provide lists of specialist food shops in the local area or stores with 'delicatessen' sections that sell 'foreign' foods or, for example, Halal or Kosher produce. Experiment with food from other countries – you may have resident experts amongst your friends who can introduce you to different cuisines.

In general, shopping in the UK is possible every day in the week, although in smaller towns this will not apply to smaller shops. The standard opening hours are from 9.00 to 17.30 although some of the bigger supermarkets remain open to 22.00 or for 24 hours a day. Prices for some items include an additional 'value-added tax' which will be included in the price printed on the sales ticket. Prices are not negotiable. However, at certain times of the year price reductions are offered in 'sales'. If an item proves to be faulty, then there are certain rights that protect the interest of the customer. You can find out more about rights and entitlements under the law at **www.tradingstandards.gov.uk/advice/consumer-advice.cfm**.

Regarding smoking and alcohol, you should be aware of specific UK legislation. Smoking is not allowed in or near public buildings. This applies to all university buildings and halls of residence. Alcohol is sold in restaurants, pubs, clubs and hotels – ID may be required as proof of age. In addition, alcoholic drinks are sold under special licensing laws in supermarkets and small general goods stores. It is an offence to be drunk in the street or to drive a car with more than 85 micrograms of alcohol per 100 millilitres of blood.

Transport

Walking and cycling are options if your accommodation is close to the campus. Most cities have good and affordable public transport systems via bus, tram, railway or underground trains. Daily and weekly travel cards and season tickets may be cost-effective options. Your Freshers' or residences information pack will provide relevant information about discount schemes for students.

Being a pedestrian or a driver in the UK may seem strange to you if you come from a country where the traffic drives on the right of the carriageway. If you wish to drive you can find out more about the conventions and mandatory motor insurance and taxation on **www.ukcisa.org.uk/student/information_sheets.php#driving**. If you come from a country where the traffic drives 'on the right', then note that you also need to take care when crossing the road as a pedestrian.

✔ Practical tips for adjusting to UK culture

Come with an open mind. Things will be different; that is certain. However, come with the view that this is a life experience where you will learn much about your studies, about the culture and, most of all, about yourself. You will be reflecting on your own education, values and perspectives. Make the most of the opportunities you are offered and you will gain much. At the end of your studies you will move on – perhaps back to your own country or to somewhere else. Wherever you go, the experience of living and learning in a different culture zone will enrich you as a human being.

Find out how to travel cheaply. In the UK, there are systems which offer cheap local and rail travel to students. These provisions may vary from area to area. You may also find that there are special cheap internal UK flight 'deals' that are available to people who do not mind travelling at unsocial hours. However, be particularly aware that travelling by taxi or mini-cab (private hire) may be much more expensive than in your own country; you may find that you are charged according to how many pieces of baggage you are transporting and how many passengers are using the taxi.

Learn where to obtain specialist foods. When people are living far from home sometimes the familiarity of foods that are particular to their own country is important. Check out your university website for information about the nearest supplier of such products that you might wish to be able to buy regularly.

Take up a sport. Look out for induction sessions for gym facilities, swimming and other activities where you will be able not only to keep fit, but make a different network of friends and acquaintances with whom you have something in common.

💬 Useful language for . . . registering with services

Context: these expressions are useful for making initial approaches to reception staff.

Good morning. I am a student at the University of xxxx. I am from [country]. I'd like to register with a doctor in this practice, please. Is this possible?

Hello. I am a student at the University of xxxx and I am from [country].

I'd like to enquire about registering as an NHS patient with this dental practice, please. Could you tell me if this is possible?

Could you tell me how much I shall have to pay for dental treatment, please?

Good morning. I am a student at the University of xxxx. I am hoping to bring my family to join me. I have two sons who are 6 and 9 years old. Could you tell me if it would be possible for them to be accepted in your school? Can you tell me what I need to do to apply, please?

5 | Starting out

How to get the most out of your university's Welcome Week

So much goes on during Welcome Week (sometimes known as Freshers' Week) that it is easy to forget some of the important things you need to do. This chapter aims to help by providing a listing of important tasks.

Key topics:
→ Essential, important and optional tasks
→ Key tasks and activities for Welcome/Freshers' Week

Essential vocabulary
Department   Faculty   Fresher   Matriculation   Principal   School Student Association   Students' Union   Vice-chancellor

Most universities hold a Welcome or Freshers' Week. The main purpose is to help new students settle in quickly. As well as a number of presentations and workshops related to effective learning at university and to your chosen course, there is usually an energetic social programme, including events for new international students. Senior students will be around to help you to find your way about. Your university may send you an information pack ahead of your arrival, or direct you to their Freshers' website. Do read this material, because this may be the only time that you will be given the information and when you arrive it will be assumed that you know it. Some universities recognise that students can suffer from 'information overload' in these first few days and weeks, so they spread the transfer of information over a longer period and cover specific essential skills within taught modules.

→ Essential, important and optional tasks

All new students - undergraduates and postgraduates - need to do several things during Welcome Week:

- **Essential tasks.** These include administrative responsibilities and you *must* do these. You will find dates and times in the paperwork you will receive from the university before the academic year starts.
- **Important tasks.** These tasks, such as setting up a bank account, may depend on your personal situation, for example, whether you are new to the area or whether you are living locally. Banks will be competing for your custom, so check out all the deals before you make your choice of bank.
- **Optional tasks.** These will depend on your preferences and goals and might include joining a particular society.

You can use Table 5.1 as a checklist to ensure that you have thought of all the things you might need to do.

Table 5.1 Key tasks and activities for Welcome Week. This applies to *all* students – undergraduate and postgraduate.

Type of task	Checklist of activities	Comments
Knowing what to do, when and how	☐ Review all the university documentation sent to you through the post or via website or Virtual Learning Environment (vle) to which you may have been given preliminary access ☐ Read your Welcome Pack – this will usually contain information from the university Students' Union or Association ☐ Note all the appointments, events and activities that are relevant to you and plan what you will do each day	You will receive a great deal of important literature in the weeks leading up to your arrival at the university. All the information from the university, the faculty or college and the department or school in which you will be studying will be important. Make sure that you read it and bring it with you when you travel.
Administration at institutional level	☐ Each student must matriculate. This is sometimes called registration, enrolment or signing up ☐ Meet your Adviser/Director of Studies. In some institutions this person might be called a Personal Tutor or Course Director. Postgraduate research students will meet with their supervisor. ☐ Collect your matriculation form and follow the instructions about registering for your courses	The matriculation or enrolment process is a fundamental procedure that confirms your admission to university, initiates your academic record, your access to facilities and the production of your student identity card. The latter is proof of your status as a student within your institution, as well as to outside agencies. You will also need this card to prove your student statuos outside the university.
Administration at college, faculty, departmental, divisional or school level	☐ Attend relevant induction meetings ☐ Find out how your university is organised ☐ Find out your timetable, where you have to go and when ☐ You will probably have been given a map of the campus, so it is a good idea to check out ahead of time where lectures/labs/tutorials take place	The names used to describe the organisational units within a university differ from institution to institution. Most direct contact with students is made at the level at which the teaching is done, usually departmental or school level. Most units provide subject or course handbooks, which give details of timetables, locations and times of lectures. Some departments will have an induction meeting with new students when there will be an opportunity to meet the teaching staff.
Communicating with the university and beyond	Find out contact numbers and/or email addresses for: ☐ Your Adviser of Studies ☐ Your Personal Tutor (if different from above) ☐ Your subject department(s) or school ☐ The university library ☐ Your general practitioner (GP) ☐ Your landlord (if appropriate)	Put all these details in an address book or personal organiser. Look around mobile phone providers to obtain the best deal that you can to get low-cost/free email, surfing, free quota or unlimited calls and texts as well as any other offers that might be available for students. Consider the advantages of pay-as-you-go if you feel that you need to watch your expenditure on communication.

TOOLKIT A Adapting to a new educational experience

Category	Checklist	Notes
Accommodation	☐ Book into accommodation ☐ Check that what you are signing for in terms of an inventory of equipment is actually there and in good condition ☐ Identify additional things that you may wish to purchase for your comfort or convenience ☐ If you are in private accommodation, arrange for transfer of electricity, gas or phone services to your name ☐ Make further enquiries about Council Tax Exemption as it may be that you have to apply for this explicitly	Getting to know your flatmates is important for future relationships. Everyone has particular habits and preferences, which may or may not be shared by others – this can be an exercise in 'people skills'. If you are sharing accommodation, you will need to reach an agreement with flatmates about how services are to be paid for. Be aware that if your name is on the bill, then you are liable for all charges outstanding at the end of a rental period.
Getting to know your way around (on campus)	☐ Go on campus tour (see p. 50) ☐ Apply for a student rail card/bus or tram travel permit ☐ Find on-campus facilities, e.g. library, sports hall, chaplaincy, parking zones ☐ Apply for/purchase a parking permit to park on campus if this is possible ☐ Apply for a season ticket for local parking	Finding your way around a tight-knit campus is usually quite easy, but many universities are dispersed widely and finding the cheapest and fastest method of travelling to your campus site is an important budgeting measure. Travel passes provide some help and some universities run free 'shuttle' buses between different campuses. Many students prefer to cycle to their classes. For some people the only travel option is by private car, but to park on university property you will need to purchase a permit. Note that some universities do not provide parking for students' vehicles.
Getting to know your way around (off campus)	☐ Go on city or town tour ☐ Go on supermarket tour ☐ Find out about off-campus facilities, e.g. post office, laundrette ☐ Research special student discount deals and loyalty card offers ☐ Find out bus, tram and train times for your journey to and from the university ☐ Find out how long it will take you to make the journey at different times of the day and week	Universities or their students' unions/associations offer tours of the local area. This will help you to find key landmarks, including the local supermarkets and best places to buy food.

Table 5.1 (cont'd)

Type of task	Checklist of activities	Comments
Preparing to participate in the life of the university	❑ Attend welcome from the Vice-chancellor/Principal ❑ Attend Societies' Fayre ❑ Join societies and clubs	There are usually two occasions in student life when you will assemble as a body. These landmark occasions are not to be missed. They are the welcome to the institution as you step out into uncharted territory with all the hopes and concerns that are to be expected; and graduation day, which marks the end of that journey and the fulfilment of those early hopes. In between these two dates, you have the opportunity to join societies, such as your own subject society, participating in international friendship schemes and many others. They contribute to the richness of university social and cultural life. Students' unions/associations usually organise some kind of 'Societies' Fayre' where you can enrol.
Getting ready for learning	❑ Purchase an academic diary ❑ Join the library and sign up for a library induction tour ❑ Participate in a library induction presentation or tour ❑ Attend IT induction and log in to your IT account ❑ If you are unsure about your IT skills, sign up for computing training sessions as appropriate	Many universities and students' unions or associations publish a university diary that contains useful information about that institution, such as term/semester and vacation dates, where to go for information, sports facilities and much more.
Looking after yourself	❑ Register with a local GP practice. Representatives of local medical practices are often present at some of the Welcome Week events and you should be able to sign up with them at that time. Note: students from some countries may be required to have a chest X-ray or courses of injections. This may also depend on your subject of study	As an international student, you can find out how to go about registering with a doctor in the UK by visiting a practice of your choice (see p. 39); you also need to know that in Britain, if you are ill, the first place you need to contact is your doctor's surgery; hospitals are for emergencies only or for referral by your GP.
Police registration	❑ International students from certain countries must register with the Police within seven days of arriving in the UK	See the UK Border Agency (UKBA) website (www.ukba.homeoffice.gov.uk) for further details. Note that you will have to pay the necessary fee in cash (not by cheque or credit card). You will also need to take your passport and other documents with you.

Getting street-wise	☐ Get personal safety leaflets ☐ Buy a personal alarm - often available at discount price in Students' Union/Association shops ☐ Make yourself aware of fire drill regulations in your accommodation	Most institutions provide information and advice on personal safety, including protecting your belongings as well as protecting yourself and your health. These are real-world issues and it is important to be aware of what you might encounter in the social scene on your campus. Many institutions or students' unions sell personal alarms and offer leaflets on drugs, sexually transmitted diseases, date-rape, theft, and other issues commonly found in the community at large. Counselling services exist in all university institutions to support all students from every background, nationality, gender orientation and creed. Counselling is free and confidential.
For students with disabilities	☐ Make contact with the disability service in your institution to make them aware that you have arrived ☐ Check that facilities you have identified as being necessary for you are in place ☐ Students can choose whether they wish to disclose a condition that might be classified as a disability. It may be advantageous to disclose such information in order to obtain the most effective help. The information will be kept confidential until you authorise disclosure to others	If you have a disability, you need to consider how this might impact on your life as a student. You will probably have prepared for coming to university by contacting the disability service in your institution ahead of the beginning of the academic year, but you should make contact again. Your university has a legal responsibility to provide adequate facilities, and this will be put into action if you disclose relevant information.
Developing your language skills if English is not your first language	☐ Register for an English-language test if required ☐ Sign up for a course in English for Academic Purposes ☐ If you are a postgraduate international student who uses English as an additional language, look out for courses to help you with dissertation or thesis writing	In some institutions, if you are an international student and English is not your first language, you may be obliged to take a language test as a matter of routine. If it is considered that you need to continue to develop your English language, courses may be available to you. In some cases, fees will be charged; in other cases, courses will be free of charge. Even if you have met the English language qualification for your university, remember that this is simply a benchmark requirement - your lecturers may suggest that you continue language study in addition to your discipline studies, so that you can deal competently with the reading, writing, listening and speaking required of you.

Be prepared for matriculation/registration/enrolment

Your first few days at university can be confusing and sometimes even frustrating as you get used to a new environment and deal with administrative matters. Things will go more smoothly if you:

- read carefully all the documents you have been given
- work out where to go and when
- plan your daily activities well
- decide what you want to say and to whom
- make sure you are on time for any appointments
- bring the right paperwork
- are prepared to queue.

✔ Practical tips for new international students

If you are living in university halls, work at getting to know your fellow students. Everyone is new, so just a little extra effort can make a difference, both for you and for others.

- Go out of your way to introduce yourself and speak to others.
- Leave your door open so you can greet those going past.
- Propose an evening event, such as a floor party or an international meal.
- Look out for people who look lonely and invite them along to whatever you're doing.
- Make a special effort to join in, even if you are confused by cultural and language differences.
- Find out if people play the same sports as you and set up a match with them.

Join in campus activities. This will help you become a part of the university community and is especially important if you are living off-campus. If you have your family with you, there are often events that they will be able to attend too. This will not only give them a chance to become involved, but also a better idea of what you do and where you study.

Buy a cheap filing system. You'll get lots of paperwork before you arrive and during the first few weeks of term or semester. There'll be too much to look at straight away, but some of the literature, such as course handbooks, will be very useful later on. Spend some time sifting through all the papers you receive, put aside what you *think* you won't need (you might need it later after all) and store the rest in a logical order.

Don't spend money on impulse. During Welcome Week there will be pressure on you to spend money: for example, to participate in events, join clubs and societies, buy textbooks, and more. Unless you are confident in your interests and needs, save your cash until you are more certain about things. Therefore:

- do you really need to join lots of clubs? There will be many demands on your time during the term/semester and you can't be an active member of them all. Select the one(s) likely to be of main interest to you. You can always join others later.

- will you really need your own copy of all the books on your reading lists? There will usually be plenty of copies of each text in the library and if a book is peripheral you may only need to consult it a few times.

 Useful language for . . . registering for your course

Context: the formal process of registering may be called enrolling, matriculating or signing up, depending on institution. The following expressions could be used with those you meet at this stage.

[Asking for and giving information] Please cay you show me [on the compus map] where matriculation is taking place?

[Introducing yourself to an administrator] My name is xxxx. I have been accepted to study [course] Here are my documents.

[In a queue where you arrived first] Excuse me. I think I was first.

[In a queue where you arrived after another person] I think you were here first [often accompanied by an open-handed gesture, to suggest that the person moves ahead of you].

GO And now . . .

5.1 Prioritise your activities for Freshers' Week. Use the checklist in Table 5.1 to help you decide on a set of activities to accomplish each day. By the end of the week you should have all the main checklist items sorted out.

5.2 Set up a regular time to communicate with home. Your family will be keen to know how you are getting on. If you always do this at a particular time or on a particular day, this will make sure you keep in touch.

5.3 Set up a list of contacts. If you haven't already got one, invest in an address book or personal organiser, so you can keep details of all your contacts in one place. Staff contact details are available on faculty or departmental/school web pages and are also in course handbooks. You may also wish to add key phone numbers to your mobile phone memory.

6 | Campus orientation

How to identify the key facilities at your university

Knowing your way around campus is essential if you don't want to waste time or miss lectures or meetings, but it isn't always straightforward. Familiarising yourself with your new university environment will be easier if you follow the tips within this chapter.

Key topics:
→ Campus tours
→ Key buildings and locations
→ Town information
→ Transport information

Essential vocabulary
Alumni   Campus   Matriculation   Students' Union   Yellow Pages

The physical area covered by university buildings is usually referred to as a campus. Some universities are in the middle of cities, while others are located at a distance from city life. Your university may have a traditional layout with quadrangles and lawns, or its buildings may be placed within busy city surroundings. Often, universities are spread over more than a single campus.

Whatever kind of campus you inhabit, initially you will need to find your way about. Lectures and tutorials often take place in buildings that are widely dispersed and you'll need to recognise these buildings, learn the shortest routes between locations, and find out where certain key resources are housed. Often buildings are named after important benefactors or famous alumni or researchers who have a connection with the institution. Campus maps usually have a key, with these names in alphabetical order. Signposting is generally provided at key points around a university campus and if all this fails, then simply ask someone.

→ Campus tours

You may find that your university's website has a virtual tour of the campus, which will help you explore it online before you arrive.

Universities usually run campus tours in the early days of Welcome Week. These tend to be led by senior students, so you get the chance to ask questions and benefit from their knowledge. Even if you are local, it is unlikely that you will have discovered the inner parts of the university campus, so it is worthwhile attending. It's also a good way to meet people and explore in company.

Maps

Most universities provide transport directions and campus maps with their enrolment documentation; these are also available electronically on university websites. Most campuses are well signposted but, if you are in doubt, enquire at the central reception facility, or simply stop someone and ask. An A–Z-style of street map for the town may be a useful addition to help you find your way around the surrounding area.

After you've done the tour, it's worth going walkabout with your maps to ensure that you know how to get to the places you'll need to go to regularly. Note how long it actually takes to move from one place to another – make allowance for extra time needed when paths and roads may be busy as people move from class to class. You'll find out where your lectures and other learning activities will take place from the timetable given out when you matriculate or when you register for a specific course.

→ Key buildings and locations

Among the important buildings to identify in your first few days are:

- where to matriculate and/or register for classes;
- where your lectures will be held;
- where tutorials, practicals and labs will take place;
- where IT facilities can be accessed;
- where to eat and socialise (for example, the Students' Union);
- where you can study.

The checklist below includes these and itemises additional buildings and locations that you should be able to find.

Some key buildings and locations – a checklist

- ❏ Bookshops
- ❏ Buildings where your lectures will be held
- ❏ Buildings where your tutorials or labs will take place
- ❏ Buildings where you will research or study
- ❏ Campus bank and/or cash dispenser (ATM)
- ❏ School/faculty building for your discipline
- ❏ School/faculty (administrative) office
- ❏ Finance/cash office
- ❏ Informal learning spaces
- ❏ International Advisory Office

- ❏ IT suites
- ❏ Main or subject library
- ❏ Registry/academic administration office
- ❏ Residences (accommodation) office
- ❏ Students' union or association
- ❏ Student 'help desk'
- ❏ Support services
- ❏ Student Union shop
- ❏ University health centre

Some buildings will be large and navigation skills will be required to find your way around inside. For example, the university library is one place where, initially, you may feel rather lost. The librarians will be happy to answer queries about facilities at any point in the year, but in the early weeks of the academic year they usually offer special library tours. These are valuable not only because they show you where books and other resources are kept, but also because they show you how to use the library catalogue to find out what resources are held and how to access them (**Ch 22**).

→ Town information

Depending on the size of the local town or city, universities often run bus tours to help students who are not local to become familiar with the local area and community. This is important if you do not want to become too campus-oriented with your activities.

Another useful source of local information is the people who work in your institution. They will often live locally and will be able to provide you with information that might otherwise be difficult to find. For example, they might be able to tell you where would be the best place to buy a set of second-hand pots and pans, or where you can find a shop selling halal or kosher food.

Some useful community locations – a checklist

Maintenance:	Public facilities:	Entertainment:
❑ Bank	❑ Police station	❑ Cinemas
❑ Post office	❑ Public library	❑ Theatres
❑ Medical practice/surgery	**Travel:**	❑ Football grounds
❑ Supermarkets	❑ Bus station	❑ Sports centres
❑ Chemist	❑ Rail station	❑ Swimming pools
❑ Cobbler (shoe repair)	❑ Airport links	❑ Restaurants
❑ Launderette	❑ Taxi ranks	❑ Clubs and pubs

Speaking with students living at home will also help you find your way about, since they have local knowledge and will be able to help people new to the area to find their bearings.

→ Transport information

You'll need to work out how best to travel from your accommodation to the campus. This may be a simple walk or cycle ride, but if you live some distance away from the campus it may be necessary to find out about public transport options. The local *Yellow Pages* will have contact details under 'Bus, coach and tramway services' and 'Train information'. Associated websites advertised alongside may offer online public transport timetables and route-planning information. Local tourist offices will also have this kind of information, including places to go and things to do within the area. Investigate student travel offers and discounts.

Where students have to travel between campuses, or between a residence and the campus, some universities may provide shuttle buses timed to fit in with lecture schedules. If you will have to undertake such trips regularly, make sure that you know the timetable as well as the pick-up and drop-off points.

Practical tips for getting to know your campus and university town

Plan your days ahead. Before you get to know your routine and the tracks you'll need to make between teaching venues, use your street map and the campus map to work out the shortest routes in advance.

Always carry your matriculation (ID) card when you are on campus. This is usually required for access to buildings and facilities, such as the library and students' union.

Take care over personal safety. Exploring a new town or city is interesting, but it is better to do this in company, particularly at night. Students' unions often run late-night bus services so that it should not be necessary to walk alone at night. If you feel a personal alarm would make you feel safer, these are normally sold in campus shops such as those run by students' unions.

Useful language for . . . finding your way around campus

Most fellow students will be happy to help you. Look for people who seem at ease or to know where they are going. However, avoid those obviously in a rush to a lecture, tutorial or lab. At night, take care who you select to approach.

Context: asking for directions

Excuse me. I wonder if you could help me? I'm trying to find [name of place]. I'm not sure where I am on this map. Could you show me how to get there on the map, please?

Hi! Do you know where matriculation is?

Hi! I need to get to [name of building or lecture theatre]. Do you know where it is from here?

GO And now . . .

6.1 Visit university websites, including international student and Freshers'/Welcome Week areas, and watch online video tours of the campus. These will help you feel more at home when you eventually move there.

6.2 Ask someone you know who is already a student to show you around when you arrive. They'll know all the shortcuts on the campus and be able to offer useful advice.

6.3 During Freshers'/Welcome Week, time your journeys. This will allow you to work out, for example, when you'll need to set your alarm and get up, when you need to leave home, or whether you have time for a snack or coffee between venues.

7 | Getting organised

How to interact with the university and prepare for study

Universities are large organisations, frequently with long traditions that have evolved over many generations. As an international student, you may not be aware of relevant customs and expectations. This chapter outlines ways in which you can prepare yourself so that you have a good start to your studies.

Key topics:
→ Communicating with the institution
→ Organising yourself
→ Developing your academic skills
→ Organising yourself for study
→ Looking after yourself

Essential vocabulary
**Arts subjects   College   Counselling   Drop-in facility   Ethical   Faculty
Matriculation** *PowerPoint* **Reflect   Research postgraduate   School
Science subjects   Taught postgraduate   Virtual learning environment (VLE)**

The academic community of a university consists not only of the lecturing staff who teach you, but also administrators, cleaners, janitors, secretaries, technicians, and a range of specialist staff who work behind the scenes. You will interact with many of these people as you study, maintain yourself and socialise. They will provide services for you but will expect you to do certain things to keep the system running smoothly. It will help you to understand their expectations and to try your best to meet these.

→ Communicating with the institution

The university machinery of administration is not really as complex as it sometimes seems. Your main role is to communicate with it effectively, for example by:

- matriculating (registering/enrolling) on the date and at the time given in your letter of acceptance;
- accessing your university email account regularly and responding to communications from staff members. Some departments will only communicate on coursework and routine matters through your university email account;

---

smart tip

Email accounts

It makes sense to transfer all your emails to the account assigned to you at university. This will make it easier for you to check for messages from staff since much of the ongoing course information will be distributed via email.

- making a habit of reading notices on college, faculty, school, departmental and course noticeboards as well as routinely checking announcements for courses that use the university's virtual learning environment (VLE) (**Ch 26**);
- informing your college/faculty, school or course organiser of absence through illness and providing medical certificates to cover periods of absence beyond the normal period of self-certification;
- keeping in touch with the international office, as you wish;
- letting the university know as soon as possible if you change address, or change other personal details;
- notifying your college/faculty, school or course organiser if you find yourself having to cope with exceptional personal circumstances which mean that you will be absent for a period of time – for example, bereavement of a close relative (all such information is confidential);
- responding to written communications as required.

What if your expectations of the course aren't met?

Discuss this in the first instance with your adviser/director of studies or personal tutor. If regulations allow, you may be allowed to change modules. In some universities changes can only be made in the first few weeks.

→ Organising yourself

University is an exciting place with lots of activities beyond those your course offers. You will need to make choices about how you go about enjoying these activities while maintaining the right levels of effort for your course. To do this, you will be expected to:

- organise your activities and time effectively (**Ch 9**);
- plan your workload to meet deadlines;
- engage with all the university's codes of practice, for example, on plagiarism (**Ch 32**), IT etiquette and responsible use of the Internet;
- arrange your social life around your studies;
- maintain a balance between work, study, family responsibilities and your social life.

---

smart tip

Planning ahead

To get the most out of your course, map out the things you need to do in relation to your course programme(s) in a diary, semester/term/monthly/weekly planner such as *The Smarter Student Planner* (see inside cover) or electronic diary:

- every day
- every week
- at other times.

→ Developing your academic skills

University learning in the UK may be different from your earlier experience of learning at school, college or university. You may find that you have to adjust your approach to learning to respond to UK methods and standards. For example, you will be expected to be willing to:

- adapt to new ways of studying;
- challenge your existing perceptions and receive new ideas with an open mind;
- think independently and develop analytic skills; and
- think logically and see issues from different viewpoints.

You will find more on relevant skills in **Ch 8** and on critical thinking in **Ch 21**.

Be prepared to state your own point of view about a topic

The ability to present your own views objectively is an important aspect of UK higher education. Expressing your own view is expected in arts subjects almost from the start, and becomes progressively more important in the science subjects once a base of factual knowledge and practical skills is established. Stating personal views may feel strange or even uncomfortable if your past learning experiences have expected you to copy the thinking of your teachers. It requires effort and skill. Your views must be based on reading course materials, analysing them for yourself and making conclusions based on the evidence. You need to be able to communicate your views clearly and succinctly and to cite your sources. Much of the guidance contained in this book is designed to help you refine these skills.

→ Organising yourself for study

Different levels of study require different approaches, and these are outlined in Table 7.1. You should select the section of this table that is appropriate to your situation and reflect on how prepared you feel to carry out the tasks it contains. A further factor is your learning style.

Table 7.1 Expectations of staff on students at different levels in UK higher education. Cross-referenced chapters provide greater detail and further guidance.

Undergraduate students
Requirements will depend on the field of study, but normally undergraduates are expected to:
• prepare for lectures and other learning activities by doing some background reading. This may include printing out lecture notes or *PowerPoint* handouts for use in the lecture (**Chs 14-16**)
• attend and take notes as appropriate (**Ch 16**) in all scheduled lectures and programmed class or group meetings
• follow up lecture and other activities by doing supplementary reading, worked examples, or reviewing and condensing notes (**Chs 16** and **25**)
• contribute fully in all forms of teaching and assessment, for example, by asking and answering questions (**Ch 20**)

Table 7.1 (*cont'd*)

Undergraduate students (*cont'd*)

- engage fully with teaching materials and other activities offered online. For example, in order to participate in class discussion you should look at any VLE modules over the week and read any updates or announcements (**Ch 26**)
- submit work on time
- participate in field trips or activities as appropriate to your study (**Ch 19**)
- ensure that you register for examinations at the appropriate time (**Ch 35**)
- provide feedback on your course and participate in the student representation processes for your course

Postgraduate students on taught courses

Taught postgraduates will normally have an intensive programme and will be expected to:

- attend all lectures, seminars, tutorials or additional presentations that are part of the course programme (**Chs 14** and **20**)
- attend group meetings (in the sciences) and postgraduate training courses
- identify the librarian with responsibility for supporting students on your course and seek advice on how to access the library resources (**Ch 22**)
- source material from specialist literature that goes beyond the course, reading list
- keep up to date with all the reading required for the course, since lectures will usually not provide everything that you need for assessment purposes
- think independently and recognise the fundamental difference between undergraduate and postgraduate study in the UK – students have to show in assessed work that they have gone beyond the lecture material in their thinking (**Ch 21**)
- work on developing English for academic purposes (**Ch 27**), for example, attend special training workshops on dissertation writing (note that these may include students for whom English is a first language)

Postgraduate research students

Research students are expected to follow a more independent approach to study and so need to:

- attend postgraduate training courses provided by the university
- attend lectures if recommended
- attend group meetings and other special seminars that may be arranged, even when these are not directly related to your research topic
- meet regularly with supervisor(s) by appointment (**Chs 42** and **43**)
- appraise ethical considerations relating to research topic and methodology (**Ch 41**)
- identify the librarian with responsibility for supporting students in your discipline and seek advice on how to use the library resources (**Ch 22**)
- undertake background reading and source material through use of specialist archives, databases and other media as appropriate (**Ch 22**)
- prepare and write research proposals and progress reports at regular prescribed intervals (**Chs 42-44**)
- be prepared to contribute to the research of others who may require your participation as a subject in their research projects
- work on developing English for academic purposes (**Ch 27**), for example, special training workshops on thesis writing (note that these may include students for whom English is a first language)

→ Looking after yourself

Universities are not as anonymous as they might seem on the surface and if you find yourself in difficulties there is usually someone to whom you can turn for help or advice that is freely available and confidential (see p. 79). You'll find information about these services from noticeboards, your university's website and from information leaflets that will be displayed in prominent places in university buildings.

Typical services available in most universities

Note that the names of the units involved in these services may be different in your university or college.

- **Academic skills/advice service:** providing support for academic writing, learning strategies, exam techniques and coping with academic issues.
- **Advisory service:** covering among other things finance, hardship, tenancy issues, leases and other matters relating to day-to-day life.
- **Careers service:** offering careers advice often along with 'job shop' information for finding part-time work, placements and internships, and vacation employment.
- **Chaplaincy centre:** welcoming people of all faiths and those who do not subscribe to any particular faith. The chaplaincy usually provides a range of facilities and activities not necessarily related to religion.
- **Counselling service:** supporting students with personal emotional problems such as stress, being homesick or loneliness.
- **International service:** providing cultural activities and care support for international students.
- **Residence service:** dealing mainly with university accommodation. May also have information about other property available for rent.
- **Sport and well-being centre:** for keeping fit, playing sports, meeting people and generally unwinding.
- **University health service:** providing on-campus health care and advice, including mental health issues.

It's expected that, if you need help, you will take the initiative in asking for it. This should not be about crisis management, but about recognising potential queries, issues or difficulties before they become problems. Seeking advice at an early stage is not a sign of weakness, but a mature decision in problem-solving.

Most services are run on an appointment basis, although in some cases, there may be a 'drop in' facility.

Punctuality when meeting staff

In the UK, when a time is mentioned for a meeting or appointment, this is *always* meant as the fixed starting time. Arriving late is regarded as bad manners and should be avoided by careful planning of journeys and prior engagements. If circumstances do mean that you are unavoidably late, you should always apologise to the person and/or group. Punctuality is expected for lectures and tutorials. Similarly, it is expected that students do not leave before the end of the teaching period.

Funding out about where to obtain information or support

For many international students, the first person they would turn to for assistance when they require it – regardless of whether this is academic or personal in nature – would be one of their lecturers. In the UK, the expectation is that students would consult the university web pages or pick up leaflets available at key points on their campus or read notices about the many free services provided. This readily available material ensures that students can more quickly access the help or information they require.

 Practical tips for dealing with the university system

Recognise that going to a UK university is like moving to a new community.
Each university has its own culture and conventions. Although it might seem confusing at first, the information you need is usually available somewhere. A good starting point is the institution's web pages. From the university's home page, you can usually find what you want by using the search facility or A–Z index.

Think for yourself. Whether you are an undergraduate or a postgraduate student, you will be expected to organise your time for yourself. Undergraduate and taught postgraduate students will have timetabled classes and procedures given in course handbooks. However, they are expected to create and follow planned private study independently of others.

Seek help promptly with any academic issues. Ensure that you speak to your course director/adviser of studies/personal tutor or academic skills advice centre (sometimes called learning support centre) if you have difficulty with your course or recognise that you may need to develop your learning skills, including your academic writing for essays, reports, dissertation or thesis. Information about learning advice is usually available through your university's web pages.

If you have any queries, ask. If you don't know who to approach, or are in doubt about what needs to be done and when, ask the departmental secretary or administrator.

Get together. If you feel that you don't understand course materials, probably there are others in the same boat. Ask around and discuss the difficulty with fellow students. Between you, it may be possible to work out the answer. If this doesn't work, ask a lecturer or tutor for help.

Seek pastoral support at an early stage. If you find that personal issues are beginning to interfere with your studying, then go to the support service that seems most appropriate for advice. It is better to seek advice while things are less critical than wait until the issues become big problems.

Useful language for . . . asking for support

You may need to make requests in a number of different situations. Here are some examples.

Context: to the academic support tutor

My supervisor (lecturer) says that I need to improve my academic writing. Can you help me, please?

Context: to a project or research supervisor

How often will I meet with you to discuss my research?

Context: asking for assistance from a librarian

Could you show please me how to access the specialist resources for my subject?
How can I find the electronic journals on my reading list?

Context: making general requests

I'd like to meet with the [for example, Student Counsellor]. Please may I make an appointment?
The information I've been sent is not correct. Can you change it please?

GO And now . . .

7.1 Get into the habit of using a diary or planner. Use this to keep notes of what you have to do and when and where, and to plan ahead for large-scale assignments. Research students should keep a research diary (**Ch 42**).

7.2 Plan your study and research ahead. In the UK on many taught courses, assignments are often 'clustered' within a very narrow time-frame. This means that it is important to create a time-management plan that will allow you to meet each submission date (**Ch 30**). This should include research time, planning, drafting and crafting (see Toolkit D). Research students will have different kinds of deadlines, but the strategy of long-term planning similarly applies.

7.3 Find out more about your university's support services. Take note of what is offered and where you can seek advice, perhaps via leaflets and websites. These services aren't just for help with crises – for example, they organise voluntary work, and arrange social events and outings. You may also gain from services without visiting their offices, for example, via websites.

TOOLKIT B

MANAGING YOURSELF IN THE UK

How to communicate what you will gain from being at university

What you learn at university is as much about the skills you'll use in later life as it is about the subject you have chosen to study. This chapter provides an overview of the skills and attributes that could apply to your situation, introduces some of the terms used to describe them and explains how they might be recorded for use in job applications.

Key topics:
→ Key skill areas
→ Reviewing and recording your skills and achievements

Essential vocabulary
Curriculum vitae (CV) Employability Graduate attributes Graduateness HEAR Key skill Personal development plan (PDP) Progress file Trait Transferable skill

The term 'graduate attributes' is now commonly used in UK higher education. It describes the skills and personal qualities that have been developed in a student by the end of their period of study. Some universities outline common attributes that should be present in all graduates, and particular courses may also focus on discipline-specific skills that are enhanced through study.

The reason for this emphasis is that employers who recruit graduates expect more from a member of their workforce than their professional skills as chemists, historians or engineers, for example. Employers are looking for someone who possesses a range of skills and attributes that can be applied in different situations. These are sometimes called 'transferable skills'. Combined with your subject knowledge and other personal qualities, such skills will contribute to your 'employability' – your ability to gain employment and move forward on your chosen career path.

If you hope to get a good or better job as a result of your qualification, it is important that you are aware of both the concepts and terms related to employability. This awareness will help you to communicate your skills to potential employers after you graduate. It will also help you to understand more deeply the aims of the exercises and assessments you will be asked to complete while studying.

Attributes, skills and personal qualities

Although they may be interpreted slightly differently in different universities, commonly accepted definitions of these terms are:

Attribute - a skill or a personal quality (see below)

Skill - a thing you are able to do, for example, organise and deliver an effective spoken presentation. A skill may be learned and developed, often through practice. Skills are sometimes called competencies.

Personal quality - a natural aptitude or trait that is a part of your personality, for example, motivation or patience. A quality can't really be learned, but may develop through time.

→ Key skill areas

Many different skills can be developed at university and there are many ways of describing them. Figure 8.1 illustrates five key areas in which transferable skills might be positioned. The five skill areas highlighted are:

- personal development skills;
- interpersonal skills;
- communication skills;
- technical skills;
- intellectual skills.

→ Reviewing and recording your skills and achievements

Figure 8.1 can be used as a reference checklist when reviewing your skills. You may be asked to do this as part of personal development planning (PDP) activities that may be encouraged by your university. This process will involve reflection on the current status of your skills and how you might improve them, for example, by attending training events organised by the university.

You will also have to consider your skills and personal qualities when you apply for a career position. In part, your curriculum vitae, or curriculum vitae (CV), will provide this information. However, as part of a personal statement or application letter, you will be expected to match your personal profile to the job description. Both in the application letter and at interview, you will be expected to provide evidence for any claims you make.

Figure 8.1 Skills and attributes. Here is a fairly comprehensive list of what are commonly called personal transferable or key skills. Tick all the boxes where you think you already have some degree of skill, then highlight all those with or without ticks that you think you could or should develop further while at university.

Personal development skills

Self-development – ability to:
- set personal goals
- develop self-confidence
- use creative talents
- be flexible
- work under pressure
- meet deadlines
- respond positively to change
- exercise self-discipline
- appreciate environmental issues
- adopt an international outlook

Assertiveness – ability to:
- stand up for oneself
- approach others
- make polite requests
- agree/disagree
- take risks
- challenge established ideas

Survival skills – ability to:
- organise accommodation
- develop home-management skills
- develop cooking skills
- maintain healthy lifestyle
- implement basic first aid
- build networks: social and business
- balance work/study/family/ friends
- make appointments
- make own transport arrangements
- organise banking/finance

Interpersonal skills

Teamwork skills – ability to:
- participate in/form a team
- engage with group/team
- demonstrate commitment
- give instructions
- display loyalty
- conduct meetings
- persuade by sound argument/evidence
- negotiate
- reach compromises
- speak concisely
- give/receive feedback
- motivate others

Interactive skills – ability to:
- be culturally aware
- integrate with others
- participate in a team
- develop self-confidence
- take responsibility
- develop problem-solving skills
- participate in community activities
- exercise (self-)discipline

Management/leadership skills – ability to:
- act as a leader
- manage time
- identify achievable targets
- set meeting objectives
- manage resources

Cross-cultural awareness – ability to:
- recognise conventions and value systems of host community
- recognise that opportunity to mix across all cultures is enriching and valuable in employment contexts
- retain or modify own values as appropriate to situation
- avoid isolation from the host community and be prepared to learn about other cultures
- recognise turn-taking conventions in dialogues with native speakers
- be aware of and observe body language and related conventions
- be aware of and observe punctuality conventions

Figure 8.1 (cont'd)

Communication skills

Written – ability to:
- write for academic purposes
- write for specific contexts
- write formal articles/papers
- give a poster presentation
- write a product evaluation report
- write a project/technical report
- take minutes of meetings
- conduct correspondence
- construct a CV
- work accurately

Visual and aural – ability to:
- listen to the views of others
- construct and deliver a *PowerPoint* presentation
- make a poster presentation
- use design techniques

Verbal – ability to:
- speak formally/informally to a range of people
- converse confidently
- present case/project
- debate formally and informally
- contribute to discussion in meetings
- conduct telephone interactions and negotiations
- use another language

Technical skills

Computing skills – ability to:
- use a keyboard
- organise file storage
- word process
- manage a database
- use a spreadsheet
- produce graphics
- use desktop publishing
- handle statistical data
- search the Web

Numerical – ability to:
- understand numerical terms
- handle numerical information
- present numerical results
- produce numerical reports

Technical/creative – ability to:
- appreciate the aesthetic
- be creative
- drive a vehicle
- use work-related technology

Intellectual skills

Problem-solving – ability to:
- collect data
- summarise information
- analyse
- evaluate information
- reason objectively
- think critically
- work on own initiative
- reflect on own learning
- develop learning strategies to suit personal learning style
- undertake career planning
- generate new ideas
- redesign and restructure
- understand task organisation
- organise and plan
- evolve problem-solving strategies
- research

Personal qualities

This list provides examples of personal qualities that an employer might look for in a potential employee.

Adaptability	Flexibility	Patience
Coolness under pressure	Health and fitness	Perseverance
Determination	Honesty and integrity	Self-discipline
Energy	Leadership	Tenacity
Enthusiasm	Motivation	Thoroughness

If you were asked to provide evidence about your honesty and integrity, you might, for example, discuss your experience as the treasurer for a society or club.

When you graduate, universities in the UK will provide a certain amount of information to verify your performance and to assist you to gain employment. A transcript is always provided along with your qualification certificate. This provides details of the modules you have taken and the grades you have obtained in any assessments. In some cases your university may verify extracurricular activities you have done and which it is willing to verify. Together some or all of these may be used to make up your Higher Education Achievement Record, or HEAR.

Vocabulary used in relation to recording skills and achievements

The terms used in the UK may be different from those familiar to you.

Employability – the blend of subject knowledge, skills and personal qualities that will help a graduate gain employment and advance in their chosen career

Graduateness – the sum of the skills and characteristics of a person with a university degree

Personal development planning – the process of reviewing and recording your qualities, achievements and skills and clarifying your personal and career goals in the context of your learning

HEAR – the Higher Education Achievement Record that may be provided by your university to record your achievements (this may be called a progress file)

Transcript – an official, certified list of a student's academic record. This may be provided in the form of a European Diploma Supplement.

UK universities offer a Careers Service, open to all students and at any level of study. Here, in confidence, you can discuss your employment goals with a trained advisor and obtain guidance about:

● careers available to you, both in the UK and internationally;
● vacancies;
● how to apply for a job;
● how to write a CV (resumé) in appropriate formats and style.

This (free) service is worth visiting at an early stage in your studies so that you are aware of opportunities available to you and what you will need to do to be considered for specific jobs.

Practical tips for enhancing your skills and recording your achievements

Consult your course handbooks for references to key skills. These will probably highlight opportunities for you to gain and develop skills, and will indicate the terminology in favour at your institution and in your discipline.

Identify which extra-curricular activities and experiences could contribute to your skills. Make sure you add details of these to your CV.

Bear skills in mind when you consider optional elements of your course. For example, don't pick a supplementary module just because it is 'easy' – choose one that will enhance your skills.

Sign up for workshops and training courses. First-aid courses, IT workshops, short language courses and training for mentoring are all examples of readily available training options that you could use to develop your skills.

Talk to others about your career plans. Discuss your options and opportunities with as wide a range of people as possible, including personal tutors, academic staff and careers service advisors, as well as friends and family. This will help you to develop your thoughts and explore new options.

Useful language for . . . discussing employment and employability

These expressions might be used when discussing your employment aims with careers service staff.

Context: seeking advice

I've drafted a CV in the format advised on the career service website. Please could you have a look at it and comment on how it might be improved?

My long-term aim is to work in the xxxx industry. Please can you tell me about international opportunities in that field of work?

What opportunities might I have for working in the UK?

And now . . .

8.1 Audit your key skills. Using Figure 8.1 as a framework, decide which of the skills listed you could say that you already possess and then consider whether you could develop them further. How? When? Where? What skills do you feel are weak? How might you address those?

8.2 Look for subject benchmarking statements. The Government's Quality Assurance Agency for Higher Education has created benchmarking statements that list the skills and knowledge expected in any graduate in a particular discipline. They can be found at: **www.qaa.ac.uk/students/guides/ UnderstandCourses.asp**

8.3 Update your CV. It's always a good idea to keep your CV up to date. It is especially valuable to keep track of the skills you have developed, the stage you are at with them and detail the evidence you can quote to show that you are competent.

How to organise your activities effectively

Managing your time effectively is an important key to making a success of your time studying in the UK. This chapter provides ideas for organising your activities and tips to help you focus on important tasks.

Key topics:
→ Diaries, timetables and planners
→ Listing and prioritising
→ Routines and good work habits
→ How to avoid putting things off

Essential vocabulary
**Asterisk   Displacement activity   Perfectionism   Prioritising   Procrastination
Subconscious   Swot   Time management   Writer's block**

Successful students tend to have the ability to focus on the right tasks at the right time, the capacity to work quickly to meet their targets, and the knack of seeing each job through to a conclusion. In short, they possess good time-management skills. Time management is a skill that can be developed like any other. This chapter presents some simple routines and tips that can help you improve your organisation, prioritisation and time-keeping. Evaluate the following ideas and try to adopt those most suited to your needs and personality.

As a student, you will need to balance the time you devote to study, family, work and social activities. Making the necessary decisions is a challenging task. Table 9.1 demonstrates just how easy it is for students' study time to evaporate.

→ Diaries, timetables and planners

Organising your activities more methodically is an obvious way to gain useful time.

Diaries and student planners

Use a diary or planner to keep track of your day-to-day schedule (for example, lectures, sports activities) and to note submission deadlines for university work.

- Work your way back from key dates, creating milestones such as 'finish library work for essay' or 'prepare first draft of introduction'.
- Refer to the diary or planner frequently to keep yourself on track and to plan out each day and week. Try to get into the habit of looking at the next day's activities the night before and the next week's work at the end of the week. If you use a diary

Table 9.1 Some of the ways in which students' study time evaporates. Do you recognise any of these traits in yourself?

Personality type	Typical working ways . . . and the problems that may result
The late-nighter	Lee likes to work into the small hours. He's got an essay to write with a deadline tomorrow morning, but just couldn't get down to doing it earlier on. It's 2.00 a.m. and now he's panicking. Because the library's shut, he can't find a reference to support one of his points; he's so tired he won't be able to review his writing and correct the punctuation and grammatical errors; and he feels so shattered that he'll probably sleep in and might miss the 9.00 a.m. deadline . . .
The extension-seeker	Elena always rationalises being late with her assignments. She always has good reasons for being late, and it's never her fault. This is beginning to make her tutors impatient. This time her printer broke down just before submission, last time she had tonsillitis and the time before she had to visit the visa office. She's asked for an extension, but will lose 10 per cent of the marks for every day her work is late. It's only a small amount, but as she's a borderline pass in this subject, it could make all the difference . . .
The stressed-out non-starter	Shahid has to give a presentation to his tutorial group. Only thing is, he's so intimidated by the thought of standing up in front of them, that he can't focus on writing the talk. If only he had his *PowerPoint* slides and notes ready, he'd feel a whole lot more confident about things, but he can't get going because of his nerves. Maybe if he just goes out for a walk, he'll feel better placed to start when he comes back . . . and then, maybe another cup of coffee . . .
The last-minuter	Mitsuko is a last-minute person and she can only get motivated when things get close to the deadline and then she produces her best work when the adrenaline is flowing. However, her final-year dissertation is supposed to be a massive 10,000 words, there's only a week to go and she hasn't felt nervous enough to get started until now . . .
The know-it-all	Marcus has it all under control. The lecture notes are all on the Web, so there's really no need to go to the lectures. He'll catch up on sleep instead and study by himself later on. Then he'll just stroll to the exam looking cool, get stuck in and amaze everyone with his results. Trouble is, at her first lecture the professor gave out a sheet changing the learning outcomes, missed out one of the topics (which Marcus has revised carefully) and told the other students that the exam format now involves two compulsory questions . . .
The perfectionist	Elizabeth wants to do really well at uni. She signed up for a vocational degree and has plans to land a top job on graduation to start her climb up the career tree. Her parents want her to do really well in her assignments and it's vital that the essay that she's working on starts with a cracking first sentence. Just can't phrase it right though – she's tried 15 different ways and crossed them all out. Time is running out now, and she will have to put off going to the Globetrotter's Dance. Well, who needs a social life anyway . . .
The juggler	Jeff is a mature student and is working part-time to make ends meet. Although his job started as 10 hours a week, it's now up to 25. He's juggling his shifts so he can attend lectures and tutorials, and might be able to do a bit of coursework in the breaks at work, providing the staffroom is empty. He can't get into the library to work on the short-loan material, so he'll have to miss that out. And he's so tired at the end of each day, he just can't summon the energy to read the core texts. Doesn't know how long he can keep going like this . . .

with the 'week-to-view' type of layout, you will be able to see ahead each time you look at it.

- Number the weeks, so you can sense how time is progressing over longer periods, such as a term or semester.
- Consider also numbering the weeks in reverse 'count down' fashion to key events such as end of semester/term exams and assignment submission dates.

Choosing a diary or planner

Some UK universities and many bookshops sell diaries that cover the UK academic year from September to August. Alternatively, some sell academic planners, such as *The Smarter Student Planner* (see inside cover), which provide templates for planning that allow you to keep track of assignment dates, plan for exam revision as well as providing reviews of key points of grammar, spelling, punctuation and maths.

Timetables

Create a detailed timetable of study when you have a big task looming (e.g. before exams, or when there is a progress report or literature survey to write up). The use of revision timetables is covered further in **Ch 50**, and the same principles apply to other tasks. You could:

- break the task down into smaller parts;
- space these out appropriately;
- schedule important activities for when you generally feel most intellectually active (e.g. mid-morning).

One advantage of a timetable is that you can see the progress you are making if you cross out or highlight each mini-task as it is completed.

Wall planners

These are another way of charting out your activities, with the advantage, like a timetable, that you can see everything in front of you.

Keeping a project or research notebook

The main purpose of these notebooks is to record your ideas, note important references and record data. However, they can also be used to organise your activities and work more efficiently. Depending on your discipline, you can:

- make simple 'to do' lists for each day's activity;
- note down questions for your supervisor ahead of meetings;
- record follow-up actions after meetings and seminars;
- create pages with 'recipe'-like instructions for carrying out repeated lab procedures, such as making up a solution or carrying out a procedure.

If you organise your time well, you will:

- keep on schedule and meet deadlines;
- reduce stress caused by a feeling of lack of control over your work schedule;
- complete work with less pressure and fulfil your potential;
- build your confidence about your ability to cope;
- avoid overlapping assignments and having to juggle more than one piece of work at a time.

Being organised is especially important for large or long-term tasks because it seems easier to put things off when deadlines seem a long way off.

→ Listing and prioritising

At times you may run into problems because you have a number of different tasks that need to be done. It is much better to write these tasks down in a list each day, rather than risk forgetting them. You will then have a good picture of what needs to be done and will be better able to prioritise the tasks.

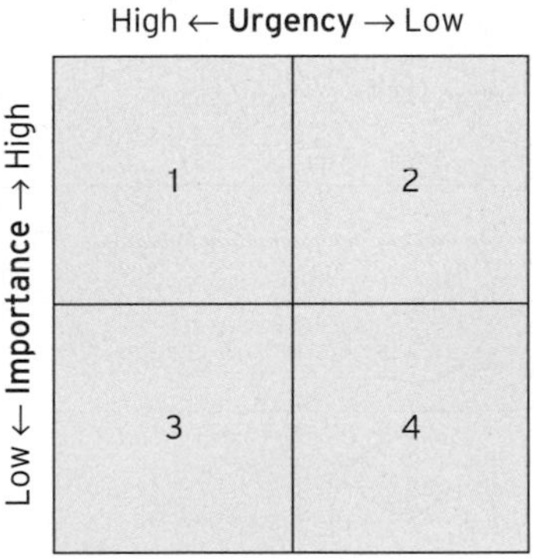

High ← **Urgency** → Low

1	2
3	4

Low ← **Importance** → High

Figure 9.1 The urgent-important approach to prioritising. Place each activity somewhere on the axes in relation to its importance and urgency. Do all the activities in sector 1 first, then 2 or 3, and last 4.

Once you've created a list, rank the tasks by numbering them from 1, 2, 3 and so on, in order from 'important and urgent' to 'neither important nor urgent' (see Figure 9.1). Your 'important' criteria will depend on many factors: for example, your own goals, the weight of marks given to each assessment, or how far away the submission date is.

Each day, you should try to complete as many of the listed tasks as you can, starting with number one. If you keep each day's list achievable, the process of striking out each task as it is completed provides a feeling of progress being made, which turns into one of satisfaction if the list has virtually disappeared by the evening. Also, you will become less stressed once high-priority tasks are tackled.

Carry over any uncompleted tasks to the next day, add new ones to your list and start again – but try to complete yesterday's unfinished jobs before starting new ones of similar priority, or they will end up being delayed for too long.

Deciding on priorities

This involves distinguishing between important and urgent activities.

For example, in normal circumstances, doing your laundry will be neither terribly important nor particularly urgent, but if you start to run out of clean underwear, you may decide otherwise. Hence, priorities are not static and need to be reassessed frequently.

→ Routines and good work habits

Many people find that carrying out specific tasks at special periods of the day or times of the week helps them accomplish things on time. You may already adopt this approach with routine tasks like doing your food shopping every Tuesday morning or playing a sport on Sunday afternoons. You may find it helps to add work-related activities to your list of routines – for example, by making Monday evening a time for library study, working on whatever assignment is next on your list.

Good working habits can help with time management:

- **Do important work when you are at your most productive.** Most of us can state when we work best (Figure 9.2). When you have worked this out for yourself, timetable your activities to suit: academic work when you are 'most awake' and routine activities when you are less alert.

- **Make the most of small scraps of time.** Use otherwise unproductive time, such as when commuting or before going to sleep, to jot down ideas, edit work or make plans. Keep a notebook with you to write down your thoughts.

- **Keep your documents organised.** If your papers are well filed, you won't waste time looking for something required for the next step.

Time period	Alertness rating
am	
pm	
pm	
pm/am	

Figure 9.2 Are you a morning, afternoon, evening or night person? Rate yourself (marks out of 10) according to when you find yourself most alert and able to study productively.

- **Make sure you always have a plan.** Often, the reason projects don't go well is because there is no scheme to work to. Creating a plan for an essay, report or project helps you to clarify the likely structure behind your efforts. Writing a fairly detailed plan will save you time in the long run.

- **Extend your working day.** If you can deal with early rising, you may find that setting your alarm earlier than normal provides a few extra minutes or hours to help you achieve a short-term goal.

Being time-conscious

In UK academic life, punctuality is very important. If you come from a country where the time that is given as a starting time is interpreted very loosely, then you may need to become more time-conscious in your new environment. Staff will expect you to arrive promptly for appointments, lectures, seminars and meetings. They will be disappointed and possibly angry if you are repeatedly late. In UK social life, timings are less rigid. For example, if you are invited to someone's home for a meal in the UK, it is expected that you might arrive 10–15 minutes after the time stated (but not later).

→ How to avoid putting things off

One of the hardest parts of time management is getting started on tasks. Procrastination is all too easy, and can involve the following:

- convincing yourself that other low-priority work is more important or preferable;
- switching frequently among tasks, and not making much progress in any of them;
- talking about your work rather than doing it;
- planning for too long rather than working;
- having difficulty starting a piece of writing (having 'writer's block');
- spending too long on presentational elements (e.g. the cover page or a diagram), rather than the content of the project.

A particular type of procrastination involves displacement activity – doing things that help you to avoid a difficult or distasteful task. For example:

- Do you really need to check and answer all your texts and emails or update your social networking profile before getting down to work?
- Do you really need to watch that TV programme or have another spell at that computer game?
- Why are you cooking tonight, rather than eating fast food and getting down to your studies much quicker?
- Why are you drawing such a neat diagram, when creating a less tidy one will let you get on to the next topic?
- Why are you so keen to chat to your friends rather than go to the library?
- Why are you shopping today, when you could easily leave it until later?

The first step in preventing the syndrome of procrastination, and especially displacement activity, is to recognise what your subconscious is doing. You need to make a conscious effort to counteract this side of your personality, by analysing your behaviour and possibly setting yourself time or other targets with 'rewards' to tempt you into meeting these. For example, 'I'll take a break when I've written the next section, 200 words . . .'

You might also make a list of things that need to be done and prioritise these into 'immediate', 'soon' and 'later' categories. Convince yourself that you will not start

Table 9.2 Ten tips for getting started on academic tasks and completing them on time

1 **Improve your study environment.** Your focus and concentration will depend on this.
   - Create a tidy workplace. Although tidying up can be a symptom of procrastination, in general it is easier to start studying at an empty desk and in an uncluttered room.
   - Reduce noise. Some like background music, while others don't – but it's generally other people's noise that really interrupts your train of thought. A solution might be to go to a quiet place like a library.
   - Escape. Why not take all you need to a different location where there will be a minimum of interruptions? Your focus will be enhanced if the task you need to do is the only thing you can do, so take with you only the notes and papers you require.

2 **Avoid distractions.** If you are easily tempted away from tasks by your friends, you'll have to learn to decline their invitations politely. Hang up a 'do not disturb' sign, and explain why to your friends; disappear off to a quieter location without telling anyone where you will be; or switch off your phone, TV or email program. One strategy might be to say to friends, 'I can't come just now, but how about having a short break in half an hour?'

3 **Work in short bursts while your concentration is at a maximum.** After this, give yourself a brief break, perhaps by going for a short walk, and then start back again.

4 **Find a way to start.** Breaking initial barriers is vital. When writing, this is a very common problem because of the perceived need to begin with a 'high-impact' sentence that reads impressively. This is unnecessary, and starting with a simple definition or restatement of the question or problem is perfectly acceptable. If you lack the motivation to begin work, try thinking briefly about the bigger picture: your degree and career, and how the current task is a small but essential step to achieving your goals.

5 **Focus on the positive.** You may be so anxious about the end point of your task that this affects your ability to start it. For example, many students are so nervous about exams or speaking in public that they freeze in their preparation and put the whole thing off. One way to counter this would be to practise – perhaps through mock exams or rehearsing an oral presentation with a friend. Focus on positive aspects – things you do know, rather than those you don't; or the good results you want to tell people about, rather than those that failed to provide answers.

6 **In written tasks, don't feel you have to work in a linear fashion.** Word-processing software allows you work out of sequence, which can help get you going. So, for a large report, it might help to start on a part that is 'mechanical', such as a reference list or results section. Sometimes it's a good idea to draft the summary, abstract or contents list first, because this will give you a plan to work to.

7 **Cut up large tasks.** If you feel overwhelmed by the size of a job and this prevents you from starting it, break the task down to manageable, achievable chunks. Then, try to complete something every day. Maintaining momentum in this way will allow you to divide the job in small pieces.

8 **Work alongside others.** If you arrange to work alongside others, you can encourage each other on with sympathy, humour and the promise of a drink or coffee after each study period.

9 **Ask for help.** You may feel that you lack a particular skill to attempt some component of the task (e.g. maths, spelling, or the ability to use a software program) and that this is holding you back. Don't be afraid to ask for help. Rather than suffering in isolation, consult a fellow student, lecturer, or skills advisor; or visit one of the many websites that offer assistance.

10 **Don't be too much of a perfectionist.** We all want to do well, but doing your very best takes time – a commodity that should be carefully rationed so that all tasks are given their fair share. Perfectionism can prevent or delay you getting started if you feel your initial efforts need to be faultless (see 4, above). Also, achieving fault-free work requires progressively more effort, with less return as you get nearer to perfection. The time you need to spend to attain the highest standards will probably be better used on the next task.

TOOLKIT B   Managing yourself in the UK

on the 'soon' and 'later' categories until you have fulfilled all those items on the 'immediate' list. And don't be tempted to think that if you get the smaller things out of the way that will free up your mind for the bigger issues – all that will happen is that even lower-category issues will creep into your attention.

Delaying completion of a task, in itself a form of procrastination, is another aspect of time management that many find difficult. It's a special problem for those afflicted by perfectionism. Good time managers recognise when to finish tasks, even if the task is not in a 'perfect' state. At university, doing this can mean that the sum of results from multiple assignments is better, because your attention is divided more appropriately, rather than focusing on a single task at the expense of others.

Tips for getting started on tasks and completing them on time are provided in Table 9.2.

 Practical tips for managing your time

Invest in items to support your time management. Helpful items could include a diary, wall planner, personal digital assistant (PDA), mobile phone with diary facility, and alarm clock.

Investigate how you really use your time. Time-management experts often ask clients to write down what they do for every minute of several days and thereby work out where the productive time disappears to. If you are unsure exactly what you waste time on, you might like to keep a detailed record for a short period, using a suitable coding for your activities. When you have identified the time-wasting aspects of your day, you can then act to reduce these (or cut them out). If you are more numerical you might wish to construct a spreadsheet to do this and work out percentages spent on different activities. Once you have completed your timesheet, analyse it to see whether you spend excessive amounts of time on any one activity or may not have the balance right. As you think about this, remember that universities assume you will be carrying out academic-related activities for approximately 40 hours per week.

Create artificial deadlines. Set yourself a finishing date that is ahead of the formal submission deadline for your assignment. That way you will have the time to review your work, correct errors and improve the quality of presentation.

Build flexibility into your planning. You may end up rushing things because the unexpected has interrupted a timetable that is too tightly scheduled. To avoid this, deliberately introduce empty slots into your plans to allow for these contingencies.

Try to prioritise the items on your 'to do' list. If you produce a daily list of tasks, spend some time thinking about how you wish to prioritise and order them through the day. You might adopt a numerical system or one using asterisks, for example.

Ask yourself whether your lifestyle needs radical surgery. You may find that little in this chapter seems relevant because your non-study time is dominated by a single activity. This might be socialising, caring for others, outside employment or travelling, for example. In these cases, you may need to make fundamental changes to your lifestyle to place greater emphasis on your studies. In some cases a student counsellor might be able to help you decide what needs to be done.

Here are some ways of explaining situations related to deadlines and time-keeping.

Context: asking to be excused and presenting apologies

I'm sorry, I can't go to [name of event]. I've got a big assignment due in tomorrow and I have hardly started it. Perhaps next week?

I have to go to the library tonight to work on that project for [subject]. Would you like to come along to meet later when I've made some progress?

Would it be possible for me to have an extension for the next assignment, please?

I'm sorry I'm late. My bus was running late/I overslept/I thought we began later.

(Note: It is better to give a reason after your apology . . . and, of course, the reason should be genuine.)

GO And now . . .

9.1 Analyse your time-management personality. Read through this chapter and particularly Table 9.1. Can you recognise any character traits that are preventing you from organising your time effectively? Might any of the 'Practical tips' help you become better at time management? How could you adapt them to your own situation?

9.2 Experiment with listing and prioritising. If you haven't used this method before, test it out for a week or so. Make a list of all your current and future tasks, assignments, appointments and social events. If they are large, subdivide them into smaller components. Rearrange the list in order of priority. Take special care to take account of events that depend on other jobs being completed. Now try to complete the different components, ticking them off the list as you go. After your trial period, decide how effective the method was in organising your activities and helping you to ensure that tasks were done on time.

9.3 Declutter and reorganise your life. If you reckon disorganisation is a reason for lack of progress (Table 9.2), make a determined effort to tidy things up. Start with your room and study environment, and if necessary invest in files and boxes to help you organise things. Keep out only that which is relevant to current activities and carefully store the rest. Decide how you can better arrange your affairs to keep on top of routine tasks. Now you should be in a better mental and physical position to get started on your next assignment.

10 | Budgeting and banking

How to organise your finances in the UK

For many international students, managing their finances is one of the hardest parts of student life. This chapter provides information to help you predict likely costs, advice on keeping costs down and hints on what to do if your budget isn't working out.

Key topics:
→ Creating a budget
→ Banking options
→ Term-time and vacation work
→ What to do if your finances seem out of control

Essential vocabulary
Budget   Building society   Contingency   National Insurance Number   Overdraft

Being at university in the UK will place you in a changed financial position. Much depends on your personal circumstances and, in particular, the degree of support your family is able to provide. However, being an international student restricts your earning potential and almost certainly increases your expenses. This chapter will explain about banking systems in the UK and suggest ways to keep to a restricted budget.

→ Creating a budget

A budget contains predictions about your income and your expenditure over a defined period. The main reasons you should set up a budget are:

● you will have a realistic view of the costs of being a student, especially in relation to less easily predicted expenses (**Ch 5**);

● by forecasting expenditure on essentials, you can have a better idea of any surplus available for lower priority or luxury items;

● you can reserve sums of money for anticipated costs;

● you can feel more confident that any debt you do incur will be controlled.

Studying and living in a large city

This can be much more expensive than at a campus-based or smaller-town university. Additional costs arise mainly from food, accommodation and transport (it is often difficult or very expensive to live near the campus). For example, costs in London are estimated to be about 18 per cent higher than elsewhere.

Table Z.1 in the Appendix on p. 459 can be used as the basis for a budget over weekly, monthly or yearly periods. To predict your costs, you should:

- use past expenditure as a guide, adding a suitable amount for inflation;
- use other sources of information, such as Figure 3.1 (p. 26), agreed rental contracts and student-focused financial websites;
- make an intelligent guess, perhaps based on data given on websites or discussions with other students or family members.

If you feel that budgeting over short periods is inappropriate for you because your expenditure is irregular, you could try working to an annual cycle, dividing infrequent but large outgoings by 12 to give average monthly costs. You can then create a budget for each month, but you should take care to carry over any monthly surplus, rather than spending it.

smart
tip

A spreadsheet could help with budgeting

If you are familiar with this kind of program, consider using a spreadsheet to set up your budget as on p. 459. You will be able to adjust the income and expenditure headings to suit your circumstances. You can also monitor your income and outgoings more easily by updating with real values.

→ Banking options

Setting up a bank account in the UK

As an international student, you will find it essential to set up a bank account in the UK. A basic bank account can be used to pay in and take out money. You can take your money out at a cash machine or at a Post Office using the Chip and PIN card that will be provided; you can pay bills (such as fees) by standing order or direct debit; and you may be able to make purchases online or in shops. However, you cannot get credit or an overdraft and will not have a cheque book.

To open a basic bank account, you will need to visit a bank branch, taking the following identity (ID) documents:

- your passport with student visa, if that is appropriate, or your national photo ID card, if you are from an EU/EEA country;
- the letter from your university/college/school confirming your UK study details or a *'Letter of Introduction for UK Banking Facilities'* which your university or college will provide to confirm your UK study programme.

Can I open an account in the UK based on Sharia principles?

Yes, but it depends on the bank. Check websites and publicity materials or ask in a branch. Your university student funding unit will also be able to give you further information on local availability.

If you wish to open a more complex account, or an online or a telephone account, the bank may need to see more documents – ask the staff to find out what is required.

Note: if you are required to register with the police, then it is important to make your banking arrangements *before* you register as their procedure requires them to keep your passport for up to 14 days for immigration checks. Without your passport you cannot open a bank account (due to 'money laundering' legislation) and so you might not have access to your money until your passport is returned.

Most basic bank services are currently free in the UK, although there may be monthly charges for certain international student accounts. Your bank will send you statements regularly, and you should always let your bank know in writing if you change your address. You can also check your account balance and get a mini-statement from a cash machine.

In general, you will pay nothing for using cash machines, but note that there are some locations where you may be charged for withdrawing money (for example, in pubs and clubs). There will be an announcement on the screen or printed on the machine if cash dispensing is free. If there is no such information, then check to see whether you will be charged.

Banking terms in common use in the UK

Automated Credit Transfer – a direct payment into your bank account, instead of by cash or cheque to you.

Basic bank account – an account offering basic banking services. You can use this to pay in and take out money. You can take your money out at a cash machine or at a Post Office; you can pay bills by standing order or direct debit; you may be able to make purchases online or in shops (check with the bank). However, you cannot get credit or an overdraft.

Cash machine – facility allowing cash withdrawal using the 'chip and PIN' system – you present your bank card (which carries a computer chip) and enter a PIN or 'personal identification number'. These are sometimes referred to as the 'hole in the wall' (slang) or ATM (Automated Teller Machine) and may be in shops, or your students' association union as well as outside bank branches.

Cheque – a printed order instructing your bank to pay money from your account to a named individual or company. It is illegal to present a cheque knowing that there are insufficient funds in the account to make the payment. Cheques are likely to be phased out in the UK in the near future.

Current account – account that may allow a credit facility subject to your status (accounts may be called different things at different banks).

Direct debit – a payment out of a bank account which is arranged by the organisation which receives the money with the express agreement of the account holder.

ID – identity.

Standing order – an instruction by a bank's customer to the bank, to pay an amount of money regularly to another account.

Note: the information in this tip box and elsewhere in this section is based on information provided by the British Bankers' Association. For more information consult their website at **www.bba.org** (BBA leaflets) and especially the leaflet *International students: opening a UK bank account.*

Types of banks

As well as the well-known high-street banks, many building societies offer current accounts with similar facilities. While either of these types of enterprise offer online banking, there are also specialist online banks whose charges and interest rates may be better than those subsidising high-street branches.

Here are some important aspects to consider when choosing a bank:

- **Convenience and facilities.** Is there a branch or cash dispenser (ATM) on campus, or is a good telephone or internet banking facility available?
- **Costs and potential gains.** Will your account be free to run? If not, how do the charges compare with those of other banks? Might you gain interest when your account is in credit?

If you wish to bring money into the UK, a convenient way is to ask your bank in your home country to give you a cheque in sterling (UK pounds) drawn on a UK bank. Alternatively, you can transfer money from home after opening an account. When you open the account the bank may ask you who you think will normally pay money into your account, and where they are located. They will need your International Bank Account Number (IBAN) and your Bank Identifier Code (BIC). Your bank will be able to give you these codes. It is *not* recommended to bring large amounts of currency on your person or in your luggage.

Anticipate delays in money transfers

Some automated money transfers are more-or-less instantaneous. However, if you pay in a cheque, it may take up to six working days for the money to appear in your account. Always check how long things will take and have enough cash available for the transfer period. There could also be a charge and extra delay if the payment is not in UK pounds sterling. If your sponsor is from a country which is subject to sanctions and export controls, your bank might refuse the payment. Check the UK Foreign and Commonwealth Office's web pages on sanctions (**www.fco.gov.uk**).

→ Term-time and vacation work

Naturally, universities and their staff expect you to study hard to earn your degree. In fact, they expect you to put in the equivalent of a full-time working week. Not all of this is taken up in 'contact' with staff in lectures, tutorials and practicals, but it is expected that you read, revise and work on essays and other assessments during the remainder of the time. If you take on term-time paid employment, this may affect your study effort and it may reduce time you would otherwise spend socialising or in sport, leisure or rest. Many sources recommend taking on no more than 15 hours' paid work per week.

The university vacations will provide you with opportunities for longer, more intensive periods of employment, which can replenish your bank account without affecting your studies. Many of these opportunities will involve seasonal occupations, but some of these fall into the category of 'internships', which, while often less financially rewarding, may provide vital career-related experience and are worth pursuing.

University towns and universities themselves provide many opportunities for paid term-time and vacation work and there is usually a contact point at the Students' Union or support services ('job shop', or similar) where these are advertised. Alternatively, you can look for adverts in the local press, online or visit a Jobcentre Plus (**www.jobcentreplus.gov.uk/JCP/index.html**).

Rules and regulations for international student workers

The UK Council for International Student Affairs (UKCISA) also provides information on how to find work in the UK as an international student, both during and after your studies. The following information applies to work during your studies, but as this area is subject to frequent rule changes, consult the UKCISA website or your local Jobcentre Plus for the latest information, or the UK Borders Agency website at **www.ukba.homeoffice.gov.uk/studyingintheuk**.

If you are an EU/EEA student, you may work without restriction, unless from a 'new member state' or 'accession country', in which case you will need to register under the Worker Registration Scheme (see **www.ukba.homeoffice.gov.uk/workingintheuk/eea/wrs/workers/**).

If you are not from the EU/EEA, and your passport or ID card says 'no work', then you must not take paid employment or you will be in breach of your immigration conditions. If, however, your passport or ID card has a sticker stating one of the following:

- 'Restricted work, p/t term-time, f/t vacations';
- 'Restricted work in term-time';
- 'Work (and any changes) must be authorised';
- 'Able to work as authorised by the Secretary of State';

then you may take on work, but you may not work more than 20 hours in any week. Note that special rules apply to student nurses where workplace training is usually part of their course.

National Insurance Number (NI No.)

If you are permitted to work in the UK and wish to do so, you will need to obtain a National Insurance Number (NI No) when you take on work (apply at the local Department for Work and Pensions Office – see *Yellow Pages* or **www.yell.com** for location).

Employers in the UK must pay a minimum wage, and grant you certain rights by law, for example, they must comply with anti-discrimination measures, health and safety requirements, and give you breaks during work (see **http://payandworkrightscampaign.direct.gov.uk/index.html**). As an employee, you must pay UK taxes if your income exceeds the personal allowances.

→ What to do if your finances seem out of control

If your budget doesn't seem to be working out or if you are approaching or in danger of exceeding your authorised overdraft limit, it is vital to talk to someone about your problems. You might approach a family member, your university's student finance specialist (often working within student services), or people at your Students' Union/Association. Your bank advisor may be able to point you in the direction of additional sources of money (loans) or extend your overdraft facility. Most of these people will be sympathetic to your needs, perhaps surprisingly so, as long as you are open and honest with them.

---

smart tip

Always respond promptly to all communication regarding debt

Explain what you intend to do and take notes of the names of the staff to whom you spoke and what was said. Keep a note of times and dates of all communications.

 ## Practical tips for cost-saving and budgeting

Actively control your weekly or monthly expenditure. From your budget calculations (p. 459), work out how much you should be taking out of the bank each week – and try to keep to this. Limit your 'pocket' money (the cash in your pocket or purse for day-to-day expenses). That way you will not be tempted to buy small treats, the cost of which add up. If you spend more than you planned in a given period, think of it as a loan from yourself and make do with less cash in the following week(s). Bear in mind that expenditure at the beginning of an academic session is always higher, and slows down as the year progresses.

Keep track of your account balance. By doing so you can avoid going into the red or exceeding your overdraft limit. In particular, don't forget to take a note of how much you take out of the 'hole in the wall' (ATM) to top up your wallet or purse. Try to pay predictable bills by standing order or direct debit, so that you can have a better idea of your outgoings and will not receive a surprise bill – but make sure that you always have enough in your account to cover these payments and remember to cancel them when your obligation to make these payments terminates.

Keep money back for known costs and contingencies. Allocate some of your funds to known recurrent costs, predictable one-off expenses and 'emergencies'. Use only the remainder for day-to-day expenses.

Save on insurance costs. It's always worth shopping around to find the best deal and some companies have special policies for students. You should also find out whether any home-based insurance policy for contents covers your possessions while you are studying in the UK and under what circumstances and with what excesses.

Shop smartly at the supermarket. If you have to buy food, play the supermarkets at their own game to save money.

- Find out which supermarket group is the cheapest for the goods normally on your shopping list.
- Find out the times that perishable goods are taken off the main shelves to be sold cheaply before their sell-by date – and time your shopping trips to suit.
- Check which cheap or own-brand items are acceptable, and buy these, but note that some of these may represent a false economy, either because there's less in the packet or tin, or because the quality is significantly reduced.
- Be aware of supermarket strategies to encourage impulse buying. When you visit, make a shopping list and stick to it.
- Take advantage of two-for-one offers to stock up – but only if you would normally buy the product.
- Use loyalty schemes and student discounts to your advantage.
- Don't shop when you are hungry. This sounds odd, but it means you won't be tempted as much to stock up.

Useful language for . . . banking or trying to find a job

Different systems and terms are used in the UK for banking. You can start developing your 'banking' vocabulary by reading the banks' leaflets. This will familiarise you with some of the necessary language.

Context: in a bank or building society

Good morning/afternoon. I'd like to set up a basic bank account with this bank, please. I am a new student at the University of [name] and I've come from [name of your home country].

I'm sorry, I don't understand this part of the form. Please can you explain?

Context: the Job Centre (Jobcentre Plus)

Please can you tell me what opportunities there might be for obtaining part-time work close to the university?

Do I need to obtain a National Insurance Number? Can you tell me how I apply for this?

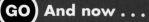

GO **And now . . .**

10.1 Check out the best deals in bank accounts. Shop around using the Web, Welcome Week literature or by visiting individual bank branches near to your campus.

10.2 Review your term-time employment options. If your visa status permits and if you feel term-time work is necessary to help balance your budget, visit your University's Job Shop or equivalent (usually associated with the Careers Service) to find a suitable position. Your Students' Association or Union and local bars, restaurants and shops may also employ students part-time.

10.3 Budget for some luxuries. Student life often requires a level of money consciousness that has the potential to become a strain. However, try to factor in some 'luxuries' or treat that ensure that life is enjoyable. These need not be expensive, but simply allow you to relax and enjoy yourself without feeling that you are being extravagout. A little pampering and sharing pleasure in relatively inexpensive ways can be just as enjoyable as more costly activities.

Social life at university

How to develop and maintain personal connections

For nearly all students, university involves great changes to their social relationships and this is especially true for international students. There will be changes to contacts with family, old friends and groups. New friendships will be formed, but they won't happen overnight. This chapter suggests ways of developing contacts and forming new relationships.

Key topics:
→ Making contacts
→ Forming new relationships

Essential vocabulary
Extra-curricular   Hall of residence   Idiom   Sports Union   Students' Association

A university is like a city within a city. Its community is populated by people who live locally as well as those who have come from other parts of the UK and other countries. It is enriched by the variety of people who live, work and study on the campus. As a member of this cosmopolitan society, you will begin to build up social and learning networks and will make many new and long-lasting friendships. However, this will not happen immediately. It takes time to create these contacts and friendship groups and that process will depend especially on where you live – on or off campus.

→ Making contacts

Many institutions try to offer international students the opportunity to live in a university residence. Here you will immediately have the potential, within a very short time, to meet a diverse range of new people, and will often live in close contact with students from different backgrounds. Although most accommodation offices try to 'match' people in the way they distribute students in residences, this is not always possible. It may take you some time to locate someone doing the same course as you, or with the same social interests, or a group of people with whom you feel comfortable in terms of personality.

One thing you may share with others is living away from the family home, so social events are usually organised to help new students to feel at home and to encourage people to mix. Some with be specifically arranged for international students. Taking part in these activities when everyone is new will help you to feel part of your new community. These events offer opportunities for networking that become less easy once people disperse to their own courses and studies. Making such contacts during the Welcome/Freshers' period also means that you can form friendships outside the narrower confines of your class or research area.

International students are sometimes routinely housed in the same residences, thus creating an international 'ghetto'. To reduce this effect, introduce yourself to home students and ask them questions about language and customs. This gives you a chance to interact with native speakers and become less reliant on your own national or ethnic group. Join societies and clubs as a means of broadening your circle of friends and experience of university life. Queuing for meals, doing your washing in the in-house laundrette or making a cup of tea also provide opportunities for meeting people and beginning conversations.

You may have chosen to live in shared private rented accommodation. This has the potential advantage of introducing you to the closer friendship group of your flatmates. On the other hand, it may limit the number of new people you meet, and to compensate you may need to make extra efforts to take part in social activities on the campus.

Some international students choose the 'home stay' option. This arrangement, where students live as a 'guest' with a local family, is one that provides immersion in an English-speaking environment and an opportunity to integrate into the local culture.

→ Forming new relationships

Even if you are shy, you will recognise that it is important to mix and to work at forming new relationships. This is especially true for international students, who may have to overcome additional language and cultural 'barriers'. We all have different ideas of what makes someone a possible kindred spirit and, if you are a 'people watcher', you may find it interesting to look out for the personality types in Table 11.1 and decide which types are the ones you would like to associate with.

On the academic scene

Many friendships emerge by sharing experiences. The most obvious way is by meeting people who are following similar studies. You will find that you get to know people through tutorial or lab groups, as well as from striking up casual conversations as you wait outside a class or lecture room or meet in the departmental common room. In some lectures, you will be encouraged to work with people sitting around you and this is an effective way of widening your circle of acquaintances. One way of ensuring that you get to know people studying the same subject is to volunteer to be a class representative (**Ch 12**).

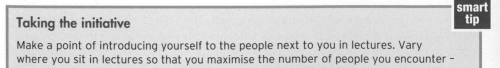

smart tip

Taking the initiative

Make a point of introducing yourself to the people next to you in lectures. Vary where you sit in lectures so that you maximise the number of people you encounter – but avoid the back row if you want to have a good view of the board and hear clearly. Sitting nearer the front ensures that you avoid some of the distraction of noise from others.

Table 11.1 Social stereotypes you may meet at university. Of course, there may be others, and it is unlikely that everyone you meet will be so well-defined as these characters.

Social stereotype	How you might relate to them socially
Those who want to be everybody's friend and flits from one group to another; seems to know and be known by everyone.	If you also are of this personality, this is alright. If you're not, accept this type of person for the open, sharing, but short-term acquaintance they may prove to be.
Those who go around in an exclusive group or clique; very difficult to join unless you share their value systems or shared experience.	If you have an 'intro' to the group through an existing member, it may be possible to break into it. These groups can start out as apparent opinion formers, but, as other (non-clique) networks are formed, their influence diminishes.
Lovely but loud extroverts – you will hear them before you see them. They always seem to need to make a noise – talking at full volume and oblivious to the fact that others are trying to work/sleep/study.	If you are this type, you will probably find and go around with others who are similar. Making friends with a person of this type allows you entry to an alternative, but often larger-than-life, world.
People who feel insecure in their own abilities and try to make up for this by working extra hard. Others who like to work may just be 'workaholics'.	These folk may come across as serious-minded, and tend to find their friendship groups among similar types. They may become isolated and miss out on wider opportunities.
Shy, modest types who frequently may give an impression of being academically weak. However, often they are highly competent, but they just don't project this loudly.	These are people to watch because they will have worked out how the course works and how best to succeed. Generally, they don't say much, but they observe a lot. If you need to know something about the course, they will probably have read all the information – and know what it means.
Those who may have swallowed all the hype about the great uni social life but may have played too hard and too long. Generally, they do not perform well and may drop out.	These people may simply have come to university because they see it as a rite of passage on to the next phase in their lives. Their priorities may not be studying towards a degree. If you find yourself mixing with such a group, you could be in danger of underperforming.
People who may live on or off campus but feel the tug of home very strongly. Consequently, they may make too few opportunities to mix with other students, preferring the security of home.	These types may find university so different from home and their previous learning environment that they return home at every opportunity or preserve their home networks to the exclusion of potential university ones.
Those who hop from party to party and generally live it up. Fatigue often takes over and they lose sight of the primary activity of studying.	These people tend to have developed a set of values and behaviours that may not equate with success or achievement of full potential. If you wish to succeed, you can certainly go along with them, but on your own terms – that is, on condition that you keep up with your academic work.
Folk who are often doing too many things: for example, by leaping from one part-time job to another part-time job in order to keep themselves financially solvent.	These types will have little time for making friends although they may need, of necessity, to cultivate a few contacts from whom they can borrow notes and general information.

On the social scene

Membership of the Students' Union or Students' Association is automatic in most institutions. This gives you access to all the facilities and activities provided within the union. These services are managed by a student executive, although some of the commercial activities such as bars, cafés and restaurants are managed by professionals. Office-bearers of the union/association are elected by the student body and the process is conducted under the scrutiny of a returning officer nominated from the staff body. You may feel that you would like to participate in this aspect of student life by standing as a year representative (**Ch 12**).

Joining one of the university's many clubs or societies is a way of finding people who share the same interests as you. The range of possible activities is vast and you will need to decide how many societies you can realistically afford to join. Being a fully participating member will not be possible for more than a few, and membership fees soon add up. Some subjects have their own societies, which may organise their own subject-specific events.

Examples of university societies

- Bridge Club
- Chemistry Society
- Computer Games Society
- Debating Society

- European Society
- Mature Students' Society
- Poker Club
- Public-speaking Club

Pubbing, clubbing and partying are all part of UK student life. You'll need to strike a balance between night-time fun and the need to be bright and attentive in daytime classes. Also, there is a limit to the amount of money you can afford to spend on these social activities. Conversely, staying in your room and being abstemious can be limiting also. It is perfectly possible to go out and *not* spend a lot of money – hard drinking is not a prerequisite for a good social life, but pub or Students' Union life may offer the setting that helps to consolidate friendship groupings. If you do not drink alcohol for religious or other reasons, you may find it difficult to meet the 'average' UK student, you'll have to find a different way to mix, such as a club or society.

Use social contact to refine your language skills

There's a tendency among international students when studying abroad to mix with students from their own country or who share a common language. You will feel more at ease doing this and will be able to converse fluently. However, you should remember that an important benefit of studying in the UK is the chance to refine your language skills – finding out more, for example, about the use of idiom, humour and slang. This may mean that you need to make big effort to meet UK students in a social context.

On the sports scene

People often quote the old saying 'a healthy mind in a healthy body' in relation to university study. In more modern language this might translate to 'work hard and play hard'. Joining your Sports Union or Institute is a way of keeping fit and making friends with people who enjoy the same sporting activities as you. It provides chances for regular social interaction and the chance to relax will also help you to perform well in your academic studies. On campus, there are numerous possibilities of sporting activities and facilities available at moderate costs. Many institutions offer family memberships, so that for mature students, for example, this is a way of involving your family in your university life.

Typical sports activities

- Badminton
- 5-a-side football
- Golf
- Hockey
- Judo
- Karate
- Keep-fit
- Squash
- Swimming
- Tennis
- Water polo

✔ Practical tips for establishing your university social life

Try to arrange things so that you can attend evening social activities. If you are living some distance from the campus, you may feel that this tends to isolate you from the social life of the university. This need not be the case. If you can manage to attend some activities that are of particular interest to you – and there are many early evening events that mean you don't have to worry about when the last bus is – you will meet people who share something in common with you.

Take the initiative by introducing yourself to others and engaging them in conversation. Ask people secondary questions about their feelings and responses to events; this usually gets the conversation going.

Try not to go around exclusively with those of a similar background. Branch out. Meet new people. Learn about different cultures and communities within the UK.

Think innovatively about different ways to meet people. You could take up an extracurricular activity (**Ch 12**), offer to act as a representative for your class, become a volunteer, join a church, cook a national dish for others, take up a part-time job, for example. Resolve to try to speak to at least one new person every day.

Be sensitive to others. Every culture has different approaches to social relationships, and you should be aware of this. To some, UK people will seem reserved and difficult to make friends with. Keep trying! They like others who are humorous, share their cultures (especially food and drink) and have a willingness to get involved (see **Ch 4**). They tend to dislike those who complain, are 'pushy' and who are unwilling to 'have a go'.

Expect to feel lonely or homesick sometimes. Having made radical changes to your lifestyle, this is only natural, especially at the beginning of your course. It is possible to feel alone in a crowd, and university might seem to be just such a place. If you do begin to feel that this is the case for you, speak to someone about how you are feeling. With a little support from your university counselling service, someone from the chaplaincy team or a personal tutor or adviser of studies, or maybe even a student who is in the year above you, you can work out some strategies to combat these feelings so that you begin to feel part of the community.

Asking questions is always a good start to a conversation but can become tiresome if the same questions (and answers) come up again and again. Here are some alternative strategies to the obvious *What's your name? Where are you from?* and *What are you studying?*

Context: taking the initiative in starting convesations

Hi. My name is xxxx. I don't think we've met before. Are you a student too?

Excuse me asking, but are you in the same class as me? I'm studying xxxx.

I think I saw you at this morning's workshop. Did you find it interesting/helpful?

Do you know anywhere where I could play [name of sport]? I'm just looking for a friendly game.

I'd like to explore more of the city/town. Are there any places that you would particularly recommend?

I'm hoping to take up learning another language. Have you any idea where I could do this?

GO And now . . .

11.1 Think about your own social networks following the example given in Figure 11.1. Give some thought to how your pre-existing networks might change with the addition of the 'new' ones. Think also how these changes might impact on you.

11.2 Look on your university or Students' Association/Union website for information about societies. If you have a real passion for an activity that does not seem to be represented, ask around and see if you can get together enough people interested in creating a new society. You can do this through your Student Association or Students' Union.

11.3 Think about signing up for some voluntary work, either through a society or through outside networks. This can give you an interest beyond your studies and is another way to make friends. It also allows you the chance to 'put something back in', whether in the university or local community. Although this means committing yourself to some regular responsibility, this can be motivating and rewarding. It's also a potential addition to your CV.

12 | Maintaining a good work–life balance

How non-study activities can contribute to your well-being

At university there are many calls on your time and it would be easy to become so focused on your studies that you lose a sense of perspective about other important aspects of life as a student in another country. This chapter offers suggestions about maintaining a balance between your studies and other interests, and explains how to deal with negative and stressful feelings when these arise.

Key topics:
→ Extra-curricular activities
→ Dealing with negative feelings
→ Coping with stress

Essential vocabulary
Extra-curricular   Nightline   Representation   Samaritans   Seasonal affective disorder (SAD)   Stress   Work–life balance

Your time in the UK is an opportunity to absorb a new culture and develop as a person. Your studies will only be a part of this experience, so the first part of this chapter outlines other activities you can do to contribute to and learn about life in the UK without neglecting your studies. Surveys reveal that, in general, the experience of international students when studying in the UK is positive. Even so, each individual will always find swings in their mood and feelings (**Fig 4.1**, p. 35). When negative, these might be associated with deadlines, personal or study difficulties or missing home life or family. The second part of the chapter provides some tips for dealing with these feelings and the stress that can sometimes result.

Extra-curricular activities

Doing things beyond your studies has the potential to contribute to the richness of your university experience and to the academic and non-academic communities around you. There is a wide range of activities to choose from, but balancing these with your academic studies is vital to your success at university.

Some students choose to pursue an 'outside interest' such as a sport or skill, some may wish to carry out charity work, while others might opt to become involved in student representation through their student union or association (see Table 12.1). Participating in these kinds of extra-curricular activities can result in life-changing

Table 12.1 Examples of extra-curricular activities in the UK

Activity	Examples
Charities	Working in a charity shop; collecting on charity days.
Exchanges	Spending a part of your summer working abroad or helping with exchange students.
Faith-based organisations	Taking part in religious observance; participating in faith-based social activities.
Internships/placements	Working for a local firm, a large company or government body.
Representation	Offering to stand for election as class representative or the executive of your students' union or association.
Skills-related	Learning a language; joining a student entrepreneurship organisation; learning to drive; gaining a First Aid qualification.
Societies	Joining and taking part in a debating society; the music group; a creative writing group.
Sports	Joining a local hockey team; playing for a university team; playing squash with friends.
Volunteering and community participation	Peer-mentoring students at earlier stages of study in your school; working on a conservation project; writing for the student newspaper.

experiences – from developing relationships to finding a vocation that influences your future career, as well as bringing a sense of balance to your life. Note that some voluntary activities may be recognised by an outside body (for example, a First Aid qualification) or certified as part of your university transcript. Some Universities give credit for activities whose extent and quality they can verify.

Opportunities to take part in extra-curricular activities will vary from campus to campus. Whatever is on offer on or around your campus will be enriching and may be the only chance ever that you will have access to so many opportunities to try something new. Many campus activities are generated for students by students. However, outside opportunities may be organised by the local community although sometimes student societies are involved in some 'outreach' charitable work. Your participation will help you to develop personal qualities and skills such as leadership, team-building and problem-solving – in short, many of the qualities sought by employers.

Another reason why students should have an outside interest is that studying is hard work and having an outlet to counterbalance any sense of pressure or stress can be a good 'de-stresser'. Doing something other than study will help because:

- you'll meet other people;
- you will relax;
- you'll being doing something totally different;
- doing things for others will keep things in your own life in proportion;
- you'll find that some of the 'problems' are reduced to manageable when you go back to your studies.

Charities and volunteering in the UK

British society is one where supporting charity is an important activity. Charities often provide support in areas not covered by state provision (paid through taxation) or supplement such state provision as exists. It is commonplace for people to volunteer to raise money for charities through special campaigns, charity shops or other activities. Anyone acting as a volunteer collector will carry an identity badge; without this form of identification, they cannot collect in the street or by calling at homes. British charities provide support over a wide range of needs: research into life-threatening illnesses, practical care for people suffering from such illnesses, protection of vulnerable children, specific animal protection, people who suffer from poverty or other hardship.

If you would like to work with a charity, then ask for some contact numbers and addresses at the local public library, Citizens' Advice Bureaux or online, since many charities have generic websites. If there is no obvious interest you can identify, why not find out more about the history and culture of the area you are living in? This will help you gain from your experience in the UK and understand the background of many of your fellow students. Start with the local tourist office or public library to find out more. For some activities involving children and older people, it may be necessary for volunteers to undergo a criminal record check (sometimes called 'disclosure'). This can take some time and there is a cost implication for the organisation wishing to recruit you as a volunteer. You should check this over with your chosen organisation when you volunteer in case you have to wait for a long period before being able to participate.

Creating new friendships

smart
tip

Research indicates that students with friends at university feel positive about their learning experience and are less likely to drop out. This is probably even more true for international students as they may be very distant from past social networks. However, making fresh acquaintances and converting these into friends takes energy. Although many friendships start off with a chance remark or casual invitation for a coffee, you shouldn't expect others to make all the moves: you need to be proactive. Joining some of the university clubs and societies where you will meet others with similar interests is always a good starting point.

→ Dealing with negative feelings

As with any new experience, once the initial feeling of excitement subsides, people can become unsettled. This can happen for some students, but not for others. Those it affects can feel slightly isolated and lonely. If this happens to you, then you need to realise that others may have similar feelings – and they won't all be in the international community either. UK students can be living away from home too and be experiencing exactly the same feelings.

Things that could be causing you to feel unhappy might include:

- changes in the people you see and relationships in general. You may become slightly distant from your family and old friends. Some existing relationships may fail to survive the lack of contact, leading to break-up;

- other worrying events that occur for some students include illness and death of relatives at home, and parental problems, including divorce;

- you may be worried about your course and whether you are going to make the grade;

- financial worries (see **Ch 10**);

- you might be suffering from SAD – Seasonal Affective Disorder – without knowing it.

Ways of keeping negative feelings under control include:

Are you feeling SAD?

SAD can affect home and international students alike. SAD stands for Seasonal Affective Disorder and is a condition that affects many people in northern European countries during the months between September and April. It is said to result from shorter hours of daylight in the winter months and to make people feel low in spirit. Fortunately, as the days lengthen, and the days become brighter and sunnier, people feel better.

If you suspect that the climate is causing you to feel 'low', then you should visit your GP or University Health Service for advice.

- Looking at the 'bigger picture' – whatever is making you sad will not last forever. Think of things that you can look forward to with pleasure – for example, a day out with friends; a trip to the cinema or the ice rink; a cycle ride or even just a long walk. Look for the positive.

- Interacting with your fellow students (**Ch 11**). Not only will this provide company, it can also enhance your learning experience (**Ch 17**). Take active steps in making and maintaining contact with others, for example, through sport and other activities external to the univesity.

- Keeping in regular contact with family and friends back home. Although this can remind you of what you are missing, normally this can counteract feelings of isolation. Remember too that those in your home country will be missing you as much (if not more) than you are missing them and they will be eager to hear your news.

If you are experiencing difficulties with happenings in your home country, this can be frustrating and stressful as appropriate and normal actions may be outside your control. There is no easy answer and you may need to rely on others back home to help, such as relations and family friends. If matters are extreme, you may need to return home. However, don't forget to inform staff in your department or school and ask their advice on, for example, delaying submission of assignments.

Obtaining help and support as a responsible student

In the UK university system there is a wide range of specialist support on campus. It is there for a reason – to help students – and it is there because, in the UK, asking for assistance is regarded as the normal, responsible approach to confronting a difficulty. Some international students take exactly the opposite action by starting to miss lectures, struggling along on their own by reading source material either in their own language or that is inappropriate to the course. This strategy cannot work because they miss the discussion points given in the lecture, they never hear the correct language being modelled and become isolated and unhappy.

If you do find that academic stress becomes an issue for you, then taking action at an early stage is wise. You will be respected for doing this and showing that you are a responsible student. As a first step, make an appointment to meet with a study advisor, a lecturer or the school secretary, who will be able to arrange support for you. You might also wish to make an appointment to see your doctor.

→ Coping with stress

Being a student exposes you to a number of events that can lead to stress – for instance, living away from home, entering new relationships, organising your finances. Within your academic context, stress can arise from the need to meet deadlines, compile written progress reports and take new-style exams. However, for many international students there may be additional stresses. For example, the knowledge that your family may have made financial and personal sacrifices to allow you this opportunity may cause you to fear failure, because this might bring disappointment and possible shame to them. Another factor might be that you have been sponsored by your company or government and, if you fail to do well, then you will face disgrace and your career may be blocked.

Therefore, recognising and dealing with stress is important. If you can detect the physical symptoms associated with stress, then you can develop strategies to deal with these. For example, characteristics of stress might include: loss of appetite, feeling of panic, nausea, shaking, sweating and dry mouth. Behavioural changes may occur and you may become more irritable, lose concentration, feel depressed or have difficulty sleeping. Especially at the start of your UK university experience, you may feel stressed in a number of ways and for a number of reasons.

If you feel that any of the above factors or events are stressful to you, or are likely to become so, it is important to respond positively. The practical tips in this chapter include suggestions for dealing with stress in an active and constructive manner. It's also vital that you don't suppress your feelings, so you should try to share them with others, either informally with friends, family or with professional counsellors or an academic responsible for your studies.

General stress factors

These may include some of the following:

- Practical issues including not liking your accommodation; feeling lonely, alternating between having too much and too little to do; having noisy neighbours; and feeling uncomfortable with your study facilities - because it seems that your interests and values differ from those around you (see **Ch 4**).
- Outside influences are putting you under pressure to perform - for example, fear of failure.
- Too many things are being demanded of you at the same time - for example, deadlines clustered within the same time span.
- You have never before had to deal with the kind of stresses that you are encountering - you have no strategies for dealing with the feelings of stress.
- There is a difference between the way things are and the way you would like them to be, you may feel insecure - because the learning situation is different and you have still to work out effective strategies to deal with these.
- You have little control over events but care greatly about the way they might turn out - therefore you spend a lot of time becoming stressed about things you have no power to change.
- You have been under low-level pressure for a long period - but you have had no 'time out' to recharge your energy levels.
- You run out of time and have a task to do in too short a period - because your time management skills are less well-developed.
- You fear that you will not achieve to your own high standards - you have yet to learn how to moderate your perfectionism.
- You fear criticism of others - this may include your peers, academic staff, your family and your employer (if applicable).
- Specific academic pressures - for example:
  - dealing with new teaching methods, such as lectures and tutorials;
  - lecturing staff who make incorrect assumptions about your knowledge or abilities;
  - expectations that you have to learn by yourself without the detailed guidance you are used to;
  - expectation that you will have a high standard of English and reasoning skills;
  - the sheer volume of work creating problems;
  - the prospect of assessment deadlines and impending exams.

What if you feel really, really bad?

For some, the stresses of student life are such that they consider dropping out or even harming themselves in some way. Talking about your situation is the best way to counteract these feelings. You can do this anonymously and/or confidentially through:

- The Samaritans (**www.samaritans.org.uk**)
- Nightline (**www.nightline.niss.ac.uk**)
- Your university's medical or counselling services (**www.studentcounselling.org**).

These sources provide contact telephone numbers and 24/7 online guidance.

- You can also speak with your School Secretary, your Advisor of Studies or a lecturer who you feel would be understanding.

Practical tips for dealing with stress

You may find one or more of the following tips appropriate to your situation and/or personality.

General strategies

Try not to worry about things over which you have no control. If necessary, recognise your personal limitations. Accept life as you find it and try to find positive ways around each problem.

Share your problem. Simply talking about your problems can help you confront them, put them in perspective or work out a solution, while keeping them to yourself may make them worse. You might wish to speak to a friend about your feelings; or talk to a receptive member of academic staff (who will have seen most problems before); or seek a session with one of your university's counsellors or approach someone in your local faith centre or community if you think that you would feel more comfortable about discussing this. Consider new approaches that are suggested to you and act on those that will help you resolve your problem.

Try to forget about your problem. Some problems (not all, certainly) simply disappear with time as events move on or circumstances change. What was a problem on Friday morning may have disappeared by Monday morning. Go out to the cinema or watch a DVD for some escapism. Get some sleep and see how you feel in the morning.

Confront your problem. OK, so you have a tough essay to write for the end of the week and you feel stressed. Well, start studying and writing! Or if someone is being a nuisance, tell them so, explaining why their actions are causing you problems. Running away from a problem means you avoid the issue rather than face it.

Don't be afraid to have a good cry. This is a very natural way to relieve stress in some situations – and this applies to both sexes.

Reward yourself. Instead of feeling that you are always doing things you don't like, or find hard or take ages, give yourself a break and do something you know you will enjoy. You will probably find that when you return to your stressful task you are in a much better frame of mind to conquer it.

Learn how to meditate. Try out yoga or other methods of relaxation. Some people find this is a great tool for de-stressing.

Do something physical. This is great for removing the symptoms of stress. Go for a jog or swim or join a fitness class. This provides an outlet for the jangled nerves and hormones that your body has unconsciously prepared in anticipation of a stressful event.

Academic issues – taking control by changing your attitude

Try to manage your time better. See **Ch 9** for more information.

Learn to prioritise. If you are stressed because you have too much to do, make out a list and put it in order based on urgency and importance (see **Ch 9**).

Change your learning pattern. If you are having problems because of skipping lectures, the remedy is obvious – get there! If you can confess to laziness in other ways, increase your work rate. Decide to study longer hours or study the same hours more effectively. Cut out activities that are preventing you from achieving your goals.

Put things in perspective. Look around you and see how others are coping. There is always someone worse off than you are, and some people battle through against amazing odds. If they can manage, why not you?

Try not to be a perfectionist. Accept a lesser standard if this means your life is more balanced.

Recognise that you can't please everyone. Accept that you may have to act selfishly or in a focused way. You may find that others are far more accommodating than you thought they would be, if you simply explain and apologise.

 Useful language for . . . talking about your work-life balance

These expressions cover a wide range of situations you might encounter.

Context: arranging extra-curricular activities

I'd like to volunteer to work for a charity involving animals. Could you give me some local contacts, please?

I'm interested in working with Riding for the Disabled. Is there a branch near here? How would I get in touch with them?

[At the Careers Service, perhaps] *I've got the chance to go on a placement related to my course. I'd like to work with a charity as an intern. Have you a list of charities that might accept me?*

Context: talking to a counsellor or friend about feeling low-spirited and stressed

I've not been sleeping and I'm worrying all the time about the situation in my country. I'm thinking about going home.

I'm tired all the time and I can't concentrate on my work.

The lectures are too difficult for me to understand. I'd rather read the textbook. I'm worried that I'll fail my exams. I don't know what to do.

Context: talking about steps to overcome stress

I'd like to change my modules. Is this possible?

I can't keep to the deadlines – it takes me too long to do the reading. Is there anyone who can help me with this?

I'd like to work on improving my grades but I don't know where I'm going wrong. Can you help me, please? Could you give me some tips?

12.1 If you can, make sure you influence things. You may be able to remove the cause of stress. For example, if noisy neighbours are causing you stress in halls, ask for a move to a different room or floor in your residence, or, if you are experiencing financial problems, visit the student advisor who specialises in financial matters. This may require determination and assertiveness on your part. Putting the blame on others is tempting, but you may have the solution in your own hands. For example, you may think others are being unfriendly, when in fact you are expecting them to make all the approaches, rather than being outgoing yourself.

12.2 Use your university's counselling service. The mere fact that a counselling service exists should tell you something: others have been here before. This service will be staffed by professionals, expert in their job. They will make you feel at ease, assist you to work out your own solution, and put you in contact with others who can help. You can rest assured that the service will be fully confidential and independent from the academic side of university life.

12.3 Make an appointment to see a doctor or nurse if your problem involves your health. In the past, you may have left this sort of thing to your parents, but now you will need to take on this responsibility. As a first step, visiting your University Health Service to see a nurse or doctor will provide you with the chance to discuss your health with professionals who understand the University Environment.

DEVELOPING YOUR LEARNING SKILLS FOR THE UK CONTEXT

Studying independently

How to organise yourself and develop good study habits

One of the distinctive traditions of the UK university system is that students are expected to set their own learning agenda within the confines of their course of study. For some international students, this may require adjustment to previous approaches. This chapter covers practical ways for organising yourself for study, and ways of organising the material you need to support your learning, assignments, exam revision or research.

Key topics:
→ Sources of information for your subjects
→ Organising your study space and your notes
→ Developing your skills
→ Getting down to the task
→ How to study actively
→ Understanding your learning style

Essential vocabulary
**Annotate Aural Chronological Displacement activity Glossary Kinesthetic
Learning objective/outcome Learning style Mnemonic Practical Reflect**

In UK universities, learning depends on the initiative of the student. You are expected to organise yourself by planning ahead, prioritising different study activities, and making sure that you meet deadlines. You may also need to decide what to learn and how deeply you need to understand it (**Ch 21**). An audit of what resources you will require and what needs to be done will help you to organise yourself. Examining learning objectives/outcomes (**Ch 53**) and taking account of assessment feedback in the context of marking criteria (**Ch 48**) are good ways of assessing whether you are hitting the right level with your work.

Adjusting to expectations

Some international students will find the style of UK higher education teaching very 'distant' in that staff will rarely tell you what and how to study. Even for home students, there may be a contrast between the extent of guidance given to them at school and in higher education. If you are not aware of these differences right from the start (**Chs 2-3**), you are likely to feel disorientated and to perform less well.

→ Sources of information for your subjects

In taught courses at a UK university, most key information is given in written format and students are expected to read this intensively in order to plan their own schedule of personal study. The most common places for finding relevant information include:

- **Course handbook:**
  - gives information about lecture topic, numbers of lectures, names of lecturers;
  - gives dates and venues of practicals, lab dates and tutorials;
  - gives reading lists for written work, for tutorial or practical work;
  - gives some guidance on subject-specific or preferred referencing styles;
  - may give some guidance on essay-writing as required in that subject area;
  - provides learning objectives/outcomes;
  - refers to marking criteria (**Ch 53**).

- **College/faculty/school timetable:** gives venues and times of classes and exam dates.

- **Noticeboards:** give important information, including late changes to printed information. You should find out where the relevant departmental, faculty and school noticeboards are and consult them regularly.

- **Emails:** provide updates, reminders and other information. Group and individual emails are the preferred means of communication with students. Thus, it is essential to keep checking your university email account regularly.

- **Virtual learning environment:** gives access to much of the above information, online. Course information may be posted on the electronic noticeboard or announcement page. You need to check such announcements frequently to keep up-to-date with what is happening on your courses.

Coping with language difficulties

For all students, university-level study involve learning new terms, idioms and jargon. This process is even more difficult for non-native English speakers, who will need to spend extra time interpreting lecture notes, handouts and books, and creating their own glossary of key words (see Table Z.2). You may need to allocate more study time for this process. For example, it will help considerably if you download lecture notes, if available, and read them before the lecture.

→ Organising your study space and your notes

Everyone needs a place to study, and, ideally, this should be a location that is exclusively 'yours'. For example, most research students will be allocated desk or bench space. However, this is not possible for undergraduates, so investigate facilities such as study rooms in your department or study zones in your library. Alternatively, some students find that going to a public library or another specialist library on the campus provides the anonymity that allows them to study uninterrupted. Working in a comfortable temperature with adequate light and ventilation is important. Your desk and chair should be complementary in height so that you are not sitting in a crouched position; conversely, if you are 'too comfortable' it is easy to drop off to sleep – easy chairs or on top of your bed are not recommended.

Keeping your work organised is something that some people do intuitively, while others need to work hard at it. Each theme you study on your course will generate a lot of paper. Table 13.1 gives practical ideas for organising the vast amount of information that you will gather.

Table 13.1 Tips for organising key information arising from your studies

Day-to-day 'housekeeping'
• Use time when you are at an 'energy low' to undertake routine clerical activities by writing up and filing your notes; use your 'high energy' time for intensive study (see Figure 9.2).
• Be systematic – date everything as you receive or create it.
• Store your material in an organised way – invest in a series of large ring-binder folders, one per subject, with coloured dividers to section different elements of the course. This will help you to retrieve things quickly. You could arrange the subjects alphabetically or chronologically, for example. This is a matter of personal preference. The important thing for retrieval purposes is to be consistent.
• As soon as you start to use material from any kind of source, *always* note down all the reference information required to relocate the source should you need it at a later point. This information will also be needed should you wish to cite some of the information from this source in your text. This means that you should record all the information required for the reference system you may customarily use, for example, the Harvard Method of referencing (**Ch 31**).

Language and formulae
• Create a glossary using the format shown in Table Z.2 (p. 460) for each of your subjects by listing all terms that are unfamiliar and use dictionary, textbook and internet searches to compose an explanation that is accurate and makes sense to you. Make sure you follow definitions provided by your lecturers if there are differences among sources.
• If you feel it would be useful, you may wish to create a 'key phrases' file that includes useful ways of stating things in English. This might include, for example, text where respective cultures take a different approach to the order and logic of wording, or combinations of words and phrases that you feel explain things well.
• In subjects with a mathematical element, you may be introduced to a range of new formulae (equations). A 'formula sheet' listing these can be useful for revision and should include a note of what all the symbols mean and when the equation should be used. Notation may differ between your country and UK. Ask for guidance if symbols used by your lecturers are not the ones you recognise.

Electronically retrieved or created material
• Create separate folders for each topic within the course you are studying. This will make it easier for you to locate work.
• Save your material using a file name that will make sense to you even when you try to locate it several months later. It may be useful in some cases to add a date reference to the file name, for example: Dental caries 170211.doc
• Keep a back-up of all work done on a personal computer. This includes saving any electronic work that you have to submit so that you can produce additional copies if required to do so.
• Insert page numbers and the date on which you last worked on the document as a footnote (some packages can be set to alter the date automatically every time you work on a document). This will avoid confusing different versions.
• Explore the software package you are using to find out how to print the file name and complete pathway in the footer section of your document for ease of reference.

→ Developing your skills

Initially, early on in your study period in the UK, it will help you tremendously if you review the learning and studying skills you need to develop. These include:

- learning how to use IT facilities (**Ch 26**);
- being competent in relatively advanced features of a word-processing package – Microsoft Word is possibly the most commonly used package on most university networks (**Ch 26**);
- learning how to use subject-specific software (**Ch 26**);
- using a keyboard skilfully (**Ch 26**);
- knowing the location in your library of books, reference materials and other subject-specific resources (**Ch 22**);
- being able to use your library efficiently by accessing its electronic catalogue and other electronic resources (**Ch 22**);
- internet searching for reliable source material at the correct level (**Ch 22**, **Ch 26**);
- being able to organise, structure and write a competent piece of text appropriate to the higher-level learning in your subject area (**Ch 27–Ch 34**).

Being able to do these things to some degree of competence will be of enormous value to you in your academic studies. If you feel that you need further assistance in any skill mentioned, go to the relevant service in your university and make enquiries about courses or inductions that will help you to develop your skills. You will find information on how to access support services on the university home page. Look for:

- **IT support service:** word-processing, software packages or keyboard skills.
- **Learning or study advice centre:** for help from study advisors.
- **Library:** for a familiarisation or induction programme. For specific queries, there will be an information desk position where you can get help with your search or query.

→ Getting down to the task

Think about what you need to do, work out how much time you can allocate to completing the task, decide how you are going to tackle the task and then get on with it. You may find that the first ten minutes is hard going, but then you become involved in the subject.

Types of studying to be done

Studying is a multifaceted activity and one that differs according to discipline and subject. The first thing you need to consider is what you need to do to learn within your specialism. This could include:

- reviewing new material from lectures by annotating or re-framing notes;
- finding and reading related hard-copy material in textbooks or journals as appropriate;
- finding material on a virtual learning environment or other web-based source;

- preparing or writing up reports or essays;
- preparing for exams.

Once you work out for yourself the activities that are necessary for learning in your field, then you will be able to assign the time and priority you give to each activity.

Recognise the importance of *thinking* about the subject material as a vital part of studying (**Ch 21**) rather than simply passively reading it and/or memorising it. Table 21.1 (on p. 163) summarises the different types and 'levels' of thinking that tutors expect you to be doing.

Displacement activity

As noted in **Ch 9**, displacement activity is a form of procrastination where you find other ways of using your time to avoid getting down to work. Examples include:

- persuading yourself that you can study in the sun (or the pub!);
- phoning, emailing or social networking;
- going window-shopping;
- tidying your DVD collection or room.

Planning and overplanning are other kinds of displacement activity. Although planning is essential, there is the risk of overplanning: try to achieve the right balance between planning and productivity.

If the total number of displacement tasks or the time that you allocate to them is preventing you from making real progress with your studies, maybe you need to make serious decisions about time management (**Ch 9**).

Asking questions

Although learning is up to you at university, if you are studying on a taught course and do not understand something even after you have attended the relevant lectures, delved into the recommended texts and spoken to others on the course, go to your department and ask to see someone who can help you. Departmental secretaries are usually good people to speak to first in order to find out about availability of academic staff. Otherwise, email your lecturer to make an appointment or to pose the question directly. Staff like being asked academic questions and within a few minutes may resolve the difficulty for you. This could also highlight to the staff member that a topic may need to be revisited with the whole class. If you are a research student, make sure you keep a list of questions you wish to ask your supervisor at your next meeting. Your supervisor will appreciate this organised approach to your research.

→ How to study actively

It's all too easy to go through the mechanics of studying by copying out notes or reading a chapter from beginning to end. While this could be *part* of process, it's important to think about what you're doing and why. Table 13.2 lists some typical activities along with the questions you should be asking yourself as you do them. Being aware of these different aspects of studying will prevent you from working 'automatically' and will help you to absorb the content of your reading and writing.

Table 13.2 Typical study activities, with questions to ask yourself as you do them. For research activities, see **Chs 41-43**.

Rewriting notes from lectures (see also Ch 16)
• What are the key ideas? • Do I need to reorganise these to create a logical sequence that matches my understanding? • Is this taking up too much of my time? If so, try to take original notes more neatly. If rewriting notes helps you to learn, could you synthesise the notes into bulleted lists/flow charts/diagrams rather than lengthy sentences?
Making notes from texts (see also Ch 25)

• How is the information organised?
• How can I identify the key ideas quickly to provide an overview?
• How can I restructure detailed information into concise notes?
• How much detail do I need for:
  - learning about the topic?
  - eliciting information for an assignment?
  - revising for exams?
• What is the best method for framing my notes?

Thinking/reflecting (see also Ch 21)

• What do I think about this topic? It's important that you don't just take what someone else tells you as the only approach on the topic. Think critically by questioning your own ideas. Be prepared to redefine your view in the light of new interpretation, information or evidence.
• What should I be looking for - information or concepts? If information, how reliable is the source and can you cross-check from another resource? If concepts, what evidence is there for each viewpoint? How good is the evidence? What other evidence might be available? Where will you find this?
• Are any patterns emerging? Look for relationships or themes, such as:
  - cause and effect (reason and result);
  - comparisons and similarities, contrasts and differences;
  - threads of arguments, supporting evidence and counter-arguments;
  - problem and solution information.

Working through problems and examples (see also Ch 37)
• Is the answer sensible and are the units correct? • Have I done what has been asked? • Is there anything else asked for? • Have I used the correct formula? • Have I used all the information given in an appropriate way?

smart tip

Using your 'visual' brain

Generally, most people tend not to exploit their visual memory. If you use highlighters for headings and sticky place tabs on key sheets in your file, this will help you find things more readily and also help you remember content because of the layout of the page or the positioning of notes within your file.

→ Understanding your learning style

As a student, it is worthwhile thinking about how you learn best and how this relates to your personality. This will help you reflect more deeply about how you tackle learning activities, from note-taking (**Ch 16**) to revising (**Toolkit F**). There are numerous ways of categorising learning styles and several tools, some available free online, to help you determine what kind of learner you are. These have the potential to help you:

- identify your academic strengths and weaknesses;
- study more effectively;
- approach problem-solving more flexibly, especially when working with others.

It is said that a person's learning style has already evolved significantly by the age of three, and through education, it is influenced by the behaviours you learnt. Trying to be true to your learning style may have been difficult in your past educational experience, especially if it involved rigid teaching methods. At university in the UK, however, there may be more scope for personal choice over what you learn and how you learn it. If you know more about your preferences for learning, you will be in a better position to adopt approaches that suit you.

> **Definition – learning style**
>
> This is the way a person takes in information, processes it, remembers it and expresses it. Some people refer to this as a learning preference. Categorising learning styles is not an exact science and whatever the method used, it is probably true that no one category fits any person perfectly. We all have elements of more than one learning style in our make-up and we may change through time.

VARK learning preferences

A learning coach called Neil Fleming has developed this simple system. It has four main categories, giving the mnemonic VARK:

- **Visual learners** – these show a preference for learning from visual media. They like highlighting their notes and like using books with pictures and diagrams. They will gain from using mind-maps and concept diagrams.
- **Aural learners** – these prefer discussion. They like attending tutorials and lectures rather than reading textbooks. They can learn well by talking to others about their subject.
- **Read-write learners** – these like learning from text in all formats and language-rich lectures. They will like using headings and bullet points in their notes and revision and have a tendency to convert diagrams to text.
- **Kinesthetic learners** – these use their senses to learn and learn best when remembering or imagining experiences and things that (might have) happened.

You can find out which of these categories you would be assigned to by taking a quick online questionnaire at **www.vark-learn.com**. You may find that this categorises you as 'multimodal' learner, meaning that you show aspects of more than one style in your character. This website provides study strategies that should suit each learning style.

Know your best time to study. You are at your most effective as a student at particular times (**Ch 9**); exploit this by doing intensive learning activities at these times.

Check out the hours that facilities are open. Find out the library, study centre or computing facility opening times. Plan your study periods around those if you prefer studying in these settings.

Plan ahead. Keep an eye on things you have to do over the following week/month and plan your time to fulfil all the assignments, lab and tutorial work on time (**Ch 9**).

Develop a personal filing system. Learn to be methodical in the way that you store notes, handouts and any other printed material within your filing system (**Ch 16**).

Do not allow new vocabulary or language difficulties to get in the way of learning your subject. Any problems should be dealt with at an early phase of assimilating the material. If possible, acquire a subject-specific dictionary (p. 228) that will help develop your subject-specific vocabulary. Alternatively, use the glossaries provided within specialist textbooks.

Think about the underlying principles involved in your learning. Keep your focus on the bigger picture and avoid becoming bogged down in the minutiae.

Take breaks. When working on your own it is essential to take breaks. It is also important to maintain your social networks, and taking regular short breaks with colleagues helps you to maintain perspective on your work.

Work with a buddy. Although studying is something that you need to do primarily on your own, coming together with another person doing similar studies or research can help the learning of all involved. For example you could compare notes, confirm understanding of more difficult points and discuss a set assignment or research procedure. This process will contribute to the consolidation of your learning and help identify gaps in your knowledge (**Ch 17**, **Ch 54**).

Reinforce your learning. You will need to be able to use the language of your subject appropriately and make sure terms are spelled correctly; if studying a quantitative subject, you may need to master key formulae so that they become second nature to you. Such competence is a reflection on your command of your subject. Make a habit of checking through your glossary or formulae lists frequently so that you can make a conscious effort to learn how to spell the more difficult words or lay out formulae accurately.

Tackle tutorial questions. Do *all* the examples in a set of tutorial questions, even when you don't have to submit them. Check your answers from the answer key, if provided. If you have difficulty in working out a particular solution, ask one of your lecturers or tutors to give you some guidance – staff will often go to considerable lengths to help with difficulties. Once you are satisfied that you have the correct answers, file the tutorial sheets alongside the related topic notes.

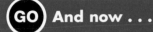

Useful language for . . . asking staff about subject material

Context: you might use these examples when asking a librarian or member of staff to help you.

I'm looking for material about xxx. Could you show me where I could find this?

Where can I find bilingual technical dictionaries?

I'd like to get some help in using spreadsheets. Is there a course I could do to learn about this?

This [paragraph/slide/topic] here is causing me problems. I'm not sure I understand. I think it means [give explanation]. Is that right?

I'm sorry. I still don't understand fully. I'm not sure what the word xxx means exactly. Could you please explain?

GO And now . . .

13.1 Go through your subject handbooks. Note down all the topic areas that will be covered on your course. Use these topics as headings for the dividers for your files so that you have an allocated space for the notes that will apply to these areas when you receive them or compile them for yourself.

13.2 Visit your subject departments. Find out where the noticeboard for your year is; visit the department electronically by looking at its home pages to find out if there is any special area that provides routinely updated information for students; visit your virtual learning environment and explore any sites that have been set up to support your learning in your subjects. Familiarising yourself with sources of information at an early stage in the course will save you a lot of time later when you may be under greater pressure.

13.3 Review your skills and learning patterns. If your word-processing is weak or you are not quite sure of how to search a resource database such as a library catalogue, make it a priority to upgrade your skills. Consult Table 13.2 and consider whether your approach to study activities is helping you to study as effectively as you might. Could you improve on these approaches?

14 | Lectures

How to learn effectively from this teaching method

The lecture is the fundamental component of most campus-based university teaching in the UK. For many students, lectures represent a new way of learning. You'll need to decide how to deal with different lecture styles and how to adapt to a wide range of different approaches to the use of lecture time in modern higher education.

Key topics:
→ What is a lecture?
→ Key facts about lectures
→ What you are meant to do in lectures
→ Different lecture formats
→ Visual aids used in lectures

Essential vocabulary
**Discipline   Monologue   Overhead transparency   Practical   References
Virtual learning environment**

The English word 'lecture' comes from the Latin word *lectura* - a reading; it is worth remembering that, even in modern times, a lecture begins its life as a piece of text and that some lecturers do, indeed, read their lectures from that text. However, many academics adopt a less formal delivery and use their notes simply as a reference rather than as a text that they read aloud.

Timing of lectures

The timetable of lectures is based on a framework organised at institutional, faculty or school/department level. Tutorials, practicals, laboratory and fieldwork are all normally timetabled by schools/departments. Generally, lecturers have no say about when or where the lectures or other learning activities take place, as these are usually decided by a central timetabling unit on the basis of availability of the facilities required.

Lecture conventions

Tutorials, seminars and lectures begin at specific times - usually five minutes past the hour and finish five minutes before the hour. Entering a lecture late is regarded as discourteous. Similarly, leaving a lecture early or going out and then returning is not well-regarded since this disrupts the attention of other students and can distract the lecturer from their train of thought. Students should arrive promptly and not leave until the lecturer has indicated that the lecture is finished.

→ What is a lecture?

The normal pattern is that a lecture:

- usually lasts for 50-60 minutes;
- is given by a subject specialist;
- provides different perspectives on learning depending on the topic and discipline – this could be factual information, ideas, analysis, argument, contrasting viewpoints, methods or examples;
- guides you in your study of a topic – this means that you may have to do a lot of supplementary reading on your own, or that you need to work through examples, or conduct experiments, to add to your understanding and knowledge;
- may provide introductory or complementary material that is later followed up in tutorials, laboratory practicals, fieldwork or site visits;
- may relate to some form of assessment, either in class or in an e-learning format after the lecture.

→ Key facts about lectures

People have differing expectations of where lectures fit into the learning within a particular subject area. Here are some key facts that will help you to understand and adapt to this form of course delivery.

- What you hear in the lecture will not necessarily be found in textbooks.
- A lecture is not meant to be a comprehensive treatment of any topic. The aim is generally to give an overview of the key issues or topics and a framework to assist you with further study.
- Lecturers may present views that do not necessarily represent their own position; they may simply be exploring different approaches and attitudes within the field.
- Although some lecture notes are made available through virtual learning environments (VLEs), these notes will not reflect exactly what was said in the corresponding lecture.
- Approaches differ between one lecturer and another, even in the same subject area.
- Style of delivery differs from one subject to another and from one discipline to another (**Ch 15**).
- Some lectures are compulsory, for example, in vocational subjects, such as law, medicine or nursing. Even if they are not, it is important to attend as listening to your lecturer explain the topic (**Ch 15**) lays down the foundation for understanding and recall.

In some disciplines, the programme of lectures is divided into topic areas, with different lecturers taking responsibility for the delivery of their specialist topic.

→ What you are meant to do in lectures

Although students do not generally participate in the delivery of the lecture in terms of interaction with the lecturer, sometimes they are asked to perform some kind of task, perhaps in collaboration with someone sitting beside them. Otherwise, students are expected to take responsibility for exploiting the information covered in the lecture, and, in particular, to take a personal set of notes (**Ch 16**). Some important ways in which students can contribute before, during and after the lecture are given in Table 14.1.

What should I derive from a lecture?

International students sometimes think that they have to write down and remember everything that they hear in a lecture so that they can reproduce this in examinations. This is not necessary, because in the UK this would not be rewarded highly. Generally, the key ideas in the lectures act as a guide rather than provide comprehensive information for exam purposes.

→ Different lecture formats

Be prepared to experience different lecture formats – not all will involve listening and note-taking. While some lecturers may consistently follow a particular format, others may alter their delivery depending on the topic, the size of the class, or the stage in the module that has been reached. Some typical formats are:

- **Traditional lecture:**
  - 50-minute non-stop monologue;
  - aims of the lectures are listed;
  - the method of approach is explained;
  - the content is covered in detail;
  - the key points are summarised.
- **'Split' lecture:**
  - 25-minute lecture; then
  - 5-minute break, allowing students to catch up with colleagues on any points that have been missed in the first phase of the lecture; then
  - 25-minute lecture, giving further coverage by the lecturer.
- **'Activity' lecture:**
  - 20 minutes (approximately) of content; then
  - 10 minutes of in-class activity (possibly working with partner(s)); then
  - 15 minutes' general discussion relating to the work with partners; then
  - 10 minutes' summary by the lecturer of key issues arising from the lecture, small group work and plenary: this could consist of clarification of points, identification of argument and counter-argument and balance of argument.

Table 14.1 Ideas for getting the most from lectures

Before the lecture	In the lecture	After the lecture
General information about lectures is usually available in the course handbook or on the VLE.	• Always write the name of the lecturer, the subject and the date on your lecture notes. This helps you to keep your files organised sequentially and will aid your revision.	• Soon after the lecture, go over your notes. Some people completely rewrite their lecture notes: they feel rewriting notes is a valuable means of consolidating the information and ideas. However, others regard this as a pointless and time-consuming exercise. Their view is that the time would be better spent doing supplementary reading on the lecture content.
• Find out when and where your lectures are – be there. Lectures provide the framework of the knowledge base of your course. If you miss lectures, your understanding rapidly becomes incomplete.	• Ensure that you keep a written record of each lecture:	
	– If the lecturer gives handouts, highlight, underline or make additional notes on the handout as the lecture progresses. This is called 'annotating'.	• Clarify any points you didn't understand. Ask a fellow student, consult a text or website and, if still in doubt, speak to the lecturer.
• Find out how changes in the timetable are notified to students, e.g. via noticeboards or as email or VLE announcements.	– If you are not given handouts, choose a note-taking style that is appropriate to the content and discipline of the lecture. Take the lecturer's style into account as well (**Ch 16**).	• Follow up references and think about the ideas that were covered in the lecture. As your course progresses you should then begin to think about connections between topics and the theory that relates to them.
• Identify the lecture topic and prepare by doing some basic reading beforehand.		
• Prepare by checking over the vocabulary likely to be used in the lecture. Recognising and understanding technical terms and jargon will help you absorb the context more easily.	• Evolve your personal abbreviations for note-taking. This could include some contraction of words, text-message language or standard abbreviations drawn from mathematical or punctuation symbols (**Ch 16**).	• There may be additional material and coursework to complete after the lecture – make sure you do this as it will almost certainly be related to later assessment (**Ch 53**).
• Review the learning objectives or outcomes for the lecture or topic. This will help you to focus your attention on key aspects.	• Look at the lecture template in **Ch 15** (Table 15.2) and listen for the statement at the beginning of the lecture that outlines the aims and the way that the lecturer intends to achieve these and the 'signpost' words that are used to provide a transition from one phase to the next within the lecture.	• Try matching the lecture content with the learning objectives or outcomes. This helps you understand the fuller context of your course; what you are being taught and why; and, specifically, where any particular lecture fits in the greater scheme of things.
• Note how many lectures are allocated to each topic. This can often be important in balancing your effort when it comes to revising.		
• Be on time. Late arrivals are disruptive and interrupt the lecturer's flow of thought and this will affect the delivery. You should aim to be sitting in your seat five minutes before the start of the lecture.	• Note any particular points of emphasis – these topics may crop up later in assessment.	• Get into the habit of noting down your own ideas and questions in your notes in a way that allows you to remember that these were not part of the lecture but your reaction to what you heard. Think about such issues further, as these points show your ability to think critically.
• Switch off your mobile phone.	• Learn to adapt your note-taking style to the different styles of delivery you encounter (**Ch 16**).	
	• Note any references (usually author surname and date) and do follow up reading from them.	

Introductions and summaries

Most lectures begin with an outline of what will be covered; if you miss this, you could fail to understand the logic of the lecture structure and content. Don't be late – you may miss the whole point of the lecture for the sake of a few minutes. Often key 'housekeeping' announcements occur at the start and you may miss these too. Lecturers usually summarise key issues, facts, theories or processes at the end of the lecture and sometimes introduce their next lecture in general terms to demonstrate the linkage between one phase of their teaching and the next. Apart from being discourteous, leaving early means that students miss this key guidance and interpretation of the lecture series.

→ Visual aids used in lectures

Some lecturers will appear to talk spontaneously without prepared notes, but lectures are not off-the-top-of-the-head streams of words. They are the product of planning and research, as well as careful thought about the best way to present the topic.

Many lecturers use visual aids to assist them in their explanations. These may include:

Overhead projector and board

While some lecturers continue to use acetate sheets on an overhead projector ('overhead transparencies'), this is becoming increasingly rare. However, some lecturers still prefer to write up notes as they proceed through the lecture, and may use a projector to magnify the image. In some subjects (maths, for example), staff may prefer to use a chalk board or white board. Handwritten notes may cause problems because of difficult-to-read handwriting – ask your fellow student or the lecturer as soon as possible to complete any 'missing' text.

Slides

In some disciplines there is a strong reliance on visual images that cannot be reproduced readily except on photographic slides, for example, where the lecturer might wish to show you examples of anatomical sections or fine art. In such instances, it is helpful to note details of each slide and a record of the comments that are made by the lecturer, both as an aid to recall and in case you have a question afterwards. The examples and conclusions may be extremely important to the topic.

PowerPoint presentations

Many lecturers now structure their presentation around projected slides of this kind. *PowerPoint*-style slides are beneficial in that they allow you to listen, rather than write. However, it is vital not to switch off – the points on the slides will only be the skeletal framework and if you have a printout, you should be annotating this throughout the lecture, adding detail or personal interpretation.

Recording lectures

If your English language skills are not as strong as you would like, you may be tempted to record lectures. However, in the UK recording lectures is not the norm and you must ask permission from each lecturer before the lecture if you wish to do this. Some lecturers may refuse to give permission for reasons of copyright. Visually or aurally impaired students can make special arrangements.

If you are dyslexic, or have an aural, visual, physical or other disability

There may be special arrangements in place to help you with lectures. For example, you may be entitled to ask for larger print handouts or may be permitted to record lectures or have the service of a scribe. Ask for information from a lecturer or from the disability support service on your campus, or consult your university's website.

✔ Practical tips for learning effectively from lectures

Approach the lecture experience with a positive, open-minded attitude.
For example, you can bring:

- motivation for learning (**Ch 13**);
- an interest in the subject (**Ch 3**);
- prior knowledge of the subject (**Ch 25**);
- understanding of the learning objectives, gained from the course handbook (**Ch 53**);
- critical thinking skills (**Ch 21**).

Prepare for the lecture. You will need appropriate materials for your chosen subject: paper, pens, highlighters, calculator, dictionary. Particularly in topics you find difficult printing out and reading any published notes, reading the textbook or revising relevant vocabulary before the lecture will greatly improve what you gain from lectures.

Attend all lectures. You may be tempted to miss them for a number of reasons, but in most cases the lectures are the foundation of your course. If you miss even one lecture, it is very easy to continue this practice so that, in the end, you don't attend any. This is not advisable as it is difficult to catch up with the material later on. Don't rely entirely on the lecture material accessible from the VLE. These printed notes are simply outlines – there is no substitute for hearing what was actually said. Moreover, don't assume that the lecture content is all that you have to learn for assessment in assignments or exams; lectures provide a framework for learning but you are expected to develop your understanding by further reading and critical thinking.

Listen intelligently. This means recognising the lecturing style of the lecturer, the structure of the lecture and the thought process that is being demonstrated (**Ch 15**). This will enable you to identify key points and adapt your note-taking strategy to the style, method of delivery and lecture format.

Relate to your lecturers. Adopting positive body language sends the signal that you are engaged with the lecture topic. Making eye contact and nodding as you understand points shows your lecturer that you are relating to the content of the lecture.

Take account of the importance of visual information. If you are shown something on a photographic slide, a *PowerPoint* slide, an overhead transparency or on the chalk-/whiteboard, then you should write the important details down. Your lecturer would not present it to you visually if this information were not important.

Note down references. Take particular note of any references that are given by the lecturer. Often only the author will be mentioned, possibly by surname (family name) only and maybe the date of publication. You will usually find full details in the course handbook. Make a point of consulting the references as soon after the lecture as possible. Add any notes you gain from these sources to your lecture notes.

Useful language for . . . discussing lectures with fellow students or staff

Lecturing has its own jargon which you will need to understand to get the most out of this teaching method.

Context: to a fellow student

I didn't catch the bit where [s]he was talking about [topic]. Did you get good notes then? Please could I photocopy that part of your notes? It would help me a lot.

Context: to a lecturer

I'm sorry, but I found it very difficult to take notes while you were talking about [topic]. Could you recommend a textbook that would help me go over the material myself?

[Perhaps representing a number of students] I'm sorry, but you are talking a little too fast for all the students from [name of country]. We would like to ask you if it would be possible either to slow down a little or to provide some supporting notes that will help us understand.

14.1 Find out about course texts. Locate the sections in your course handbook that relate to the recommended texts or course books. If you familiarise yourselves with these references, when they are mentioned in the lectures, you will know what they are and possibly where to find them in the library.

14.2 Identify what is meant by critical thinking. Read **Ch 21** and **Ch 23** to raise your understanding of thinking processes and ways of evaluating information. A feature of UK university learning is that you don't simply accept what you are told just because the person who told you is an academic or because you read it in a book or on the internet. You are being trained to question and enquire, to look at the strengths and weaknesses of evidence you find for yourself or you have presented to you. When you have evaluated this evidence, then you can form your own opinion based on a sound understanding of the issues.

14.3 Practise 'intelligent listening'. You can do this by watching a discussion or current affairs programme on television or listening to something similar on the radio. Listen for the introduction to the topic to be presented, listen for the key points and note how speakers summarise these at the end of their interview or speech. This is a strategy that is used in many fields where people need to get ideas across to others in a short time.

How to understand what lecturers say and how they say it

Lectures are about passing on information, ideas and arguments. This chapter introduces you to some different lecturing styles; suggests strategies for adapting to each of these examples; and provides some illustrations of the language frequently used to frame and structure lectures.

Key topics:
→ Lecturing styles
→ The structure and language of lectures

Essential vocabulary
Banter   Drone   Egotist   Fidget   'Lose the thread'   Peer   Signpost word   Smokescreen   Take-home message

In the course of your academic career you'll encounter many lecturers; some good, some less so, some you will like and some you will not. But it is the lecture content that is important, and whatever you think about the lecturer or the topic, you will need to engage with the material that is being delivered.

→ Lecturing styles

You will find some common lecturing approaches given in Table 15.1. This table also provides strategies for dealing with these delivery styles. These examples are only a selection of lecture types – each lecturer has a unique approach. Your challenge is to adapt your listening strategies and note-taking style to meet the idiosyncrasies of each lecturer. Listening carefully and developing an ability to take meaningful notes comes with practice. As you develop this skill you will be able to evaluate and extract what is relevant from each lecture.

---

smart tip

Differing preferences for lecturing styles

One person's ideal lecture is another person's nightmare. Some people like a measured, systematic delivery, while others dislike this intensely and find a more dynamic delivery more stimulating. As an international student you will need to take time to develop your listening skills. You will need to adapt to the different styles you encounter.

Table 15.1 Examples of lecturing styles and the strategies that can be used to cope with them

Type of lecturer	Potential strategies
The entertainer. This sort of lecturer tells good jokes and can 'ad lib' them throughout the lecture. Many people like these lectures, but what you need to do is separate the ideas from the 'banter'. Good lecturers who adopt this style are not comedians, but are usually simply using humour as a method of delivering their ideas by keeping the listeners' attention.	Listen for the 'signpost' words and phrases in their lecture, that is, when they state how they are going to deal with the topic, and then pick these out as the lecture unfolds (see Table 15.2). Keep a note of the lecture structure as an aid to revision and a record of your understanding. Remembering the jokes may help you remember the content afterwards, although it may also create a smokescreen that you need to see through.
The drone. This type of lecturer specialises in a monotonous delivery, that is, without any modulation of voice or expression. Material to be covered may be difficult to absorb, even if it is fundamentally interesting.	You have to listen carefully for the specific words used that express meaning rather than rely on the intonation to highlight changes in the stages of a lecture, for example, when the lecturer is moving on to another theme.
The rambler. Some lecturers ramble. They appear to stray from the point, get carried away by their own eloquence or simply lose the thread. However, in some instances what seems like a series of disjointed thoughts may be pulled together as underpinning for a tight and logical argument.	Don't 'switch off' – take notes! Listen for the individual points and note these down as the lecture progresses. Gradually, the rationale may become clearer and you will have the key points made at the earlier stage to support the conclusions. Later, imposing your own order on the content of the lecture, perhaps by referring to the recommended texts, may help you to make the material more easily remembered.
The mumbler. Not everyone is a gifted public speaker and lecturers are no exception. Some very gifted and talented people just do not perform well in front of large groups of people. Consequently, they may not project their voices well (they 'mumble'). The bigger the lecture theatre, the more this becomes a problem.	In this case coping strategies are less easy to evolve. Sitting near the front of the room will at least place you nearer the speaker and this may assist a little. A more subtle approach is to make eye contact with the lecturer, smile and look interested. This confidence-building strategy may encourage the lecturer to speak more clearly. Another strategy might be to raise the issue with your class representative who can draw it to the attention of the department concerned. Otherwise, simply make an appointment to speak with the lecturer to explain the difficulty – they may be unaware that they cannot be heard beyond the third row.
The fidget. Some people think best when they move around. It may be that, as they deliver the lecture, they move back and forth across the dais or wave their arms like windmills or absent-mindedly 'play' with equipment.	The lecturer's mannerisms can be distracting, but try to rise above these irritations and follow the flow of information coming your way. Try to identify whether this idiosyncrasy is a form of 'code'. For example, does the lecturer use hand, arm or body movements as a means of reinforcing important points? Watching the lecturer as you take notes can be important to obtaining the most from the lecture.

Table 15.1 (cont'd)

Type of lecturer	Potential strategies
The techno-wizard. Some lecturers thrive on the use of gadgetry and you may find that your lecturers prefer the medium of slides, video, or *PowerPoint* presentation instead of the traditional oral presentation. Good teachers use the medium that is best suited to their message and sometimes *PowerPoint* presentations provide greater clarity and precision than the traditional acetate slides. One advantage is that it is possible to obtain handouts of the *PowerPoint* presentation (sometimes available on the module VLE facility), but do not assume that this will always be the case.	Getting down the detail of the *PowerPoint* slides may be difficult and it might be helpful to request that the slides are made available on the course VLE, if this is used, so that you can look at the presentation again later and print it out if you feel that it would be useful. *PowerPoint* presentations might provide a good opportunity for some team work. If the slide is packed with information, agree with a fellow student that one of you will make a note of what is said about the slide while the other will copy down what is on the slide. In this way, you can share the notes later, confident that you have the complete information that was delivered – both oral and visual.
The egotist. Many of the people who lecture to students are so absorbed in their own ideas that they sometimes ignore the bigger picture. They may have been asked to deliver the lecture series because of their expertise and research background. However, this can result in a rather narrow perspective on a topic and you need to be aware that there may be other viewpoints or approaches to be considered in order to achieve a balanced perspective.	Listen carefully for references to the work of others. After the lecture, check the library catalogue for other 'big names' in the field. Look particularly for recent publications on the same topic area. Look at journals for articles by your lecturer and identify from the reference list other experts in the field.

→ The structure and language of lectures

Although lecture styles differ among disciplines and from one lecturer to another, it is possible to identify some common features that apply to most. Table 15.2 links these typical structural elements with the characteristic language that is associated with them.

The implication is that you should not only be listening to what is being said, but also thinking about what is being said. This can help greatly when deciding what type of notes to take (**Ch 16**).

---

smart tip

Disability issues

If you are a person who is assisted by a scribe, it is important to discuss with your scribe some of the lecture elements and corresponding language shown in Table 15.2. This will help ensure that your scribe recognises and notes down important information for you.

Table 15.2 Structural elements of lectures and their characteristic 'signpost' language.
These speech samples are typical examples your lecturers might use. This is not a comprehensive list of elements of a lecture; nor will all of the elements appear in every lecture. Once you have developed the capability to listen for such phrases, you can use this information to create better notes (**Ch 16**). For example, you can hear when a list is being initiated; when a definition requires to be taken down exactly as spoken; or when emphasis is being given to an important point.

Lecture element	Characteristic language
At the beginning of the lecture	
Introduction – outlining the topic to be covered	'In today's lecture I'll be considering . . .'
Aims – defining what the aim of the lecture is	'I'm going to look at a number of aspects of . . .'
Lecture format	'I'll begin by . . . and then I'll go on to . . . and I'll end by . . .'
In the body of the lecture	
Providing a definition	'I'm going to start by defining . . .'
Giving examples	'Let's look at some models of . . .'
Describing: • processes • events • position	'The first stage is . . .' 'To begin with . . . then . . .' 'At the centre is . . .'
Presenting a theory or argument: • stating the key points in support • explaining the perspective of each point • justifying the evidence supporting these points • presenting a counter-argument • justifying the evidence supporting these points	'This viewpoint is supported by . . .' 'This means that . . .' 'It can be seen from this evidence that . . .'; 'This evidence suggests that . . .' 'The opposing viewpoint is that . . .'; 'This contradicts the view that . . .' 'It can be noted that there is some variance with . . .'
Drawing logical connections	'Thus, it can be seen that . . .'
Identifying main issues	'The critical factors are . . .'
Stressing importance	'It is essential that . . .'
Repeating a point for clarification or emphasis	'Let me put that in another way . . .'
Moving on to a new theme	'Passing on to the next theme in my discussion . . .'
At the end of the lecture	
Concluding – drawing together the lecture's key messages	'To summarise the key aspects I've covered, let's remind ourselves of . . .'; 'The "take-home messages" are . . .'

The language of summary

British people often summarise ideas by using different language from their original explanation. International students can be confused by this and think that new points are being made. Listen particularly for expressions such as: 'to summarise . . .'; 'just to go over that again . . .'; 'to sum up, . . .'; 'let's just run over that again . . .' which indicate that facts or concept are being repeated in a different way.

 Practical tips for better listening

Think about where in the lecture theatre suits you. Sitting near to the front may allow you to hear better, but it may not be the best spot to see visual aids. Try not to sit next to others who may distract you.

Understand the jargon. Your comprehension will be better if you are familiar with the technical terms and jargon being used – so a little preparation before the lecture may help, for example, by reading the appropriate chapter of the textbook and consulting a dictionary.

Be well organised. Make sure you can devote all your attention to the lecture rather than finding pens and paper.

Don't try to take down all the lecturer's words as if they were dictation. There may be spells when this is appropriate, and the lecturer should make this obvious. Otherwise, listen to the main points of what is being said and recast this in words that you understand (**Ch 16**). If you hear a word that is unfamilar, write it down phonetically (as it sounds) and then after the lecture ask a native speaker to repeat the word and suggest a meaning.

Useful language for . . . listening to lectures

During lectures you will hear characteristic language and afterwards, you may wish to ask questions.

Context: phrases you may hear your lecturers say (see also Table 15.2).

I've put the notes for this lecture on the VLE [often refers to PowerPoint slides].

If anyone didn't follow that, there's a further explanation in Chapter x of your textbook [Note: they may use the name of the author(s), rather than the title of the book].

It's important that you understand [or follow] this. [Might be taken as a hint about what to revise for exams].

Context: what you might say to a lecturer if you are having some difficulty with lectures.

I'm sorry but I didn't understand xxxx. Please could you explain it again? [Alternatively: Please may I make an appointment to discuss this further?]

I'm sorry, I find it difficult to hear your lectures because of the background noise. Would it be possible for you to use the microphone in the lecture theatre?

And now . . .

15.1 Analyse lecturing styles. Thinking about your own experiences as a student, decide whether you have any lecturers who match any of the types described in Table 15.1.

15.2 Arrive at a strategy for getting the most from each lecturer's delivery style. Consider how you cope with each lecturer and compare the strategies you have used with those suggested in Table 15.1. Should you adjust your approach?

15.3 Apply your strategy. If, as yet, you have not tried the particular strategy given in Table 15.1, try to apply it in the next lecture with that lecturer/type. If you can, ask a friend to follow the same method and then meet after the lecture to compare notes and to evaluate the effectiveness of the approach.

16 Note-taking in lectures

How to refine what you hear into note form

The aim of lectures, regardless of discipline, is to present a topic for study in ways that introduce key points and develop understanding through explanation, provision of examples or citation of references for further reading. This chapter outlines approaches to attending lectures, and taking notes from what you hear and see during the lecture.

Key topics:
→ Your role in lectures
→ Approaches to note-taking

Essential vocabulary
Annotate   Concept map   Learning personality   Mind map   Verbatim

Lectures should be seen as a guide to a topic rather than the definitive or final word on a subject (**Ch 14**). The university lecture provides essential information delivered in a particular sequence for a particular course. In many subjects, the lecture is an introduction to the topic rather than a comprehensive analysis. For some subjects, lectures are often compulsory. This may be dictated by professional associations that validate many professional qualifications and is not simply a university regulation. Some students visiting the UK may have their attendance monitored as part of UKBA regulations (p. 23).

→ Your role in lectures

Lectures are not intended to provide you with a full understanding of the subject, and certainly not the total requirement for exam revision. Thus, some input on your part is assumed. Since you will attend many lectures in a week, maybe several in a day, it makes sense to keep some record of what you have seen and heard. It is important to consider what your purpose is when you take notes, since this will affect your strategy. For example, you may wish to write up the notes in a style that is more comprehensive and comprehensible to you. Alternatively, you may use the original lecture notes as the basis for note-making from texts cited from the reading list. In many subjects, this practice is assumed as part of the learning process.

Routine lecture note housekeeping

In each lecture:

- note the date;
- note the lecturer's name;
- note the lecture topic or title;
- number pages 1, 2, 3 . . . ;
- note down the aims of the lecture as outlined at the beginning of the lecture.
- keep a full record of what was said for future reference and exam revision;
- note key points to allow you to do follow-up reading on the topics in your own time;
- as appropriate record a constructed argument, a sequence of ideas or a process;
- as appropriate record information that will help you derive a proof or formulae.

Think about who you accompany in lectures

If you sit alongside students who are native speakers of English, then you will be in a better position to ask them for help with particular words or with comparing notes that you each took. If you sit with others from your own language community, then you might be able to discuss the points more fluently using your own language, but that means that you are not practising talking about your subject in English. Both strategies have merits and you need to decide which is better for you.

→ Approaches to note-taking

How you write down notes in lectures will depend on:

- your ability to listen for specific information and the thread of an argument, discussion or sequence of a process (**Ch 15**);
- the neatness of your handwriting;
- your particular learning personality or style (**Ch 13**);
- the styles of delivery you encounter in lectures (**Ch 15**);
- the subject you are studying and its conventions;
- the specific lecture content.

Notes made as a result of reading provide you with the chance to design a layout that reflects your learning style and understanding (**Ch 25**). This is less possible in a lecture because you are following someone else's logic without having the chance to reflect on this too much. As a result, the design of your lecture notes has to be spontaneous and is less under your control. However, as you become a more experienced note-taker, you will become more attuned to ways in which the format of the lecture can be adapted to particular types of note-taking design.

Table 16.1 outlines four different lecture delivery modes that are commonly used and makes suggestions as to how you might extract key information for your notes.

Table 16.1 Note-taking scenarios. Each lecture is unique and the strategies adopted by the lecturers will vary from individual to individual, topic to topic and according to discipline conventions. You will need to adapt your note-taking style to the mode of presentation, the style of the individual lecturer and the content. Four possible scenarios that you might encounter are shown in this table.

Scenario 1	Scenario 2	Scenario 3	Scenario 4
'Straight' lecture: delivered without handouts or special visual aids	Lecture supported with printed handouts	Lecture delivered using notes on a board or overhead transparencies	Lecture delivered using *PowerPoint* software
Listen for: • Aims of lecture or outline of structure of lecture. • Names of authors, dates of publication. This is the usual way of citing sources in a lecture. You will need to consult the reading list for details of title, chapter or page references. • Key personalities, dates or events relating to specific aspects of the topic. • Discourse markers – the signpost words (**Ch 15, Ch 29**) that indicate stages and shifts of emphasis within the lecture. • Structuring of an argument and the supporting evidence; stages of a process; sequence of events. • Repetition of points or oral emphasis using exaggerated stress or intonation. • Summarising of points at mid- and end-points in the lecture.	If handouts are available before or at the lecture: • Use highlighters to mark key points. • Use a contrasting colour, e.g. red or green, to annotate notes with additional information, examples or explanations given in the lecture. This will make it easier to distinguish from the printed text. • Make additions as described in scenario 1. If handouts are available after the lecture, use your own notes taken in the lecture to expand the lecture notes. **Warning:** Notes from lectures, whether borrowed from a colleague or made available by the lecturer, are not a substitute for attending the lecture. Lecturers expand on certain points or add examples to clarify understanding. They may also deviate from the notes and expand points outside the notes.	Follow scenario 1 but in addition: • Copy points shown on overheads as the skeleton for your own expanded notes. • For this kind of presentation it is sometimes helpful to work with a friend where one person copies the slide and the other notes what is said when the lecturer 'talks to the slide'. After the lecture merge the notes to create a more comprehensive record of what was actually covered in the lecture. To do this, you will need to work together in order to agree the synthesis of your notes and this will offer opportunities to discuss and clarify points. This process will reinforce your learning.	Use of this software provides a slick and professional presentation that permits good images of the detail of graphs or diagrams, and the lecturer can build these up stage by stage. However, this approach can often create an amount of detail that is very difficult to note down completely in the lecture. If this is the case for you, try to follow the steps for scenario 1 and ask for the *PowerPoint* slides to be made available for downloading before or after the lecture. This has cost implications but note that there are options to print out slides as handouts of two, three, four, six or nine slides to a page using greyscale or black and white rather than colour (**Ch 26**).

Figure 16.1 illustrates four possible formats for notes and suggests ways in which these different strategies can be used to suit different note-taking needs within lectures. Adding to these strategies, note-making approaches are covered in **Ch 27**.

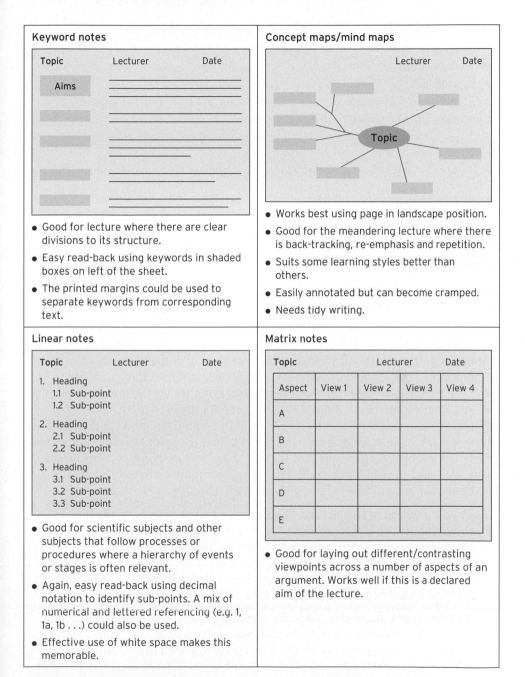

Keyword notes

Topic   Lecturer   Date

Aims

- Good for lecture where there are clear divisions to its structure.
- Easy read-back using keywords in shaded boxes on left of the sheet.
- The printed margins could be used to separate keywords from corresponding text.

Concept maps/mind maps

Lecturer   Date

Topic

- Works best using page in landscape position.
- Good for the meandering lecture where there is back-tracking, re-emphasis and repetition.
- Suits some learning styles better than others.
- Easily annotated but can become cramped.
- Needs tidy writing.

Linear notes

Topic   Lecturer   Date

1. Heading
   - 1.1 Sub-point
   - 1.2 Sub-point
2. Heading
   - 2.1 Sub-point
   - 2.2 Sub-point
3. Heading
   - 3.1 Sub-point
   - 3.2 Sub-point
   - 3.3 Sub-point

- Good for scientific subjects and other subjects that follow processes or procedures where a hierarchy of events or stages is often relevant.
- Again, easy read-back using decimal notation to identify sub-points. A mix of numerical and lettered referencing (e.g. 1, 1a, 1b . . .) could also be used.
- Effective use of white space makes this memorable.

Matrix notes

Topic   Lecturer   Date

Aspect	View 1	View 2	View 3	View 4
A				
B				
C				
D				
E				

- Good for laying out different/contrasting viewpoints across a number of aspects of an argument. Works well if this is a declared aim of the lecture.

Figure 16.1 Note-taking strategies. Four models of note-taking showing the benefits of each style.

Tips for good note-taking

- Listen for and note the key ideas – avoid trying to write down every word (verbatim notes). It's impossible – you'll miss out on understanding ideas, explanations and examples.
- Develop a note-taking style that will provide you with notes that will be meaningful in six days, weeks or months.
- Cultivate your own 'code', for example:
  - underlining or highlighting points emphasised by the lecturer;
  - asterisks (*) for points or new words to look up later;
  - BLOCK CAPITALS for sub-headings or keywords;
  - special abbreviations for your subject that are in general use or that you create for yourself;
  - a symbol (e.g. #) that indicates your thought or response to a point made by the lecturer.

✔ Practical tips for attending lectures and taking notes

Prepare for the lecture. Try to read some fundamental background information on the topic. This could be the introduction to that topic in a basic recommended textbook or from a good encyclopaedia. Beware of internet sources, because these can be unreliable in terms of accuracy and truth.

Obtain supporting material. Some lecturers make use of virtual learning environments available in many universities to provide lecture notes, handouts, overhead transparency or *PowerPoint* slides before or after the lecture. Downloading this kind of material when it is made available may assist you to make more comprehensive notes. Note that the provision of this material remains at the discretion of the lecturer. If you have a hearing impairment, are dyslexic or have another visible or invisible disability, you may be able to request that lecture notes or handouts are made available to you before lectures. You should consult the disability support service in your institution with regard to any special needs you may have.

Select your position in the lecture. Choose a seat that allows you to see the whiteboard, projection screen or television monitor easily. Avoid sitting near the door, the back of the room (most commonly inhabited by the chatterers and latecomers) or underneath noisy air-conditioning vents. If you have a disability, you can ask for special arrangements to be made to enable you to access a lecture theatre or room without difficulty and also, if necessary, to ensure that a particular seat is reserved for you.

Use an appropriate paper size. A4 is the standard paper size for handouts and printers and so it makes sense to be consistent by using A4 paper and file size for your own notes. It is probably more economical to use narrow-lined paper with a margin, as this allows you to optimise the use of paper. Some subjects might require blank rather than lined paper to allow for diagrams and mathematical calculations. Otherwise, your own handwriting style and ability to write neatly at speed will dictate your choice.

If you are neat by nature, lined or unlined paper is probably not required (you can get more text on unlined paper!); if you are generally untidy in your writing, the lines will discipline your note-taking. Small reporter-style notebooks are not recommended, because the volume of notes that you will generate will fill one of those pads in a very short time.

Store your notes carefully. Decide on a strategy for filing your notes that is systematic and foolproof. Foolscap or A4 files with two holes are the most readily available and therefore cheaper. You may prefer to keep separate thinner files for each subject, or to use a single lever arch-file for a subject and use colour-coded section dividers to separate topics within the subject area. Get into the habit of filing notes immediately after the lecture so that they are not lost.

Adapt your style. There is no single way to take notes that will suit all styles, content or circumstances. You will need to adapt your style to suit individual delivery styles as well as content.

Write up lecture notes after the lecture. Views differ on this. You need to ask yourself a difficult question – what do you gain from this exercise? Some people feel that this is an essential aspect of the learning process, is an aid to understanding and aids their recall. Others start off by re-writing notes but quickly find that there is simply not enough time to revisit lecture notes in order to remodel them to make them neater, more legible or more meaningful. If writing up lecture notes is just to make your notes look neat, colourful or simply pretty, you need to consider whether the time might not be better spent doing some follow-up reading using your 'raw' lecture notes as a guide and possible skeleton for notes you make from sources (see **Ch 25**).

💬 Useful language for . . . discussing your notes

Context: these points might be discussed with a fellow class member.

My notes from that lecture are a complete mess [slang phrase]. Can I get together with you some time to discuss what you took out of the lecture?

I've found a good book in the library that covers this topic really well.

I'm going to experiment with a new type of note-taking this lecture. I'm going to try mind mapping. In case it doesn't work, would you mind if I copied your notes after the lecture?

16.1 Check availability of handout notes, overhead transparency or PowerPoint slides. Some lecturers will make these available before the lecture as handouts or as online files. If this is not the practice, you might consider asking as a group for this to be considered as an aid to learning.

16.2 Develop your note-taking skills. As with all skills, that of note-taking will not be acquired immediately. You will need to work at it and, if you are able to do so, you can do this by practising taking notes from one of the principal news broadcasts on radio or television. If you do this over a week or so, this will give you the chance to experiment with different layouts. If you listen to a broadcast at 6.00 p.m., for example, you can check your notes against a similar broadcast at a later hour in the same evening.

16.3 Collaborate on note-taking. Arrange with another student on your course to pair up for note-taking together in a lecture. For the first half of the lecture one of you takes the written notes, the other simply listens. At a mid-point in the lecture, change roles. At the end of the lecture, together work on the two half-sets of notes; develop these by adding your individual recollections for both listen-only periods. Photocopy the revised notes so that each of you has a copy. The value of this approach in that you will both have a richer, more detailed record of the lecture and you will have had to think further about the content and discuss the salient points. Overall, this will enhance your understanding and your learning.

17 | Co-operative learning

How to study successfully with others

Increasingly, British academics are using teaching techniques where students are expected to work in groups. In addition, students often set up their own informal study groups, and this is encouraged. This chapter examines some aspects of good practice for these activities.

Key topics:
→ Formal (staff-selected) groups
→ Informal (student-selected) groups

Essential vocabulary
Assertive   Devil's advocate   Facilitate   Group dynamic   Peer   Study buddy

Learning in a group has advantages – principally because people learn from each other by interacting, comparing ideas, challenging each other's viewpoints as well as processing new information together. Everyone has something to contribute to group work and international students often bring a fresh perspective, so you should view this as a useful opportunity to participate.

Speaking out in groups

International students often say that they feel inhibited in group work because their language skills are weaker than those of native speakers. Indeed, language development does require a period of time when people listen more than they converse. However, although you'll improve your passive language (your understanding) by listening, you'll also improve your productive language (speech) by participating in group discussion. If you don't contribute to the discussion, then people will think you don't want to take part and may ignore you and your views. So, show that you're willing to share your ideas – even if you make mistakes. Other people will probably use similar language structures (correctly) in the discussion – and so the process will help you to learn.

→ Formal (staff-selected) groups

Studying formally as a group normally means that you are participating in a learning activity that has been initiated by an academic staff member. This could be a formal tutorial, lab activity or practical facilitated by a tutor, or it may take the form of a group project that is conducted independently of the staff member. In all these situations, it is likely that you will have had little choice in the composition of the group. For effective learning to take place, however, you will have to adopt the basic practices described in this chapter.

Staff-led groups

- Ensure that you are prepared adequately for the group activity.
- Participate in the discussion and do not leave one or two people to dominate.
- Have the confidence to express your views, even if these seem to be different from others.
- Be prepared to defend your views or suggestions with reasoned argument supported by well-considered evidence.
- Use the group-learning experience as an opportunity to explore issues or ideas in greater depth with an expert to guide you.
- Recognise that a tutor may act as 'devil's advocate' to push you into exploring alternative scenarios, options or strategies.
- Take notes in these meetings, as these will complement your lecture notes and additional reading.

Unsupervised student groups

- Agree some ground rules, such as setting goals, responsibilities and deadlines.
- Offer to do a specific task at an early stage of the discussion.
- Ensure that the work allocation is evenly distributed across the group.
- Create a positive learning environment by addressing the task in hand.
- Engage in analytical thinking to tackle the task in hand.
- Encourage everyone to contribute ideas.
- Encourage exploration of ideas, their implications and also counter-arguments.
- Be assertive by stating your views firmly rather than tentatively.
- If you don't understand something, ask others in the group if they can explain it to you.
- If more than one meeting is required, ensure that the assigned contributions are completed for presentation at the next meeting.
- If you have real unresolved difficulties within your group, approach the staff member who set up the activity to discuss these with the whole group.

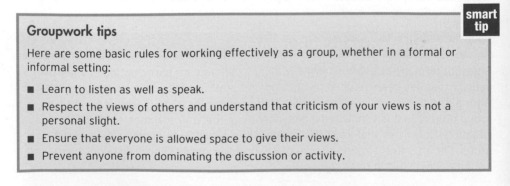

smart tip

Groupwork tips

Here are some basic rules for working effectively as a group, whether in a formal or informal setting:

- Learn to listen as well as speak.
- Respect the views of others and understand that criticism of your views is not a personal slight.
- Ensure that everyone is allowed space to give their views.
- Prevent anyone from dominating the discussion or activity.

Advantages of unsupervised group learning

This learning context:

- allows people to learn from each other.
- encourages a positive-thinking approach to the task.
- broadens the horizons of thinking.
- breaks down barriers.
- supports weaker students and develops the mentoring abilities of stronger students.
- allows all members to be less inhibited in presesting ideas, opinions or solutions.

→ Informal (student-selected) groups

Studying informally as a group is more likely to have come about because a self-selected group of students has decided to tackle a particular issue or topic independently of staff input. Such groups are less likely to need to agree ground rules and a method of working, because the very creation of the group is evidence of a less formal social arrangement. Some tips for working in this way include:

- Allocate a specific time and location to tackle the task you've decided to address.
- Select an appropriate location – for example, the open discourse area of the library rather than the union bar where distractions could interfere with the purpose of the group. Increasingly institutions are providing seating in 'open-space' locations that are relatively quiet to enable students to work together informally.
- Agree targets and work towards fulfilling these within a certain time span.
- Recognise that not all the things you wish to tackle can be solved in this way and that it is sometimes appropriate to seek help from a staff member.
- Accept that people work at different speeds and so try to accommodate this in how the group breaks down the tasks it wishes to fulfil.
- If the group works well, try to maintain the co-operative spirit by sharing resources, debating lecture issues, and exploring new techniques or approaches that you encounter in your learning.

How can you set up your own study group?

Here are some possibilities to consider. In each case, explain what you are trying to set up and ask if anyone would be interested in participating.

- Speak to your lab partners or fellow members of formal groups.
- Speak to people before or after lectures, or as you walk between lecture theatres.
- Place a message on a discussion board on your virtual learning environment.
- Email fellow class members.
- Ask your class rep or the lecturer to make an announcement ('anyone interested meet after the lecture . . .').

The interplay in informal groups can be complex and rewarding, as the example in Table 17.1 illustrates: that students who help others at one level can also benefit from the process. Although Gary is a UK student, his situation is very similar to that of some international students.

Table 17.1 Case study: Gary's informal study group

The problem and a solution
Gary came to university from a local college.
He is finding it really difficult to grasp some aspects of the new topic being covered in lectures. He has done this subject before at college, but it was taught in a completely different way. Gary is a direct-entry student, which means that he has gone straight into second year at university. He thinks he's possibly missed out on something that everyone else has covered in first year. After a bit of soul-searching, he plucks up the courage to ask a couple of other students, whom he knows only by sight, if they are also finding the topic difficult. Their response indicates that they too are finding it difficult, but less so than Gary, so he suggests that they meet up after the lecture to try a couple of tutorial questions together.
By pooling their knowledge, these three are able to work through the new topic and method of tackling it. The others are able to explain the missing bit of Gary's knowledge and he is able to explain from his college learning some aspects the others don't quite understand. As a result, the learning that the group gained from working with others on the problem areas was probably much deeper than if they had each studied alone. The three decide to meet up again when it is time to revise for the end-of-module exam.

Underlying message
If you work with other students, you will learn more deeply. When students explain particular learning points to their peers, everyone benefits. Colleagues develop their own understanding and language when they have to work out how to explain something to someone else.

Some points for you to consider
• In Gary's case, he decided that he would ask some of his fellow students to work with him. This is acceptable in UK culture. How might an international student solve this problem if they were in a similar situation? • British students can be reticent about showing other people that they are having difficulty. How would someone from your culture feel about letting others know they are in difficulty? • British students will make the first move if they felt that they knew some people well enough to identify the problem and to suggest working together. What strategy might you use in this situation?

Suggestions
• Ask some of the people in your class if they are having problems. • If you are not sure about asking people directly, then you could post a message on the discussion board on your module area within the virtual learning environment. • If you are not sure about either of these options, then you could consider approaching your class representative who might be able to identify others in the same position and help you to form a study-buddy group. • Of course, you could email your lecturer or course director explaining that you have some difficulty understanding; you could ask for a meeting or a special tutorial for a small group of people who may also be having difficulty.

✔ Practical tips for studying in groups – in both formal and informal settings

Remember effort in; benefit out. What you gain from working in a group will reflect the effort that you and your colleagues put into the activity.

Believe in yourself and your ideas. Your ideas are as valid as anyone else's. Do not be put off by the person who sounds extremely eloquent and well read – sometimes there is little substance behind what they say.

Treat group-working as a positive learning experience. Use the group experience as an opportunity to explore your own ideas, and learn from those of others.

Know when to ask for help. Sometimes groups simply do not work as a functioning entity – there may be no explicable reason and the 'fault' may not be attributable to any individual or group of individuals within the group. The group dynamic simply fails. If this seems to be happening, talk to a member of staff who may have some strategies to resolve the situation.

Learn more about how groups and teams work. This topic is covered in more detail in **Ch 18** and **Ch 54**.

Useful language for . . . taking part in informal and formal study groups

You may need to be relatively assertive for both types of group. For informal groups, the hardest part may be setting up the group in the first place. In formal groups, especially if they are large, you may struggle to make your views heard. This can be done in subtle ways.

Context: signalling your wish to contribute to a discussion:

Could I just make a comment here?

Could I suggest another point of view?

My view is quite different.

I think that there is another way to look at this.

I think you're missing the point there. What it really means is . . .

Context: making your viewpoint heard:

Did anyone else find that lecture hard? I think I need to do quite a lot of work on that one. Is anyone else in the same boat [slang]? How about we meet in the Union at 4 o'clock to work through our notes?

I'm not sure I agree with what you are saying there. You see, what I've read [quote source] suggests that [give alternative interpretation]. What do you think about that explanation?

I don't agree with that. I've read in [quote source] that [give alternative interpretation]. What do you think?

I think what x is saying is more logical because [reason]. What y is saying does not fit with the information we've been given, because [reason].

17.1 Become an observer of human interaction within learning groups. In the next group work activity in which you participate, watch to see just how a group dynamic can be affected by the levels of participation within the group. If things don't seem to be working, suggest that the group stops the activity and discusses what could be done to make the process more effective. Although you may think that this would be outrageous, what you'll probably find is that people would much rather work in a group that was operating effectively than be trying to meet the targets set in a dysfunctional group.

17.2 Expand your understanding. There are several publications on group behaviour. Possibly one of the more readable authors in this area is Desmond Morris whose book *Peoplewatching: The Desmond Morris Guide to Body Language* (2002) gives some interesting insights about how people interact in different situations, including in groups. This complements information on Belbin's nine team roles explained in Table 18.1 on p. 143.

17.3 Reflect on a group activity in which you have been involved. This need not be a university activity. Think first of all about what the target task was. Then think about how well the group worked to achieve the target. What were the strengths? What were the weaknesses? Finally, think about what you would do differently if you had to perform the target task again. If possible, discuss your thoughts with others who participated in this group. This analysis will help you to work more effectively in other groups because you will be more aware of what works and what doesn't work; it will, for example, help you to know what sorts of things to avoid in similar situations in the future.

18 Participating in a team

How to make a contribution when working with others

Working within a team is a rewarding way to learn and it can reflect workplace practice. This chapter introduces the theory of team roles and discusses some essential teamwork skills.

Key topics:

→ Team roles
→ Essential teamwork skills
→ Making sure that your team works well together

Essential vocabulary

Clique   Creative person   Critic   Delegate   Extrovert   Leader   Manipulative   Milestone   Organiser   Painstaking   Team role   Worker

---

There are many situations at university where you will be expected to act as a member of a team – sometimes in the academic context and sometimes in a sporting or social situation. The academic focus is usually on assessed group exercises, but the principles are applicable in other areas, such as club membership or employment. Generally, your team will be expected to work together to produce some outcome such as a poster or report. Your actions within the team may be assessed by your tutors and in some cases by your fellow group members (peers).

You may already have built up teamwork skills without realising it. Perhaps you have played team games, been a member of a fund-raising group, organised a social event or been employed as part of a team. This experience will help greatly as you learn more about your character as a team worker and develop the necessary skills even further.

→ Team roles

Research suggests that there are many distinct team personalities and that each of us has a 'natural' team role. During group work at university you can discover which role suits you best. Thinking about your group activities will help you develop as a team member. What you find out about yourself may even influence your eventual choice of career and job.

A part of the tension in being a team member is that you, or a fellow member, may be asked to play a different role from the one that is natural. This can lead to problems as you try to adapt to the requirements of the role, or when someone else tries to assume a different role from the one they have been assigned. Also, when you work in a small team, you may be asked to play multiple roles or to switch between roles at different times as the project progresses.

Examples of teamwork at university

■ Preparing a group poster (**Ch 46**).

■ Writing a joint report (**Ch 44**).

■ Some types of problem-based learning (**Ch 35**).

■ Practical and project work (**Ch 19**, **Chs 41–43**).

■ Running a society or sports club (**Ch 11**).

Table 18.1, which is based on the work of Meredith Belbin, gives a breakdown of main team roles and the personality features associated with them (Belbin, 2006). His analysis recognises that there are both 'good' character traits and 'allowable weaknesses' for each role. This latter notion is valuable, because it eliminates the feeling that any one role is superior. For example, you may have the impression that 'team leader' is the star role in any group, and perhaps one to which you might want to aspire. However, leader types are generally poor at coming up with ideas and can be weak at putting them into practice (Table 18.1); these are functions vital to the success of the group and they may well be your strength.

To help decide which role might suit you, think whether you would describe yourself as action-oriented, people-oriented, or as a thinker. Belbin classified the nine roles in this way and, by narrowing the options, this may help you to decide which fits you best:

● Those who prefer action should be a shaper, implementer or a completer–finisher (types B, F or G in Table 18.1).

● Those who are people-orientated should be a co-ordinator, a resource investigator or a team worker (types A, E or H in Table 18.1).

● Those who are thinkers should be an innovator, a monitor–evaluator or a specialist (types C, D or I in Table 18.1).

Simplified team roles

You may feel that the analysis of roles in Table 18.1 is too complex and detailed for your needs. A simplified grouping of roles, using the role numbering of that table, could be:

■ Leader: A + B

■ Creative person: C + E

■ Organiser: F + G

■ Worker: H + I

■ Critic: D

Delegation

If you like to be 'in control' of your work, giving over tasks to others can be stressful. In teamwork, you should accept that others may take a different approach from you and allow them to learn from their mistakes.

Table 18.1 The nine team roles identified by Belbin. Use this table to identify the role(s) that best fit your personality. Refer also to **Ch 13** regarding learning styles and their relevance for team-work roles.

Team role	Key attributes and beneficial functions in a team	Allowable weaknesses
A The co-ordinator	A 'caring' leader type who is calm and authoritative. Takes a balanced view and displays sound judgement. Makes the team work towards its shared goal. Good at spotting others' talents and at delegation.	May be less creative or intelligent than others and have no special expertise.
B The shaper	A 'manipulative' leader type who is a dynamic go-getter but impatient for results. Good at generating action, troubleshooting and imposing a pattern. Provides drive and realism to team activities.	Can be headstrong, emotional and impatient with others.
C The innovator	An intelligent, creative, ideas person, who generates solutions to problems and often uses unusual approaches. A source of originality for the group's activities.	May work in isolation and ideas may be impractical. May not communicate well.
D The monitor-evaluator	The 'critic' who analyses what the team is doing in a detached and unemotional way. Good at evaluating the group's ideas and making sure they are appropriate.	May lack drive and have a low work-rate. Critical comments may act to demotivate others.
E The resource investigator	An extrovert, communicative sort, who enthusiastically investigates new information and ideas. Good at exploiting resources and developing external relations.	Can be over-optimistic and may have a short attention span.
F The implementer	A hard worker who uses energy, discipline and common sense to solve problems. Turns ideas into actions. Good at making sure things get done.	May lack flexibility and resist new ideas.
G The completer-finisher	A conscientious individual who is anxious that tasks are completed to a high standard. Painstaking, orderly and well-organised. Good focus on fulfilling objectives.	Obsessive about details and may wish to do too much of the work to control quality and outcome.
H The team worker	A social type whose aim is to support others and provide cohesion to the team. Perceptive of others' feelings – helpful and diplomatic in approach. Promotes team spirit.	Doesn't like to lead or make decisions.
I The specialist	The kind of person who provides essential expertise and skills to the group. Adds a professional dimension but can be single-minded and may not suffer fools gladly.	Narrow outlook. Can be obsessed by technical detail and not see the big picture.

Communication

The success of any team depends on its ability to communicate. The larger the group, the more important this becomes, as shown in Figure 18.1. Group members need to understand what is expected of them by the team and by the teaching staff who have set the task. Time frames have to be defined, as do team roles, arrangements for meetings and the interchange of information or files. Face-to-face meetings are usually important at some early stage; thereafter, email, mobile phones and discussion boards are useful ways of keeping in touch. Agreeing and setting up these communication channels should be one of the first things your group does, for example, by exchanging email addresses.

Time management

There will always be a deadline for your team's work and this implies that planning will be required to meet your goal (**Ch 9**). You may find it difficult to arrange mutually suitable meeting times if the group members have diverse timetables and responsibilities, so intermediate targets (milestones) and diary dates should be set as early as possible. This is an important responsibility of the co-ordinator or shaper.

Compromise

Give and take is essential to team function at many levels. One concession you may need to make is in the team role(s) you adopt, as discussed above: this may require self-awareness and flexibility on your part. In addition, you may not have chosen your team and you may not even like some of its members – but to succeed as a group you will have to get along together. This may require diplomacy and tact. Team membership requires everyone to be able to give and receive criticism constructively and not as personal disapproval. If you are a perfectionist, you may need to accept that some aspects of the group's activities may be below your normal standards – but this may be essential to ensure that the team as a whole fulfils its remit.

Focus and commitment

Teamwork exercises are often demanding in time and effort; everyone needs to show commitment and a high work rate if the highest standards are to be achieved. Your group must keep its collective eye on its goals and targets, otherwise the overall mark may suffer. Facilitating this is one of the leader's duties.

---

smart tip

Finding the right person for the job

At different times your team will need someone to co-ordinate the task; someone to come up with bright, inventive ideas; someone to keep everyone else on target; someone who can find useful facts; someone who is good at design; someone who can organise materials; and someone to act as a spokesperson. If the right person does each of these tasks, the overall output from the team will be improved.

Adding value from your background

Since cultures operate in different ways, as an international student within a mixed group you can often contribute to a team effort by demonstrating a different approach, way of thinking or specific skill. It's a good thing to discuss differences in perspective and their origins openly, as they may help the group arrive at a consensus view or a new agreed way of working.

→ Making sure that your team works well together

Issues can often be anticipated and defused before they become problems. Difficulties are best treated by discussing them as soon as they become apparent, either within the team or with the staff supervising the task.

- Try to ensure that team members have sufficient time collectively to complete the task. If this is not possible, you may need to consider how you modify the task or the method you have agreed upon. This may result in an outcome less ambitious, but still of a high standard.

- If some members do not feel sufficiently motivated, the group as a whole may lack drive. One of the leader's roles is to stimulate the group. If this is your responsibility, from time to time remind the team of the relevance of the task and the rewards for doing it well.

- Where possible, try to ensure that people are assigned roles that fit best with their personality. Otherwise, they may feel uncomfortable.

- Sometimes, personalities clash when it is felt that someone is not pulling their weight, or when someone acts as an outsider (or is treated as one). Early discussion is essential and a 'team worker' may need to act as mediator.

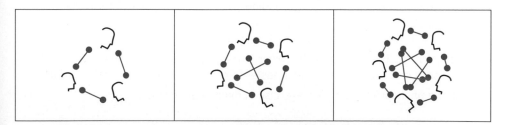

Figure 18.1 Team interactions. As the number of people in a group increases, so does the complexity of potential contacts between them. With three people, the number of one-to-one relationships possible is three; with four people it is six and with five it is ten. The larger your group, the more important communication becomes.

✔ Practical tips for being a successful team member

Behaviour:

- Be considerate by respecting the different abilities and contributions of others.
- Be positive, praise others' work whenever you can and discourage ridicule of other team members' ideas.
- If you feel you need to be critical, try to do this without arousing hostility.
- Don't form cliques within teams.
- Remember that if someone has flaws in some areas, they may be compensated for in other areas (and perhaps at a later time).
- From time to time, reflect on your contribution and the role you are playing.

Communication:

- Make sure you talk to other team members and try to encourage them to talk to you.
- Distribute mobile numbers and email addresses; reply promptly to messages.
- Talk through all problems as soon as possible.
- Understand that other team members may be shy or nervous.
- Contribute if your team has to 'defend' your work.
- Learn to listen to others and recognise that views which differ from your own may have value. Don't monopolise discussions or impose your views.

Effort:

- Try to 'do your bit'. Don't be a lazy team member.
- Produce work of the highest quality you can.
- If you feel your contribution is overloading you or is disproportionate to the contribution of others, call the group together, explain the problem and explore some solutions with the whole team participating.
- Tailor your collective effort to the reward on offer, remembering that good marks in assessed coursework can make it easier to gain a pass or good grade overall.
- Keep the final objective of your exercise in mind at all times.

Assessment and evaluation:

- Make sure you know how the activity will be assessed, and use this information to the team's advantage.
- Be scrupulously fair in your assessment of colleagues, if this is required.
- Don't award peer-assessment marks from loyalty if they are not deserved.
- After the event, think about what you learned from it – not only about the subject, but about your own behaviour and teamwork in general.

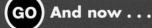

Useful language for . . . working in a team

Context: be assertive when you feel you have something to contribute. Ask questions when you don't understand why certain decisions have been made.

I'd like to volunteer for that task. I did something similar back home and I think I know how to do it.

Can I help you with that job? What part would you like me to do?

Sorry, but I don't understand why we are planning to do it that way. May I suggest an alternative plan? [Then explain]. This would have the following advantages [list them].

I'd like to do that but I don't think I could do that on my own because of my language skills. Would anyone be willing to do it with me? I'm good at the . . . aspect.

GO And now . . .

18.1 Reflect on your last teamwork activity. What were your major contributions? Looking at Table 18.1, what role or roles did you adopt? How did the team perform as a whole? How might you use this experience to modify your approach to your next team exercise?

18.2 Focus on communication channels. For your next teamwork activity, especially if the group is relatively large, place special emphasis on communication and meetings.

18.3 Establish your 'ideal' teamwork role. Categorise yourself as action-oriented, people-oriented or a thinker (see p. 143), then decide which of Belbin's categories best fit you (Table 18.1). It may be helpful to ask a friend or past teamwork colleague what they think, although be prepared for a different answer from the one you were expecting!

19 Laboratory sessions and field visits

How to gain hands-on experience and skills

Many courses, especially in the sciences, include laboratory sessions and field visits. These practicals provide valuable opportunities to observe specimens, carry out standard procedures and refine a range of valuable skills. You can gain a lot from these parts of the curriculum if you approach them correctly.

Key topics:
→ Preparing for practical sessions
→ Appropriate conduct in the lab and field
→ Carrying out instructions and noting results

Essential vocabulary
COSHH   Demonstrator   EU   Schedule   Scientific method

In many scientific subjects, more than a third of the course time in undergraduate courses may be allocated to laboratory sessions and/or field visits. This proportion will also be reflected in the marks given for related in-course assessments and formal practical exams, so you should treat these practical elements just as seriously as lectures and tutorials.

Practical work is given emphasis because it:

- allows you to see and interact with real examples of organisms, specimens, artefacts, processes and reactions;
- helps you to develop new skills in areas such as observation, measurement, manipulation and data analysis;
- lets you gain an appreciation of 'scientific method', perhaps by imitating original experiments carried out in your field;
- demonstrates equipment and gives you 'hands-on' experience of using it;
- allows you to explore field locations relevant to your studies;
- gives you practice in writing up your work in formats that you may use to report project work or incorporate into your dissertation or thesis at a later stage.

In many cases, practical sessions are carried out in pairs or as part of a small group, so there is a chance to learn from your fellow students and to work as a team (**Ch 17, Ch 18**).

Examples of skills covered in practicals and field visits

- Observation
- Handling samples and organisms
- Using equipment
- Designing experiments
- Working safely

- Measuring and recording
- Creating tables and graphs
- Data analysis
- Reporting in written and spoken forms
- Teamwork

→ Preparing for practical sessions

If you want to gain the most from your practicals, effective preparation is essential. Often lab sessions and field visits are tightly scheduled and you may be expected to be 'up and running' almost from the start. Practicals may also involve new concepts and terms and if you don't understand these, you may not gain much from your efforts.

- Read through the schedule beforehand, making sure you understand the terminology – try to gain an overall impression of what you will be expected to do, and why.
- Consult textbooks or websites if you don't understand any of the underlying theory.
- Make sure you have the appropriate equipment ready to take to the practical.
- Ensure you arrive at the lab or assembly point in good time.

→ Appropriate conduct in the lab and field

Any rules associated with lab or fieldwork will have your safety as their primary concern, so you must pay attention to them. You may be asked to work with toxic chemicals, dangerous instruments or in hazardous environments, so care is essential. At an initial meeting of your class, you will be introduced to basic safety measures and legislation, told about the fire drill and shown relevant hazard symbols (Figure 19.1).

In the lab, you will be asked to wear a lab coat – which should always be buttoned up – and, if you have long hair, asked to tie it back. Eye protection goggles may also be necessary, and those who normally wear contact lenses may be subject to special rules because vapours of corrosive laboratory chemicals may be trapped between the lens and the cornea of the eye. You should never eat or smoke in a lab. You should also keep your bench space tidy and quickly dispose of specimens or sharps as instructed.

Explosive

Oxidising agent

Extremely or
highly flammable

Toxic or very toxic

Corrosive

Harmful or irritant

Dangerous for
the environment

Figure 19.1 **Some of the main EU hazard symbols**

Definition: COSHH

This stands for 'Control of Substances Hazardous to Health' – a UK regulation that came into force in 1999. It lays out the legal framework for risk assessment whenever hazardous chemicals, agents or procedures are used. Normally the person in charge of your lab or field visit (an academic or senior lab technician) will carry out a COSHH assessment, which should be displayed prominently and/or communicated to you. In certain situations you may be asked to complete the paperwork yourself, but will be given guidance on how to do this.

Where hazardous materials or procedures are involved, you will be told about any risk assessment that needs to be carried out, including, where appropriate, a COSHH risk assessment (see box above), and you have a duty to read this carefully.

When working with chemicals or live organisms like bacteria, take appropriate precautions:

- note where eye washes and emergency showers are located in your lab and understand the appropriate procedures when you come into contact with chemicals;
- make sure you know what type of fire extinguisher or fire blanket to use for the reagents being used, and where these are located, also note fire exits;
- be aware of possible modes of ingestion, including inhalation by nose or mouth, ingestion by mouth, absorption through exposed skin, inoculation through skin;
- know what to do if you spill any chemicals;
- take special care with procedures such as pipetting or transferring samples between vessels;
- always wash your hands thoroughly after each lab session.

For field visits, you will be advised about appropriate clothing. You should take special care to use appropriate footwear and be prepared for a change of weather conditions. If in a group, you should stay close to the main body of people; otherwise, try always to work with a partner, rather than alone. Any fieldwork group should:

- take a first aid kit;
- consult a weather forecast before they leave, and if working on the seashore find out about the state of the tides;
- leave full details of where they are going and when they expect to return.

You *must* obey any instructions regarding safety, whether given by a staff member, technician or postgraduate demonstrator.

→ Carrying out instructions and noting results

Lab and field visit schedules usually contain the following components:

- **Theory, background and aims.** This contains information essential to your understanding of the practical interpretation of instructions and approach to any assessed components, so do not be tempted to skip this and move directly to the instructions.

- **Instructions.** The language used here is generally very precise and should be followed to the letter or number. Success will often depend on, for example, the precision with which you measure out reagents, or the exact timing or temperature you use. When reading the schedule beforehand, you may wish to highlight key points in the instructions so you can follow them better during the session, or lay out tables ready to record your data. Before you start, the person in charge of the lab may tell you about any late changes that have had to be made – it is therefore important to arrive in good time and to listen carefully while this is done, making appropriate notes.

- **Results section.** This part provides space for you to record observations, data and comments.

Increasingly, a 'workbook' style of lab schedule is provided, with spaces and prompts for drawings, results and conclusions, but this is not always the case, and, especially in later years and at postgraduate level, you will be expected to organise your own notes.

---

smart tip

The language of practical reports

This is worth paying attention to as there are specific conventions that should be adopted. In the 'Introduction' and 'Materials and methods', the **past tense**, **passive voice** and **third person** (see **Ch 44** for definitions) are generally used (for example, 'Sturrock and Dodds (1984) **were** the first to show . . .' and 'the data **were recorded** at 5-minute intervals'). However, **present tense** might be used when describing figures and tables (for example, 'Table 3 **shows** the relationship between . . .'). Read research reports in your subject area to gain a feel for the style usually adopted.

Being able to record accurately what you see and measure is a vital skill in the sciences, and will be practised and tested throughout your university career. The following are key tips for recording your observations:

- Don't rely on your memory – write everything down.

- Never write on scraps of paper (you'll lose them) – use a proper lab book.

- Always date each page and provide full details of the specimen or experiment.

- If recording data, develop the skill of writing this information clearly – for example, ones and sevens are easily confused and you may wish to adopt the practice of crossing the latter (i.e. 7).

- If you are recording numbers, use an appropriate number of significant figures (**Ch 37**) to take account of the precision (or, perhaps more strictly, the lack of precision) of your method.

- If drawing diagrams, make sure these have a descriptive title and are well-labelled.

- In the field, be prepared for bad weather – buy a special wet weather notebook or take a clear plastic bag to enclose your notebook, and use a pencil as this will write on damp paper.

- Write down any final answers or results *in the form specified* – you may lose marks otherwise.

- Draw any graphs or tables according to the normal scientific conventions (**Ch 29**).

Defined report formats

If you are asked to use a specific format or template for writing up lab or field sessions, make sure you do this, or you may lose marks (and the sympathy of your marker!).

You may be asked to submit a selection of completed workbook schedules for marking. In some cases, you will be required to hand in lab reports. Table 19.1 details the key components of a typical lab report and outlines what's expected for each part. Further advice on practical assessments and oral exams is provided in **Ch 40**.

?

How should I title my report?

This is something that many students get wrong. The title should be a simple descriptive summary of what you are reporting, for example:

- Effect of Chemical X on Response Y of Specimen Z;
- The relationship between factor A and factor B under condition C;
- Yield of reaction P in the presence of different catalysts Q, R and S;
- Characteristics of specimens of C found in location D.

If no other hints or tips are provided, you should consult the literature in your subject area for typical examples of style.

Practical tips for getting the most from laboratory sessions and field visits

Focus on the aims and 'learning outcomes' of the session. When reading schedules beforehand, or listening to your lecturer introducing a procedure, make sure you understand what the purpose and likely 'take-home message' of the session is going to be. This will help you work much more effectively during the practical.

Use lab assistants and demonstrators fully. These people are generally paid to help you, so make the most of them. Often, they may be recent graduates, and sympathetic to any problems you may be facing. If in doubt, ask – it could save you lots of time and help you gain marks. Be prepared to ask questions yourself rather than wait to be asked – but don't expect the demonstrator to give you the answers directly. They will be under instruction to make *you* do most of the thinking, but will be happy to help you along the way.

Learn how to draw up informal tables and figures quickly. Rough tables will help you to record your results neatly and quickly, while 'instant' graphs will give you an early visual indication of how the experiment is proceeding. Your tables should include a column describing what is being measured or the number or timing of the measurements, and include sufficient 'cells' in the rows for each replicate or repeated measurement you will make. When constructing graphs, you will need to assess the largest and smallest figures you are likely to obtain, so you can determine what the

Table 19.1 Typical components of a lab or field report. This is the standard format used for scientific reports (see also **Ch 44**): for write-ups of single experiments or a laboratory practical, normally only the parts marked * in column 1 would be included. *Always adopt the precise format specified in your course handbook or by your supervisor.*

Section or part	Expected content
Title page*	A descriptive title that indicates what was done and sometimes describes the 'headline' finding. Also the full names of the author or authors, the module title or code if applicable and the date.
Abstract	A brief summary of the aims of the experiment or series of observations; the main outcomes (in words) and conclusions. This should allow a reader to understand your main findings and what you think they mean.
Abbreviations	A list of any abbreviations for technical terms used within the text (for example, 'DNA: deoxyribonucleic acid'). These are also given within the text at the first point of use, for example, '. . . deoxyribonucleic acid (DNA)'.
Introduction*	An outline of the background to the experiment, the aims of the experiment and brief discussion of the techniques to be used. Your goal is to orientate the reader and explain what you have done and why.
Materials and methods*	A description of what was done. You should provide sufficient detail to allow a competent person to repeat the work.
Results*	A description of the experiments carried out and the results obtained, usually presented in either tabular or graphic form (never both for the same data). You should point out meaningful aspects of the data, which need not be presented in the same order in which the work was done.
Discussion (or conclusions)*	A commentary on the results and an outline of the main conclusions. This could include any or all of the following: • comments on the methods used; • mention of sources of errors; • conclusions from any statistical analysis; • comparison with other findings or the 'ideal' result; • what the result means; • how you might improve the experiment; • where you would go from here, given more time and resources. Sometimes you might combine the results and discussions sections to allow a narrative to develop – to explain, for example, why one result led to the next experiment or approach. Remember that a large proportion of marks may be given for your original thoughts in this section.
Acknowledgements	A list of people who helped you.
References	An alphabetical list of sources cited in the text, following one of the standard formats (**Ch 31**).

limits of the graph axes should be. For all tables and figures, no matter how quickly drawn up, remember to state the measured quantity and the units of measurement.

Take plentiful notes and provide detailed labels. Note down anything that might be useful at a later date – and be prepared to use most of your senses, with caution: note colours, sounds and feel, but only taste and smell when specifically instructed. Label any diagrams fully and add a time and date. As well as stating what a component is, add relevant detail such as colour and texture. All diagrams should include a scale.

Use 'empty' time effectively. During lab experiments, there may be delays between parts of your work as reactions develop, or gaps if you are ahead of the rest of the class. Use this time to look ahead in the schedule to see what you will be doing next, to create tables or graphs ready for recording your results, or jot down ideas for your conclusions.

Write up your practical work when it is fresh in your mind. You may be tired after a lengthy lab session, but if you delay for too long you may forget useful details.

 Useful language for . . . working in a laboratory or in the field

Context: take care to learn the technical terms for the various pieces of equipment you will be expected to use and make sure that you thoroughly understand any safety aspects.

Can you tell me where the [name of piece of equipment] is? Please can you show me how to use it? I've never seen one like that before.

Is this the result that I should be expecting?

How do you think I should tabulate [or graph] these results?

GO And now . . .

19.1 Make up a checklist of items to take to your practicals. This will depend on your subject. Refer to the list before you leave for each session to ensure you don't forget anything.

19.2 Rehearse safety scenarios. Taking into account the safety information provided in your lab handbook, lab notices and lecturers' announcements, imagine what you would do in different situations, such as if there were a fire, if a fellow student swallowed a toxic chemical, or if someone cut themselves. This will make you more aware of the dangers of the lab or field environment and might help you react faster if needed.

19.3 Find out how your practical or fieldwork will be assessed. This assessment may be through reports or a special practical exam. Try to track down past papers or model answers, if these are available. Knowing the format and question style ahead of time will help you get the most from the sessions.

20 | Tutorials

How to prepare and participate

Tutorials are a method of gathering a small group of students together to discuss a topic or tackle problems related to a particular aspect of their course. This chapter outlines approaches to the conduct of tutorials that you may encounter in your studies.

Key topics:
→ Preparation for tutorials
→ Participating in tutorials
→ Strategies for dialogue in tutorials

Essential vocabulary
Devil's advocate   Freelance   Gambit   Monologue   Tutor   Tutorial

The tutorial system is one that is historically embedded in UK university education. Its function is to involve students actively in the learning process by meeting in small groups in order to address a set topic or problem.

Most tutorials will involve 5–12 students, although there are some universities where tutorials are conducted on a one-to-one basis. The tutor's role is to facilitate discussion or, for problem-solving tutorials, to assist students encountering difficulties. In addition, the tutor may be required to make an assessment of your participation and performance.

Who are my tutors?

Generally, it is unlikely that the people who deliver your lectures will conduct your tutorials. Some may be freelance experts who are brought in for the sole purpose of leading tutorials; others may be postgraduate students who are studying in your department (this may be an element of their postgraduate training).

It is worth thinking a little more strategically about what you can learn from tutorials beyond the subject-based agenda on which your group will work. For example, a tutorial is a kind of meeting and through your participation you will be expected to develop interpersonal skills that will transfer to meetings in other professional contexts once you graduate.

Tutorial types

There are essentially two types of university tutorial in the UK. One is common in subjects related to arts, social sciences, law and social work, for example. In this kind of tutorial a pre-set topic is considered in a discussion format. The second type of tutorial is more common in scientific and engineering disciplines, and is conducted alongside the lecture and practical programme. Here, students discuss answers to a series of problems or calculations under the guidance of a tutor. This approach is also found in numerical subjects such as accountancy.

→ Preparation for tutorials

Your tutorials will be held at regular intervals over a term or semester. You will normally be allocated to a tutorial group by the course director or administrator, and details of dates, times and venues for these meetings will be provided in your course handbook, on the departmental noticeboard or posted on your university's virtual learning environment. Tutorial topics and problems will be given to you under the arrangements set up by your department. For example, sometimes this information is provided in handout form, sometimes it is included in the course handbook.

Ch 39 outlines how your tutorial performance may be assessed.

Preparing for tutorials

Particularly for tutorials that involve working through examples or problems, it may be helpful to prepare for the tutorial with others. If you work together on problems that have been tricky, you might find a solution together. If not, then asking as a group for help from the tutor will ensure that your problems are addressed and may guide the meeting to cover key issues for your learning.

Before each tutorial, depending on the subject you are studying, you will be expected to have done some preparation.

- **For discussion-style tutorials in non-scientific subjects, you should have:**
  - done the required reading;
  - identified and analysed the topic or theme;
  - reflected on the key issues that arise;
  - considered the topic from different angles, for example, arguments for and against a particular set of ideas or proposals.

- **For tutorials in practical or numerical subjects, you should have:**
  - tackled the full set of problems or done the prescribed reading;
  - where required, submitted answers on time;
  - thought about difficulties that you may have found with the tutorial problems or about possible issues that might arise in the discussion;
  - reflected on how this topic or set of problems fits into the wider course structure and learning process.

Informal 'one-to-one' meetings

There are occasions when you might have a meeting with a lecturer on an informal basis to go over a particular piece of work or to ask for an explanation of a point covered in lectures that you have had difficulty understanding. This type of meeting is conducted more as a conversation than as a tutorial in the sense outlined in this chapter.

→ Participating in tutorials

How you participate in tutorials will very much depend on what kind of a student you are and what type of tutorial you are attending. No two students are the same and it is the richness represented within a student group that can make a tutorial a stimulating experience. There can be a time lapse between one tutorial and the next, and it may be that you don't meet your fellow tutees except in that tutorial situation. Some people may not feel as comfortable about participating in problem-solving or debating issues with relative strangers as they would among friends. This may be because they feel unsure of the situation as well as feeling unsure of the mode of learning that they are experiencing.

→ Strategies for dialogue in tutorials

Most communication is a two-way process, where one person speaks and the other listens. In tutorials, the situation is much the same except that there are more listeners, all with views of their own and all with something to say, if given the opportunity. You will need to develop some skills in interpersonal communication to ensure that you have the chance to be both a speaker and a listener. Table 20.1 introduces some tutorial 'characters' and suggests ways in which you can interact with them by using appropriate conversational gambits that are part of the turn-taking in group dialogue (see also the tips in **Ch 17**). These strategies are not only useful in tutorials – they can apply in meetings and group work situations.

Can I ask my tutor to explain things I wasn't sure about in the lecture?

This is not really the function of a tutorial in most subjects. In fact, your tutor may have no first-hand knowledge of your lecture course and will not be in a position to undertake discussion of any queries you might have. If you do have questions about the lectures, it is advisable to seek an appointment with the lecturer either via email or through the departmental secretary.

Table 20.1 Tutorial characters. Tutorial groups comprise many different types of student with different personalities, views and experience. Learning to interact with these individuals can be as challenging as the content of the tutorial. The column on the far right presents some approaches that might be useful to stimulate an even balance of participation in tutorials.

Tutorial character	Characteristic behaviour in tutorials	Typical language strategies	Language gambits in response
The quiet student	Shy and retiring. Never, or rarely, offers an opinion on topic. Takes lots of notes. Avoids eye contact with others. Speaks only when spoken to.	• I don't know. • Says nothing.	• What do you think about this? • What do you think about X's theory?
The know-it-all student	Has an opinion on almost everything. May have done reading but no reflection on deeper meaning; or has done problems but omits key steps.	• In my opinion . . . • I think . . . • It's my view that . . . • If you ask me . . .	• I think you're taking rather a narrow view on this. What about . . . ?
The centre-stage student	Likes to be the centre of attention. Attempts to monopolise the attention of the tutor and prevents others from asking questions or from contributing.	• I see this breaking down into 10 areas. The first one is . . . ; the second one is . . . the tenth one is . . .	• Could I come in here? • Actually, I have a related point . . . • I'd like to make a point here.
The conversation-monopolising student	Has read up about the subject and thought about it a lot, therefore has a lot to say and goes on and on. Is so preoccupied with his/her own thoughts that he/she tends to forget that others might wish to make their own points.	• My understanding of X's work is that . . . furthermore . . . on the other hand . . . I'd also like to say that . . .	• Could we hear other views? • Let's summarise what you've said so that I can make sure I understand your point.
The interrupting student	Not a good listener. Keeps talking over others or interrupting when others are speaking.	• If I could come in here . . . • I can't let that point go unchallenged . . .	• Could I just finish my point? • That's really a digression.
The uncertain student	Not very confident of own understanding or abilities – usually unfairly. Doesn't ask questions to confirm understanding. Rarely offers opinion except when asked directly.	• I'm not sure. • I don't think I know.	• How would you tackle this? • That's a really good point. • I quite agree with you.
The uninterested student	Only took the subject to make up the module numbers at matriculation. Gazes out of the window, plays with mobile phone.	• Don't know. I'm only here until the union opens. • This is really boring, isn't it?	• Ignore.
The active student	Contributes and listens. Has done the preparation; sorted out some of the ideas; not too sure about some points. Asks for clarification.	• Could you explain . . . ? • There are three points to make. • What do other people think?	• I think that is a well-considered point. • Could you expand on it further? • That's an interesting question. • What do others think about this?

✔ Practical tips for participating in tutorials and meetings

General pointers for problem-solving tutorials

Think about the underlying principles involved in the exercises. Consider how the examples fit into the wider scheme of things, especially your lectures.

Make sure that you have done the full set of examples beforehand. Identify those that have caused difficulty or raised questions in your mind so that you can discuss these points with the tutor.

Don't feel that your question is stupid. The chances are that there will be other students in the group who will be having the same difficulty.

Get your question in early on in the session. Make sure you ask your question before people who may not have done the preparatory work divert the tutor's attention with trivial or irrelevant questions.

Useful general pointers for tutorials based on discussion

Make sure that you do contribute. It is better to say something that you have an opinion about rather than be asked a direct question by the tutor about something where you have very little knowledge to support an opinion.

Make your points clearly and objectively. While you may hold strong views on a topic, you will be expected to explain these on the basis of supporting evidence and argument, not on emotion.

Don't take criticism of your ideas personally. This is an objective academic exercise and the tutorial would be dull and possibly pointless if everyone agreed.

Be aware that your ideas are as valid as anyone else's. This means that you can contribute effectively to the discussion.

Learn to listen as well as to speak. The convention in tutorials is that everyone has space to speak and be heard. Although you may not agree with the views of others, at least listen to what they have to say and consider their argument for its merits as well as its flaws.

Don't assume that your tutor is expressing a personal view when they present a point. Tutors may be taking the role of 'devil's advocate' simply to stimulate discussion.

Think ahead. When tutorial performance is assessed, each student must contribute in order to have a mark recorded (see also **Ch 39**). Therefore, before the tutorial you should think about how you would frame your ideas on the tutorial topic. This will help you 'rehearse' particular phrases so that you can focus on ideas rather than language.

Useful language for . . . speaking in tutorials

Context: in addition to the gambits shown in Table 20.1, the following are potential ways of getting your points across.

To prepare for this topic, I read the paper [or book] by [name]. She has a different view from the one outlined in our textbook. She suggests that [describe viewpoint]. I'm inclined to agree with that because [quote supporting evidence].

I recognised this problem as one that could be solved by using xxxx's equation [or law]. We are given data for all the variables except [name]. So, by rearranging the equation, we can find the unknown [name variable] and answer the question. The answer I obtained was [give figure and units].

Doesn't this topic connect with the one we did last semester? In the previous case, the outcome of [xxxx] was [xxxx], whereas in this case, the outcome was [xxxx]. I think the outcomes are different because . . .

GO And now . . .

20.1 Check out the dates, times and locations of your tutorials. Enter details for each subject for the term/semester and note this information in your diary or on your wall planner. Make sure you know exactly where the tutorials will take place and, if the location is unfamiliar, make a point of finding it so that you know where to go on the day.

20.2 Create a work plan that includes doing the preparatory reading or examples for your tutorial meetings. This will almost certainly have a big effect on your performance (**Ch 39**).

20.3 Identify tutorial 'characters'. Read through Table 20.1 and see if any of the tutorial personalities outlined there are present in your group(s). Think about how these characters interacted in previous tutorials. Might some of the gambits noted in Table 20.1 have assisted in creating a more balanced discussion? What kind of a character are you? Would it be helpful to your learning, and that of others, if you modified your behaviour in tutorials? In the next tutorial, do a little observation of your own about how people use body and oral language to make their points and to ensure that they have their say. Note any particular strategies that you think you could adapt or adopt to help you participate fully in tutorials in general.

21 | Thinking critically

How to develop a logical approach to analysis and problem-solving

The ability to think critically is probably the most transferable of the skills you will develop at university – and your future employers will expect you to be able to use it to tackle professional challenges. This chapter introduces concepts, methods and fallacies to watch out for when trying to improve your analytical capabilities.

Key topics:
→ Thinking about thinking
→ Using method to prompt and organise your thoughts
→ Recognising fallacies and biased presentations

Essential vocabulary

Analysis Anecdotal Bias Critical thinking Description Dichotomy Euphemism Fallacy Pejorative Propaganda 'Straw man' Value judgement

How can you apply theory and technique to help you think better? Many specialists believe that critical thinking is a skill that you can develop through application of theory and practice – and this assumption lies behind much university teaching. Your experience of the educational system probably tells you that your marks depend increasingly on the analysis of facts and the ability to arrive at an opinion and support it with relevant information and evidence, rather than the simple recall of fact. If you understand the underlying processes a little better, this should help you meet your tutors' expectations. If you are unsure how to tackle a new task, adopting a methodical approach can be useful in helping to work out a suitable approach.

→ Thinking about thinking

Benjamin Bloom, a noted educational psychologist, and colleagues, identified six steps involved in learning and thinking within education:

- knowledge;
- comprehension;
- application;
- analysis;
- synthesis;
- evaluation.

Bloom *et al.* (1956) showed that students naturally progressed through this scale of thought-processing during their studies (Table 21.1). Looking at this table, you may recognise that in your earlier education, much of the focus was on knowledge, comprehension and application, while your university tutors tend to expect more in terms of analysis, synthesis and evaluation. These expectations are sometimes closely linked to the instruction words used in assessments, and Table 21.1 provides a few examples. However, take care when interpreting these, as processes and tasks may mean different things in different subjects. For example, while 'description' might imply a lower-level activity in some subjects, it might involve high-level skills in others.

Definition: critical

People often interpret the words 'critical' and 'criticism' to mean being negative about an issue. For university work, the alternative meaning of 'making a careful judgement after balanced consideration of all aspects of a topic' is the one you should adopt.

Some disciplines value creativity as a thinking process, for example, art and design, architecture, drama or English composition. In such cases, this word might take the place of 'synthesis' in Table 21.1. In certain cases creativity could be ranked as surpassing 'evaluation' in the table.

When you analyse the instructions used in writing assignments (**Ch 28**, especially Table 28.2) and other forms of assessment (**Ch 36-Ch 47**), you should take into account what type of thinking process the examiner has asked you to carry out, and try your best to reach the required level. To help you understand what might be required, Table 21.2 gives examples of thought processes you might experience in a range of areas of study.

Contexts for thinking critically

Examples of university work involving high-level thinking skills include:

- essay-writing in the arts and social sciences
- problem-based learning in medicine and nursing
- engineering problems based on real-life machines and buildings
- cases in law
- project-based practical work in the sciences.

→ Using method to prompt and organise your thoughts

Imagine that you recognise that critical thinking is required to solve a particular problem. This could be an essay question set by one of your tutors, an issue arising from problem-based learning, or even a domestic matter such as what type of car to buy or where best to rent a flat. The pointers below help you to arrive at a logical answer. Think about the different stages and how they might be useful for the specific

Table 21.1 Classification of thinking processes by Bloom *et al.* (1956) (Bloom's Taxonomy)

Thinking processes (in perceived ascending order of difficulty)	Typical question instructions
Knowledge. To know a fact, to be able to have it at your disposal and to *recall* or *recognise* it. This does not mean you necessarily understand it at a higher level.	• Define • Describe • Identify
Comprehension. To comprehend a fact means that you *understand* what it means.	• Contrast • Discuss • Interpret
Application. To apply a fact means that you can *put it to use.*	• Demonstrate • Calculate • Illustrate
Analysis. To analyse information means that you are able to *break it down into parts* and show how these components *fit together.*	• Analyse • Explain • Compare
Synthesis. To synthesise, you need to be able to *extract relevant facts* from a body of knowledge and use these to *address an issue in a novel way* or *create something new.*	• Compose • Create • Integrate
Evaluation. To reach *a judgement* based on its importance relative to the topic being addressed.	• Recommend • Support • Draw a conclusion

issue under consideration and your own style of work. Adopt or reject them as you think appropriate, or, according to your needs, alter their order.

- **Identify the exact problem.** An important preliminary task is to write down a description of the problem or issue – if this is not already provided for you – taking care to be very precise with your wording. If a specific question has been given as part of the exercise, analyse its phrasing carefully, to make sure you understand all possible meanings (**Ch 28**). If you are working in a group, ideally all members should agree on the group's interpretation.

- **Organise your approach to the problem.** You might start with a 'brainstorm' to identify potential solutions or viewpoints. This can be a solo or group activity and typically might consist of three phases:
  - **Open thinking.** Consider the issue or question from all possible angles or positions and write down everything you come up with. Don't worry at this stage about the relevance or importance of your ideas. You may wish to use a 'spider diagram' or 'mind map' to lay out your thoughts (**Ch 16** and **Ch 25**).
  - **Organisation.** Next, you should try to arrange your ideas into categories or sub-headings, or group them as supporting or opposing a viewpoint. A new diagram, table or grid may be useful to make things clear (see Figures 25.1-25.7 for examples of layout).
  - **Analysis.** Now you need to decide about the relevance of the grouped points to the original problem. Reject trivial or irrelevant ideas and rank or prioritise those that seem relevant.

Table 21.2 Examples of Bloom's classification of thinking processes within representative university subjects

Thinking processes (in ascending order of difficulty)	Law	Examples	
		Arts subjects, e.g. History or Politics	Numerical subjects
Knowledge	You might know the name and date of a case, statute or treaty without understanding its relevance	You might know that a river was an important geographical and political boundary in international relations, without being able to identify why	You might be able to write down a particular mathematical equation, without understanding what the symbols mean or where it might be applied
Comprehension	You would understand the principle of law contained in the legislation or case law, and its wider context	You would understand that the river forms a natural barrier, which can be easily identified and defended	You would understand what the symbols in an equation mean and how and when to apply it
Application	You would be able to identify situations to which the principle of law would apply	You might use this knowledge to explain the terms of a peace treaty	You would be able to use the equation to obtain a result, given background information
Analysis	You could relate the facts of a particular scenario to the principle to uncover the extent of its application, using appropriate authority	You could explain the importance of the river as a boundary as being of importance to the territorial gains/losses for signatories to the peace treaty	You could explain the theoretical process involved in deriving the equation
Synthesis	By a process of reasoning and analogy, you could predict how the law might be applied under given circumstances	You could identify this notion and relate it to the recurrence of this issue in later treaties or factors governing further hostilities and subsequent implications	You could be able to take one equation, link it with another and arrive at a new mathematical relationship or conclusion
Evaluation	You might be able to advise a client based on your own judgement, after weighing up and evaluating all available options	You would be able to discuss whether the use of this boundary was an obstacle to resolving the terms of the treaty to the satisfaction of all parties	You would be able to discuss the limitations of an equation based on its derivation and the underlying assumptions behind this

- **Get background information and check your comprehension of the facts.** It's quite likely that you will need to gather relevant information and ideas – to support your viewpoint or position, provide examples or suggest a range of interpretations or approaches. You also need to ensure you fully understand the information you have gathered. This could be as simple as using dictionaries and technical works to find out the precise meaning of key words; it might involve discussing your ideas with your peers or a tutor; or you could read a range of texts to see how others interpret your topic.

- **Check relevance.** Now consider the information you have gathered, your thoughts and how these might apply to your question. You may need to re-analyse the question. You will then need to organise the evidence you have collected – for example: for or against a proposition; supporting or opposing an argument or theory. You may find it useful to prepare a table or grid to organise the information (see Figure 25.6 for an example) – this will also help you balance your thoughts. Be ruthless in rejecting irrelevant or inconsequential material.

- **Think through your argument, and how you can support it.** Having considered relevant information and positions, you should arrive at a personal viewpoint, and then construct your discussion or conclusion around this. When writing about your conclusion, you must take care to avoid value judgements or other kinds of expression of opinion that are not supported by evidence or sources. This is one reason why frequent citation and referencing is demanded in academic work.

- **Get cracking on your answer.** Once you have decided on what you want to say, writing it up should be much easier.

→ Recognising fallacies and biased presentations

As you consider arguments and discussions on academic subjects, you will notice that various linguistic devices are used to promote particular points of view. Identifying these is a valuable aspect of critical thinking, allowing you to rise above the argument itself and think about the way in which it is being conducted.

There are many different types of logical fallacies, and Table 21.3 lists only a few common examples. Once tuned in to this way of thinking, you should observe that faulty logic and debating tricks are frequently used in areas such as advertising and politics. Analysing the methods being used can be a useful way of practising your critical skills.

One way of avoiding bias in your own work is consciously to try to balance your discussion. Avoid 'absolutes' – be careful with words that imply that there are no exceptions, for example, *always*, *never*, *all* and *every*. These words can only be used if you are absolutely sure of facts that imply 100 per cent certainty.

Definitions

- **Fallacy:** a fault in logic or thinking that means that an argument is incorrect.
- **Bias:** information that emphasises just one viewpoint or position.
- **Propaganda:** false or incomplete information that supports a (usually) extreme political or moral view.

Table 21.3 Common examples of logical fallacies, bias and propaganda techniques found in arguments. There are many different types of fallacious arguments (at least 70) and this is an important area of study in philosophical logic.

Type of fallacy or propaganda	Description	Example	How to counteract this approach
Ad hominem (Latin for 'to the man')	An attack is made on the character of the person putting forward an argument, rather than on the argument itself; this is particularly common in the media and politics	The President's moral behaviour is suspect, so his financial policies must also be dubious	Suggest that the person's character or circumstances are irrelevant
Ad populum (Latin for 'to the people')	The argument is supported on the basis that it is a popular viewpoint; of course, this does not make it correct in itself	The majority of people support corporal punishment for vandals, so we should introduce boot camps	Watch out for bandwagons and peer-pressure effects and ignore them when considering rights and wrongs
Anecdotal evidence	Use of unrepresentative exceptions to contradict an argument based on statistical evidence	My grandmother was a heavy smoker and she lived to be 95, so smoking won't harm me	Consider the overall weight of evidence rather than isolated examples
Appeal to authority	An argument is supported on the basis that an expert or authority agrees with the conclusion; used in advertisements, where celebrity endorsement and testimonials are frequent	My professor, whom I admire greatly, believes in Smith's theory, so it must be right	Point out that the experts disagree and explain how and why; focus on the key qualities of the item or argument
Appeal to ignorance	Because there's no evidence for (or against) a case, it means the case must be false (or true)	You haven't an alibi, therefore you must be guilty	Point out that a conclusion either way may not be possible in the absence of evidence
Biased evidence	Selection of examples or evidence for or against a case. A writer who quotes those who support their view, but not those against	My advisers tell me that global warming isn't going to happen	Read around the subject, including those with a different view, and try to arrive at a balanced opinion
Euphemisms and jargon	Use of phrasing to hide the true position or exaggerate an opponent's – stating things in mild or emotive language for effect; use of technical words to sound authoritative	My job as vertical transportation operative means I am used to being in a responsible position	Watch for (unnecessary) adjectives and adverbs that may affect the way you consider the evidence
Repetition	Saying the same thing over and over again until people believe it. Common in politics, war propaganda and advertising	'Beans means Heinz'	Look out for repeated catchphrases and lack of substantive argument
Straw man/ false dichotomy	A position is misrepresented in order to create a diversionary debating point that is easily accepted or rejected, when in fact the core issue has not been addressed	Asylum seekers all want to milk the benefits system, so we should turn them all away	Point out the fallacy and focus on the core issue

Originality

Your ability to bring originality of thinking to your work will be highly prized in the UK university system. Some international students may find it difficult to express ideas in an original way because their schooling system rewards repetition of facts as provided by teachers or textbooks. At university in the UK, you will be expected to demonstrate the processes of analysis, synthesis and evaluation. This will help you confirm your own thoughts on an issue, based on evidence and assess the thinking of others.

Value judgements

These are statements that reflect the views and values of the speaker or writer rather than the objective reality of what is being assessed or considered (**Ch 27**). For example, if the person is sympathetic to a cause they may refer to those who support it as members of a 'pressure group'; if they disagree with the cause, its members become 'activists'; similarly, 'conservationists' versus 'tree-huggers'; 'freedom fighters' versus 'insurgents'. Value judgements often imply some sense of being pejorative (negative). For example: 'Teenagers are unreliable, unpredictable and unable to accept responsibility for their actions'.

✔ Practical tips for thinking critically

Focus on the task in hand. It is very easy to become distracted when reading around a subject, or when discussing problems with others. Take care not to waste too much time on preliminaries and start relevant action as quickly as possible.

Write down your thoughts. The act of writing your thoughts is important as this forces you to clarify them. Also, since ideas are often fleeting, it makes sense to ensure you have a permanent record. Reviewing what you have written makes you more critical and can lead you on to new ideas.

Try to be analytical, not descriptive. By looking at Table 21.1, you will appreciate why analysis is regarded as a higher-level skill than description. Many students lose marks because they simply quote facts or statements, without explaining their importance and context, that is, without showing their understanding of what the quote means or implies.

When quoting evidence, use appropriate citations. This is important as it shows you have read relevant source material and helps you avoid plagiarism (**Ch 32**). The conventions for citation vary among subjects (**Ch 31**), so consult course handbooks or other information and make sure you follow the instructions carefully, or you may lose marks.

Draw on the ideas and opinions of your peers and tutors. Discussions with others can be very fruitful, revealing a range of interpretations that you might not have thought about yourself. You may find it useful to bounce ideas off others. Tutors can provide useful guidance once you have done some reading, and are usually pleased to be asked for help.

Keep an open mind. Although you may start with preconceived ideas about a topic, you should try to be receptive to the ideas of others. You may find that your initial thoughts become altered by what you are reading and discussing. If there is not enough evidence to support *any* conclusion, be prepared to suspend judgement.

Balance your arguments. If asked to arrive at a position on a subject, you should try to do this in an even-handed way, by considering all possible viewpoints and by presenting your conclusion with supporting evidence.

Avoid common pitfalls of shallow thinking. Try not to:

- rush to conclusions;
- generalise;
- oversimplify;
- personalise;
- use fallacious arguments;
- think in terms of stereotypes;
- make value judgements.

Keep asking yourself questions. A good way to think more deeply is to ask questions, even after you feel a matter is resolved or you understand it well. All critical thinking is the result of asking questions.

Look beneath the surface. Decide whether sources are dealing with facts or opinions; examine any assumptions made, including your own; think about the motivation of writers. Rather than restating and describing your sources, focus on what they *mean* by what they write.

 Useful language for . . . explaining your thoughts and analysing others' thoughts

Even native speakers can find it difficult to put their own thoughts into language. Thus, for everyone, writing down a few words and phrases that will help frame the ideas you want to explain will help in discussion.

Context: contributing ideas to a debate or tutorial discussion

[For sequencing points in an argument] Firstly, . . . Secondly, . . . Finally, . . .

I've read several things on this. I think that the ideas of X are the strongest, because . . .

I think there's a fallacy in that argument. The evidence is mostly anecdotal. He (she) hasn't looked at all the published evidence.

21.1 Practise seeing both sides of an argument. Choose a topic, perhaps one on which you have strong views (for example, a political matter, such as state support for private schooling; or an ethical one, such as the need for vivisection or abortion). Write down the supporting arguments for both sides of the issue, focusing on your least-favoured option. This will help you see both sides of a debate as a matter of course.

21.2 Analyse the instruction words in past exam papers. Note which types of instruction words are commonly used. First check that you understand what is expected in relation to each word (**Ch 28**, p. 235), then, taking into account the subject and the way in which it has been taught, what level of thinking you are expected to demonstrate in your exam answers. If you are in doubt, ask a subject tutor to explain.

21.3 Look into the murky world of fallacies and biased arguments. There are some very good websites that provide lists of different types of these with examples. Investigate these by using 'fallacy' or 'logical fallacies' in a search engine. Not only are the results quite entertaining at times, but you will find the knowledge obtained improves your analytical and debating skills.

How to make the best use of the facilities

At university you will find that you will be expected not only to seek out the books and other source material on your reading list, but also to source additional material for yourself. Learning more about information literacy and how to access resources is a priority. Libraries and the information you can access from them are constantly changing. Thus detailed institution-specific information soon becomes outdated. Hence, this chapter focuses on key aspects of information retrieval and related skills.

Key topics:
→ First steps for new students
→ The range of facilities and resources
→ What you need to know as a borrower
→ Regulations and codes of conduct
→ Key information literacy skills

Essential vocabulary
**Code of conduct   Copyright   Dewey decimal system   Ebrary
Library of Congress system   Reciprocal arrangement   Regulations**

The library is a key resource for any student. A modern university library is much more than a collection of books and journals – it co-ordinates an electronic gateway to a massive amount of online information. Accessing these resources requires library skills that are essential for your studies.

→ First steps for new students

- Visit the university library and activate your membership. This usually cannot be done until you have matriculated/enrolled.

- Find out when library tours that are offered to new students take place. Register for one of these, since this will introduce you to the layout and facilities available.

- Obtain leaflets or library layout maps to which you can refer later when you explore the library on your own.

Your library record

When you join your university library, a record is established in your name. Most libraries use an electronic system that allows you to check your record of books out on loan at any time.

Deciding whether or not to buy textbooks

Sometimes reading lists are long and the recommended textbooks can be expensive. However, it may not be necessary to buy some of the books because these will be available in the university library. In some cases, you may wish to buy your own copy of a book that you will need frequently, because demand for the library copies may be high and you may find it difficult to obtain the book on loan. If you can't afford to do that, an alternative is to find books with similar content also in the library by using the library catalogue.

→ The range of facilities and resources

Most university libraries offer the following facilities:

- quiet study areas;
- groupwork areas where discussion is allowed;
- photocopiers and printers;
- computing terminals, and possibly a wireless network;
- online catalogue access;
- support from expert staff, both in person and via the library website.

Apart from books, most UK university libraries will also hold some of the following, in hard copy form:

- selected daily and weekly newspapers;
- periodicals and academic journals;
- reference materials;
- slides (e.g. for art or life sciences);
- video and DVD resources.

Table 22.1 indicates the type of content you can expect from these resources. The precise holdings will depend on factors such as the degrees taught, any teaching specialisms, the research interests of staff and past bequests of collections. Each library is unique and, in this respect, will hold particular archive material that is not available elsewhere.

Digital and web-based resources

Many current items are now available online in each of the categories listed in Table 22.1. For example, libraries take out subscriptions to e-book repositories, e-journals, e-newspapers and online dictionaries and encyclopaedias. Your institution will have its own method of giving access to these digitised and web-based resources, probably via the library electronic desktop. A password may be required.

The main advantage of this method of accessing information is that it is available 24 hours per day from any computer connected to the internet. In some cases, more than one person can access the e-book at any one time. Some e-book facilities, such as ebrary, offer additional facilities, including searching, note-making facilities and linked online dictionaries for checking the meanings of words.

Table 22.1 Some of the types of content that can be obtained from library resources. These may be available as hard copy or online.

Type of resource	Examples	Indication of content
Books	Prescribed texts	Provide linkage with the course content
	General textbooks	Give an overview of the subject
	Supplementary texts	Discuss subject in greater depth
Reference books	Standard dictionaries	Provide spelling, pronunciation and meaning
	Bilingual dictionaries	Provide translation of words and expressions in two languages
	Subject-specific dictionaries	Define key specialist terms
	Thesauri (plural); Thesaurus (singular)	A–Z versions are easier to use than the original Roget's Thesaurus. The A–Z versions give synonyms (words similar in meaning) and, in some, antonyms (words opposite in meaning).
	General encyclopaedias	Provide a quick overview of a new topic
	Discipline-specific encyclopaedias	Focus on in-depth coverage of specific topics
	Biographical material	Sources of information on key figures both contemporary and in the past
	Yearbooks	Provide up-to-date information on organisations
	Atlases	Provide geographical or historical information
	Directories	Provide up-to-date access to information on organisations
Newspapers	Daily or weekly newspapers	Provide coverage of contemporary issues
Periodicals and academic journals	Discipline- or subject-specific publications produced three or four times per year	Provide recent ideas, reports and comment on current research issues
Popular periodicals	*Nature*; *New Scientist*; *The Economist*	Provide coverage of emerging themes within broad fields, such as their titles suggest
Search engines and databases	Electronic repositories of academic journals and other material	Access will depend on the journal subscriptions held by your library

Electronic databases make it easier to access information from public bodies, and much of that kind of information is also now more readily available online. For example, statistical population details are available through the UK National Statistics website (**www.statistics.gov.uk**), while papers and publications produced by the UK Houses of Parliament can also be accessed electronically (**www.parliament.uk**).

Shared library resources

Many university libraries share resources with those of neighbouring institutions and all are linked to the British Library, the national library of the UK. This receives a copy of every publication produced in the UK and Ireland, and its massive collection of over 150 million items increases by 3 million items every year. Some university libraries are designated as European Documentation Centres (**http://ec.europa. eu/europedirect**). These centres hold key documents of the European Union although much of this material is now available online.

→ What you need to know as a borrower

You should find out the answers to the following questions regarding book borrowing.

- **How many books can you borrow at any one time?** This depends on your status as a borrower: staff and postgraduate students can usually borrow more books than undergraduate members.

- **What is the maximum loan period?** This will depend on the type of resource you wish to borrow. For example, some books that are heavily in demand because they are prescribed texts may be put on a short-loan system within the library. The basic idea is that readers are limited to a shorter borrowing time for these books. This period may be as short as a few hours, or perhaps a few days. Standard loans are usually for several weeks.

- **What are the fines if you keep a book after the due date?** Fines usually apply to all borrowers, whether they are staff or students. The fine will be dictated by the status of the book that is overdue. Short-loan books have higher fines; standard loans are lower. While a few pence may not seem much on a standard loan, if you have 10 books all overdue for two weeks, you can be looking at a double-figure in pounds.

- **How can you renew the loan?** Most libraries accept telephone renewals, but, increasingly, online facilities enable you to renew books from wherever you access the university home page.

Electronic book tagging

To protect their valuable assets, most universities operate a system of electronic 'book tagging' to ensure that resources cannot be withdrawn without being logged out to a particular user. This means that all books need to be 'de-activated' before you can take them out of the library, otherwise an alarm may be triggered at the exit.

→ Regulations and codes of conduct

All libraries have regulations and codes of conduct; they generally serve to protect the resources and respect the needs of other library users. You will be alerted to these rules by notices, leaflets and websites. In particular, you have important legal responsibilities under copyright law, which sets out limits on the amount of material you can photocopy from a single source (**Ch 32**).

→ Key information literacy skills

Information literacy has been defined as: *'knowing when and why you need information, where to find it, and how to evaluate, use and communicate it in an ethical manner.'* (Information Literacy Group, 2009). Seven key information skills are associated with information literacy (SCONUL, 2009), namely the ability to:

1 recognise a need for information;
2 distinguish ways in which the information 'gap' may be addressed;
3 construct strategies for locating information;
4 locate and access information;
5 compare and critically evaluate information obtained from different sources;
6 organise, apply and communicate information to others in appropriate ways; and
7 synthesise and build upon existing information, contributing to the creation of new knowledge.

You should think about how well you can perform each of these skills.

In terms of the ability to locate and access information, these are the basic skills you will need to master:

- **How to use the electronic catalogue.** Most systems offer a function where you can search by author, by title, or by subject, although there may be more alternatives on the system you will use.

- **How to find a book or periodical.** When you identify the book that you want from the catalogue, then you need to be able to find where it is shelved in the library. This means that you need to take a note of two things: the location (the book might be shelved in another site library, for example) and the class number (not the ISBN number, which is irrelevant). The catalogue number may comprise a sequence of letters and/or numbers depending on the system used in your library. This number corresponds to the number on the spine of the book – universities generally use one of two systems (see tip box opposite). Books are shelved sequentially according to these numbers, in stacks labelled to assist you to find what you want. If you have difficulty in locating a particular book or other resource, library staff can help.

Catalogue searches for named authors

There are often several ways to spell surnames in the UK, for example Brown/Browne or Nichol/Nicol/Nicoll. To find a book by an author's name that you may only have heard mentioned in a lecture, you may have to try various options in order to find the one you want. Check with the book list in your course handbook, as this may give details, including catalogue information. Make sure you are checking the catalogue for the surname (usually the last one) and not a personal (first) name.

- **How to borrow a book or journal from another library.** Sometimes books are not available in your own library and you may wish to request a loan from another UK library. There will be a particular librarian responsible for inter-library loans who will arrange this. However, there are cost implications in this process. Usually, the cost is borne by the borrower.

- **How to access your university library's e-resources.** This is normally done via the library's website. Some resources are open-access, but others will require a password that allows publishers to verify that your library has subscribed to an e-resource and that you have access rights. Systems may vary but information and training on how to access material using e-resources will usually be available to students in a special training session during a lecture or your library may provide independent training sessions that you can attend. The important thing is not to be puzzled by the range of resources available to you. Ask a librarian to help you find your way around this 'e-world'.

Library cataloguing systems

The system your library uses will be explained in leaflets or during the library tour. The two main possibilities are:

- **The Dewey decimal system:** each book is given a numerical code. For example, editions of *Hamlet* by William Shakespeare are filed under 822.33.
- **The Library of Congress system:** each book is given an alphanumeric code. For example, editions of *Hamlet* by William Shakespeare are filed under PR2807.

Additional numbers and letters may be used to define editions and variants on a subject area. Each system may be interpreted slightly differently in different libraries.

Of course, finding information within the library and associated online facilities is only the first step in using it for your studies. The next stage is to evaluate it (**Ch 21** and **Ch 23**) and use it appropriately in your academic writing (**Ch 28, Ch 29**), note making and revision (**Ch 25, Ch 51**). In these contexts, citing sources of information correctly (**Ch 31**) is important, to avoid plagiarism (**Ch 32**).

✔ Practical tips for making the most of library resources

Go on a library tour. Be prepared to ask questions if you are shown things that you don't understand or that seem strange to you. University libraries are unlike public libraries in many ways and have much more to offer. This is a chance to learn about these opportunities. If tours are not available, see if a virtual tour can be made from your university library's website.

Take advantage of reciprocal arrangements. Some university libraries have agreements with other similar libraries in the area, including national libraries. This enables you to use and sometimes, depending on the agreement, borrow books from partner libraries.

Find and join the local public library. This may hold some texts that would be relevant to your course and will not be so heavily in demand as those in the university library.

Explore all the library locations available to you. You may find different areas that are more convenient or that suit your moods, learning preference or personality. You may find spots that are out of the way and quieter or zones with a buzz that gets you going.

Evaluate library resources carefully – for example, just because a resource is newer, this does not mean it is better. Sometime 'old' books can be more valuable than 'new' sources like websites. Each resource needs to be considered on its merits (see **Ch 23**).

💬 Useful language for . . . studying in the library

Context: all the questions noted below could be addressed to library staff, for example, at the reception or help desk.

Excuse me. I'm looking for this book [show title]. It doesn't seem to be in the electronic catalogue. Can you tell me how I might obtain a copy?

How much of this book am I allowed to photocopy?

Can you tell me how late the library is open tonight? Is there an alternative study area open later than that?

I've looked for this book but the numbers on the shelves don't seem to go that high. Is there another area that this book might be shelved in?

My library account does not seem to be available. Could you sort that out for me, please?

And now . . .

22.1 Spend some time becoming thoroughly acquainted with the electronic library resources. Look, in particular, at any subject-specific resources that are provided on the catalogue system or via the library website.

22.2 Explore the shelves covering your subject area. Identify this area from the library catalogue and the information on shelving aisles. 'Browsing' the books and catalogues may reveal interesting resources you might not find by other searching methods. Citing sources that are not on the recommended list can enhance your work, but be sure that any material you have used to support your discussion is well-regarded, has academic provenance and is not out of date. This means that you have to explain your point and identify how the cited source supports or contradicts it.

22.3 Find out about alternative library facilities. In some cases, there may be satellite libraries on different campuses or in different buildings. Some of these may be departmental libraries, containing specialist resources. These can contain duplicate holdings of books in the main library.

How to filter and select reliable material and discuss it appropriately

Since so much information is available nowadays, through many different media, the evaluation of evidence, data and opinions has become a core skill. This chapter will help you understand the origin of information and ideas, the reliability of sources, and differences between fact, opinion and truth.

Key topics:
→ The origin of information and ideas
→ Assessing sources of 'facts'
→ Facts, opinions and truth
→ Backing up your own opinion or conclusion

Essential vocabulary
Argument   Citation   Conjecture   Multifaceted   Objectivity   Opinion   Premise/premiss   Primary source   Provenance   Scepticism   Secondary source   Subjectivity   Tenet   Value judgement

Whatever subject you are studying at university, the ability to evaluate information and ideas is essential. This is a multifaceted skill that will differ according to the task in hand. Your analysis may centre on the accuracy or truth of the information itself, the reliability or potential bias of the source of the information, or the value of information in relation to some argument or case. You may also come across contradictory sources of evidence or conflicting arguments based on the same information. You will need to assess their relative merits. To do any or all of these tasks, you will need to understand more about the origin and nature of information.

→ The origin of information and ideas

Essentially, facts and ideas originate from someone's research or scholarship. These can be descriptions, concepts, interpretations or numerical data. At some point, information or ideas must be communicated or published, otherwise no one else would know about them. Information and ideas usually appear first in the primary literature and may be modified later in the secondary literature (Table 23.1). Understanding this process is important when analysing and evaluating information and when deciding how to cite evidence or references in the text of your own assignments (**Ch 31**).

Table 23.1 Characteristics and examples of primary and secondary sources of information

Primary sources: those in which ideas and data are first communicated.	• The primary literature in your subject may be published in the form of papers (articles) in journals. • The primary literature is usually refereed by experts in the authors' academic peer group, who check the accuracy and originality of the work and report their opinions back to the journal editors. This system helps to maintain reliability, but it is not perfect. • Books (and, more rarely, articles in magazines and newspapers) can also be primary sources, but this depends on the nature of the information published rather than the medium. These sources are not formally refereed, although they may be read by editors and lawyers to check for errors and unsubstantiated or libellous allegations.
Secondary sources: those that quote, adapt, interpret, translate, develop or otherwise use information drawn from primary sources.	• It is the act of recycling that makes the source secondary, rather than the medium. Reviews are examples of secondary sources in the academic world, and textbooks and magazine articles are often of this type. • As people adopt, modify, translate and develop information and ideas, alterations are likely to occur, whether intentional or unintentional. Most authors of secondary sources do not deliberately set out to change the meaning of the primary source, but they may unwittingly do so. Others may consciously or unconsciously exert bias in their reporting by quoting evidence only on one side of a debate. • Modifications while creating a secondary source could involve adding valuable new ideas and content, or correcting errors.

→ Assessing sources of 'facts'

Not all 'facts' are true. What you read could be misquoted, misrepresented, erroneous or based on a faulty premise. This is particularly true of web-based information because it is less likely to be refereed or edited. Logically, the closer you can get to the primary source, the more consistent the information is likely to be with the original. Clearly, a lot depends on who wrote the source and under what patronage (who paid them?). Hence, another important way of assessing sources is to investigate the ownership and 'provenance' of the work (from whom and where it originated, and why).

● **Authorship.** Can you identify who wrote the piece? If it is signed or there is a 'by-line' showing who wrote it, you might be able to judge the quality of what you are reading. This may be a simple decision, if you know or can assume the author is an authority in the area; otherwise a little research might help (for example, putting the name into a search engine).

Of course, just because Professor X thinks something, this does not make it true. However, if you know that their opinion is backed by years of research and experience, you might take it a little more seriously than the thoughts of an unknown web author. If no author is cited, this may mean that no one is willing to take responsibility for the content. Could there be a reason for this?

The nature of evaluation

In 'scientific' subjects you will need to interpret and check the reliability of data. This is essential for setting up and testing meaningful hypotheses, and therefore at the core of the scientific approach.

In 'non-scientific' subjects, ideas and concepts are important, and you may need to carry out an objective analysis of information and arguments so that you can construct your own position, backed up with evidence.

● **Provenance.** Is the author's place of work mentioned? This might tell you whether there is likely to have been an academic study behind the facts or opinions given. If the author works for a public body, there may be publication rules to follow and they may even have to submit their work to a publications committee before it is disseminated. They are certainly more likely to be in trouble if they include scurrilous or incorrect material. Another question to ask is whether a company or political faction may have a vested interest behind the content.

Table 23.2 gives a checklist for assessing the reliability of information you may read.

Using more than one source

In the UK, students are usually required to use several sources of material in their reading for coursework and tutorials. This is part of the process of analysing and synthesising material. A good strategy for a new topic is, first of all, to find a textbook or other reputable source that covers the topic in a general way so that you have an overall understanding of the issues within the area. Then, you can select more detailed material and be able to read it within the framework provided by the general textbook.

→ Facts, opinions and truth

When dealing with a large reading list and a wide diversity of viewpoints, you can easily become confused and lose sight of the differences between fact, opinion and truth. Becoming aware of this issue is fundamental to study in many subjects, particularly in the arts, social sciences and law.

In many fields, for example, in arts and social sciences, there is often no 'right' or 'wrong' answer, simply a range of stances or viewpoints. It is therefore possible that your answer may differ significantly from the viewpoints of your fellow students and possibly also that of your tutor. You will probably be given credit for constructing your own argument with evidence to substantiate your position, rather than simply following a 'line' expounded in lectures or a standard text. Even if your tutors disagree personally with your conclusions, they will mark your work according to the way you have presented it.

Table 23.2 A checklist for assessing the reliability of information. These questions are based on commonly adopted criteria; the more 'yes' answers you can give, the more trustworthy you can assume your source to be.

Assessing authorship and the nature of the source	Evaluating the information and its analysis
❏ Can you identify the author's name?	❏ Is the source cited by others?
❏ Can you determine what relevant qualifications they hold?	❏ Is the date of the source likely to be important regarding the accuracy of the information? For example, is it contemporary to events, or is it written with the benefit of hindsight?
❏ Can you say who employs the author?	❏ Have you focused on the substance of the information presented rather than its source?
❏ Do you know who paid for the work to be done?	❏ Is the information fact or opinion?
❏ Is this a primary source rather than a secondary one?	❏ Have you checked for any logical fallacies in the arguments?
❏ Has the source been refereed or edited?	❏ Does the language used indicate anything about the status of the information?
❏ Is the content original or derived?	❏ Have possible errors associated with any numbers been taken into account?
❏ Does the source cite relevant literature?	❏ Have the data been analysed using appropriate statistics?
❏ Have you checked a range of sources?	❏ If there are graphs, are they constructed fairly?

However, in some subjects, such as History, Politics and Economics, it is very easy to stray into opinionated and biased conclusions. Sometimes these might be referred to as 'value judgements' (see p. 166). If your work includes these unsubstantiated viewpoints, you may be marked down.

Truth is a concept that can be problematic, because it involves a host of philosophical concepts, which may be confusing. In debate, something is only true when all sides of the argument accept it. If a particular line of argument can be shown to lack credibility or to be in some way unacceptable, this will add weight to the counter-argument.

Concepts of truth and fact involve the notions of objectivity and subjectivity:

● **objective** means based on a balanced consideration of the facts;
● **subjective** means based on one person's opinion.

Most academics aim for a detached, objective piece of writing. Nevertheless, it is important to state your own opinion at some point in the work, particularly if some of the evidence might point to a contrary view. The key is to produce valid reasons for holding your opinion.

The provisional nature of information

There are countless examples where what was once seen as an unassailable 'fact' is now seen as ridiculous (consider the once-accepted orbit of the Sun around the Earth); and where what was once considered ridiculous is now generally accepted (for example, continental drift in the field of plate tectonics). In other cases, the mainstream view of society may change through time, such that it radically alters the whole frame of discussion (for example, on slavery or emancipation of women). For this reason, one of the central tenets of academia is that it is seen as acceptable and often desirable to challenge accepted fact and opinion. Keeping an open and enquiring mind is therefore valued, so long as a viewpoint is supported by up-to-date reference points.

→ Backing up your own opinion or conclusion

Your grade will probably depend on how convincing your argument is and how well you use supporting evidence to support your position. Evidence comes in many forms: from statistical/numeric sources, from quotations, or from observation. You should assess all potential evidence for relevance and value, and you must make sure you cite the source of the information in your own writing, otherwise the evidence may be invalidated by the marker and you may be accused of plagiarism (**Ch 31**, **Ch 32**).

Above all, you should try to produce a *balanced* conclusion. This is one where you are open about counter-arguments and counter-evidence that does not, at least on the face of it, support your case. You must explain what others think or might think, then explain why you have arrived at the conclusion you have made.

Example: fact and opinion

The world record for the 100-metre sprint in athletics was 9.56 seconds at 16 August 2009. This is a *fact*. The record may change over time, but this statement will still be true. Some claim that many world records are created by athletes who have taken drugs to enhance their performance. This is an *opinion*. There is evidence to back up this position, but recent controversies have highlighted the problem of proof in these cases. Claims about drug misuse are open to conjecture, claim and counter-claim, not all of which can be *true*. Your task might be to identify the difference between fact and opinion and write with that knowledge. Do not avoid the controversy, but be clear about the facts, the truth and your opinion of the evidence.

✔ Practical tips for evaluating information

Be selective in your choice of sources you cite. Always try to read and cite the primary source if you can. Do not rely on a secondary source to do this for you, as you may find the author uses information selectively to support their case, or interprets it in a different way than you might.

'Triangulate' uncertain information by making cross-referencing checks.
This means looking at more than one source and comparing what is said in each.

The sources should be as independent as possible (for example, do not compare an original source with one that is directly based on it). If you find the sources agree, you may become more certain of your position. If two sources differ, you may need to decide which viewpoint is better.

Consider the age of the source. 'Old' does not necessarily mean 'wrong', but ideas and facts may have altered between then and now. Can you trace changes through time in the sources available to you? What key events, works or changes in methods have forced any changes in the conclusions?

Look at the extent and quality of citations provided by the author. This applies particularly to articles in academic journals, where positions are usually supported by citations of others' work. These citations may indicate that a certain amount of research has been carried out beforehand, and that the ideas or results are based on genuine scholarship. If you doubt the quality of the work, these references might be worth looking at. How up to date are they? Do they cite independent work, or is the author exclusively quoting him/herself or the work of one particular researcher?

Assess substance over presentation. Just because information is presented well, for instance in a glossy magazine or particularly well-constructed website, this does not necessarily tell you much about the quality of its content. Try to look beyond the surface.

Analyse the language used. Words and their use can be very revealing. Have subjective or objective sentence structures been employed? The former might indicate a personal opinion rather than an objective conclusion. Are there any telltale signs of propaganda? Bias might be indicated by absolute terms, such as 'everyone knows . . .'; 'I can guarantee that . . .'; or a seemingly unbalanced consideration of the evidence. How carefully has the author considered the topic? A less studious approach might be indicated by exaggeration, ambiguity, or the use of journalese and slang. Always remember, however, that content should be judged above presentation.

Try to maintain a healthy, detached scepticism. However reliable the source of a piece of information seems to be, it is probably a good idea to retain a degree of scepticism about the facts or ideas involved and to question the logic of arguments. Even information from primary sources may not be perfect – different approaches can give different outcomes, for reasons not necessarily understood at the time of writing. Also, try not to identify too strongly with a viewpoint, so you can be detached when assessing its merits and failings.

Try to distinguish fact from opinion. To what extent has the author supported a given viewpoint? Have relevant facts been quoted, via literature citations or the author's own researches? Are numerical data used to substantiate the points used? Are these reliable and can you verify the information, for example, by looking at a source that was cited? Might the author have a hidden reason for putting forward biased evidence to support a personal opinion?

Spot fallacious arguments and logical flaws. Concentrate on analysing the method being used to put the points over, rather than the facts themselves. Perhaps you can see one of the common fallacies in arguments that indicate a flaw in logic (**Ch 21**).

Look closely at any data and graphs that are presented and the way they have been analysed. If the information you are looking at is numerical in form, have the errors of any data been taken into consideration, and, where appropriate, quantified? If so, does this help you arrive at a conclusion about how genuine the differences are between important values? Have the appropriate statistical methods been used to analyse the data? Are the underlying hypotheses the right ones? Have the results of any tests been interpreted correctly in arriving at the conclusion? Look closely at any graphs. These may have been constructed in such a way as to emphasise a particular viewpoint, for example, by biased selection of axis starting points.

Don't be blinded by statistics. Leaving aside the issue that statistical methods don't actually deal with proof, only probability, it is generally possible to analyse and present data in such a way that they support one chosen argument or hypothesis rather than another ('you can prove anything with statistics'). To deal with these matters, you will need at least a basic understanding of the 'statistical approach' and of the techniques in common use.

Look at who else has cited the author's work, and how. For example, in scientific subjects you can use the Science Citation Index to find out how often an article or author has been cited and by whom. You may then be able to consult these sources to see how others have viewed the original findings. Works that review the same area of study, published after your source, may also provide useful comments.

Useful language for . . . evaluating information

Context: tutorials and other similar teaching methods offer chances to try out different approaches. This requires a certain amount of confidence, but do not hesitate to make your suggestion or offer an opinion. Your contribution could enliven the discussion and improve learning for everyone.

I don't think [name of author] was the first to come up with that idea. I've found an earlier paper by [name] which mentions it several years earlier.

I don't think we can rely on that piece of information. It's from a wiki type website that might not be very reliable, because there is no indication of who wrote the material and on what basis.

To begin with I thought that too. However, I've been reading other material and I think that my first ideas were subjective. I think that now I can be more objective about this topic. So, now I think . . .

And now . . .

23.1 Use the checklist in Table 23.2 to assess a source about which you are uncertain. If you are unable to establish its reliability, you should research further around the topic.

23.2 Analyse the nature of your sources. Each time you are provided with a reading list for a tutorial, assessment exercise or for background reading, decide whether the sources on it should be considered as primary or secondary, and why (see Table 23.1). If secondary, do they quote any of the primary sources? Try to get a copy of one of the primary sources, if available, and see if this reveals anything to you about the nature of knowledge in your discipline, how it arises and how it can be modified during translation.

23.3 Find out about how articles in your subject area are published. Next time you are looking at a journal in the primary literature, look out for the 'information for authors' section. This appears every three months or so in current (unbound) volumes, or on specific web pages for e-journals. This will provide valuable insights and background information about the submission, refereeing and editing process for contributions to the primary literature.

How to read efficiently and with understanding

Whatever your discipline, you will find that you are required to do a lot of reading as a university student. This chapter explains how to develop the speed-reading skills that will help you to deal more effectively with academic text.

Key topics:
→ Surveying the overall organisation of a text
→ How to examine the structure of the writing itself
→ Speed-reading techniques
→ Reading online resources

Essential vocabulary
**Blurb   Finger tracing   Gist   Take-home message   Terminator paragraph
Topic paragraph   Topic sentence**

Much of the material you will read as part of your studies will be books, chapters and perhaps journal articles written following traditional academic style. This may appear, at first glance, to be difficult to absorb. However, if you develop an understanding of how text within these references is structured, you should find it easier to read the pages of print. This will help you gain an understanding of the content while saving you time.

smart tip

Reading and note-taking

This chapter is concerned mainly with reading and comprehension as a prelude to note-making (**Ch 25**). While it is possible to read and make notes at the same time, this is not always the most effective form of studying, as your notes may end up simply as a rewrite of the source text. Notes framed after you have scanned the prescribed section of text will be better once you have a clearer idea of their context and overall content.

→ Surveying the overall organisation of a text

Your lecturers will recommend certain texts, but in addition you may come across a resource in the library that looks as if it might be relevant. In either case, carry out a preliminary survey to familiarise yourself with what it contains. You can use elements of the structure to answer key questions about the content. Some of these you can respond to instantly, while others will require more careful consideration.

● **Title and author(s).** Does this text look as though it is going to be useful to your current task? Are the authors well-known authorities in the subject area?

- **Publisher's 'blurb'.** Does this indicate that the coverage suits your needs?
- **Publication details.** What is the date of publication? Will this book provide you with up-to-date coverage?
- **Contents listing.** Does this indicate that the book covers the key topic areas you need? Do the chapter titles suggest the coverage is detailed enough?
- **Index.** Is this comprehensive and will it help you find what you want, quickly? From a quick look, can you see references to material you want?
- **General impression.** Does the text look easy to read? Is the text easy to navigate via sub-headings? Is any visual material clear and explained well?

The answers to these questions will help you to decide whether to investigate further: whether you need to look at the whole book, or just selected parts; or whether the book is of limited value at the present time.

What is your reading goal?

It is always a good idea to think about your purpose before you start reading any piece of text (see 'question stage' in Table 24.3).

- If you are looking for a specific point of information, this can often be done quickly, using the index or chapter titles as a guide.
- If you wish to expand your lecture notes using a textbook, you might read in a different way, which might result in note-making (**Ch 25**).
- If your aim is to appreciate the author's style or the aesthetics of a piece of writing, perhaps in a work of fiction, you may need to read more slowly and re-read key parts.

Sometimes, different methods may be required, for example, in English literature, 'close reading' techniques. These specialised methods will probably be taught as part of your studies.

→ How to examine the structure of the writing itself

Well-structured academic texts usually follow a standard pattern with an introduction, main body and conclusion in each element. Sometimes the introduction may comprise several paragraphs; sometimes it may be only one paragraph. Similarly, the conclusion may be several paragraphs or only one. Figure 24.1 shows a layout for a piece of text with five paragraphs, comprising an introduction and conclusion with three intervening paragraphs of varying length.

Within the structure of the text, each paragraph will be introduced by a 'topic sentence' stating the content of the paragraph.

Reader as author

The points in the main text about the organisation of printed material and the structure of text are important for you as a reader or decoder of text, and they also become relevant when you become an academic author and have to put your own ideas clearly – they help your reader (often 'the marker') to decode your written text.

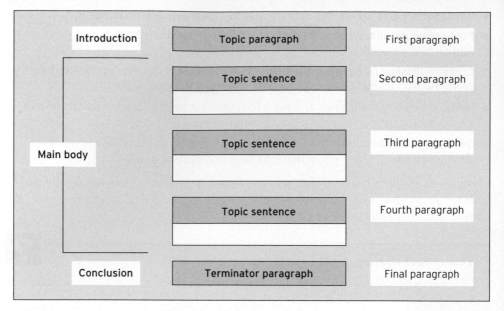

Figure 24.1 Sample textual layout. Most academic texts will be similarly organised.

Each paragraph performs a function. For example, some paragraphs may describe, others may provide examples, while others may examine points in favour of a particular viewpoint and others points against that viewpoint. For more about paragraph types, see p. 195.

The function of these paragraphs, and the sentences within them, is usually signalled by use of 'signpost words', which guide the reader through the logical structure of the text. For example, the word 'however' indicates that some contrast is about to be made with a point immediately before; 'thus' signals that a result or effect is about to be explained. A breakdown of text structure is given in Table 24.1.

Use this knowledge of text structure to establish general meaning.

● Read topic and terminator paragraphs, or even just their topic sentences, to gain a quick overview of the text.

● Scan through the text for key words related to your interest. This may indicate particular paragraphs worthy of detailed reading. Sometimes headings and sub-headings may be used, and these will facilitate a search of this kind.

● Look for signpost words identify the underlying 'argument'.

Origin of speed-reading

The basic techniques were developed in the 1950s by Evelyn Wood, an American educator. She set up institutes to teach students to develop an ability to read hundreds of words per minute. Those who have studied her method include businessmen and politicians, who have to learn to read lengthy papers quickly but with understanding. US Presidents Jimmy Carter and John F. Kennedy were both regarded as famous speed-reading practitioners.

→ Speed-reading techniques

Before describing techniques for improving reading speed, it is useful to understand how fast readers 'operate'. Instead of reading each word as a separate unit, these readers use what is called peripheral vision (what you see, while staring ahead, at the furthest extreme to the right and the left). This means that they absorb clusters of words in one 'flash' or 'fixation' on the text, as shown in Figure 24.2(a). In this example, four fixations are required to read that single line of text.

A reader who does this is reading more efficiently than the reader who reads word by word (Figure 24.2(b)). This reader makes 12 fixations along the line, which means that their reading efficiency is low. Research has also indicated that people who read slowly in this way are less likely to absorb information quickly enough for the brain to comprehend. Therefore, reading slowly can actually hinder comprehension rather than assist it.

As a practised reader, you will probably have developed these fast-reading skills to some degree in your own language. In English, you can improve your speed reading by using techniques like the 'eye gymnastics' exercise in Figure 24.3. Other things you can do include 'finger tracing', where you run your finger below the line of text being read to follow your eyes' path across a page, starting and stopping a word or two from either side. This is said to increase your eye speed, keep your mind focused on the words being read and prevent you from skipping back to previous sentences or jumping forward to text that follows. Some people find it helpful to use a bookmark or strip of paper placed horizontally along the line they are reading, because it makes a useful guide that prevents the eye jumping ahead of the text they are reading.

The average reading speed of someone proficient in the relevant language is said to be 265 words per minute (wpm). Reading speeds for university purposes may be slightly lower, as aspects including difficulty of the text, unfamiliarity with the terminology used and the complexity of the concepts being discussed in the text have the potential to slow down reading. However, as you become more familiar with the specialist language of the subject and the issues being covered in your course, then your reading speed will increase.

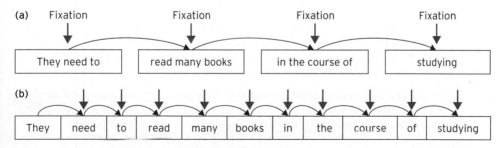

Figure 24.2 Eye movements when reading. (a) Reader who makes eye fixations on clusters of words. (b) Reader who reads every word one by one.

Table 24.1 Sample reading text, showing reading 'signposts'. This text might represent the introduction to a textbook on modern communications in electrical engineering, journalism, marketing or psychology. The light shaded areas indicate the topic sentences; darker shading indicates the signpost words. You can also use this text of 744 words to assess your speed of reading (see Table 24.2).

Introduction	Technological advances and skilful marketing have meant that the mobile phone has moved from being simply an accessory to a status as an essential piece of equipment. From teenagers to grandmothers, the nation has taken to the mobile phone as a constant link for business and social purposes. As a phenomenon, the ascendancy of the mobile phone, in a multitude of ways, has had a critical impact on the way people organise their lives.	Topic sentence
Topic paragraph		
	Clearly, the convenience of the mobile is attractive. It is constantly available to receive or send calls. While these are not cheap, the less expensive text-message alternative provides a similar 'constant contact' facility. At a personal and social level, this brings peace of mind to parents as teenagers can locate and be located on the press of a button. However, in business terms, while it means that employees are constantly accessible and, with more sophisticated models, can access internet communications also, there is no escape from the workplace.	Topic sentence Signpost word Signpost word
	The emergence of abbreviated text-message language has wrought a change in everyday print. For example, pupils and students have been known to submit written work using text message symbols and language. Some have declared this to mark the demise of standard English. Furthermore, the accessibility of the mobile phone has become a problem in colleges and universities where it has been known for students in examinations to use the texting facility to obtain information required.	Topic sentence Signpost word Signpost word
	The ubiquity of the mobile phone has generated changes in the way that services are offered. For instance, this means that trains, buses, and restaurants have declared 'silent zones' where the mobile is not permitted, to give others a rest from the 'I'm on the train' style mobile phone conversation.	Topic sentence Signpost words
Transition paragraph	While the marked increase in mobile phone sales indicates that many in the population have embraced this technology, by contrast, 'mobile' culture has not been without its critics. Real concerns have been expressed about the potential dangers that can be encountered through mobile phone use.	Topic sentence Signpost words
	One such danger is that associated with driving while speaking on a mobile. A body of case law has been accumulated to support the introduction of new legislation outlawing the use of hand-held mobile phones by drivers while driving. The enforcement of this legislation is virtually impossible to police and, thus, much is down to the common sense and responsibility of drivers. Again, technology has risen to meet the contingency with the development of 'hands-free' phones that can be used while driving and without infringing the law.	Topic sentence Signpost word

Table 24.1 (*cont'd*)

	A further danger is an unseen one, namely the impact of the radiation from mobile phones on the human brain. Research is not well advanced in this area and data related to specific absorption rates (SARs) from the use of mobile phones and its effect on brain tissue is not yet available for evaluation. Nevertheless, although this lack of evidence is acknowledged by mobile phone companies, they advise that hands-free devices reduce the SARs levels by 98 per cent.	Topic sentence Signpost word	
	Mobile phone controversy is not confined only to the potential dangers related to the units alone; some people have serious concerns about the impact mobile phone masts have on the area surrounding them. The fear is that radiation from masts could induce serious illness among those living near such masts. While evidence refuting or supporting this view remains inconclusive, there appears to be much more justification for concern about emissions from television transmitters and national grid pylons, which emit far higher levels of electro-magnetic radiation. Yet, little correlation appears to have been made between this fundamental of electrical engineering and the technology of telecommunications.	Topic sentence Signpost word Signpost word	
Conclusion Terminator paragraph	In summary, although it appears that there are enormous benefits to mobile phone users, it is clear that there are many unanswered questions about the impact of their use on individuals. At one level, these represent an intrusion on personal privacy, whether as a user or as a bystander obliged to listen to multiple one-sided conversations in public places. More significantly, there is the potential for unseen damage to the health of individual users as they clamp their mobiles to their ears. Whereas the individual has a choice to use or not to use a mobile phone, people have fewer choices in relation to exposure to dangerous emissions from masts. While the output from phone masts is worthy of further investigation, it is in the more general context of emissions from electromagnetic masts of all types that serious research needs to be developed.	Topic sentence Signpost words Signpost words Signpost word Signpost word	

---

smart tip

Things that can reduce your reading speed

As well as trying methods to read faster, you should be aware of circumstances that might slow you down. These include:

- distractions such as background noise of television, music or chatter (see Table 9.2 on p. 76);
- sub-vocalisation (sounding out each word as it is read aloud);
- reading word by word, perhaps because of unfamiliar vocabulary;
- over-tiredness;
- poor eyesight – if you think your eyes are not 20:20, it might be worth going for an eye test; your eyes are too important to neglect and a pair of reading glasses may make a huge difference to your studying comfort;
- poor lighting – if you can, read using a lamp that can shine directly on to the text; reading in poor light causes eye strain and this, in turn, limits concentration and the length of reading episodes.

Learning to read quickly   is a skill   that needs to be developed.

If you have to read   a new piece of text,   you will find it useful

first of all   to read   the first paragraph

and the last paragraph of the section, chapter or article.   From this

you should be able   to gauge   the context

and general outline   of the topic under discussion.   While it is true

that all academic texts   should have been well edited   before publication,

it does not follow   that every text   will follow these conventions.

However,   a well-written piece   of academic writing

should follow this pattern   and, as a reader   you should exploit

this convention   in order to help you   to understand

the overall content   before you embark   on intensive reading

of the text.

When you are about to   take notes from texts   you should not begin

by sitting   with notepad ready   and the pen poised.

Certainly   make a note of   publication details needed

for your bibliography,   but resist the temptation   to start taking notes

at the same time as   beginning   your first reading of the text.

It is better   to read first,   reflect, recall

and then write notes   based on   what you remember.

This gives you   a framework   around which

you ought to be able   to organise your notes   after you have read

the text intensively.   People who start   by writing notes

as soon as   they open the book   will end up

copying   more and more from the text   as their tiredness increases.

In this case   very little   reflection or learning

is achieved.

Figure 24.3 'Eye gymnastics' exercise. Try to read the above text quite quickly. Read from left to right in the normal way. The aim of the activity is to train your eyes to make more use of your peripheral vision when you are reading. In this way, you will learn to make fewer fixations on the text by forcing your eyes to focus on the centre of a group of words, which are printed in naturally occurring clusters – usually on the basis of grammatical or logical framing. It may be that you experience some discomfort behind your eyes, which indicates that they are adjusting to this less familiar pattern. If this is the case, you should keep practising using this text as a means of developing the speed of your eye movements.

Increasing your reading speed using finger tracing

■ Select a reading passage of about two pages in length (you could use the sample text in Table 24.1). Note your starting and finishing time and calculate your reading speed using Method B in Table 24.2.

■ Take a break of 40–60 minutes. Return to the text and run a finger along the line of text much faster than you could possibly read it.

■ Repeat, but more slowly, so that you can just read it ('finger tracing'). Again, note your starting and finishing times, and work out your reading speed. You should find that your reading speed has increased from the first reading.

■ Carry out this exercise at the same time of day over a week, using texts of similar length and complexity.

You can assess your normal reading speed using either method described in Table 24.2. The text of Table 24.1 is a suitable piece of writing whose word length is already known, should you wish to try method B. If your reading speed seems slow, you can work on improving it by using a similar level and length of text at the same time each day. Go through the reading speed process and, gradually, you should see your average creeping up.

Table 24.2 How to calculate your reading speed. Two examples.

Method A (specified reading time)	
a Select a chapter from a textbook (this is better than a newspaper or journal because these are often printed in columns)	
b Calculate the average number of words per line, e.g. 50 words counted over 5 lines	= 10 words per line
c Count the number of lines per page	= 41 total lines
d Multiply (b × c) = 10 × 41	= 410 words per page
e Read for a specific time (to the nearest minute or half-minute) without stopping	= 4 minutes' reading
f Number of pages read in 4 minutes	= 2.5 pages read
g Multiply (d × f) = 410 × 2.5	= 1025 total words read
h Divide (g ÷ e) = 1025 ÷ 4	= **256 words per minute**
Method B (specified text length)	
a Find a piece of text of known word length (see method A)	= 744 words
b Note the time taken to read this in seconds	= 170 seconds
c Convert the seconds to a decimal fraction of minutes = 170 ÷ 60 = 2.8 minutes	
d Divide (a ÷ c) = 744 ÷ 2.8	= **266 words per minute**

Other strategies you can develop to read and absorb content quickly include:

● **Skimming.** Pick out a specific piece of Information by quickly letting your eye run down a list or over a page looking for a key word or phrase, as when seeking a particular name or address in a phone book.

● **Scanning.** Let your eye run quickly over a chapter, for example, before you commit yourself to study-read the whole text. This will help you to gain an overview of the chapter before you start.

- **Picking out the topic sentences.** As seen above and in Figure 24.1 and Table 24.1, by reading the topic sentences you will be able to flesh out your overview of the text content. This will aid your understanding before you study-read the whole text.
- **Identifying the signpost words.** As noted above, these help guide you as the reader through the logical process that the author has mapped out for you.
- **Recognising clusters of grammatically allied words.** Subliminally, you will group words in clusters according to their natural sense. This will help you to read by making fewer fixations and this will improve your reading speed. You can improve your speed by using the eye-gymnastics exercise (see p. 192).
- **Taking cues from punctuation.** As you read, you will gain some understanding by interpreting the text using the cues of full stops and commas, for example, to help you gain understanding of what you are reading. The importance of punctuation to comprehension is vital (**Ch 27**, p. 226).

To be effective, reading quickly must be matched by a good level of comprehension; reading too slowly can hamper comprehension. Clearly, you need to incorporate tests of your understanding to check that you have understood the main points of the text. One method of reading that incorporates this is called the SQ3R method – survey, question, read, recall and review (Table 24.3). This is also a helpful strategy for exam revision as it incorporates the development of memory and learning skills simultaneously.

Table 24.3 Reading for remembering: the SQ3R method. The reader has to engage in processing the material in the text and is not simply reading on 'autopilot', with very little is being retained. SQ3R and note-making are covered in **Ch 25**.

Survey stage
• Read the first paragraph (topic paragraph) and last paragraph (terminator paragraph) of a chapter or page of notes • Read the intervening paragraph topic sentences • Focus on the headings and sub-headings, if present • Study the graphs and diagrams for key features
Question stage
• What do you know already about this topic? • What is the author likely to tell you? • What specifically do you need to find out?
Read stage
• Read the entire section *quickly* to get the gist of the piece of writing; finger-tracing techniques may be helpful at this point • Go back to the question stage and revisit your initial answers • Look especially for keywords, key statements, signpost words • Do *not* stop to look up unknown words – go for completion
Recall stage
• Turn the book or your notes over and try to recall as much as possible • Make key pattern headings/notes/diagrams/flow charts (**Ch 25**) • Turn over the book again and check over for accuracy of recall; suggested recall periods – every 20 minutes
Review stage
• After a break, try to recall the main points

The role of paragraphs in understanding text

The first paragraph/last paragraph technique suggested in Table 24.3 acknowledges the role of the introductory and concluding paragraphs. However, each of the other paragraphs in a text will perform a role also. For example, they may describe (appearance, position, process, time), define, classify, generalise, give examples, hypothesise, identify cause/effect or comparison/contrast relationships, or list features. In your skim-reading identifying these roles will help you to develop a better understanding of the content of the text and allow you to focus on particular aspects of the text that are important for your purpose.

→ Reading online resources

Of course, you can always print out material sourced from the Web, in which case, similar principles apply to those described elsewhere in this chapter. However, due to cost or environmental considerations, or simply the fact that that you need to assess the material before committing yourself to a printout, you may prefer to read directly from the screen. The following points are worth considering when doing this:

- Web page designers often divide text into screen-sized chunks, with links between 'pages'. This can make it difficult to gain an overall picture of the topic being covered. Make sure you read through the whole of the material before forming a judgement about it.

- One benefit of web-based material is that it is often written in a 'punchy' style, with bulleted lists and easily assimilated take-home messages, often highlighted with graphics. Bear in mind, however, that this may lack the detail required for academic work, for example, in the number and depth of any examples given.

- The ease of access of web-based materials might cause a bias in your reading – perhaps towards more modern sources, but also, potentially, away from the overtly academic – always check to see whether 'standard' printed texts are advised on reading lists or are available in your library.

- The skimming method described on p. 193 can be accelerated if you use the 'find' function (control + F in MS Word and Internet Explorer) to skip to key words.

- If you are likely to spend lengthy spells at a screen, make sure you are positioned well, with your eyes roughly level with the mid point of the screen.

- Take frequent breaks – stand up, walk around for a while and then return to the task.

- If you wear spectacles, you may find that an additional pair for use when reading on-screen material is helpful. You can find out more about this from your institution's health and safety office or from an optician.

If you do decide to print out a resource, check on the screen for an icon that might give you a 'print-friendly' version.

✔ Practical tips for reading effectively and with understanding

Be selective and understand your purpose. Think about why you are reading. Look at the material you have already collected relating to the subject or topic you aim to study. For example, this should include lecture notes, which ought to remind you of the way a topic was presented, the thrust of an argument or a procedure. Are you reading to obtain a general overview or is it to identify additional specific information? Use a technique and material that suits your needs.

Adjust your reading speed according to the type of text you have to read. A marginally interesting article in a newspaper will probably require less intensive reading than a key chapter in an academic book.

Grasp the general message before dealing with difficult parts. Not all texts are 'reader friendly'. If you find a section of text difficult to understand, skip over that bit; toiling over it will not increase your understanding. Continue with your reading and when you come to a natural break in the text, for example, the end of a chapter or section, then go back to the 'sticky' bit and reread it. Usually, second time round, it will make more sense because you have an overview of the context. Similarly, don't stop every time you come across a new word. Read on and try to get the gist of the meaning from the rest of the text. When you have finished, look the word up in a dictionary and add to your personal glossary.

Always check on meanings. If English is not your first language, then you may find that you can guess new or unfamiliar words from the context in which you find them. However, it is wise to check on meanings, particularly if the word is used frequently or seems central to the meaning of the text. There are many instances of similar-looking words that have subtle or not-so-subtle meanings in different languages (for example, the Spanish *colegio* for primary school, might easily be mistaken for the English *college*, more usually applied to higher education and perhaps better translated as *Universidad* in Spanish).

Take regular breaks. Reading continuously over a long period of time is counterproductive. Concentration is at a peak after 20 minutes, but wanes after 40 minutes. Rest frequently, making sure that your breaks do not become longer than your study stints.

Follow up references within your text. When you are reading, you need to be conscious of the citations to other authors that might be given in the text; not all will be relevant to your reading purpose, but it is worth quickly noting the ones that look most interesting as you come across them. You'll usually find the full publication details in the references at the end of the chapter/article or at the end of the book. This will give you sufficient information to supplement your reading once you have finished reading the 'parent' text.

Develop your vocabulary for reading complex texts. Creating a 'language family' for a piece of text is a useful way of consolidating the relevant vocabulary in your own mind. Figure 24.4 shows an example. You could insert the meanings in your own language alongside each word if you wish. You can use this record as a reference while reading a text. It will help to save time because you will not have to repeatedly look up the same words in your dictionary.

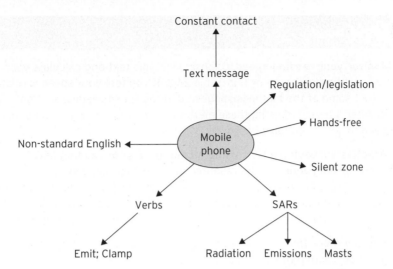

Figure 24.4 A language family diagram. This is a type of mindmap (Ch 16), in this case for words related to mobile phones created from the text given in Table 24.1.

Context: you might need to use these when speaking to a language tutor.

This text is very difficult for me to understand. It has lots of words that are new to me. I understand most of the words, but it takes me a long time to read because I have to look up many of the technical words. Could you recommend a text that may be easier for me to read?

I calculated my reading speed using the methods described in this book, and it was xxx words per minute. That seems slow compared with the values given in the book. How do you think I can improve?

I cannot find a bilingual subject-specific dictionary. Have you any suggestions?

I like reading for pleasure in my own language. Do you think reading books in English for pleasure would help me with my academic reading?

GO And now . . .

24.1 Monitor your reading speed. Choose a suitable text and calculate your speed using either method A or B in Table 24.2. If you feel your speed is relatively slow, try out some of the methods suggested in the speed-reading section of this chapter. After a period of using these methods, and deciding which suit you, check your speed to see if you have improved.

24.2 Practise surveying a text using a book from your reading list. Rather than simply opening your reading resource at the prescribed pages, spend five or ten minutes surveying the whole book. Think about how the author has organised the content and why. Keep this in mind when reading the text, and reflect on whether this has improved your comprehension and assimilation of the content.

24.3 Become more familiar with the visual reading cues embedded within texts. As shown within this chapter, conventions of grammar, punctuation and spelling are useful in providing clues to meaning for the reader (see Table 24.1, for example). If you would like to look into these topics further, consult appropriate texts on English grammar.

How to create effective notes for later reference

Keeping a record of the content of your reading is essential when you are a student. There is simply too much information to remember and retain. This chapter outlines practical ways in which you can keep a record of what you read and think in appropriate note form so that it is meaningful to you at a later date. You should also note connections, critical thoughts and ideas that arise while you read.

Key topics:
→ Why are you making notes?
→ What do you need to record?
→ How are you going to lay out your notes?

Essential vocabulary
**Annotate   Citation   Citing   Concept map   Fishbone   Flow-chart
Keyword   Landscape orientation   Linear   Matrix   Mnemonic
Portrait orientation   Timeline**

Most courses provide a reading list of recommended resources. Depending on your subject, these include textbooks, journal articles and web-based materials. Sometimes you will be given specific page references; at other times you will have to find the relevant material in the text for yourself. The techniques described in **Ch 24** will help you identify the most relevant parts of the text quickly and provide basic information for your note-making.

You will develop note-making skills as you progress in your studies. It takes time and experimentation to achieve a method that suits you. This will need to fit with your learning style (**Ch 13**), the time that you can allocate to the task and be appropriate for the material and the subject area you are tackling. This chapter suggests a range of methods you can choose from in order to abstract and write down the key points from your sources.

smart tip

Note-making formats

Sometimes notes may be better suited to being laid out on paper in the landscape rather than the portrait position. This page orientation clearly suits methods such as mind maps (Figure 25.5). Similarly, you can take advantage of the landscape format when making matrix (grid) notes (Figure 25.6) by creating columns across the page.

→ Why are you making notes?

Students usually make notes for assignment writing and/or revision. Therefore, some texts will simply be 'dip in and out', while some will require intensive reading. You need to decide what your purpose is in making the notes. For example, it may be to:

● frame an overview of the subject;

● record a sequence or process;

● enable you to analyse a problem;

● extract the logic of an argument;

● compare different viewpoints;

● borrow quotes (with suitable citation – see **Ch 31**);

● add your own commentary on the text, perhaps by linking key points with what has been discussed in a lecture or tutorial.

This will influence the style, detail and depth of your notes.

---

smart tip

Essentials of note-making

It will save time if you develop good practice in making your notes.

■ On all notes record the full details of source, that is:
  - author surname and initials;
  - title in full with chapter and pages;
  - date of publication;
  - publisher and place of publication.

  You will need this information to enable you to cite the source if you decide to refer to any of this material in your own writing (**Ch 31**).

■ Add the date(s) you made the notes.

■ Your notes have to be as meaningful in six days, weeks or months. Personalise them by using:
  - underlining;
  - highlighting;
  - colour coding;
  - numbered lists;
  - bullet points;
  - mnemonics;
  - distinctive layout;
  - boxes for important points.

→ What do you need to record?

One of the pitfalls of making notes is that people often start off with a blank sheet, pen in hand, and then begin to note 'important' points as they read. Within a short time, they are rewriting the source book. To avoid this, the trick is to:

- identify your purpose;
- decide on the most appropriate note-making style and layout for the task;
- scan the section to be read;
- establish the writer's purpose, for example:
  - a narrative of events or process
  - a statement of facts
  - an explanation of reasoning or presentation of a logical argument
  - an analysis of an issue, problem or situation
  - a critique of an argument;
- work out their view on the subject, and how this relates to your purpose;
- jot down ideas that arise during your reading;
- make links between this text and others, if any;
- ensure you paraphrase in your own words rather than transcribe, and if you do transcribe, use quote marks and note reference details (**Ch 31**, **Ch 32**).

→ How are you going to lay out your notes?

There are several strategies that you might consider using. Figures 25.1–25.7 illustrate some examples (see also **Ch 16**). Not all will be relevant to your subject, but some will. Some techniques may not seem directly suitable, but, with a little adaptation, they may work for you. Table 25.1 compares the advantages and disadvantages of each method.

It may be that one of these note-making strategies has attractions for you because it seems to fit with your learning preferences (**Ch 13**). For example, a 'visual learner' might prefer the concept map (mind map) shown in Figure 25.5. Other methods might suit a specific task: an assignment that requires you to analyse a complex set of viewpoints or positions might best be approached using the matrix approach shown in Figure 25.6, while one that asked you to review two sides of an argument could be tackled using the fishbone map idea shown in Figure 25.7, or a variant of it.

Table 25.1 A comparison of the different methods of note-making from texts (illustrated in Figures 25.1-25.7)

Note type	Figure	Advantage	Disadvantage
Keyword notes	25.1	Good as a layout for easy access to information	Dependent on systematic structure in text
Linear notes	25.2	Numbered sequence - good for classifying ideas	Restrictive format, difficult to backtrack to insert new information
Time lines	25.3	Act as memory aid for a sequence of events; stages in a process	Limited information possible
Flow-chart notes	25.4	Allow clear path through complex options	Take up space; may be unwieldy
Concept maps/ mind maps	25.5	Good for recording information on a single page	Can become messy; can be difficult to follow; not suited to all learning styles
Matrix notes/ grid notes	25.6	Good layout for recording different viewpoints, approaches, applications	Space limitations on content or amount of information
Fishbone maps	25.7	Good for laying out opposing sides of an argument	Space limitations on content or amount of information

Topic: DEPOPULATION OF THE COUNTRYSIDE   Source: Ormiston, J., 2002. Rural Idylls.
Glasgow: Country Press.

Problem: Population falling in rural areas
Traditional communities disintegrate
Incomer settlement – dormitory villages

Reasons: Mechanisation of farming
Creation of farming combines
Bigger farms, fewer employed
Decline of traditional farming & related activities

Effects: Families dispersed – fewer children
Closure of shops, post offices, schools, surgeries
Transport links less viable

Solutions: Housing subsidies to encourage families to remain
Diversify economic activity, e.g. tourism/action holidays
Stimulate rural economy – farm shops, farmers' markets
Diversify from traditional crops – seek new markets

Figure 25.1 Example of keyword notes

Topic: OBESITY IN CHILDREN

Source: Skinner, J., 2001. Diet and Obesity. Edinburgh: Castle Publishing.

1. Lifestyle
   1.1 Television, computer-games generation
   1.2 Unsupervised leisure time – sedentary
2. Diet
   2.1 Constant 'grazing' – junk food
   2.2 Additives/processed foods
   2.3 Lack of adequate fresh food, including fruit & vegetables
3. Exercise
   3.1 Sport by spectating rather than participating
   3.2 Decline in team sports in schools
   3.3 Children over-protected from 'free play' outdoors
4. Family
   4.1 Parents overeat; children likewise
   4.2 Instant food
   4.3 Food as an incentive & reward
5. Schools
   5.1 School meals spurned in favour of snack bar/chip shop
   5.2 Healthy-eating programmes as part of curriculum
6. Health service
   6.1 Less emphasis on prevention
   6.2 Limited health education of parents and children

(a)

Topic: GENERAL FEATURES OF ORGANIC MATERIALS

Source: Barker, J., 2001. Chemistry for University. Manchester: Midland Publishing.

1. Solid state – molec. crystal – powder, poly. Thin films
2. Unique physical properties – exploit for high-tech applications
3. Advantages
   3.1 Versatile properties – reg. by organic chemistry
   3.2 Readily accessible – via organic synthesis
   3.3 Low cost – cheap raw materials
   3.4 Tractable – fusable, soluble: easy to fab.
4. Disadvantage
   4.1 Relatively fragile
5. Important types
   5.1 Conducting CT salts
   5.2 Conducting poly

(b)

Topic: OPERATIONAL AMPLIFIERS

Source: Scott, D.I., 1977. Operational Amplifiers. Coventry: Circuit Publishers.

1. Usually an integrated circuit; can be discrete
2. Uses all technologies: bipolar; FET; MOS; BI-FET
3. Effectively a highly stable differential amplifier
4. Advantages
   4.1 High voltage gain – typ. 100,000
   4.2 High input impedance – typ. 1 $M\Omega$ – can be much higher, FET, MOS
   4.3 Low output impedance – typ. 600 Ω
   4.4 Low drift, BI-FET best
   4.5 Wide voltage supply range
5. Disadvantages
   5.1 Relatively narrow bandwidth – GBP typ. 1 MHz (but operates to DC)
   5.2 Very unstable in discrete versions – requires matched transistors
6. Common types
   6.1 741 – most common
   6.2 LM 380 – common AF AMP
   6.3 TDA 2030 – common power amp. – 20 W into 4 Ω

(c)

Figure 25.2 Examples of linear notes. These are drawn from three diverse disciplines where topics lend themselves to hierarchical approaches.

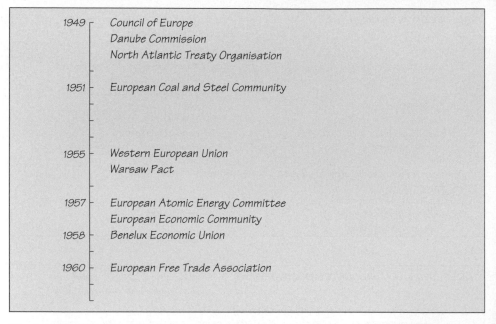

1949   Council of Europe
          Danube Commission
          North Atlantic Treaty Organisation

1951   European Coal and Steel Community

1955   Western European Union
          Warsaw Pact

1957   European Atomic Energy Committee
          European Economic Community
1958   Benelux Economic Union

1960   European Free Trade Association

Figure 25.3 Example of time-line notes. This design is good for showing a sequence of events, in this case, the development of European organisations.

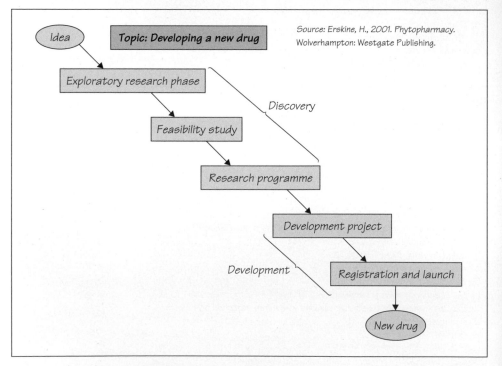

Figure 25.4 Example of flow-chart notes. These are particularly useful for describing complex processes in visual form.

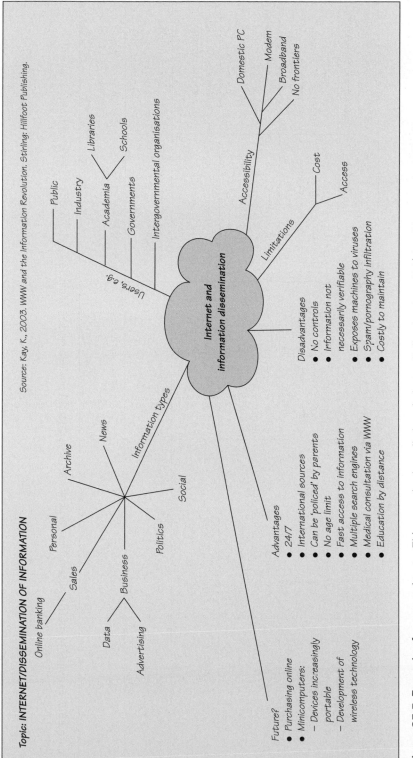

Topic: *INTERNET/DISSEMINATION OF INFORMATION*

Source: Kay, K., 2003. WWW and the Information Revolution. Stirling: Hillfoot Publishing.

Figure 25.5 Example of a concept map. This may also be called a mind map. Suits visual-spatial/visual learners (see **Ch 13**).

Topic: TRAFFIC CONGESTION

Source: Walker, I.M.A., 2005. Urban Myths and Motorists. London: Green Press.

Solutions	Council view	Police view	Local business view	Local community view
Pedestrianisation	+ Low Maintenance – Initial outlay	+ Easier to police + Less car crime + CCTV surveillance easier	+ Safer shopping and business activity – Discourages motorist customers	+ Safer shopping + Less polluted town/city environment
Park and ride schemes	+ Implements transport policy – Capital investment to initiate – Car park maintenance	+ Reduce inner-city/town traffic jams + Reduce motor accidents – Potential car park crime	– Loss of custom – Lack of convenience – Sends customers elsewhere	+ Less polluted town/city environment – Costly
Increase parking charges	+ Revenue from fines – Costly to set up	– Hostility to enforcers	– Loss of custom – Delivery unloading problematic	– Residents penalised by paying for on-street parking
Restrict car journeys, e.g. odd/even registrations on alternate days	+ Easy to administer	+ Easy to police	+ Seek exemption for business vehicles	+ Encourage car-sharing for daily journeys – Inconvenience
Levy congestion charge for urban journeys	+ Revenue raised – Cost of implementing tracking system	– Traffic jams on alternative routes	– Cost of loss of custom	– Inhibit work/leisure activities – Cost

Figure 25.6 Example of matrix notes. This particular analysis lays out positive (+) and negative (–) viewpoints on an issue from a range of different perspectives.

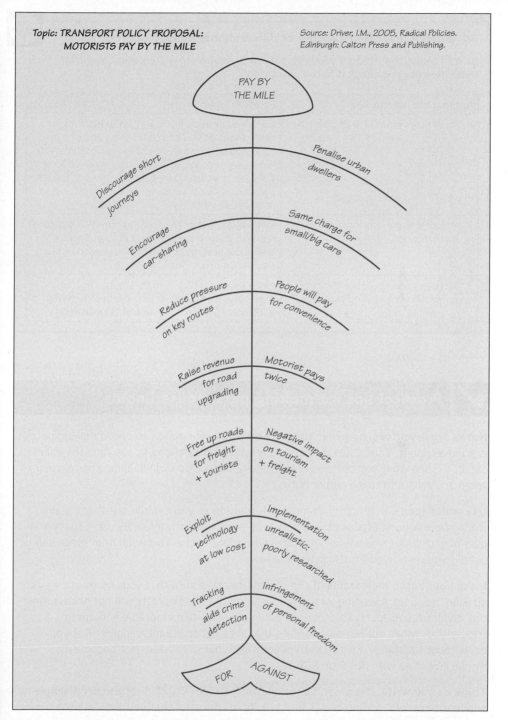

Topic: TRANSPORT POLICY PROPOSAL: MOTORISTS PAY BY THE MILE

Source: Driver, I.M., 2005, Radical Policies. Edinburgh: Calton Press and Publishing.

PAY BY THE MILE

Discourage short journeys

Penalise urban dwellers

Encourage car-sharing

Same charge for small/big cars

Reduce pressure on key routes

People will pay for convenience

Raise revenue for road upgrading

Motorist pays twice

Free up roads for freight + tourists

Negative impact on tourism + freight

Exploit technology at low cost

Implementation unrealistic: poorly researched

Tracking aids crime detection

Infringement of personal freedom

FOR   AGAINST

Figure 25.7 Example of a fishbone map. This design is good for showing, as in this case, two sides to an argument. May be particularly appealing to visual learners (see **Ch 13**).

Advantages and disadvantages of different note-making approaches

As an international student you have options in relation to note-making. You might find that different options suit different instances.

Approach to note-making	Points to consider
1. Make notes entirely in English	Helps you develop fluency in writing about your subject in English. Note that as you advance in your studies, you may not have the vocabulary in your own language to write at the required level in a subject-specific manner. Thus, writing in English consolidates your competence in writing for your professional area.
2. Make notes entirely in your own language	May make it easier to record information but does not help in developing your control of English. Means duplication of effort through each of the translation processes.
3. Make notes in English with annotation in your first language	Helps develop practice in the use of English expression; provides a bridge between first and additional (English) language development.

✔ Practical tips for making personalised notes

Notes are resources, so never throw them away. The time you spend making notes is an investment. Your notes make good revision material and by the time the exam comes around what you perhaps only partially understood will become crystal clear when you return to these earlier notes.

Use white space. Don't cram as much information as you can on to a sheet; leave white space around lists or other important items of information. By using the 'visual' part of your brain, you will recall information more easily. This additional space can be used if you wish to add further detail later.

Make your notes memorable. It's important to make sure that your notes are visually striking. However, spending lots of time making them look pretty will not necessarily pay dividends. Again, try to achieve a balance – visually memorable enough to trigger your recall but not so elaborate that they become a meaningless work of art without substance. Ensure that 'decorating' your notes does not become a displacement activity (**Ch 9** and **Ch 13**).

Think as you write. It is essential for deeper learning (**Ch 21**) that you don't simply summarise others' writing and thoughts in note form, but that you evaluate the facts and ideas that you are reading. You need to make connections between different sources, between your reading as a whole and the task you have been set.

Develop your own 'shorthand'. Some subjects have their own abbreviations, for example MI (myocardial infarction) or WTO (World Trade Organisation) and, of course, there are standard abbreviations – e.g., i.e., etc. However, you will also develop your own abbreviations and symbols drawn from your own experience, for example, maths symbols, text messaging or words from other languages. As long as these are memorable and meaningful to you, then they can be useful tools in making and taking notes (**Ch 16**).

Save time by using a photocopy. Sometimes you may find that the extent of notes you require is minimal, or that a particular book or other resource is in high demand and has been placed on short loan in the library. It may be convenient to photocopy the relevant pages, which can then be highlighted and annotated. Remember that there are photocopying restrictions imposed on readers due to copyright law (**Ch 32**) – details will be posted prominently in your library. However, note also that as a learning technique this type of activity is essentially passive, and, if your note-making is meant as an aid to revision or for memorising, one of the more active methods described in this chapter or in **Ch 51** may be better.

Take care when using material straight from the text. It is important that, if you decide to use an excerpt from a text as a direct quotation, you record the page number on which that particular piece of text appeared in the book or article you are citing. You should then insert the author, date of publication and page number alongside the quotation. More information on citing sources is given in **Ch 31** and **Ch 32**.

💬 Useful language for . . . talking about lecture notes

Context: these are focused on discussions you may have with your fellow students on this topic.

I do/don't like using mind maps for making notes. How do you make notes?

Do you like the core textbook? I'd like to find something easier to understand. Have you found an easier book?

I find it difficult to make notes from reading e-books on the screen. How do you make notes from e-books?

25.1 Find out about abbreviations. Find a general dictionary that gives a comprehensive list of English abbreviations and identify ones that you might use; find a subject-specific dictionary and identify whether it provides lists of specialist abbreviations. This will mean that you'll know where to look if you come across an abbreviation that is unfamiliar to you.

25.2 Compare notes with a friend. Everyone has a different method of note-making that they have personalised to suit their own style. Compare your note-making style with that of another student on your course, preferably on the same piece of text. Discuss what you have recorded and why – this may bring out some differences in reasoning, understanding and logic.

25.3 Try something new. You may feel that you already have a fairly reasonable note-making strategy in place, but as time goes on you may find that it is not quite as suitable for the type of reading you are now required to do. If this turns out to be the case, try out some of the alternative styles demonstrated in this chapter to see if these are better suited to your study tasks and contexts.

26 | Using technology for learning

How to make the most of online resources

Information and communications technology (ICT) is a vital element of modern university education. In particular, e-learning systems offer you many useful facilities and the capacity to access course materials at a time and place of your choosing. This chapter discusses how to adapt your study methods to learn more effectively from online course components.

Key topics:
→ Effective e-learning
→ The range of e-learning facilities and how to use them
→ Useful skills with 'office'-type software
→ Online assessment

Essential vocabulary
**Back-up   Browser   E-learning   Etiquette   Network   Online   Scam
Virtual learning environment (VLE)   WiFi**

Every higher education course in the UK is now supported by learning technology, based on networked computers and the internet. In your UK university, you will be expected to use specific websites, access online journals or use a virtual learning environment (VLE). You will also be expected to use 'office' software to present assignments and may find that much of the assessment, especially in early years, is carried out online.

Most UK universities have therefore invested heavily in the computing facilities that will support your learning. This includes computer suites, wireless internet connections (WiFi), network systems and file storage facilities. They will also have purchased licences for the software that you will use. As a signed-up student you will have access to these facilities free of charge, but of course will have to obey certain rules as to their use. The facilities and rules of use will probably be introduced to you as part of your induction process (**Ch 5**).

'E-learning' is a term used to cover a range of online methods of delivering materials and resources for learning. Most universities use a web-based VLE, such as Blackboard or WebCT. Others favoured in the UK are Moodle, First Class and Desire2Learn. These platforms provide an integrated route to learning resources from a single login. Systems for computer-aided assessment (also known as online assessment) may be provided in addition. You may be given online access to all these facilities via a portal, which you might be able to customise.

Online teaching is often mixed with traditional on-campus teaching – so-called 'blended learning'. Alternatively, and especially if you are a distance learner, you may find that nearly all of your course material is delivered online. Whatever the mix, you will need to adapt to the specific challenges of the web-based component.

Definitions: e-learning terminology

Blended learning: a mix of e-learning and traditional teaching methods.

Computer-aided assessment (CAA): tests and exams delivered (and marked) using software. If delivered via the Web, also known as **online assessment (OA)**.

Computer-based learning (CBL) or **computer-aided learning (CAL):** software-driven interactive learning activity.

Portal: a web-based gateway to various useful web services, from your learning environment to online news.

VLE (virtual learning environment): online software system that delivers educational materials and facilities for students. May include lecture notes, email and discussion boards, groupwork areas, communication tools, assessments and grade books.

→ Effective e-learning

There are four basic requirements if you are to make the most of your e-learning opportunities:

- You must have access to the Web through a reasonably speedy link.
- You will require basic IT skills to navigate websites and manipulate files.
- You will need to make frequent visits to your portal or VLE.
- You should participate actively.

Access

Your university will provide a range of on-campus computing facilities and will specify minimum requirements for online access from home or other accommodation, probably at broadband data transfer rates (2 megabits per second or greater). Local authorities also provide free or low-cost facilities in libraries and study centres.

What are the minimum competencies I will require for e-learning?

These include basic skills with:

- keyboard and mouse;
- file management and printing;
- word-processing and printing;
- use of a web browser;
- web searching.

Depending on your subject, you may also require knowledge of programs such as spreadsheets, databases and computer languages (see Table 26.1).

Skills

E-learning systems generally require only basic competence in computer use. If you are a computer novice, it is essential that you learn how to use these facilities, as so much of your future work will require this – and most universities offer some form of IT induction and training. Even if you feel fully conversant with computing from experience at school and home, these sessions will inform you about the special features of your local network and systems.

Visiting and participating in your VLE modules

You should visit each VLE module or portal on a daily basis if you can. If you fail to do this, you may miss out on announcements, messages, new work deadlines, ongoing discussions and fresh materials. Where opportunities are given, you should participate in online discussions, self-assessments and the like: these will have been designed by your tutors to add to your knowledge, experience and skills.

→ The range of e-learning facilities and how to use them

It's worth setting aside some study time early in the term or semester to investigate all the different VLE features that have been activated by staff – you will then know how to use these to your advantage later on. Components offered within a typical VLE module include:

- **Course information.** This may include the syllabus, timetable, learning outcomes and details about the teaching and administrative staff – it may take the place of the traditional course handbook. Aspects of using these elements are covered in **Ch 53**.

- **Announcements.** Information from the course administrator(s) may appear on the opening page of the VLE or portal, which is a good reason for checking this frequently. They may alert you to late timetable or location changes, forthcoming coursework deadlines, and events such as departmental seminars.

- **Lecture notes.** Such notes may include files from *PowerPoint* presentations. If lecturers use the VLE to let you access summary notes or slides from their lectures in advance, printing these out with space for your own extra notes will allow you extra time to follow the

> **smart tip**
>
> **Taking notes from *PowerPoint* presentations**
>
> If you use the three-slides-per-page handout format (accessible from the 'File > Print > Print What > Handouts > Slides per page > 3 > OK' options) you can obtain a printout that looks like the following, with space for your notes beside each slide.
>
>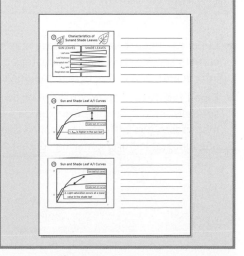

emphasis and take-home messages during the lecture, rather than simply transcribing what is covered (**Ch 15**, **Ch 16**).

● **Links to websites and e-books.** These provide you with supplementary information. Lecturers may help you by moderating or commenting on these website resources. You can use their critical remarks to improve your own skills for evaluating information (**Ch 23**).

● **Tailored resources.** These will support your learning and will include multimedia presentations, quizzes and interactive software. These resources can be extremely valuable as a substitute for a practical or other hands-on experience. Most will have self-contained instructions for their use, or this information will be given in the course handbook.

● **Learning tools.** Tools such as an online dictionary/thesaurus, online study guide or links to the library catalogue can be valuable when you are working on assignments, so it is worth the investment of time to learn what they contain and how to use them.

● **Discussion boards and chatrooms (both synchronous and asynchronous).** These are used to allow you to exchange comments and queries, and can be a useful way to sense how far ahead or behind you are with your learning. They are also used to facilitate groupwork, providing a forum for the team to exchange ideas and files. Don't be hesitant to start a new thread or to respond to someone else's query or comment. The system only works well if everyone takes part. However, when participating in online discussions, make sure you respect others' views and are polite about your peers and lecturers.

Definitions: discussion-board terminology

Synchronous discussion: occurs in real time and may take the form of an online tutorial when it is moderated by a tutor.

Asynchronous discussion: allows you to post queries or comments to which others can reply when convenient.

Thread: a sequence of postings on a specific topic, allowing you to access relevant discussions more easily.

● **Links to support services.** These may range from the students' association to the careers service. This may be a faster and more convenient method of accessing information and contacts than the university website.

● **Email facilities.** You may have your own account or links to the university's specialist email software. This can be a very convenient part of the VLE because many tasks you will carry out online may be facilitated by using email – e.g. asking questions of lecturers, making contact with your peers in the class.

Email and discussion-board etiquette

The main routes of online communication are email and discussion boards. These allow you to communicate with tutors and classmates, giving each person the choice of when and where they contribute. Take care with the etiquette of these systems, as it is easy for misunderstandings to develop.

- Check your university email account and discussion boards frequently (preferably daily). You may receive important messages from tutors in this way (for instance, changes to lecture locations).
- Bear in mind that without the normal conversational body language and voice tone, e-messages can seem abrupt and may be misconstrued. Always read through a message after you have written it with this in mind, before sending. If in doubt, leave it for 30 minutes or so, perhaps using the 'send later' function, and then reconsider.

smart tip

Developing your language through online discussion

If English is not your first language, take the chance to put up an idea online. In their response, another contributor may rephrase the language in a modified format which will help you to develop your use of language as well as make a contribution to the discussion. Avoid 'spectating' during e-discussions that is, reading contributions from other students but not making any contribution yourself. Contribute positively if you can. Even if someone has already said something you would have liked to have said, agreeing with them may help to continue the e-conversation.

- **A digital 'dropbox'.** This is a convenient way of submitting files containing coursework online. Follow the instructions carefully to ensure your work is delivered safely.
- **Gradebooks.** These allow you to see the marks that have been recorded for your coursework and final assessments. For obvious reasons, you will have read-only access. You are not able to see the grades of other students.
- **Mechanisms for providing feedback on teaching.** If feedback questionnaires are presented on the VLE, this gives you a chance to provide considered comments in your own time, and in privacy. The VLE may also provide information about class representatives and a means of contacting them (for example, by email or discussion board).

smart tip

Use VLE-based scheduling facilities with care

Your VLE or portal may include a personal calendar. This may be configurable to your own needs, although you may prefer to use your own handheld device, the system available with your email program, or a traditional paper-based diary. It is probably best to keep only one source of diary information unless you can be sure of interchanging or transferring the information regularly.

The three core 'office'-type programs deal with word-processing, spreadsheets and delivering presentations. Table 26.1 summarises useful applications of word-processing and spreadsheets in university coursework. Use of presentation software is covered in **Ch 61**. Databases are included in many software suites, but are more specialised and generally harder to learn to use (but see the spreadsheet section of Table 26.1 if you only need basic database functions).

Table 26.1 Key word-processing and spreadsheet skills for university coursework. How many of these do you feel competent about?

Word-processing skills	Spreadsheet skills
You will be expected to use word processors to write and edit written coursework. Key elements include:	If your coursework involves numbers or graphs in any form, a spreadsheet can be a valuable time-saving resource. Key elements include:
• **Word count and page numbering.** Many submissions will be limited to defined length and these functions will help you keep track of your progress.	• **Arithmetical and mathematical calculations.** Error-free addition and multiplication, and the capability to use complex formulae to calculate results. Of course, formulae need to be set up correctly to get the right answers, so always test them with a dummy set of data for which you know the expected answer.
• **Spellchecker.** Helpful for a quick check of glaring errors, but *not* a substitute for a careful read through at draft stage, as words you can easily mistype like 'form' and 'from' will not be highlighted (**Ch 33**). Also, the default spellcheckers may suggest Americanised spellings (like Americanized, for example), which may not be suitable.	• **Repeated calculations.** Excellent when you need to repeat a calculation from different starting values. Just set up a formula and enter fresh values to obtain instant results.
• **Thesaurus.** Great for adding variety to your vocabulary and finding a word that you can't recall.	• **Formatted calculations.** For example, financial statements, financial analysis and projections in accountancy.
• **Grammar checker.** Helps spot basic errors, like sentences without verbs, but do not rely on its advice as it can be faulty; moreover, you will frequently wish to reject some of its valid suggestions as these may not be tuned to academic or technical styles of writing.	• **Graphs.** Probably the most valuable spreadsheet application. Takes tabular input and uses it to create a range of graph types to suit your needs. Useful for trying out different graph styles without having to redraw. It's worth learning how to manipulate aspects like axis presentation and background, as automatic settings tend to be set up for 'business' use. Integrated 'office' suites allow export of graphs to a word-processed document.
• **Print preview.** Valuable for seeing how your work will look on the printed page and can help you to save on print costs.	
• **Copy and paste.** Useful for moving blocks of text around your document at review stages (**Ch 33**) – but use with extreme caution for copying and pasting text or images from electronic sources because of plagiarism and copyright issues (**Ch 31**, **Ch 32**).	• **Elementary database functions.** Spreadsheets can be used to carry out simple database functions (for example, you can sort number and text columns). You can also use alphanumeric and logical functions to 'interrogate' bodies of text/number information.
• **Tables.** Apart from the obvious, useful for laying out your work in columns and grids. You may wish to alter borders if set automatically.	
• **Drawing facilities.** Useful for creating simple diagrams.	• **Statistics.** Many statistical needs are catered for, including calculation of descriptive and hypothesis-testing statistics. These functions save a lot of calculation time, but you need to know some statistical theory to use them most effectively.
• **Footnotes.** Handy for some styles of citation and referencing (**Ch 31**).	

→ Online assessment

Online assessment is increasingly used at university, especially for large classes in early years. The different sorts of questions commonly on offer are outlined in **Ch 36** and **Ch 37**. If you have the chance to test the program being used beforehand, do so, as this will make it easier to sit real high-stakes assessments, which are generally carried out under exam conditions within IT suites using identical software. In any case, you will probably find that formative online tests are a good way to learn, especially if they are 'open book' and you are allowed to look at notes and texts as you answer.

Definitions: assessment terminology

Formative assessment: usually a 'low stakes' test – mainly used to train you in the types and depth of questions normally asked and to give you feedback on your performance at the required standard.

Summative assessment: counts a reasonably large amount for your final module or degree grade and may be referred to as a 'high stakes' test.

Practical tips for effective learning online

Check on the status of your home computer facility. Your access to online facilities from home will be greatly dependent on such factors as the speed of your internet connection, computer memory and what plug-ins you have installed. Each institution will publish a set of 'minimum standards' that they assume you will have, and instructions for downloading and enabling software.

Enrol on a course or workshop. If you do feel you need to update your skills or expand the range of software you feel competent to use, you may be able to enrol on an ICT module to improve your skills or attend special workshops. Enquire at the ICT helpdesk or reception to find out what is available.

Take basic computer security and safety precautions.

- Be extremely cautious when opening files attached to emails from unknown sources – they may contain viruses.
- Never give away any information about bank accounts, even if the request appears to come from your bank – this will be a scam, as your bank will never request information in this way.
- Always make a back-up copy of important files.
- Do not circulate 'round-robin' or chain-letter emails – they can clog up the system.
- Take care with food and drink next to computers – spilled drinks can short-circuit electrical components and food can make keyboards dirty, for example.
- At home, make sure you have installed appropriate firewall and virus detection software (university networks are protected centrally).

When working online, keep aware of the risks of plagiarism and copyright infringement. Although it is technically easy to cut and paste material into your own documents and essays, this is regarded as cheating and may be illegal (**Ch 37**). You should not contemplate plagiarism for moral reasons, but if tempted, you should also realise that lecturers nowadays have a range of sophisticated packages for detecting it, and the penalties for identified plagiarism are severe.

Take time at the start of each module to explore the online resources. Although some features may not be activated immediately, it will be valuable to know the scope of the resource at your disposal and to consider this in relation to your assessment tasks.

Organise your online learning resources. You could do this by grouping them within folders using the bookmark facility on your browser. This will keep the browser interface uncluttered and help you access the resources quickly, without having to remember or enter URLs.

Get into a daily routine for visiting your VLE and doing the necessary work. There may be a convenient time at the start of the day or between lectures for you to look at emails and announcements. If you get into the habit of doing this on a daily basis, you won't miss important new information. Allocate some specific times to study online – your course outcomes may require a significant and ongoing input.

Bear in mind that your tutors may be monitoring your activities. Although they may not contribute, lecturers may be able to see what you have written on discussion boards, for example. They may also be able to use the number of times you have visited the VLE as an indicator of your participation in the course (although generally speaking if they are going to do this, they should tell you beforehand).

Save on ink costs. When printing out lecture notes based on *PowerPoint* presentations or similar, you may wish to select 'Pure Black and White' from the 'Color/Grayscale' options on the 'Print' menu, or you are liable to use up a lot of coloured ink printing the slide backgrounds.

Remember to keep using 'traditional' sources of information. When a large proportion or all your teaching is provided online, it is important not to overlook conventional sources such as books and research journals. Increasingly, even these are available online, and many can be evaluated and reserved online, before visiting your library.

 Useful language for . . . talking about computing facilities

Context: these might be valuable when talking to IT support staff or lecturers.

I wonder if you could help me, please? I can't access the wireless network with my laptop.

I'd like to report a problem with my email. I've forgotten my password and have not been able to gain entry to my messages. Could you tell me how I can reset the password, please?

I've never used a virtual learning environment [or specific software package] before. Is there an induction course I could attend to learn more?

26.1 Organise your e-learning activities. Carry out the following three simple
steps to enhance your online learning:

- Bookmark your learning resources on your browser and spend some time
  thinking about how best to organise your web favourites within appropriately
  named folders.

- Decide when in each day you will visit your VLE, and try to get into a routine of
  carrying this out.

- Allocate some time for fully exploring the resources on each online module at
  your disposal.

**26.2 Set up a (better) system of folders for organising your files and
favourites.** This will repay the effort as the number of files you create expands.
You can also rearrange favourites within the folder in your browser. This will allow
you to move quickly between URLs to access your favourite search engines, news
providers, and so on.

26.3 Think about your approach to learning with online resources. When using
blended e-learning and fully online (e.g. distance-learning) approaches, lecturers
may make assumptions about the ways you are using the material. Make sure you
appreciate what is expected of you. Also, check that you are using the material
actively, rather than trying to absorb it passively (see **Ch 51** for relevant tips).
Take time to use a search engine to find websites that could be useful in your
studies, such as your university library website, textbook-support websites, writing
and learning skills websites, sites related to specific course topics, and sites
recommended by your tutors. Bookmark these and collate them in a folder.

27 English as an academic language

How to apply what you have learnt in new contexts

Writing for academic purposes is a vital skill, yet the stylistic codes you need to follow are rarely comprehensively defined. This chapter will help you, as an international student, understand what it means to write in an academic style and outlines some of the things to do and some of the things you ought not to do.

Key topics:
→ Being objective in your writing
→ Shaping your text
→ Punctuation and layout for academic purposes
→ Ensuring your use of words is accurate and appropriate

Essential vocabulary
**Ambiguous   Exemplification   Objective   Phrasal verb   Pronoun   Signpost word
Thesaurus (plural thesauri)   Unambiguous**

Academics have developed a style of writing that aims to be objective and unambiguous. This involves the use of precise and objective language to express ideas. It must be grammatically correct, and is more formal than the style used in speech, novels, newspapers and informal correspondence. The key to writing within these conventions is to ensure that you write clearly, simply and with a clear purpose and direction. Many native speakers of English think that academic writing must involve the use of long sentences and complex language. In fact, the opposite is the case.

→ Being objective in your writing

When writing academically, it is essential that your personal involvement with your topic does not overshadow the importance of your commentary or your discussion. The main way of demonstrating detachment and lack of bias (**Ch 21**) is by using impersonal language. There are four key ways in which this can be done:

1 Avoiding personal pronouns: I/me/you (singular and plural)/we/us. For example: *I carried out the experiment during the day* becomes *The experiment was carried out during the day.*

2 Using the passive rather than the active voice, so that you write about the action rather than the actor (the person who performed the action), so that **We applied** *pressure to the wound to stem the bleeding* becomes **Pressure was applied** *to the wound to stem the bleeding.*

3 Using noun structures, so that: **We applied** *pressure to the wound to stem the bleeding* becomes **The application of** *pressure to the wound stemmed the bleeding*.

4 Using 'neutral' structures, so that sentences are introduced by expressions such as: '*It is . . .*' and '*There are . . .*'. However, beginning a paragraph with 'it' is not advised as this word, by definition, has to refer to a preceding word or ideas; a new paragraph should introduce a new point. To avoid this, the initial 'it' position can be changed by amending, for example, '*It is important to note . . .*' to '*The important point to note is . . .*'.

Another key way to demonstrate objectivity is the appropriate use of references to support your writing. This aspect is covered in **Ch 31**.

→ Shaping your text

As already noted in **Ch 24**, paragraphs and their component sentences are the building blocks of text. Each paragraph performs a particular role within the text. Thus, paragraphs can describe (position, time, process, appearance), define, classify, give examples, generalise, list, relate cause and effect, as well as compare and contrast.

As an academic writer you will develop skills in constructing these different types of paragraph and in sequencing them to create logically organised text that helps the reader to understand your line of reasoning (one reason for planning your writing carefully, **Ch 28**). In addition, you need to be aware that both sentences and paragraphs can be ordered in different ways to establish the structure of the discussion in your text, that is, deductively or inductively.

- **Inductive model of text structure**: the writer presents the supporting information and concludes with the main point.

- **Deductive model of text structure**: the writer moves from the key idea and follows it with supporting information or evidence.

Inductive and deductive logic in writing

The sequences of statements shown here could represent the themes of sentences within a paragraph.

Inductive model - moving from examples to general principle(s):

1 Lecturer A wears out-of-date clothes from the 1980s;
2 Lecturer B wears out-of-date clothes from the 1990s;
3 Lecturer C wears out-of-date clothes from the 2000s;
4 Therefore, all lecturers wear out of date clothes of one type or another.

Deductive model - moving from general principle(s) to particular instances:

1 All lecturers wear out-of-date clothes of one type or another;
2 Person D is a lecturer;
3 Therefore, Person D will wear out-of-date clothes.

To help with establishing logic and flow (linkage) within the structure of your chosen method, 'signpost words' are used. Table 27.1 provides examples of these expressions. **Ch 28** explains some different structural models that you might use when writing assignments at university.

Table 27.1 Signpost words in text

Type of link intended	Examples of signpost words
Addition	additionally; furthermore; in addition; moreover
Cause/reason	as a result of; because (mid-sentence)
Comparison	compared with; in the same way; in comparison with; likewise
Condition	if; on condition that; providing that; unless
Contrast	although; by contrast; conversely; despite; however; nevertheless; yet
Effect/result	as a result; hence; therefore; thus
Exemplification	for example; for instance; particularly; such as; thus
Reformulation	in other words; rather; to paraphrase
Summary	finally; hence; in all; in conclusion; in short; in summary
Time sequence	after; at first; at last; before; eventually; subsequently
Transition	as far as . . . is concerned; as for; to turn to

Punctuation is an essential component of writing that has evolved as an aid to the reader to help convey meaning, emphasis and style. The following examples show the extent to which punctuation can alter meaning and lead to ambiguity (double meaning). For example:

- The inspector said the teacher is a fool (reports what the inspector said).
- 'The inspector,' said the teacher, 'is a fool' (reports the exact words the teacher used).
- The inspector said, 'The teacher is a fool' (reports the exact words the inspector used).

Clearly, punctuation has a role to play in making meaning precise. Hence, in academic writing, the rules of punctuation are followed closely. Learning how to use punctuation marks correctly and consistently will contribute to your skill as a writer.

Three cases where punctuation is sometimes used inappropriately are: overuse of brackets; overuse of exclamation marks; and incorrect use of ellipsis (. . .):

- Brackets are sometimes a symptom of 'lazy' writing. Sometimes these are included to add more detail than is actually necessary. In many cases, the 'extra' material within the bracket can either be omitted or included in a new sentence.
- Exclamations in academic writing are rare! This can be seen in the previous sentence where the emphasis added by the exclamation is unnecessary. If you normally use exclamation marks a lot, these can usually be replaced with a full-stop, to remove the unnecessary emphasis.
- Ellipsis (. . .) is used to indicate where words have been missed from a quotation (**Ch 32**). However, some international students use the three dots as the end of the final sentence of an essay or report. This is a use that is simply not understood in British English and should be avoided.

Avoiding contractions

For international students, one of the measure of English language competence in speech will be the ability to use contractions with ease – for example, *you're*, *can't*, *isn't*, *there'll*. However, in academic writing, this use of the contraction is regarded as too informal for most disciplines. British students generally will know not to use contractions in formal writing. This is less easy for international students – you may have spent many study hours learning these structures, but, for writing purposes at least, will have to 'unlearn' them.

Another area where punctuation conventions are not always clearly understood is in the use of bulleted and numbered lists. These can be formulated either with minimal punctuation or as part of a sentence. Note that the use of lists in text is not favoured in some disciplines; it may be acceptable, however, to state points by starting a sequence of observations with 'Firstly, . . .'; 'Secondly, . . .'; 'Thirdly, . . .', and so on.

Punctuation: examples of bulleted and numbered lists

Bullet list

(Minimal punctuation)

The causes of migration include:

- drought
- famine
- disease.

The list as a sentence

(Colon + semi-colon + no initial capital letters)

Population decreases because:

1. drought dries up pastures;
2. people do not have food;
3. lack of food lowers resistance to disease; and
4. people either die or migrate.

Numbered list (Example 1)

(Minimal punctuation. Capitals for each point because items are names of organisations)

Famine relief agencies:

1. UN
2. OXFAM
3. Save the Children.

Numbered list (Example 2)

(Colon + semi-colon + no initial capital letters)

To save an amended document:

1. click on File;
2. select Save As;
3. select directory;
4. create a new file name; and
5. click on Save.

→ Ensuring your use of words is accurate and appropriate

Good academic writing involves careful thought about your choice of words. Precision in wording is vital in academic English if you are to describe what you mean with the clarity expected. The appropriate discipline-specific vocabulary must be used to explain facts and ideas.

British English (BE) versus American English (AE)

Academic writing in the UK nearly always adopts BE. The differences are most evident in spelling, for example, 'colour' (BE) and 'color' (AE). However, there are also differences in vocabulary, so that in AE people talk of 'professor' for 'lecturer'; and, in language use, so that in AE someone might write 'we have gotten results', rather than 'we have obtained results' as in BE. In some disciplines, there is an attempt at international standardisation, for example, in chemistry, the spelling of 'sulphur' (BE) has become 'sulfur' (AE). Some citation and referencing systems will also follow the American tradition even in British contexts – as in the American Psychological Association (APA).

If English is not your first language, then you will be well aware of the different language learner dictionaries that are available. What you will discover very quickly is that these do not provide the breadth of vocabulary that you will need for your academic studies. Hence, it is important to understand what other dictionaries exist which could help you to broaden your vocabulary. The following brief checklist outlines some alternatives:

- **Bilingual dictionary**: gives equivalent words from two languages, often arranged in two sections, translating from one language to the other, and vice versa.
- **Collocation dictionary**: gives words that are often positioned together. This is useful when you find yourself searching for one word usually used alongside (collocated) another.
- **English learner's dictionary**: primarily intended for those learning English as an additional language, but very useful for all because they normally include examples of use, including idioms and a pronunciation guide.
- **Pronunciation dictionary**: gives a phonetic version of the headword. Work out the phonetic code from the symbols that are usually given at the front of the dictionary.
- **Spelling dictionary**: gives correct spellings as well as frequently misspelt versions with the correct spelling alongside.
- **Subject-specific dictionaries**: provide specialist terms, their pronunciation and examples of their use. Many such words will not be used in standard dictionaries. Bilingual subject-specific dictionaries might be less easy to find and there is a strong argument that suggests that using a subject-specific dictionary actually helps the user to rehearse the forms of expression in English, since this is the medium of teaching and learning for students in the UK.

---

smart tip

Thesaurus (plural thesauri)

These are collections of words that are similar in meaning (synonyms); sometimes they also include words opposite in meaning (antonyms). The words are sometimes organised thematically and sometimes in A–Z order. While a thesaurus can be useful, a collocation dictionary (see above) will provide better guidance on how to use words and expressions so that you will have a better understanding of which synonym is more appropriate to your particular meaning.

Take care when using electronic dictionaries

These are often used by international students as they can provide quick and convenient access to the target word or phrase in both first language and English, but note that they also have limitations and do not always produce the correct word or the appropriate form for the user's purpose. Monolingual dictionaries may provide you with a more detailed overview of the use of a particular word or phrase.

There is an organisation in the UK called the 'Plain English Campaign' that supports the use of clear, unambiguous writing. To achieve this, the Campaign recommends that words of Latin origin should be replaced with their Anglo-Saxon, or spoken alternatives. These are often phrasal verbs. However, their use does not always help the style and precision needed in academic writing. For example, consider:

If we **turn down** the volume, there will be no feedback. (i.e. reduce) alongside
If we **turn down** the offer from the World Bank, interest rates will rise. (i.e. reject)

Both sentences make sense, but the meanings of **turn down** clearly differ. Hence, there is an argument in academic writing contexts for using the Latin-based language, in these examples 'reduce' and 'reject'. This particular recommendation contradicts the Plain English Campaign position, but it should be remembered that their advice relates to clarity in business and commercial writing rather than in academic English.

Table 27.2 provides an example of writing that would not be considered to be 'academic' in style, and shows how it might be converted into more appropriate text. Developing an academic style like this for your writing will be something that will develop gradually. Some native speakers also find this difficult and it is one reason why much of the early assessment at university involves this form of writing. When you are given feedback on your writing, consider this carefully (**Ch 48**) and try to learn from each exercise you are given.

smart tip

Gender-free language

The Council of Europe recommends that, where possible, gender-specific language is avoided and this is now favoured in academic writing. Attempts to do this can seem clumsy, such as: *S(he) will provide specimens for his/her exam*. However, by transforming the sentence into the plural, this problem can be resolved and any offence avoided, thus: *They will provide specimens for their exam*.

Table 27.2 Example of converting a piece of 'non-academic' writing into 'academic' style. This table demonstrates some of the key points that are made in this chapter in an example where a piece of 'non-academic' is converted into academic style. Note that the conversion results in a slightly longer piece of text (43 versus 37 words); this emphasises the point that while you should aim for concise writing, precise writing might be more important.

Original text (non-academic style)	'Corrected' text (academic style)
In this country, we have changed the law so that the King or Queen is less powerful since World War I. But he or she can still advise, encourage or warn the Prime Minister if they want.	In the United Kingdom, legislation has been a factor in the decline of the role of the monarchy in the period since World War I. Nevertheless, the monarchy has survived and, thus, the monarch continues to advise, encourage and warn the Prime Minister.
Points needing correction	**Corrected points**
• Non-specific wording (*this country*) • Personal pronoun (*we*) • Weak grammar (*But* is a connecting word and should not be used at the start of a sentence) • Word with several meanings (*law*) • Duplication of nouns (King or Queen) • Inconsistent and potentially misleading pronoun use (*he or she, they*) • Informal style (*can still*)	• Specific wording (country specified: *in the United Kingdom*) • Impersonal language (*legislation has*) • Appropriate signpost word (*nevertheless*) • Generic, yet well-defined term (*legislation*) • Singular abstract term (*monarchy*) • Repeated subject (*monarchy*) and reconstructed sentence • More formal style (*continues to exercise*)

✔ Practical tips for developing your academic writing style

Vary sentence length. A sentence 'mix' of short and long sentences is probably more reader-friendly than lines and lines of unbroken text. As a general rule, if a sentence runs into three or four lines of typescript, consider restructuring it in some way or breaking it up into two smaller sentences.

Finding the right balance in paragraph length. The length of the paragraph depends on the content, but generally extra-long paragraphs will have some topic shift within them. If you find that your paragraph seems disproportionately long, read it aloud and listen for a 'natural' break point. This is probably a good place to start a new paragraph.

Use signpost words. These words are used to assist your reader by moving them through the logic of your text (see pp. 190–1). Some words are most frequently used at the beginning of sentences: for example, however, moreover, furthermore, nevertheless. These words are nearly always followed by a comma.

Learn the correct spelling of the key words in your discipline. Specialist terms need to be accurately spelt. For example, if you are studying politics, it is advisable to learn how to spell 'parliament' correctly. Likewise, if you are studying a scientific subject, it is important to know that the plural of 'formula' is 'formulae' and that 'data' is a plural word with the singular 'datum'.

Check on the correct form of a word. As an international student you may find that you are uncertain about the different grammatical forms that can be taken, especially for unfamiliar words. For example, 'different types of transporter' differs from 'different types of transport'; both 'transporter' and 'transport' are nouns but they have different meanings. Check correct forms of words using your English language learner's dictionary.

Ask for clarification from the person who has assessed your work. If the person who has evaluated your written work has noted that your grammar or language has caused you to lose marks, then, if it is possible, ask for some specific detail so that you can go back to the grammar books and work on these particular points. Seek help if this is consistently mentioned (see 27.3 opposite).

💬 Useful language for . . . discussing academic writing

Context: these might be used when discussing your competence in writing academic English with staff or friends.

I've found a collocation dictionary but I'm not clear how to use it. Could you show me, please?

If I write in shorter sentences, will this mean that I will lose marks?

How can I develop my vocabulary further so that my academic writing comes up to the standard required?

And now . . .

27.1 Ask a friend to work with you on your writing style. Swap a piece of writing and check over your friend's writing style and ask them to do the same for yours. When you have done this, compare the points you have found. Try to explain what you think could be improved. Together you may be able to clarify some aspects that you were unaware were problematic.

27.2 Learn from published academic writing in your discipline. Look at a textbook or journal article – especially at the section that discusses results, evidence or recommendations. Identify the way that the writer has organised the structure of the discussion – inductive or deductive (see pp. 224-5).

27.3 Find out what academic support is available in your university. Most universities have staff in specialist units who have expertise in the teaching of academic writing. They will be able to give you some guidance on how to improve your writing so that it meets the standards required in the UK. This service is usually free and you may also be able to attend workshops on specific aspects of academic writing – for essays, reports, dissertations and theses.

28 | Tackling writing assignments

How to get started

Assignments at university challenge you to write in different forms. This chapter looks at the fundamental stages in preparing to respond to any assignment. It takes you through a step-by-step process to help you plan the structure of your submission.

Key topics:
→ Realistic time-planning
→ Recognising the elements of the task
→ Exploring the topic
→ Finding the material and selecting what's relevant
→ Adopting an analytical approach

Essential vocabulary
Analyse   Argue   Brainstorm   Describe   Restriction   School of thought   Topic

Written university assignments take different forms. Examples include essays, reports, project dossiers, short-answer mini-essays, case studies or dissertations (see **Toolkit E**). The purpose of these exercises is to give you an opportunity to demonstrate several things:

● your knowledge and understanding of a topic;

● your ability to research a specific aspect of the topic set in the assignment;

● your ability to organise supporting information and evidence in a structured piece of academic writing.

Especially for a longer piece of writing, or one that will count towards a module or degree assessment, it is worth planning your work carefully and ensuring that you approach the task in a focused manner. If English is not your first language, then it is even more important to be organised and leave plenty of time for refining vocabulary, grammar and style.

→ Realistic time planning

Consult the course handbook for the assignment submission date. Work out how long you have between the starting point and due date, and then estimate how much of that time you can devote to completion of the work. Remember to take into account things you may need to do for other subjects, your need to attend lectures, tutorials or practicals, and any other commitments (see also **Ch 9**). Next, divide the available time into convenient working periods and decide how much time you wish to allocate to

Table 28.1 Subdivisions of a large writing task and their estimated timing. A possible method of organising your time when planning a lengthy written assignment. Time allocated for writing the first draft should include time for checking grammar and vocabulary.

Aspect of task	Time required	When I plan to do this
Analysing the task		
Doing preliminary reading		
Planning the response to the task		
Doing supplementary reading		
Writing the first draft		
Reviewing the first draft		
Editing/proof-reading the final copy		
Printing/writing out the final copy		
Time margin for the unexpected		

each aspect of the task (Table 28.1). Map these time allowances on to your available time.

Good planning ensures that you can realistically complete the work before the submission date. It also allows you to balance the time spent on different components, devote sufficient time to aspects such as editing and proof-reading (**Ch 33**) and avoid penalties that might be imposed because of late submission.

smart tip

Value of planning

Time spent deconstructing the task and planning your response will enable you to save time in the long term and, as with most jobs, the quality of the preparation will be reflected in the quality of the end-product. Therefore, ensure that you break down the question into its different elements.

→ Recognising the elements of the task

Once you have estimated the amount of time you can allocate to the work, the next phase of analysing an assignment requires you to divide the task into its component parts by asking yourself the following questions:

- **What's the *instruction*?** Many assignments are not in the form of questions but framed as instructions introduced by an instruction word (an 'action' verb). It is important to interpret these instruction words properly (see Table 28.2).
- **What's the *topic*?** This will clarify the context of the discussion you will need to construct.
- **What's the *aspect* of the topic?** This will help you define a more specific focus within the wider context.
- **What *restriction* is imposed on the topic?** This will limit the scope of your discussion.

The example in the tip box below shows you how this analysis might look for a sample question. You may already do this sort of thing subconsciously, but there is value in marking these elements out on paper. First, it helps you to recognise the scope and limitations of the work you have been asked to complete. Second, it means that you can avoid producing a piece of work that lacks focus or digresses. Once you have gone through this fairly quick process, you will be better able to work on planning your writing and on adopting a suitable framework for your assignment (**Ch 30**).

Example assignment

Assignment task: assess the importance of post-operative care in the rehabilitation of orthopaedic patients.

Instruction: assess.

Topic: post-operative care.

Aspect: importance.

Restriction 1: rehabilitation.

Restriction 2: orthopaedic patients.

Generally, instruction words fall into four categories, although this grouping may vary according to the context of the question. The list below defines these types. In broad terms, this suggests a hierarchy of approaches to tackling assignments that will dictate how you need to organise the information in your assignment (**Ch 31**).

Instruction word categories

One way of categorising instruction words is by looking at what they ask you to do:

Do: create something, draw up a plan, calculate.

Describe: explain or show how something appears, happens or works.

Analyse: look at all sides of an issue.

Argue: look at all sides of an issue and provide supporting evidence for your opinion or position.

Table 28.2 shows a range of typical instruction words, with definitions for each one. You should make sure you know what's expected of you when any of these instructions are used, not only in terms of these definitions, but also in relation to the thinking processes expected (see **Ch 21** and especially Table 21.1). However, always remember to take the whole question into account when deciding this.

→ Exploring the topic

Go back to the task and analyse the topic, its aspect(s) and restriction(s) more deeply. This is important because students often misread the task and, although they may submit a good piece of work, their response could miss the true focus of the assignment.

Table 28.2 Instruction words for assignments and exams. These words are the product of research into the frequency of use of the most common instruction words in university examinations. The definitions below are suggestions. You must take the whole question into account when answering. See also Table 21.1.

Instruction word	Definition – what you are expected to do
Account [give an]	Describe
Account for	Give reasons for
Analyse	Give an organised answer looking at all aspects
Apply	Put a theory into operation
Assess	Decide on value/importance
Brief account [give a]	Describe in a concise way
Comment on	Give your opinion
Compare [with]	Discuss similarities; draw conclusions on common areas
Compile	Make up (a list/plan/outline)
Consider	Describe/give your views on the subject
Contrast	Discuss differences/draw own view
Criticise	Point out weak/strong points, i.e. balanced answer
Define	Give the meaning of a term, concisely
Demonstrate	Show by example/evidence
Describe	Narrative on process/appearance/operation/sequence . . .
Devise	Make up
Discuss	Give own thoughts and support your opinion or conclusion
Evaluate	Decide on merit of situation/argument
Exemplify	Show by giving examples
Expand	Give more information
Explain	Give reason for – say why
Explain how	Describe how something works
Identify	Pinpoint/list
Illustrate	Give examples
Indicate	Point out, but not in great detail
Justify	Support the argument for . . .
List	Write down an organised list, e.g. events
Outline	Describe basic factors – limited information
Plan	Think how to organise something
Report	Give an account of the process or event
Review	Write a report – give facts and views on facts
Show	Demonstrate with supporting evidence
Specify	Give details of something
State	Give a clear account of . . .
Summarise	Briefly give an account
Trace	Provide a brief chronology of events/process
Work out	Find a solution, e.g. as in a maths problem

Next, create a brainstorm 'map' of the topic by writing down as many related aspects as you can in a free-flowing diagram (see Figure 25.5). Revisit the instruction word and consider how this applies to your initial response to the task. These immediate thoughts are principally your own reaction to the topic, perhaps influenced by lectures, but before your ideas have been influenced by any reading material. The most important aspect is that you are beginning to exercise your critical thinking skills (**Ch 21**), by analysing for yourself what you think is important about this subject.

Brainstorming techniques

smart tip

To create an effective brainstorm 'map', use a single sheet of A4 in the landscape position. This gives more space for lateral thinking and creativity. It also leaves more space for additions to be made at later stages. You can use highlighters of different colours to identify themes within your map – this may help you think critically about the topic.

→ Finding the material and selecting what's relevant

As a preliminary to tackling the prescribed reading list you may find it useful to obtain some general background information about the topic. Typical additional sources are shown in the information box below.

Reading the literature that supports a subject is a routine part of student activity. Generally, reading lists are extensive to give some choice; they often list basic texts and sources that go into greater depth. You are not usually expected to read everything on these lists. In some subjects, you may only be expected to look at one or two texts. In some other subjects, book lists are lengthy and the volume of reading may seem daunting, but the task will be more manageable if you approach it systematically.

Unless specific chapters or pages are cited, students sometimes think that they need to read the whole book. This is usually not the case. Use the contents page and the index in partnership to identify which sections are relevant to your topic (**Ch 24**).

Sources of information

Handouts/*PowerPoint* slides: should outline key issues and ideas, pose problems and provide solutions related to your topic.

Lecture notes: easy to locate if you've noted lecturer, topic and date.

General or subject encyclopaedias: provide a thumbnail sketch of useful background information; give key points to direct your reading in more detailed texts. Electronic versions may be available through your university library (**Ch 22**).

ebrary: readily accessible, and reliable in its validity.

E-journals: often contemporary material that is reliable in its provenance.

Library resources: the electronic catalogue will enable you to locate many resources in addition to those listed above. However, you may also find things by chance by browsing in the relevant zone of shelving in the library, where it is possible to find books and journals that may not necessarily come up from the search headings you have selected when consulting the catalogue.

Reading lists

In the UK, lengthy reading lists are provided to give students the chance to find relevant material when there is a heavy demand at times when assignments are due. Do not think that you must read everything on the reading list. It is better to read a selection of fewer books thoroughly, than read everything without much real understanding.

Some authors often put key pages in bold type in the index and this will help you to focus your reading rather than cover every reference. At this stage also, preliminary encyclopaedia reading will help you to identify sections in a book resource that are more relevant to the present task. There has been an upsurge in reference information on the Web and much of it is sound. However, it is important that you recognise that while sources like Wikipedia are convenient to use, they are not academically reviewed and entries may not be valid or accurate. It may be better to consult electronic or hard-copy versions of standard encyclopedias that have gone through a more formal editing and evaluation process.

Begin by doing the necessary reading and note-making (**Ch 22–Ch 25**). This has to be focused and you need to be reading with discrimination. As you move from basic texts to more specialist books or journal articles that give more detailed analysis, your understanding of the topic will deepen. This may mean, for example, that you begin to build up a more informed picture of events, implications of a procedure or the possible solutions to a problem. What are you looking for? This could be, for instance, facts, examples, information to support a particular viewpoint, or counter-arguments to provide balance to your analysis of the topic. As you become more familiar with the issues, the easier it will be to think critically (**Ch 21**) about what you are reading and consequently build your response to the task you have been set. Continue to add to your initial brainstorm.

smart tip

The reporter's questions

Sometimes it is difficult to identify the important from the unimportant, the relevant from the irrelevant. A well-tried strategy, for many subjects, is to ask yourself the questions that trainee journalists are advised to use:

- **Who?** Who is involved in relation to this topic, for example, people/organisations?
- **What?** What are the problems/issues involved?
- **When?** What is the time-frame to be considered?
- **Where?** Where did it occur?
- **Why?** What reasons are relevant to this issue/topic?
- **How?** How has this situation been reached?

Note that this list is advised as a way of starting the thinking process. It should not be seen as the outline structure for your assignment (see **Ch 29**).

→ Adopting an analytical approach

Knowing what information to put aside and what to retain requires a more disciplined appraisal than the more wide-ranging approach you will have followed in your initial reading. Certain questions may help you to focus on what is important to your topic. For example:

- Who are the key actors (people) in a sequence of events?
- What are the necessary events or conditions that explain particular situations?
- What explanations support a particular view?
- What patterns can be identified, for example, short-, medium- and long-term factors?

From your reading and note-making you will discover that different authors make similar or contradictory points. As you begin to identify the different schools of thought or approaches to an issue, you should start to cross-reference your notes so that you can begin to group authors who subscribe to the same or similar viewpoints.

smart tip

Direct quotation

It is important not to rely too heavily on quoting from texts. First, if this is overdone, it is plagiarism (**Chs 32**, **34**); second, it fails to give the necessary evidence that you understand the significance of the point being made.

University work needs more than simple reproduction of facts. You need to be able to construct an argument (**Ch 29**, **Ch 30**) and to support this with evidence. This means that you need to draw on the literature that you have read in order to support your position. In some instances, dependent on the topic and discipline, it may be appropriate to present differing viewpoints and evaluate arguments one over the others, and, if appropriate, address counter-arguments to these. What is important is to present a tight, well-argued case for the view you finally present as the one you favour.

Once you have evolved your own response to the task you have been set, you then need to place this within a framework that presents your interpretation in a way that is well-structured. Writing that follows a sequence of sound logic and argument will improve your potential for gaining better marks. This next stage in structuring your text is covered in **Ch 29**.

✔ Practical tips for getting started on a writing assignment

Select from a wide range of sources. In the early years of university study many students follow the same practices as they used at school, often with too much reliance on handouts and notes from a single core textbook. At university you will be expected to read more widely by identifying source material beyond titles given as a basic starting point. It is worthwhile exploring your library on foot to browse in the areas related to your studies, where you may find a whole range of material that potentially expands your reading and understanding.

Keep a record of what you read. It is annoying to know that you have read something somewhere but cannot find it again. It is good to develop the habit of noting page number, chapter, title, author, publisher and place of publication on notes you make. This makes citation and referencing much easier and less time-consuming.

Conserve what you read. In the process of looking for information for a writing task you will probably obtain some material that proves to be irrelevant or peripheral to the current writing task. Nevertheless, keep this in your filing system because this topic may come up again at a later date in a subtle way. In exam revision, this personal cache of information could be useful in revitalising your knowledge and understanding of this topic.

Stick to your planned allocation of time for reading. This is a vital part of the writing process, but recognise the dangers of prolonging the reading phase beyond your scheduled deadline. This is an avoidance strategy that is quite common. Students may delay getting down to planning the structure and moving on to the writing phase because they are uncomfortable with writing. Facing up to these next phases and getting on with them is usually much less formidable once you get started, so it's best to stick to your time plan for this assignment and move on to the next phase in the planned sequence.

💬 Useful language for . . . starting the writing process

Context: these examples might be used when discussing your approach to a written exercise with a fellow student.

Have you found enough information to help you with that essay we need to do?
I found some good stuff [slang] in [name of book(s)], but I can't find anything on [aspect of topic]. Have you been able to find any information on that?

I'm planning to finish my research for that report by Friday, then make a plan over the weekend and begin writing over next week. How are you getting on with it?

What do you think the topic for the next tutorial means? I wasn't absolutely sure what was meant by '[name instruction word]' but I asked one of the lecturers, and she said it meant [explanation].

28.1 Practise categorising instruction words. Go to Table 28.2 and mark out all those instruction words that would invite a response asking you to *do something practical*, those requiring you simply to *describe*, those that invite you to *analyse* and those that are directing you to *construct an argument*. You could use different colours of highlighter to do this.

28.2 Examine some of the assignment titles that you will have to complete in a selected subject. Taking the whole question or instruction into account, identify what type of approach is needed – doing something practical, describing, analysing or arguing. You may find that within the same question/task you will have to do some describing in order to analyse or argue. The trick is not to devote too much time to the descriptive element at the expense of analysis/argument (**Ch 29, Ch 30**). You could also do this activity with past exam papers.

28.3 Try creating for yourself the wording for a task in a selected subject. Think about the clarity of the question. Is it ambiguous? Is it unclear? Identify your topic, aspect and restriction(s). Turning the student-examiner roles around can sometimes be a helpful way of developing understanding. This could be an excellent preparation for exams because it helps with anticipating possible questions and reflecting on how you would answer them. This approach may broaden the range of possible questions you could feel comfortable tackling in exams (**Ch 53, Ch 57, Ch 55**).

Academic writing format

How to organise your writing within a standard framework

Regardless of the type of writing assignment you have to complete, the structure will follow a basic format. This chapter describes this design and explores some of the features that need to be included as you map your outline plan onto this structure.

Key topics:
→ Standard format
→ Taking word limits into account

Essential vocabulary
Annex   Appendix (pl. appendices)   Citation   Exemplify   Sub-heading

Most academic writing follows the same format, namely, introduction-main body-conclusion. It is on this basic framework that different types of academic assignment are constructed, and these are examined in detail in **Ch 30**.

→ Standard format

The basic structure follows the convention of moving from the general (the introduction) through to the specific (the main body) and back to the general (the conclusion). These will now be considered in sequence.

Introduction

Generally, this should consist of three components:

1 a brief explanation of the context of the topic;

2 an outline of the topic as you understand it;

3 an explanation of how you plan to address the topic in this particular text - in effect, a statement of intent.

This introductory section can be quite long as it may take several sentences to lay out these three dimensions. It's important to do this with some thought because this indicates to your reader where you expect to take them in the main body of text. The introduction also lays down the parameters that you have set yourself for this piece of text. For example, your topic may be multifaceted and the word limit imposed on the total piece of text will not allow you to give a comprehensive coverage of all aspects. It is better to acknowledge the extensive nature of the topic and note that you are going to limit your discussion to only some of these aspects - usually those you consider to be most important. You need to explain the reasons for this decision at this stage.

The importance of the introduction

This is the first contact that your reader makes with you as the author of the text. This means that it has to be well-organised and clear. However, to achieve this it is important to see this introductory section as 'work in progress' because, until you complete the entire text, you cannot really introduce the whole work accurately. Indeed, some people prefer to start writing the main body, move on to the conclusion, and only then write the introduction.

Main body

This section lays out your work based on the approach you decide to adopt in organising the content (as discussed in **Ch 30**). Therefore, you may need to generalise, describe, define or give examples as part of your analysis. Here it's important to keep this part of the writing as brief, yet as clear, as possible, so that you have space to present the argument or analysis in your answer. The construction of your paragraphs will be dictated by what you are trying to express at any particular point. Different types of paragraph structures are outlined on p. 195.

Putting too much description in your writing

Many students spend too much time 'setting the scene' by describing the context of their study in too much detail. This is done most commonly at the outset of the introduction. Consequently, the full text is imbalanced because there is too much description at the expense of the analysis that is required in the main body. Since it is this analysis that will earn more marks, it is important not to include too much 'scene-setting' description. For international students, this is important because it can be perceived that the language of description is easier to write than the analysis or argument. However, as long as the writing is kept clear and avoids overlong complex sentences, there is no reason that the analytical and argument sections should be any more difficult to write than the description.

Conclusion

This summarises the whole piece of work. You should review the entire text in three elements:

- a restatement of the question and what you feel are the important features of the topic;
- a summary of the specific evidence that you have presented in support of your views;
- a statement of your overall viewpoint on the topic.

What mainly distinguishes the conclusion from the introduction is language. In the introduction, your explanation should be given clearly, avoiding jargon or technical words as far as possible. In the conclusion, you will be writing about the detail of the content and, therefore, the terminology you use is more likely to contain technical or more sophisticated language because you will have introduced this in the main body. You should avoid introducing new ideas in the conclusion that have not already been discussed in the earlier part of the writing.

smart tip

Mini-conclusions

As you become immersed in the writing process you will become very familiar with the material and conclusions you have drawn along the way. By the time you come to write the conclusion to the whole work, this in-depth awareness may become diluted. To avoid this, it is a good idea, at the end of each section you write, to note down what main ideas you had considered and what your view is about these. If you note these mini-conclusions down on a separate piece of paper, these will provide the substance for your final conclusion.

→ Taking word limits into account

Word limits are imposed, not to relieve tutors of marking, but to train you to be concise in your writing and to analyse the topic carefully to decide what to keep in and what to leave out.

It's important to note that falling short of the word limit is just as bad as overrunning the maximum. Some students keep a running total of words they have used and as soon as they reach the minimum word limit, they stop abruptly. This is not a good approach because it is more likely to leave a ragged and poorly considered piece of text that comes to an unexpected halt rather than one that is well-planned, relevant and concisely written.

It's usually better to plan and write your first draft keeping only a casual eye on word count at this stage. When you come to editing that draft you can prune and reshape your writing so that it becomes a tighter piece of prose that falls within the maximum-minimum word limits imposed by the regulations.

smart tip

Counting words

Most word processors include a word-count feature. Check the 'Help' function on your software to find out how to keep check of your word count. However, it is important not to become over-concerned about word limits as you write. It is better to concentrate on getting ideas down on paper/on the screen. You can always reduce words later if necessary.

Practical tips for organising your writing within a standard framework

Keep the right proportions in your response. Make sure that the three elements within your writing framework are well balanced in extent. The main body should be the most substantial piece of the writing, whereas the introduction and conclusion should occupy much less space.

Pay adequate attention to the conclusion. By the time that you come to write the conclusion, this is often done at some speed because there may be other demands on your time, or the initial interest in the subject has palled, or you may simply be tired. Thus, conclusions often don't get the attention they deserve. Do reserve some time to give your conclusion a critical appraisal, and even consider writing this section before finishing the perhaps more 'mechanical' earlier parts. Alternatively, as suggested above, you could 'write it as you go' by keeping detailed notes or mini-conclusions, which you can use to frame your conclusion once you have written the main body.

Review the introduction. Once you have completed your draft, go back to the introduction and make sure that you have actually done what you set out to do when defining the parameters of your work and in your statement of intent. The act of writing your text may have stimulated new thoughts and your initial intentions may have altered in the process of writing. Revise accordingly.

Think about appendices. Sometimes the length of your text may be seriously beyond the word limit. This means that some drastic 'surgery' is required. One strategy might be to remove some parts of the text and, while remaining within the word limit, reduce the information contained to bullet-point lists if appropriate to your discipline. The detail can then be placed in an appendix or appendices (plural of appendix), making appropriate cross-references in the main text. In some disciplines, the use of appendices is discouraged and you may be penalised for using them. If in doubt, consult your course handbook or ask a member of teaching staff.

Think about citations. In many disciplines you will be expected to include reference to recognised authorities within the field you are studying. In law, this could be cases; in the arts and humanities, it could be work by a distinguished academic. This does not mean that you need to quote substantial pieces of text; you can summarise the idea in your own words and then follow the rules about citation that are given in **Ch 31**. All this needs to be taken into consideration in planning and drafting your writing.

💬 Useful language for . . . discussing the format of your writing

Context: these examples could be used to discuss a draft with another student or tutor.

I've been working on that essay we have to do and I'm not sure I've got the balance between the introduction, main body and conclusion right. The conclusion is very short, but I'm running up against the word limit if I increase it. I think I'll have to take out one of the examples I've quoted.

I'm way short [slang] of the word limit for that report. Have you any ideas for aspects of the topic I could cover in more detail?

Here's the plan for my essay on [topic]. As you can see I've . . . [explain how you plan to organise the text]. I also intend to include these examples [list]. Can you please advise me? Am I thinking along the right lines [idiom]?

29.1 Compare textual patterns. Go back to a chapter in a textbook and identify the proportion of space allocated to introducing the entire chapter and how much is reserved for the conclusion. This should be instructive as a model in framing your own writing.

29.2 Track the pattern of your writing. Go back to an existing piece of your own writing and try to identify whether you have the basic elements and sub-elements of the standard writing format in place. Are the introduction, main body and conclusion identifiable? Does the introduction contain the elements of context, specific focus and statement of intent? For the conclusion, is your position laid out clearly and with supporting rationale? If any of the answers are negative, try to work out how you could improve things.

29.3 Practise converting sub-headings into topic sentences. Take a piece of your own writing or a section from a textbook where sub-headings have been used. Try to create a topic sentence (**Ch 24**) that could replace that sub-heading. Decide which is more effective – the topic sentence or the original sub-heading. Consider why this is the case. Again, this should be instructive in shaping the style you adopt in your own writing.

30 | Planning writing assignments

How to respond to the task

Once you have assembled the information for your assignment, you will be able to think about how you are going to respond to the set writing task within the standard framework. This chapter outlines some of the different options that you may need to consider when structuring your response into an outline plan.

Key topics:
→ Identifying the key themes in your text
→ Adopting a structural model
→ Expanding your outline

Essential vocabulary
Brainstorm   Chronological   Fishbone plan   Hierarchical   Structural model

The basic framework of an essay was described in **Ch 29**. The next step is to think about the particular assignment that you have to tackle and how you might organise your response to the task. This chapter outlines the key steps in the process of planning a writing assignment.

People and their thought processes are different and so individual approaches to planning an outline response to an assignment will vary. For some students, this can be a highly detailed process, for others, it may be a minimal exercise. Too much detail in a plan can be restricting, while too little can fail to provide enough direction. Therefore, a reasonably detailed plan should give some guidance while leaving you the flexibility to alter the finer elements as you write.

→ Identifying the key themes in your text

Planning your writing means that you need to return to your 'first thoughts' brainstorm (**Ch 28**), which should have been developed further as you have added key points from your reading and thinking. Consider whether any themes or recurrent

Lower- or higher-order thinking?

While, for some subjects, description would be a lower-order writing activity, for others this would be considered to be a higher-order skill (see **Ch 21** and especially Table 21.1). Often written assignments require some initial description of context or process to outline the background to the topic. This is then followed by in-depth consideration of the topic, using more analytical or critical approaches.

issues are evident. It might be useful to 'colour code' all the items that are related, using a different colour highlighter for each category or theme. Then, you need to reconsider the instruction of the set task to help you construct your plan, that is, on the basis of description, analysis or argument (**Ch 28**).

→ Adopting a structural model

Brainstorming and analysing the instruction should give you some indication of how you can construct the content of your paper as a logical discussion by considering how it would fit into one of several classic structural models or approaches (Table 30.1).

Table 30.1 **The seven most common structural models for written assignments**

1 Chronological	Description of a process or sequence
2 Classification	Ordering objects or ideas
3 Common denominator	Identifying a common characteristic or theme
4 Phased	Identifying short-/medium-/long-term aspects, for example
5 Analytical	Examining an issue in depth (situation - problem - solution - evaluation - recommendation)
6 Thematic	Commenting on a theme in each aspect
7 Comparative/contrastive	Comparing and contrasting (often within a theme or themes)

By adopting one of these models, it should be possible to plan your answer in a way that provides a logical and coherent response to the task you have been set. Note that sometimes it may be necessary to incorporate one of these models within another. For example, within the common denominator approach it may be necessary to include some chronological dimension to the discussion.

Examples of each of these seven approaches are given below.

Chronological

An example of the chronological approach would be describing a developmental process, such as outlining the historical development of the European Union. This kind of writing is most likely to be entirely descriptive. You might use it, for example, with material that can easily be plotted on a time line (p. 204).

Classification

An example of this approach could be to discuss transport by subdividing your text into land, sea and air modes of travel. Each of these could be further divided into commercial, military and personal modes of transport. These categories could be further subdivided on the basis of how they are powered. Such classifications are, to some extent, subjective, but the approach provides a means of describing each category at each level in a way that allows some contrast. This approach is particularly useful in scientific disciplines. The rationale also is sympathetic to the approach of starting from broad generalisation to the more specific.

Common denominator

An example of this approach might be used in answer to the following assignment: 'Account for the high levels of infant mortality in developing countries'. This suggests a common denominator of deficiency or lack. This topic could therefore be approached under the headings:

● Lack of primary health care;
● Lack of health education;
● Lack of literacy.

Phased

An example of adopting a sequential approach to a topic might be in answer to a task that instructs: 'Discuss the impact of water shortage on flora and fauna along river banks'.

● **Short-term factors** might be that drying out of the river bed occurs and annual plants fail to thrive.
● **Medium-term factors** might include damage to oxygenating plant life and reduction in wildlife numbers.
● **Long-term factors** might include the effect on the water table and falling numbers of certain amphibious species.

Note that topics amenable to this treatment do not always prompt this sort of response directly by asking for 'results' or consequences of an event; you could decide to use it in answer to a question such as 'Explain why water shortage has deleterious effects on life in rivers.'

Analytical

This conventional approach might be used for complex issues. An example of an assignment that you could tackle in this way might be: 'Evaluate potential solutions to the problem of identity theft.' You could perhaps adopt the following plan:

● Define identity theft, and perhaps give an example.
● Explain why identity theft is difficult to control.
● Outline legal and practical solutions to identity theft.
● Evaluate the advantages and disadvantages of each.
● State which solution(s) you would favour and why.

Thematic

This approach is similar to the phased approach, but in this case themes are the identifying characteristics. Precise details would depend on the nature of the question, but possible examples could be:

● social, economic or political factors;
● age, income and health considerations;
● gas, electricity, oil, water and wind power.

Taking the analytical approach – the SPSER model

This tactic is particularly helpful in the construction of essays, reports, projects and case studies. It is also useful whenever you feel that you cannot identify themes or trends. The method helps you to 'deconstruct' or 'unpack' the topic and involves five elements, as follows:

1 **Situation:** describe the context and brief history.

2 **Problem:** describe or define the problem.

3 **Solution:** describe and explain the possible solution(s).

4 **Evaluation:** identify the positive and negative features for each solution by giving evidence/reasons to support your viewpoint.

5 **Recommendation:** identify the best option in your opinion, giving the basis of your reasoning for this. This element is optional, as it may not always be a requirement of your task.

Comparative/contrastive

This is a derivative of the themed approach. For example, consider a task that instructs: 'Discuss the arguments for and against the introduction of car-free city centres'. You might approach this by creating a 'grid' as in Table 30.2, which notes positive and negative aspects for the major stakeholders in two columns.

Table 30.2 Model grid for planning comparison-type answers

		Column A	Column B
	Stakeholders	Positive aspects	Negative aspects
1	Pedestrians	Greater safety, clean	Lengthy walk, poor parking
2	Drivers	Less stress; park and ride facilities	High parking fees; expensive public transport
3	Commercial enterprises	Quicker access for deliveries	Loss of trade to more accessible out-of-town shopping centres
4	Local authority	Reduces emissions	Cost of park and ride
5	Police	Easier to police	Reliance on foot patrols

There are two potential methods of constructing text in this comparative/contrastive approach:

● **Method 1.** Introduce the topic, then follow Column A in a vertical fashion, then similarly follow Column B and conclude by making a concluding statement about the merits and demerits of one over the other. In relation to the grid, this would result in the structure:

> introductory statement, then A1 + A2 + A3 + A4 + A5, then B1 + B2 + B3 + B4 + B5, followed by concluding statement.

- **Method 2.** Introduce the topic and then discuss the perspective of pedestrians from first the positive and then the negative aspects; now do the same for the viewpoints of the other stakeholders in sequence. This would result in the structure:

    introductory statement, then A1 + B1; A2 + B2; A3 + B3; A4 + B4; A5 + B5, followed by concluding statement.

A fishbone map, as illustrated in Figure 25.7 for pros and cons of a transport policy proposal, is an alternative method of comparing arguments prior to writing.

Comparative/contrastive structures

Each method of structuring the points has advantages and disadvantages, according to the content and the context of the assignment. For example, in an exam it might be risky to embark on method 1 in case you run out of time and never reach the discussion of column B. In this instance, method 2 would enable a balanced answer.

→ Expanding your outline

Once you have decided what kind of approach is required to cover your written assignment, then you can map this on to the main body of your essay plan and frame an introduction and conclusion that will 'top and tail' the essay. In this way, you can create the outline plan based on the introduction–main body–conclusion model that provides the framework for academic writing (**Ch 29**) in the English-speaking world.

Giving the 'right' answer

In the UK, academic staff encourage the exploration of new ideas and new approaches to old ideas. Clearly, in some disciplines, such as mathematics, there are more likely to be correct or incorrect answers. However, in many other disciplines this is not the case – there are 'good' and 'bad' answers, depending on the coherence and originality of the approach taken. International students sometimes take some time to adjust to this and can spend a lot of time seeking out the 'right' answer from either online or printed sources but also by consulting fellow students or staff to try to establish 'what is wanted' or 'what is correct'. Obviously, you must carry out the necessary research into the literature, but much time could be saved simply by evaluating what *you* think about that reading and then writing about that. Your lecturer wants to read about your ideas based on your appraisal of evidence from recognised sources and not simply a review of what the lecturer said in class or ideas from the source books. You will probably gain more marks from coming up with a 'new' response to the question based on your own original thinking than by simply repeating the lecture/textbook outlines.

Respond appropriately to question words. Not all tasks are based on instructions; some do ask questions. For instance, they may include words such as 'How . . . ?', 'Why . . . ?' and expressions such as 'To what extent . . . ?' In these cases, you will need to think about what these mean within the do-describe-analyse-argue instruction hierarchy. One way to do this is to reword the question.

For example, consider the question: 'To what extent has the disposal of sewage effluence in rivers contributed to depletion of fish stocks over the last decade?'

This might be reworded as: 'Evaluate the relationship between the disposal of sewage effluence in rivers and the depletion of fish stocks over the last decade'.

This might suggest using a phased approach to organising the content of the answer to the question.

Return to the outline plan. When you have completed your first draft it is a good idea to go back to your outline plan and check that you have not forgotten any points. You can also make sure that the links between sections that you noted in the plan have been achieved in the text.

Achieve balance in your response. Especially in the early years of university study, there is a tendency for students to adhere to the methods that succeeded at school or college. This means that written work is often descriptive rather than analytical (see **Ch 21** for explanation). Ensure that the description you give is sufficient for the task, but if the instruction requires you to analyse or argue, then make sure this is the main focus of your response.

Explain your approach. Although the models outlined in this chapter are fairly standard approaches to tackling academic issues, it is still necessary to identify for your reader which approach you intend to adopt in the piece of text. Your reader should learn at an early point in your writing of the route you intend to follow. In most cases this would be in your introduction. This is dealt with more fully in **Ch 39**.

 Useful language for . . . discussing the organisation of text

Context: these examples could be used to discuss a draft with another student or a tutor.

I know that we're not supposed to ask about the right answer for these tasks, but I don't know what you want. Do you want me to write about each of the different opinions that I've read or do you want me to just write about my own opinion? What if I get the wrong answer? Could I fail the assignment?

I'm planning to organise my answer in chronological fashion, by considering the developments one by one in sequence.

The material for this essay is really complicated. I can see common themes, depending on [state factor], so I'm going to consider each of these in a different paragraph of my essay.

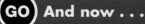

GO And now . . .

30.1 Compare textual patterns. Look at a chapter in a basic textbook and analyse the structural approach the author has taken. Identify the proportion of space allocated to 'scene-setting' using description, and to the analysis/argument/evaluation components of the text.

30.2 Identify response types. Look at some of the essay titles or report assignments you have been set. Try to identify which of the approaches given in this chapter might best 'fit' each task.

30.3 Convert questions into instructions. Look again at some of the tasks you have been set for coursework or, alternatively, look at some past exam papers to find those that have been framed as questions. Try converting them into 'instruction' tasks and decide which type they fit into in the do-describe-analyse-argue classification (**Ch 28**).

Citing and listing references

How to refer appropriately to the work of others

In academic writing at all levels you must support your discussion of a topic by referring to the relevant literature. Several styles are in use and which one you will be required to adopt will depend on the conventions within your discipline. This chapter outlines four of the more common styles, showing you how to cite your source in text and list these in your reference list or bibliography.

Key topics:
→ Why you need to cite your sources
→ Using information within your text
→ How to cite the work in the text

Essential vocabulary
Bibliography Citation Ellipsis ibid. Indentation op. cit. Reference list Superscript

When you write any kind of academic paper you must give the sources of information and ideas you have drawn from your in-depth reading on the subject. You have to give your reader sufficient information to be able to locate your source. You do this first in the body of the text at the point where you refer to (cite) the source, and then you give full details either in a footnote, endnote or separate reference list at the end of the paper. Styles vary (see Table 31.1), but the preferred style for your discipline will be stipulated in your course handbook, or may be recommended by your lecturer or supervisor. However, you must be able to recognise the alternative styles in order to interpret the information given, should you read a text that uses a style of citation that differs from the one you normally use.

---

i

Definitions

Citation: the use of the idea presented by an author and expressed *in your own words* to support a point in your own work. Rules about how to incorporate citations in your text are given in **Ch 31**.

Quotation: the use of words drawn from the source you need. The words should remain exactly as written in the original text. For layout of quotes see **Ch 24**.

Bibliography: a listing at the end of your work of all source materials that you have consulted as preparation for your paper. You do not need to have referred to all these sources directly in your text. In some styles the word 'bibliography' is used instead of the term 'reference list'.

Reference list: all the books, journals, web and online materials you have referred to in your paper. This list is usually at the end of the work.

Table 31.1 Choosing a referencing style. Departments normally specify the referencing style. Where no guidance is given, the choice is up to you. This table shows the most significant features, advantages and disadvantages of four common styles used in all forms of academic writing, including undergraduate and postgraduate assignments. It applies to all forms of writing – from essays to theses.

Method	Features	Advantages	Disadvantages
Harvard (Table 31.2)	• **Name/date** system used in the text (page number included only if making a reference to a specific quote or data) • Name of author can be included as part of the sentence (date in round brackets immediately after the name) *or* • Name and date both placed in round brackets at the end of the sentence	• Minimal typing: once-only entry in alphabetical order by author name in the reference list • Easy to identify contributors in a field from the citations shown in the text • Easy to make adjustments in the text and the reference list	• Name/date references can be intrusive in text • Not well-suited to citing archive material, e.g. historical documents, which may not have full details sufficient to comply with the system
Modern Languages Association (MLA) (Table 31.3)	• **Name/page** system in text; date at end of reference • Name of author can be included as part of the sentence (page number comes in brackets at the end of the sentence or clause) *or* • Name and page number(s) (no punctuation) both placed in brackets at the end of the sentence	• Minimal typing as details are printed only once in alphabetical order by author name in the reference list, which makes it easy to locate the source information • Easy to identify contributors in a field from the citations shown in the text	• Date of publication of source not in the text and not immediately evident in the reference list because of the position at the end of the reference • Indentation in 'follow-on' lines in the reference list can give a 'ragged' appearance to the layout of the reference list
Vancouver (Table 31.4)	• **Numerical** system with full-size numerals in brackets after the reported point • If another reference is made to a source in the text, the second and subsequent references use the number given to the reference when it was used for the first time	• Numbers are less intrusive in the text • Numbers are listed in numerical order at the end of the text, thus it is easy to locate the reference	• No bibliographical information in the text, thus difficult to gauge significance of the sources • Cumbersome to apply • Use of one number each time the source is used • Involves a considerable amount of checking and slows down the writing process
Chicago (Table 31.5)	• **Superscript numbers** used in the text • Relates superscript numbers to footnotes on the same page • Provides reference information in footnotes and reference list (note that the format differs between footnotes and reference list)	• Numbering system is unobtrusive and does not interrupt the flow of the text • Use of *op. cit.* and *ibid.* in the referencing saves retyping of bibliographical information	• First mention of a source gives full details, subsequent references give only name/page • More difficult to track the main contributors • Layout of footnote references differs from the bibliographical reference (if used) • Intensive checking to ensure that all superscript references are consistent after any changes

Academic convention requires you to give this information in order to:

- acknowledge the use of other people's work – you must demonstrate clearly where you have borrowed text or ideas from others; even if you cite an author's work in order to disagree with it, you have made use of their intellectual property and you must show that you recognise this (there is more discussion on intellectual property and plagiarism in **Ch 32**);

- help your readers understand how your argument/discussion was assembled and what influenced your thinking – this will help them form opinions about your work;

- help your reader/marker evaluate the extent of your reading. This may help them to assess your work and to advise you on further or more relevant reading;

- provide your readers with sufficient information to enable them to consult the source materials for themselves, if they wish.

In many cases, if you do not provide a reference list you will lose marks. This must be in your department's preferred style (Table 31.1).

→ **Using information within your text**

Essentially there are two means by which you can introduce the work of others into your text – by *quoting* exact words from a source, or by *citation*, which involves summarising or paraphrasing (**Ch 32**) the idea in your own words. For both, you need to indicate the source material following the chosen style of citation (Table 31.1).

Quotation in the text

There are two possibilities (see also **Ch 34**). If the quotation is a short quotation, the exact words are placed within single inverted commas within the sentence (e.g. xxxx 'zzzz zz zzzz zz zzzz' xxx). If you are using a longer quotation, usually 30 words or more, then no inverted commas are used. The status of the text as a quotation is indicated by the use of indentation (sometimes also by italicisation) where several lines quoted from another source are indented within your own text and in single-line spacing. If you deliberately miss out some words from the original, the 'gap' is represented by three dots. This is called ellipsis. For example:

xxxxxxxx xxxxx xxxxx xxxx xxx xx xxxxxxxxx xxxx xx xxxxx xx xx xxxx xxxxxx:

> . . . zzzz z zzzzzz zzzzzzz zzz zzzzzzz zzzz zz z zz zzzz z zzzz zz z zzzzzz zzzzzzzzz. zzz zz zzz zzzzzz zz zzzzzz zzz zzzz zzzzzz. zzzzzz, zzz zz zzz zzz zzz zzzzzz zz zzz zzzz.

(source)

xxxxxxx xxxx xxx xxxx xx xx xx xxxxxxxxx xxxxx xxxxxxx xxxxx xxxxxxxxxxxxxx.

Quoting within a quote: British and American English

The convention of British English is to use single inverted commas to cover the whole quotation and double inverted commas (quotation marks) for the quotation within the quotation. For example, 'xxxxxx "zzzz" xxx'. American English is the opposite.

→ How to cite the work in the text

There are essentially two ways in which to do this: the information-prominent and author-prominent methods. These depend on the style of referencing you have elected to follow. Four commonly used styles are laid out in Tables 31.2–31.5. The broad principles, following the Harvard method, are outlined below.

● **Information-prominent method.** Here the statement is regarded as being generally accepted within the field of study. For example:

   Children express an interest in books and pictures from an early age (Murphy, 1995).

● **Author-prominent method.** Here the author and date of publication form part of the construction of the sentence. This formulation can be used with appropriate reporting words (see cultural tip box) to reflect a viewpoint. For example:

   Murphy (1995) claimed that children as young as six months are able to follow a simple story sequence.

Footnotes and endnotes

In some disciplines, footnotes and endnotes, generally using superscript numbers, lead readers to the source information. However, in other disciplines, footnotes and endnotes are used simply to provide additional information, commentary or point of discussion about the content of the text. Footnotes generally appear at the bottom of the page where the link appears; endnotes are recorded in numerical order at the end of the body of the work.

Record all bibliographical details as a matter of routine. However you copy your notes – electronically, by photocopy or by writing – ensure that you record all the necessary bibliographical information, or you will waste time later on backtracking to find it.

Compile your reference list as you write. Keep a list of the works you have read. Simply create a table or list within your software package and type in the relevant details immediately you cite the source in the text. Doing this from time to time as you write saves you having to embark on a marathon of typing at the completion of the task (a table makes the formatting easier and allows easy insertion of additional records). You will need to make a decision about your choice of reference style (p. 254) at an early stage.

Don't mix referencing systems. Whichever style you use, make sure you follow its conventions to the letter, including all punctuation details. When no guidance is given, consult Table 31.1 to evaluate the possibilities.

Source quotations. If you note down a quotation speculatively for later use, make sure that you write down full reference details alongside it. Never rely on your memory for remembering reference details. Check everything and write it all down. This is important to avoid being accused of plagiarism (**Ch 32**).

Check the detail. Allow plenty of time for final checking, especially consistency of layout.

---

i

Different reference styles

Styles of citing and listing references have evolved as technology and preferences have altered. Thus, some have followed conventions using name/date, name/page, and numerical notation to cite sources within text. These different approaches reflect different conventions in the layout of the corresponding reference or bibliography lists. Styles have been dictated by disciplines and their associated research journals and this has led to modifications that create many variants of the original formats. Other styles, such as the American Psychological Association (APA) and the Modern Humanities Research Association (MRHA) used for literature and language, are extremely prescriptive. Their respective style guides extend the requirements to include a wide variety of features including such aspects as font, page layout, spelling, the use of active in preference to passive voice and much more.

The following tables illustrate four of the more commonly used styles:

- Harvard (Table 31.2, pp. 258-9);
- Modern Languages Association (Table 31.3, pp. 260-1);
- Vancouver (Table 31.4, pp. 262-3);
- Chicago (Table 31.5, pp. 264-5).

Table 31.2(a) Outline of the Harvard style for citing references. This referencing system has the advantage of being simpler, quicker and possibly more readily adjustable than other systems. It is used internationally in a wide range of fields and provides author and date information in the text. Note that there are various interpretations of the style. This one generally follows the British Standard, BS5605:1990.

How to cite the reference in the text	How to lay out the reference list or bibliography
The cause of European integration has been further hampered by the conflict between competing interests in a range of economic activities (Roche, 1993). However, Hobart and Lyon (2002) have argued that this is a symptom of a wider disharmony which has its roots in socio-economic divisions arising from differing cultural attitudes towards the concept of the market economy. Morrison *et al.* (2001) have identified 'black market' economic activity in post-reunification Germany as one which exemplified this most markedly. Scott (2004) suggests that the black economy which existed prior to reunification operated on strong market economy principles. However, Main (2003 cited in Kay, 2004) has supported the view that black market economies are not culture dependent. Statistics presented by Johannes (2000) suggest that, in the UK, as many as 23 per cent of the population are engaged at any one time in the black economy. European-wide statistics indicate that figures for participation in the black economy may be as high as 30 per cent (Brandt, 2001).	Brandt, K.-H., 2001. *Working the system* [online]. Available from: http://www.hvn.ac.uk/econ/trickco.htm [accessed 1.4.01]. *Ferry Times*, 1999. Where the money moves. *Ferry Times*, 12 April, p. 24. Hobart, K. and Lyon, A., 2002. *Socio-economic divisions: the cultural impact*. London: Thames Press. Johannes, B., 2000. Functional economics. In M. Edouard ed., *The naked economy*. Cologne: Rhein Verlag, 2000, pp. 120–30. Kay, W., 2004. *The power of Europe*. Dover: Kentish Press. Morrison, F., Drake, C., Brunswick, M. and Mackenzie, V., 2001. *Europe of the nations*. Edinburgh: Lothian Press. Roche, P., 1993. *European economic integration*. London: Amazon Press. Saunders, C., ed., 1996. *The economics of reality*. Dublin: Shamrock Press. Scott, R., 2004. Informal integration: the case of the non-monitored economy. *Journal of European Integration Studies*, 3 (2), pp. 81–9.
Quotations in the text	
The movement of money within the so-called black economy is regarded by Finance Ministers in Europe as 'a success story they could emulate' (*Ferry Times*, 12.4.99). According to Saunders (1996, p. 82), 'black economies build businesses'.	

Table 31.2(b) How to list different types of source following the Harvard style

Type of source material	Basic format: author surname | author initial | date | title | place of publication | publisher
Book by one author	Roche, P., 1993. *European economic integration*. London: Amazon Press.
Book by two authors	Hobart, K. and Lyon, A., 2002. *Socio-economic divisions: the cultural impact*. London: Thames Press.
Book with more than three authors	Morrison, F., Drake, C., Brunswick, M. and Mackenzie, V., 2001. *Europe of the nations*. Edinburgh: Lothian Press.
Book under editorship	Saunders, C., ed., 1996. *The economics of reality*. Dublin: Shamrock Press.
Chapter in a book	Johannes, B., 2000. Functional economics. In M. Edouard ed., *The naked economy*. Cologne: Rhein Verlag, 2000, 120–30.
Secondary referencing – where the original text is not available and the reference relates to a citation in a text that you have read, then refer to the latter	Kay, W., 2004. *The power of Europe*. Dover: Kentish Press.
Journal article	Scott, R., 2004. Informal integration: the case of the non-monitored economy. *Journal of European Integration Studies*, 3 (2), 81–9.
Newspaper article	*Ferry Times*, 1999. Where the money moves. *Ferry Times*, 12 April, p. 24.
Internet references including e-books	Brandt, K.-H. 2001. *Working the system* [online]. Available from: http://www.hvn.ac.uk/econ/trickco.htm [accessed 1.4.01].
Internet references: e-journals	Ross, F., 2000. Coping with dementia. *Geriatric Medicine* [online], 5 (14). Available from: http://germed.ac.ic/archive00000555/[accessed 11.01.04].

Notes:
- In this version of the Harvard style only the first word of a title is capitalised. With the exception of proper nouns, other words are in lower case. Each entry is separated by a double line space.
- If you need to cite two (or more) pieces of work published within the same year by the same author, then the convention is to refer to these texts as 2005a, 2005b and so on.
- In some interpretations of this style the first line of every entry is indented five character spaces from the left margin. However, this can create an untidy page where it is difficult to identify the author quickly.
- Titles of books and journals are italicised.
- The first date in the internet citation is the date of publication, *if available*. Thus, the 'last accessed' date as shown in the second internet reference example will always be the same or later than the published date, never earlier.

Table 31.3(a) Outline of the Modern Languages Association (MLA) style for citing references. This style provides author and page information in the text, but no date is included, only the page number(s).

How to cite the reference in the text	How to lay out the reference list or bibliography
The cause of European integration has been further hampered by the conflict between competing interests in a range of economic activities (Roche 180). However, Hobart and Lyon have argued that this is a symptom of a wider disharmony which has its roots in socio-economic divisions arising from differing cultural attitudes towards the concept of the market economy (101). Morrison *et al.* have identified 'black market' economic activity in post-reunification Germany as one which exemplified this most markedly (99–101). Scott suggests that the black economy which existed prior to reunification operated on strong market economy principles (83). However, Main has supported the view that black market economies are not culture dependent (cited in Kay 74). Statistics presented by Johannes suggest that, in the UK, as many as 23 per cent of the population are engaged at any one time as part of the black economy (121). European-wide statistics indicate that figures for participation in the black economy may be as high as 30 per cent (Brandt 12).	Brandt, K.-H. 'Working the System.' 31 December 2000. 1 April 2001. <http://www.hvn.ac.uk/econ/trickco.htm> Hobart, K. and A. Lyon, *Socio-economic Divisions: the cultural impact*. London: Thames Press, 2002. Johannes, B. 'Functional Economics.' *The Naked Economy*. M. Edouard. Cologne: Rhein Verlag, 2000: 120–30. Kay, W. *The Power of Europe*. Dover: Kentish Press, 2004. Morrison, F., *et al. Europe of the Nations*. Edinburgh: Lothian Press, 2001. Roche, P. *European Economic Integration*. London: Amazon Press, 1993. Saunders, C. ed. *The Economics of Reality*. Dublin: Shamrock Press, 1996. Scott, R. 'Informal Integration: the case of the non-monitored economy.' *Journal of European Integration Studies* 2 (2004): 81–9. 'Where the money moves.' *Ferry Times* 12 April 1999: 24.

Quotations in the text

The movement of money within the so-called black economy is regarded by Finance Ministers in Europe as 'a success story they could emulate' (*Ferry Times* 24).

Some commentators appear to give approval to non-conventional economic activity: 'black economies build businesses' (Saunders 82).

Long quotatations (normally more than four typed lines should be presented as indented text without quotation marks, that is, 2.5 cms from left margin and printed using **double line spacing**.

Table 31.3(b) How to list different types of source following the Modern Languages Association (MLA) style

Type of source material	Basic format: author surname | author initial | title | place of publication | publisher | date |
Book by one author	Roche, P. *European Economic Integration*. London: Amazon Press, 1993.
Book by two authors	Hobart, K. and Lyon, A. *Socio-economic Divisions: the cultural impact*. London: Thames Press, 2002.
Book with more than three authors	Morrison, F. *et al. Europe of the Nations*. Edinburgh: Lothian Press, 2001.
Book under editorship	Saunders, C. (ed.) *The Economics of Reality*. Dublin: Shamrock Press, 1996.
Chapter in a book	Johannes, B. 'Functional Economics.' *The Naked Economy*. M. Edouard. Cologne: Rhein Press, 2000: 120–30.
Secondary referencing – where the original text is not available and the reference relates to a citation in a text that you have read. This is the secondary source and is the one that you should cite in your reference list	Kay, W. *The Power of Europe*. Dover: Kentish Press, 2004.
Journal article	Scott, R. 'Informal Integration: the case of the non-monitored economy.' *Journal of European Integration Studies* 2 (2004): 81–9.
Newspaper article	'Where the money moves.' *Ferry Times* 12 April 1999: 24.
Internet reference	Brandt, K.-H. 'Working the System.' 31 December 2000. 1 April 2001. <http://www.hvn.ac.uk/econ/trickco.htm>

Notes:
- Successive lines for the same entry are indented by five character spaces.
- If two (or more) pieces of work published within the same year by the same author are cited, refer to these texts as 1999a, 1999b and so on.
- In some interpretations titles are *underlined* rather than *italicised*.

Table 31.4(a) Outline of the Vancouver style (numeric) for citing references.
This system is widely used in Medicine and the Life Sciences, for example. In the text, numbers are positioned in brackets, that is, like this (1). These numbers relate to corresponding numbered references in the reference list. This style has the advantage of not interrupting the text with citation information. However, this means that the reader cannot readily identify the source without referring to the reference list. The Vancouver style resembles in some ways the style adopted by the Institute of Electrical and Electronic Engineers (IEEE).

How to cite the reference in the text	How to lay out the reference list or bibliography
The cause of European integration has been further hampered by the conflict between competing interests in a range of economic activities (1). However, Hobart and Lyon (2) have argued that this is a symptom of a wider disharmony which has its roots in socio-economic divisions arising from differing cultural attitudes towards the concept of the market economy. Morrison *et al.* (3) have identified 'black market' economic activity in post-reunification Germany as one which exemplified this most markedly. Scott (4) suggests that the black economy which existed prior to reunification operated on strong market economy principles. However, Kay (5) has supported the view of Main that black market economies are not culture dependent. Statistics presented by Johannes (6) suggest that, in the UK, as many as 23 per cent of the population are engaged at any one time as part of the black economy. European-wide statistics indicate that figures for participation in the black economy may be as high as 30 per cent (7).	1 Roche P. European Economic Integration. London: Amazon Press; 1993. 2 Hobart K. and Lyon A. Socio-economic Divisions: the cultural impact. London: Thames Press; 2002. 3 Morrison F., Drake C., Brunswick M. and Mackenzie V. Europe of the Nations. Edinburgh: Lothian Press; 2001. 4 Scott R. Informal Integration: the case of the non-monitored economy. Journal of European Integration Studies. 2004; 2, 81-9. 5 Kay W. The Power of Europe. Dover: Kentish Press; 2004. 6 Johannes B. Functional Economics. In Edouard M. The Naked Economy. Cologne: Rhein Verlag; 2000; pp. 120-30. 7 Brandt K.-H. Working the System. 2000 [cited 1 April 2001]. Available from: http://www.hvn.ac.uk/econ/trickco.htm. 8 Where the money moves. Ferry Times. 12 April 1999; 24. 9 Saunders C. editor. The Economics of Reality. Dublin: Shamrock Press; 1996.
Quotations in the text	
The movement of money within the so-called black economy is regarded by Finance Ministers in Europe as 'a success story they could emulate' (8). According to Saunders, 'black economies build businesses' (9).	

Table 31.4(b) How to list different types of source following the Vancouver style

Type of source material	Basic format: author surname | author initial | title | place of publication | publisher | date
Book by one author	Roche P. European economic integration. London: Amazon Press; 1993.
Book by two authors	Hobart K. and Lyon A. Socio-economic divisions: the cultural impact. London: Thames Press; 2002.
Book with more than three authors	Morrison F., Drake C., Brunswick M. and Mackenzie V. Europe of the nations. Edinburgh: Lothian Press; 2001.
Book under editorship	Saunders C. editor. The economics of reality. Dublin: Shamrock Press; 1996.
Chapter in a book	Johannes B. Functional economics. In Edouard, M. The naked economy. Cologne: Rhein Verlag; 2000; pp. 120-30.
Secondary referencing – where the original text is not available and the reference relates to a citation in a text that you have read. This is the secondary source, which is the one you cite	Kay W. The power of europe. Dover: Kentish Press; 2004.
Journal article	Scott R. Informal integration: the case of the non-monitored economy. Journal of European Integration Studies. 2004; 2, 81-9.
Newspaper article	Where the money moves. Ferry Times. 12 April 1999; 24.
Internet reference	Brandt K.-H. Working the system. 2000 [cited 1 April 2001]. Available from: http://www.hvn.ac.uk/econ/trickco.htm.

Notes:

- If two (or more) pieces of work published within the same year by the same author are cited, refer to these texts as 1999a, 1999b and so on.
- In some interpretations of this style, superscript numbers[8] are used instead of the full-size number in brackets (8) shown in the example in Table 36.4(a).
- In this system, titles are <u>not</u> italicised and only initial letter of first word is capitalised, unless a proper noun is used in the title.
- If a source is repeated, the number reference is reused for each occurrence of the repetition, regardless of its previous position in the text.

Table 31.5(a) Outline of the Chicago style (scientific) for citing references. This is a footnote style of referencing that enables the reader to see the full bibliographical information on the first page the reference is made. However, subsequent references of the same source do not give the same detail. If the full bibliographical information is not given in the footnote for some reason, a full bibliography is given at the end of the work. To save space here, this example has been laid out in single-line spacing. The *Chicago Manual of Style* (2003) stipulates double-space throughout – texts, notes and bibliography.

How to cite the reference in the text	Quotations in the text
The cause of European integration has been further hampered by the conflict between competing interests in a range of economic activities.[1] However, Hobart and Lyon[2] have argued that this is a symptom of a wider disharmony which has its roots in socio-economic divisions arising from differing cultural attitudes towards the concept of the market economy. Morrison et al.[3] have identified 'black market' economic activity in post-reunification Germany as one which exemplified this most markedly. Scott[4] suggests, however, that the black economy which existed prior to reunification operated on strong market economy principles, while Main[5] has supported the view that black market economies are not culture dependent. Statistics presented by Johannes[6] suggest that as many as 23 per cent of the population are engaged at any one time as part of the black economy. This does not support the findings of Hobart and Lyon,[7] but it has been suggested by Scott[8] that this is probably an exaggerated statistic which it is impossible to verify. Scott[9] estimates a more modest 10 per cent of people of working age are actively involved in the black economy. Brandt[10] has conducted research into the phenomenon of the black economies of Europe but has been unable to confirm such estimates.	The movement of money within the so-called black economy is regarded by Finance Ministers in Europe as 'a success story they could emulate'.[11]

According to Saunders, 'black economies build businesses'.[12]

[11] 'Where the money moves.' *Ferry Times*, 12 April 1999, 24.
[12] C. Saunders, (ed.) *The Economics of Reality* (Dublin: Shamrock Press, 1996), 82. |
| | **How to lay out the reference list or bibliography (note that layout differs for the footnotes)** |
| | Brandt, K.-H. 'Working the System.' Available from http://www.hvn.ac.uk/econ/trickco.htm (1.4.01).
Hobart, K. and Lyon, A., *Socio-economic Divisions: The Cultural Impact*. London: Thames Press, 2002.
Johannes, B. 'Functional Economics' in *The Naked Economy*, by M. Edouard, 120–30. Cologne: Rhein Verlag, 2000.
Main, K. *Power, Politics and People*. Plymouth: Maritime Press Co., 2003, quoted in W. Kay, *The Power of Europe*. Dover: Kentish Press, 2004.
Morrison, F., et al. *Europe of the Nations*. Edinburgh: Lothian Press, 2001.
Roche, P. *European Economic Integration*. London: Amazon Press, 1993.
Saunders, C., ed. *The Economics of Reality*. Dublin: Shamrock Press, 1996.
Scott, R. 'Informal Integration: the case of the non-monitored economy.' *Journal of European Integration Studies 2*, (2004), 81–9.
'Where the money moves.' *Ferry Times*, 12 April 1999, 24. |

[1] P. Roche, *European Economic Integration* (London: Amazon Press, 1993), 180.
[2] K. Hobart, and A. Lyon, *Socio-economic Divisions: The Cultural Impact* (London: Thames Press, 2002), 101.
[3] F. Morrison, C. Drake, M. Brunswick, and V. Mackenzie, *Europe of the Nations* (Edinburgh: Lothian Press, 2001), 99.
[4] R. Scott, 'Informal Integration: the case of the non-monitored economy,' Journal of European Integration Studies, 2 (2004): 81.
[5] K. Main, *Power, Politics and People* (Plymouth: Maritime Press Co., 2003), 74, quoted in W. Kay, *The Power of Europe* (Dover: Kentish Press, 2004) 89.
[6] B. Johannes, 'Functional Economics' in *The Naked Economy*, M. Edouard, 121 (Cologne: Rhein Verlag, 2000).
[7] Hobart and Lyon *op. cit.*, 102.
[8] Scott, *op. cit.*, 83
[9] *Ibid.*
[10] K.-H. Brandt, 'Working the System.' http://www.hvn.ac.uk/econ/trickco.htm (1.4.01).

Table 31.1 ... (Citing and listing references)

The Chicago style uses footnote style referencing. Below, on the left, are the references as these would appear in the footnotes. On the right are the same references as they would appeal in a *Reference List* using the Chicago style.

Type of source material	Basic footnote format: author initial | author surname | title | (place of publication | publisher | date) | page number	Basic reference list format: author surname | author initial | date | title | place of publication | publisher
Book by one author	P. Roche, *European Economic Integration* (London: Amazon Press, 1993), 180.	Roche, P. 1993. *European Economic Integration.* London: Amazon Press.
Book by two authors	K. Hobart, and A. Lyon, *Socio-economic Divisions: the cultural impact* (London: Thames Press, 1992), 101.	Hobart, K. and A. Lyon. 1992. *Socio-economic Divisions: the cultural impact.* London: Thames Press.
Book with more than three authors	F. Morrison et al., *Europe of the Nations.* (Edinburgh: Lothian Press, 1997), 99.	Morrison, F., C. Drake, M. Brunswick, and V. Mackenzie. 1997. *Europe of the Nations* Edinburgh: Lothian Press.
Book under editorship	C. Saunders, (ed.) *The Economics of Reality* (Dublin: Shamrock Press, 1996), 82.	Saunders, C. (ed.) 1996. *The Economics of Reality.* Dublin: Shamrock Press.
Chapter in a book	B. Johannes, 'Functional Economics.' In M. Edouard *The Naked Economy* (Cologne: Rhein Verlag, 1998), 121.	Johannes, B. 1998. 'Functional Economics.' In *The Naked Economy*, M. Edouard 121-128. Cologne: Rhein Verlag.
Secondary referencing – where the original text is not available and the reference relates to a citation in a text which you have read.	Main, K. *Power, Politics and People.* (Plymouth: Maritime Press Co., 2003), quoted in W. Kay, *The Power of Europe.* (Dover: Kentish Press, 2004).	Main, K. 2003. *Power, Politics and People.* Plymouth: Maritime Press Co. Quoted in Kay, W. 2004. *The Power of Europe.* Dover: Kentish Press.
Journal article	R. Scott, 'Informal Integration: the case of the non-monitored economy,' *Journal of European Integration Studies,* 2 (1998), 81.	Scott, R. 1998. Informal Integration: the case of the non-monitored economy. *Journal of European Integration Studies* 2: 81.
Newspaper article	Craig L. Scott, 'Where the money moves,' *Ferry Times,* April 12, 1999, Financial section.	Scott, C. L. 1999. 'Where the money moves.' *Ferry Times,* April 12, Financial section.
Internet journal reference	K.-H. Brandt, 'Working the System,' *Journal of Social and Economic Policy* 36, no 3 (1999), http://www.hvn.ac.uk/econ/trickco.htm.	Brandt, K.-H. 'Working the System.' *Journal of Social and Economic Policy* 36, no 3 (August 20), http://www.hvn.ac.uk/econ/trickco.htm (accessed April 12, 2004).

Notes:
- Uses superscript numbers or full-size numbers within brackets in the text ordered consecutively. These relate to a footnote on the same page as the reference.
- Where references are repeated, then a new number is assigned each time it occurs in the text. Place the number **after a punctuation mark**.
- If you need to cite two (or more) pieces of work published within the same year by the same author, refer to these texts as 1999a, 1999b and so on.
- Some abbreviations are used in this style. They are printed in italics, because these are Latin. The most commonly used are *op. cit.* (in the work already cited) and *ibid.* (in the same place – usually in the same place as the last fully cited reference.) Thus, in the example above [9] relates to [8] which, in turn, relates to [4]
- In the footnotes the author's first name or initial precedes the surname.
- Second or further lines in the Reference or Bibliography list should be indented five character spaces.
- For secondary referencing, when compiling the reference list, cite both articles – the original source and the one that contained the reference, that is, the source you read.

Context: you may wish to address these questions to a lecturer or a librarian respectively.

Are we supposed to use Harvard or Vancouver style for our references in this exercise, or do we have a free choice?

I've lost the reference details for a paper I have read which I know is by [name author(s)], published in [year]. I think it was published in [journal], perhaps in the period 2001-2005. Can you help me find the full reference, please?

GO And now . . .

31.1 Identify the recommended referencing style for your subjects. These may differ from one discipline to another; one tutor to another. Go through your module handbooks and see what has been stated and how practices differ. Note that some subjects such as Law, History and English Literature often use specialised methods of citation and referencing. You will normally be given tuition in how to follow these practices. If no explicit information is given, analyse the way in which the list of books on your reading lists has been printed. If you compare this with the examples in Tables 31.2–31.5, you may be able to identify the style by name.

31.2 Look at textbooks or journal articles in your subject area to identify any deviations from the 'standard' referencing styles given in this chapter. You may find that in your field some modifications have been made to one of the styles outlined in this book. Discuss these modifications with a tutor in your department if you are unsure about which interpretation of a style you should follow.

31.3 Look at textbooks or journal articles in your subject area to identify which style is appropriate for quotations. Identify whether making direct quotations is common. In many academic areas, quotation from sources would be rare, and you need to be aware of this.

How to avoid being accused of 'stealing' the ideas and work of others

Many international students have only a vague understanding of plagiarism and copyright issues. However, failing to take account of them means you may risk serious disciplinary action.

Key topics:
→ What is plagiarism?
→ Strategies to ensure that you avoid plagiarism
→ How to paraphrase
→ Examples of summarising and paraphrasing
→ What is copyright infringement?

Essential vocabulary
**Copyright Paraphrasing Plagiarism Quoting Summarising Synonym
Verbatim**

Plagiarism and copyright infringement are two related topics that are extremely important academically and legally, but which are often misunderstood by international students. The use of digital scanners, photocopiers and electronic file exchange have made it simple to 'cut and paste' and copy materials. This means it is easier to commit the offence of plagiarism unknowingly. You need to be fully aware of the issues involved so you can acknowledge an author's copyright of their intellectual property appropriately and therefore avoid losing marks or being involved in further disciplinary action.

→ What is plagiarism?

Plagiarism can be defined as: 'the unacknowledged use of another's work as if it were one's own' (University of Dundee, 2005).

Hence, plagiarism is something to be avoided, and it is assumed that no one would deliberately set out to cheat in this way. The problem is that it is easy to plagiarise unwittingly. Regarding such 'unintentional plagiarism', you should note the following:

● The concept of 'work' in the definition of plagiarism given above includes ideas, writing or inventions, and not simply words.

● The notion of 'use' in the definition does not only mean 'word for word' (an exact copy) but also 'in substance' (a paraphrase of the notions involved).

Plagiarism and penalties

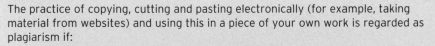

Alongside other forms of academic dishonesty, universities regard intentional plagiarism as a very serious offence. The regulations normally prescribe a range of penalties depending on the severity of the case, from a simple reduction in marks, to the ultimate sanctions of exclusion from the university or refusal to award a degree. You will find the exact penalties for your institution specified in departmental or school handbooks.

Copying an essay or other piece of work by a fellow student (past or present) is regarded as cheating. The penalty is often an assessment mark of zero *for both parties*, and further disciplinary measures may be taken. If you let someone copy your work, you are regarded as just as culpable as the 'real' cheat – so consider the risk to your academic future if you misguidedly allow someone to copy your work.

Similarly, buying an essay from the internet and presenting it as your own is also regarded as academic plagiarism.

Copying, cutting and pasting

The practice of copying, cutting and pasting electronically (for example, taking material from websites) and using this in a piece of your own work is regarded as plagiarism if:

- you do not cite the source and so imply that the ideas are your own; or
- you do cite the source material but use so much direct quotation that there is very little in the remainder of the work that is your own; or
- you use the material without citation but amending it by changing some words in the original (that is, not paraphrasing appropriately).

If plagiarism is detected, the author of the plagiarised submission will be penalised. This can be a difficult thing for international students since paraphrasing and summarising is dependent on having a fairly extensive vocabulary from which to draw. The guidance in this chapter provides several strategies that will help you to meet this challenge.

How universities identify plagiarism

Apart from your lecturers' sharp eyes, memory and in-depth knowledge of the material as they mark class assignments, there are other ways in which universities can detect where plagiarism might have occurred. These involve the use of technologies such as *Turnitin*™ which scrutinises word-processed submissions and highlights text that is potentially copied. Note that output of these programmes would always be moderated by a member of staff. In some cases, schools/departments may give access to these technical aids to students to help them recognise and understand what is acceptable use of the work of others.

Use of another's work *is* acceptable, *if* you acknowledge the source.

Once you have identified the source material that you wish to use in your assignment, the next step is to identify the function that the citations related to this material will perform in your work. For example, you will need to ask yourself whether the text you wish to cite endorses an idea, contradicts it or is neutral. In some cases you will need to make a decision about how you will incorporate the ideas from your source material within your own text. There are essentially three options:

- Quoting: where you think a particular author has said something particularly well, you can quote them directly *and* provide a reference to the relevant article or book beside the quote (**Ch 31**).

- Summarising: where you choose to provide an overview of the source material in general terms using your own works.

- Paraphrasing: where you condense the ideas from the source material in your own words but providing more detail than in summarising.

Characteristics of these methods of using sources are shown below in Table 32.1.

Table 32.1 Characteristics that typify quoting, summarising and paraphrasing

	Characteristics

For quotation (see **Ch 31**)	• 'short' quotes – include within the sentence in the text
	• 'long quotes' (usually 30+ or 40+ words) in some style guides require to be indented; in others they may also be italicised.
	• Punctuation shows direct quotation from original text
	  – Single quotation marks (British English)
	  – Double quotation marks (American English)
	  – Citation of the quoted source follows a standard form as shown in Tables 31.2a – 31.5b

For summarising	• Broad overview, briefly stating the main points from the original • Less detailed than a paraphrase • Ideas expressed using your own words • Technical terms can be retained, but otherwise ideas are expressed using different sentence structure and vocabulary
For paraphrasing	• Broad theme condensed from the original • More detailed than a summary • Ideas expressed using your own words • Technical terms can be retained but otherwise ideas are expressed using different sentence structure and vocabulary

How much quotation is acceptable?

Too much quotation is regarded as plagiarism, even if all the source information is provided. Aim to limit use of quotation to 10 per cent of the total work as an absolute maximum. In many cases the proportion will be well below the threshold.

→ How to paraphrase

1 Read the text to establish overall meaning; it may help to use the speed-reading strategy of reading *topic sentences* first of all to gain this overview (see **Ch 24**).

2 Turn over the text and note down key ideas.

3 Re-read the text intensively for greater detail.

4 Turn over the text and, from memory, note points that support the key ideas. This encourages you to use your own words and makes you less dependent on words from the text.

5 Note how you intend to use these ideas in your work.

6 Record bibliographical details for your reference list (see **Ch 31**).

Sometimes it is helpful when constructing paraphrased text to begin with the concluding idea of the text and work through the key ideas from that perspective, rather than in the logic sequence of the original. In this way you are less likely to lapse into the pitfalls of word substitution or over-quotation.

---

smart tip

Whatever the layout conventions of the citation and referencing style you are expected to adopt (**Ch 31**), to quote, summarise or paraphrase you will require the following information:

- Author(s)
- Place of publication
- Date
- Publisher
- Title
- Page number(s).

→ Examples of summarising and paraphrasing

The excerpt of original text in Table 32.2 represents material that a student might wish to use in relation to an assignment on the relative merits of e-books and traditional bound volumes. The table demonstrates poor models of summarising and paraphrasing, explains what is wrong and provides a good model of each.

---

smart tip

Avoid a word substitution exercise when citing the work of others either in summarising or in paraphrasing; this is plagiarism. You need to show that you have engaged in a critical analysis of the material and demonstrate this by using the citation material to good effect in structuring your discussion. In the good models shown in Table 32.2, the writer has processed the ideas from the original text and presented them in a fresh manner, demonstrating engagement with the meaning of the original text and hence independent thinking.

Table 32.2 Examples of summarising and paraphrasing

Original text:
E-books are a function of the internet era and make access to otherwise unattainable material possible to wide audiences. The globalisation of literature means that individual authors can present their work to a wider audience without incurring abortive publication costs. This facility constitutes a considerable threat to publishers of traditional books.
Source: Watt, W. (2006) *The demise of the book*. Dundee: Riverside Press. (p. 13)

Summarising

Poor model of summarising	Explanation	Good model of summarising
It has been suggested that '**e-books are a function of the internet era**' and that '**globalisation of literature**' allows authors to '**present their work to a wider audience**' without having to incur '**abortive publication costs**'.	*In this example, direct quotation (shown in bold) comprises 60 per cent of the total word count – this is excessive and could be regarded as a form of plagiarism. This fault is compounded because the writer has failed to give the source of the quotations.*	With the advent of e-books, individual authors are faced with new approaches to publication of their work (Watt, 2006).

Paraphrasing

Poor model	Explanation	Good model
E-books are part of the internet *age* and allow people from all over the *globe* to use them. This *means that writers show* their *writing* on the internet and so they *do not have such high publishing costs*. This *feature* means that *publishers of old-fashioned books* are *under threat* (Watt, 2006).	*In this example, use of synonyms (underlined) in a superficial manner constitutes another form of plagiarism. Despite correctly citing the source, the writer has simply 'stolen' the essential meaning without engaging in any analysis or original thinking.*	Watt (2006) notes that there is concern amongst publishers of hard-copy printed books that the advent of e-books marks the end of their monopoly of the literature market, since authors can publish directly on the internet, thus avoiding publishing costs.

→ What is copyright infringement?

Copyright law 'allows you to protect your original material and stop others from using your work without your permission' (Intellectual Property Office, 2009). Copyright infringement is regarded as equivalent to stealing, and legal rights are sometimes jealously guarded by companies with the resources to prosecute.

In the UK, authors have literary copyright over their material for their life, and their estate has copyright for a further 70 years. Publishers have typographical copyright for 25 years. This is why the copyright symbol © is usually accompanied by a date and the owner's name. You'll find this information on the publication details page at the start of a book.

Use of the copyright logo

The © symbol indicates that someone is drawing your attention to the fact that something is copyright. However, even if © does not appear, the material may still be copyright.

You will be at risk of breaking UK law if you copy (for example, photocopy, digitally scan or print out) material to which someone else owns the copyright, unless you have their express permission, or unless the amount you copy falls within the limits accepted for 'fair dealing'.

'Educational copying', *for non-commercial private study or research*, is sometimes allowed by publishers (they will state this on the material, and may allow multiple copies to be made). Otherwise, for single copies *for private study or research*, you should only copy what would fall under the 'fair dealing' provision, for which there is no precise definition in law.

Established practice suggests that you should photocopy copy no more than 5 per cent of the work involved, or:

● one chapter of a book;

● one article per volume of an academic journal;

● 20 per cent (to a maximum of 20 pages) of a short book;

● one poem or short story (maximum of 10 pages) from an anthology;

● one separate illustration or map up to A4 size (note: illustrations that are parts of articles and chapters may be included in the allowances noted above);

● short excerpts of musical works – not whole works or movements (note: copying of any kind of public performance is not allowed without permission).

These limits apply to single copies – you can't take multiple copies of any of the above items, nor pass on a single copy for multiple copying to someone else, who may be in ignorance of the source or of specific or general copyright issues.

In legal terms, it doesn't matter whether you paid for the source or not: copyright is infringed when the whole or a substantial part is copied without permission – and 'substantial' here can mean a qualitatively significant section even if this is a small part of the whole.

The same rules apply to printing or copying material on the web unless the author gives explicit (that is, written) clearance. This applies to copying images as well as text from the internet, although a number of sites do offer copyright-free images. A statement on the author's position on copying may appear on the home page or a page linked directly from it.

---

smart tip

Approved copyright exceptions

Some copying for academic purposes may be licensed by the Copyright Licensing Agency (CLA) on behalf of authors. Other electronically distributed material may be licensed through various schemes. In these cases you may be able to copy or print out more than the amounts listed opposite, including multiple copies. Your university may also 'buy in' to licensing schemes, such as those offered by the NLA (Newspaper Licensing Agency) and the Performing Rights Society. As these can refer to very specific sources, consult your library's staff if in doubt.

Private study or research

This means what it says: the limits discussed here apply to that use and not to commercial or other uses, such as photocopying an amusing article for your friends. Copying of software and music CDs (including 'sharing' of MP3 files) is most often illegal, although you are usually permitted to make a *personal* back-up copy of a track or CD you already own.

Complexity of copyright law

Note that the material in this chapter is a summary of some basic aspects of a complex body of UK law, and much may depend on individual circumstances.

✔ Practical tips for avoiding plagiarism

Avoid copying material by electronic means. You may only do this if you are prepared to quote the source. If you use the material in your work, and fail to add an appropriate citation, this would be regarded as cheating.

When making notes, always write down your sources. You may risk plagiarising if you cannot recall or find the source of a piece of text. Avoid this by getting into the habit of making a careful note of the source on the same piece of paper that you used to summarise or copy it out. Always use quote marks ('...') when taking such notes verbatim from texts and other materials, to indicate that what you have written down is a *direct copy* of the words used, as you may forget this at a later time. You do not need to quote directly in the final version of your work, but if you paraphrase you should still cite the source.

Try not to paraphrase another person's work too closely. Taking key phrases and rearranging them, or merely substituting some words with synonyms is still regarded as plagiarism.

Follow the academic custom of quoting sources. You should do this even if you prefer to use your own wording rather than a direct copy of the original. The reference to the source signifies that you are making that statement on the basis of the ideas reported there. If you are unclear about the different methods of mentioning sources and constructing a reference list, consult **Ch 31**.

Avoid overuse of quotations. Plagiarism still occurs if a considerable percentage of your assignment is comprised of quotations. In general, quotations should be used sparingly.

Double-check on your 'original' ideas. If you have what you think is a novel idea, do not simply accept that your brainwave is unique. It's common for people to forget the original source of an idea, which may resurface in their mind after many years and perhaps in a different context – this may have happened to you. Think carefully about possible sources that you may have forgotten about; ask others (such as your tutor or supervisor) whether they have come across the idea before; and consult relevant texts, encyclopaedias or the internet.

Useful language for . . . talking about plagiarism and copyright

Context: you may wish to use these examples when discussing a draft text with a tutor or supervisor, or when copying material in the library.

I plan to quote from [name author(s)]'s work quite a lot, but I don't want to overdo it. Please can you tell me how much quoting from the same author would be appropriate in this context?

I can't find a way of paraphrasing this idea – I'm afraid my English is limiting the way I can express the author's thoughts using other words. Could I ask for a little help with this, please?

I'd like to photocopy part of this book – Chapter xx to be precise. Can you tell me whether copying this much is allowed, please?

GO And now . . .

32.1 Double-check your department's (or university's) plagiarism policy. This should describe the precise situations in which you might break rules. It may also give useful information on the preferred methods for citing sources.

32.2 Next time you are in the library, read the documentation about photocopying which is often displayed beside the photocopiers. This material will provide detailed information about current legislation and any local exceptions.

32.3 Modify your note-taking technique. Highlight and put any direct transcriptions in quotes. Add full details of the source whenever you take notes from a textbook or paper source.

33 Reviewing, editing and proof-reading

How to make sure that your writing makes sense

Looking critically at your own writing is essential if you want to produce work of the highest quality. These editing skills will allow you to improve the sense, grammar and syntax of your written assignments.

Key topics:
→ The reviewing, editing and proof-reading process
→ Reviewing your answers in exams
→ The value of reviewing, editing and proof-reading

Essential vocabulary
Annotate   Expression   Justification   Skimping   Syntax   Typo

Writing is a process. It begins with a plan and it finishes with reviewing, editing and proof-reading. This means that you should read your text critically and edit it before submitting it for assessment. The effort you invest in this final stage will contribute to the quality of your work and to your assessed mark. Ideally, you should leave a gap of time between completing the writing and beginning the reviewing process, as this allows you to 'distance' yourself from the work and helps you look at it as a new reader would.

→ The reviewing, editing and proof-reading process

At this stage you are performing the role of editor. This means that you are looking critically at your text for content, relevance and sense, as well as for flaws in layout, grammar, punctuation and spelling. You should also check for consistency in all aspects, for example, in the use of terminology, in spelling, and in presentational features such as font and point size, page layout including margins (justification) and paragraph spacing, and labelling of tables and diagrams.

> **Definitions**
>
> **Reviewing:** appraising critically; that is, examining a task or project to ensure that it meets the requirements and objectives of the task and that the overall sense is conveyed as well.
>
> **Editing:** revising and correcting later drafts of an essay, to arrive at a final version. Usually, this involves the smaller rather than the larger details, such as details of punctuation, spelling, grammar and layout.
>
> **Proof-reading:** checking a printed copy for errors of any sort.

Clearly, there are many aspects to cover, and some degree of overlap in different aspects of the process. Some people prefer to go through their text in one sweep, amending any flaws as they go; others, in particular professional writers, take a staged approach, reading through their text several times looking at a different aspect each time. Here are five aspects to consider in the reviewing process:

1 content and relevance;
2 clarity, style and coherence;
3 grammatical correctness;
4 spelling and punctuation;
5 presentation.

Table 33.1 provides a quick checklist of key aspects to consider under each of these themes. This has been designed for photocopying so that you can, if you wish, use it as a checklist each time you complete a piece of work. Table 33.2 gives some strategies you can adopt when going through the editing process. Professional proof-readers have developed a system of symbols to speed up the editing and proof-reading process (see Table 33.3). You may wish to adopt some of these yourself, and you are likely to see some of them, and other 'informal' marks, on work returned by tutors.

→ Reviewing your answers in exams

In exams, the reviewing process has to be swift and efficient (**Ch 55**). Here, you will normally have time only to skim-read the text, making adjustments as you go. If you find you have missed something out, place an insert mark (Λ or λ) in the text and/or margin with your annotation, for example, 'see additional paragraph x'; then write this paragraph, clearly identified, at the end of the answer (where you will have left space for just this contingency). Similarly, if you have consistently made an error, for example, referred to Louis XIV throughout as Louis XVI, just put an asterisk beside the first occurrence of the error and a note at the end of your answer or in the margin 'Consistent error. Please read as "XIV"'. You will not lose any marks for correcting your work in these ways.

Technical notes

The word processor has made the reviewing and editing task much easier. Here are some tips for using this software effectively:

- Use the word-count facility to check on length.
- Use the 'View' facility to check page breaks and general layout before you print out.
- Don't rely entirely on the spell- and grammar checker.
- Sometimes the grammar checker will announce that you have used the passive voice. This is often a standard academic usage and, therefore, is not an error.
- Sometimes the spell-checker may accept a word because it exists but may be incorrect for your context. If you suspect this, check using a dictionary.
- Sometimes staff add comments to students' work using 'Tools/Track Changes' on the Microsoft Word software. Depending on the version you are using, feedback information can usually be accepted or rejected by right-clicking on the word or punctuation point that has been marked for alteration.

Table 33.1 **Proof-reading and editing checklists.** Each heading represents a 'sweep' of your text, checking for the aspects shown. The text is assumed to be a piece of writing produced for assessment. This table is copyright-free for use when reviewing your work.

Content and relevance	Clarity, style and coherence	Grammatical correctness	Spelling and punctuation	Presentation
☐ The intent of the instruction word has been followed (**Ch 28**)	☐ The aims and objectives are clear	☐ All sentences are complete	☐ Any blatant 'typos' have been corrected by reading for meaning	☐ The text length meets the word-count target – neither too short nor too long
☐ The question or task has been completed, that is, you have answered all sections or required numbers of questions (**Ch 28, Ch 29**)	☐ What you wrote is what you meant to write	☐ All sentences make sense	☐ The text has been spell-checked and looked at for your 'own' most often misspelled words	☐ If no word-count target is given, the overall length is as might be expected for the time you were supposed to allocate to the task (ask a tutor if uncertain)
☐ The structure is appropriate (**Ch 29, Ch 30**)	☐ The text is fluent, with appropriate use of signpost words	☐ Paragraphs have been correctly used	☐ A check has been made for spelling of subject-specific words and words from other languages	☐ Overall neatness checked
☐ The text shows objectivity (**Ch 27**)	☐ Any informal language has been removed	☐ Suggestions made by grammar checker have been accepted/rejected	☐ Punctuation has been checked, if possible, by the 'reading aloud' method (see p. 280)	☐ The cover-sheet details and presentation aspects are as required by your department (**Ch 24**)
☐ The examples are relevant	☐ The style is academic and appropriate for the task (**Ch 27**)	☐ The text has been checked against your own checklist of recurrent grammatical errors	☐ Proper names are correctly capitalised	☐ The bibliography/reference list is correctly formatted (**Ch 31**)
☐ All sources are correctly cited (**Ch 31**)	☐ The content and style of each section is consistent	☐ The text is consistent in adopting British or American English (**Ch 27**)	☐ Overlong sentences have been divided	☐ Page numbers have been included (in position stipulated, if given)
☐ The facts presented are accurate	☐ The tense used in each section is suited to the time-frame of your text and is consistent			☐ The figures and tables are in appropriate format (**Ch 29**)
	☐ The lengths of the text sections are balanced appropriately (**Ch 29**)			

Table 33.2 Editing strategies. The reviewing/editing/proof-reading process can be done in a single 'sweep'. As you become more experienced, you will become more adept at doing this. However, initially, it might help you to focus on each of these three broad aspects in a separate 'sweep' of the text. Note that the first two columns combine pairs of aspects considered in Table 33.1.

Content and relevance; clarity, style and coherence	Grammatical correctness, spelling and punctuation	Presentation
• Read text aloud – your ears will help you to identify errors that your eyes have missed. • Revisit the task or question. Check your interpretation against the task as set. • Work on a hard copy using editing symbols to correct errors (Table 33.3). • Identify that the aims you set out in your introduction have been met. • Read objectively and assess whether the text makes sense. Look for inconsistencies in argument. • Check that all your facts are correct. • Insert additional or overlooked evidence that strengthens the whole. • Remove anything that is not relevant or alter the text so that it is clear and unambiguous. Reducing text by 10–25 per cent can improve quality considerably. • Honestly and critically assess your material to ensure that you have attributed ideas to the sources, that is, check that you have not committed plagiarism (**Ch 32**). • Remodel any expressions that are too informal for academic contexts. • Eliminate gendered or discriminatory language.	• Check titles and subtitles are appropriate to the style of the work and stand out by using bold or underlining (not both). • Consider whether the different parts link together well – if not, introduce signpost words to guide the reader through the text. • Check for fluency in sentence and paragraph structure – remodel as required. • Check sentence length – remodel to shorter or longer sentences. Sometimes shorter sentences are more effective than longer ones. • Ensure that you have been consistent in spelling conventions, for example following British English rather than American English spelling. • Spelling errors – use the spellchecker but be prepared to double-check in a standard dictionary if you are in doubt or cannot find a spelling within the spellchecker facility. • Check for cumbersome constructions – divide or restructure sentence(s); consider whether active or passive is more suitable. Consider using vocabulary that might convey your point more eloquently. • Check for use of 'absolute' terms to ensure that you maintain objectivity (**Ch 27**).	• Check that you have made good use of white space, that is, not crammed the text into too tight a space, and that your text is neat and legible. • If word-processed, check that you have followed standard typing conventions (**Ch 34**). Follow any 'house style' rules stipulated by your department. • Check that you have included a reference list, consistently following a recognised method (**Ch 31**), and that all citations in the text are matched by an entry in the reference list and vice versa. • Ensure all pages are numbered and are stapled or clipped, and, if appropriate, ensure that the cover page is included. • Check that your name, matriculation number and course number are included. You may wish to add this information as a footnote that appears on each page. • Ensure question number and title are included. • Check that labelling of diagrams, charts and other visual material is in sequence and consistently presented. • Ensure that supporting material is added in sequence as appendices, footnotes, endnotes or as a glossary, as applicable.

Table 33.3 Common proof-reading symbols. University lecturers and tutors often use a variety of symbols on students' assignments to indicate errors, corrections or suggestions. These can apply to punctuation, spelling, presentation or grammar. The symbols provide a kind of 'shorthand' that acts as a code to help you see how you might be able to amend your text so that it reads correctly and fluently. In this table some of the more commonly used correction marks are shown alongside their meanings. The sample text shows how these symbols may be used either in the text or the margin to indicate where a change is recommended.

Correction mark	Meaning	Example
⌐ (np)	(new) paragraph	*Text* *margin*
≠	change CAPITALS to small letters (lower case)	The correction marks that ⌒ tutors ⌒
∼∼∼	change into **bold** type	use in students' texts are generally ⋎
≡	change into CAPITALS	made to help identify where there
⌒	close up (delete space)	have been errors of spllin or ⋌e/⋌g
/ or ⁊ or ⊢	delete	punctuation. They can often (STET)
⋌	insert a word or letter	indicate where there is lack of
⋎	insert space	paragraphing or grammatical
.... or (STET)	leave unchanged	accuracy. If you find that work is (np)
Insert punctuation symbol in a circle (P)	punctuation	returned to you with such
marks correction, then it is   ⌐⌐
plag.	plagiarism	worthwhile spending some time
⟶	run on (no new paragraph)	analysing the common errors as Sp
Sp.	spelling	well as the comments, because this
⌐⌐	transpose text	will help you to improve the
?	what do you mean?	quality of presentation and content
??	text does not seem to make sense	of your work this reviewing can ⊙/≡
have a positive effect on your
✓	good point/correct	assessed mark.
✗	error	*In the margin, the error symbols are separated by a slash (/), as in the third example down.*

→ The value of reviewing, editing and proof-reading

Many students do not appreciate the potential complexity of the review process, and prefer to submit material as soon as they have written a first draft. However, a text that is not revised in this way will be unlikely to receive as favourable a reading – and possibly as high a mark – as one that has been fully reviewed, edited and proofed. It is the mix of style, content, structure and presentation that will gain you marks, and anything you can do to increase your 'mark-earning' power will be to your advantage. In the longer term, learning how to edit your work properly will help you to develop a skill of critical analysis that will stand you in good stead throughout your career.

Importance of the reviewing process when English is not your first language

Writing in another language is never as easy as writing in your first language. This increases the importance of the reviewing stage. Especially at the start of your academic career in the UK, it may repay visiting academic support staff to see if they can provide any recommendations on your work. Initially, your aim should be to identify any repeated errors. You might also consult your English grammar books, and try to understand why you were wrong. As time goes on, and you become more proficient in English, you will be focusing more on subtle aspects of expression.

Note that academic staff will not consider correcting language errors as a routine part of their role. They will expect you to seek assistance for yourself. Information about support for academic writing will be found on notices in buildings across your campus.

 Practical tips for reviewing, editing and proof-reading your work

Make time for checking. When planning the writing, ensure that you have allowed adequate time for reviewing and proof-reading. You don't want to spoil all your hard work by skimping on the final stage. Leave some time between finishing the final draft and returning to check the whole text: you will return to your work with a fresh and possibly more critical eye.

Work from a hard copy. Reading through your work laid out on paper, which is the format in which your marker will probably see it, will help you identify errors and inconsistencies more readily than might be possible on the screen. A paper version is also easier to annotate (although this can also be done using the 'Track Changes' facility on your word processor). A printout also allows you to see the whole work in overview, and focus on the way the text 'flows'. If necessary, spread it out on the desk in front of you.

Follow the 'reading aloud' check. This is a tried and tested technique to ensure that what you have written actually makes sense. Simply read your text aloud to yourself. Your ears may hear the errors that your eyes might miss on a silent reading of the text. This will help you correct grammatical and spelling inconsistencies, as well as punctuation omissions. (Note: this method is not suitable for use in exams.)

Analyse your work to obtain an overview. 'Label' each paragraph with a topic heading and list these in a linear way on a separate paper. This will provide you with an 'overview' of your text and will allow you to appraise the order, check against any original plan, and adjust the position of parts as you feel necessary.

Check for relevance. Ensure from an early stage that you are interpreting the task, as set, sensibly and that any misinterpretation has not caused you to 'make up' another title for the task. Whatever you have written will be judged by the terms of the original task, not by the one you have created.

Check for consistency in the elements of your text. For example, ensure that your introduction and conclusion complement and do not contradict each other.

Check for factual accuracy. Ensure that all the facts are correct, for example, in a history essay that the date sequences are consistent, or in a scientific paper that a numerical answer you have reached is realistic. It is very easy to type a date erroneously or make a final slip in the transposition of an answer from one area of the page to the final answer and, thus, lose marks.

Stick to your word limits/targets. Remember that too few words can be just as bad as too many. The key point is that your writing must be clear to your reader. Sometimes this means giving a longer explanation; sometimes it means simplifying what you have written. However, at this stage, if you are over the word-count limit, check for ways in which you can reword the text to eliminate redundant words while maintaining the sense you intended to convey (see also **Ch 29**).

Create 'white space'. To help produce a more 'reader-friendly' document that will not deter the marker, try to create 'white space' by:

- leaving space (one 'return' space) between paragraphs;
- print your work using at least 1.5 line spacing (unless instructed otherwise);
- justifying only on the left side of the page;
- leaving space around diagrams, tables and other visual material;
- leaving reasonable spaces between headings, sub-headings and text.

Check that all the 'secretarial' aspects are in place. Neat presentation, punctuation and spelling all help your reader to access the information, ideas and argument of your writing. While this may not gain you marks, it will certainly ensure that you do not lose marks even indirectly by making the marker struggle to 'decode' your work.

Check other visual aspects. Diagrams, tables and figures should be drawn using a ruler, if you cannot create these electronically. Only in some subjects would freehand drawing be acceptable, for example, in the study of Architecture.

 Useful language for . . . asking staff about your writing

Context: these examples could be used when consulting academic support staff about your writing.

You can see from the feedback I received on this essay that the marker does not think I have explained this part well. Please can you explain how I could improve it?

Can you explain what this mark means – the lecturer has used it on my essay and I don't understand what it means.

The marker has said my writing is too personal. What does this mean?

My work is too long. I've gone over the word count. Can you suggest how I can shorten it without losing the meaning?

33.1 Reflect on past submissions. Look at an assignment that you have already submitted and go through it using the checklist in Table 33.1. Concentrate on two pages and, using a highlighter, mark all flaws, inconsistencies or errors. Look at the overall effect of these errors and reflect on the extent to which this may have lost you marks; then consider how you might allow for more time for the editing/proof-reading phase next time round.

33.2 Practise using the standard proof-reading marks. On the same piece of text, insert the relevant standard proof-reading symbols (Table 33.3) on the text and in the margin. Learning how to use these symbols will help you speed up the proof-reading process for yourself.

33.3 Practise condensing a piece of text. This is an acknowledged way of improving your work, though you have to bear in mind any word targets that have been set. Look at your text for irrelevant points, wordy phrases, repetitions and excessive examples; if you can reduce its original length by 10–25 per cent, you will find that you will probably have created a much tighter, easier-to-read piece of writing.

How to follow the appropriate academic conventions

The presentation of your written work may be assessed directly and it may influence the way tutors mark the content. This chapter explains how to create a polished submission that follows the established standards of academic writing.

Key topics:
→ Overall layout
→ Cover page
→ Main text
→ Citations and references
→ Quotations and formulae
→ Quoting numbers in text
→ Figures and tables

Essential vocabulary
Analogy Assignment Citation Lab Legend Qualitative Quantitative Quotation

Most marks for assignments are awarded for content, which depends on:

● activities that take place *before* you write, such as researching your sources, conducting experiments or analysing the literature;

● the way you express your ideas in writing (**Ch 28-Ch 33**).

However, some marks will always be directly or indirectly reserved for presentation, so the final 'production' phase can influence your overall grading.

Presentation involves more than layout and use of visual elements; it includes accuracy, consistency and attention to detail. For this reason it is often associated with editing and proof-reading (**Ch 33**). You'll need time to get these aspects right, so when you plan the writing-up process, you should include a final phase for tackling them. For an assignment such as a lengthy in-course essay, this could mean trying to complete the content phase at least a day ahead of the submission date.

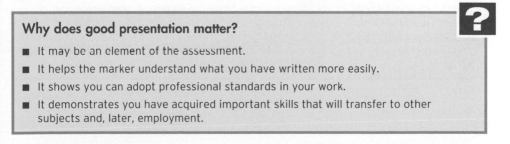

Why does good presentation matter?

■ It may be an element of the assessment.
■ It helps the marker understand what you have written more easily.
■ It shows you can adopt professional standards in your work.
■ It demonstrates you have acquired important skills that will transfer to other subjects and, later, employment.

→ Overall layout

This will depend on the type of academic writing you have been asked to produce – an essay, report, summary, case study or a worked problem. An assignment like an essay could have a relatively simple structure: a cover page, the main essay text and a list of references. A lab report might be more complex, with a title page, abstract, introduction and sections for materials and methods, results, discussion/conclusion and references (**Ch 44**). Layouts for most types of assignment also vary slightly depending on discipline. You should research this carefully before you start to write up, by consulting the course handbook or other regulations.

→ Cover page

This is important to get right because it will create a good first impression. Your department or school may specify a cover-page design that is required for all submissions. If this is the case, make sure that you follow the instructions closely, as the layout may have been constructed for a particular purpose. For example, it may aid anonymous marking or provide markers with a standard format for providing feedback (see Figure 34.1 for an example).

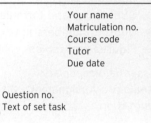

Your name
Matriculation no.
Course code
Tutor
Due date

Question no.
Text of set task

If detailed instructions for a cover page are not given, ensure that you provide your name and/or matriculation number at the head of your work. Where anonymous marking is applied, then your matriculation number only would be required. Add your course title and/or code. The tutor's name is also helpful. Give the question number and title of the question. The model layout in Figure 34.1 suggests one way to present the essential information neatly and clearly. Keep it simple: a cover sheet with fancy graphics will not add to your mark.

Figure 34.1 A model cover-page layout

Indicating your family name clearly

In the UK, where you are required to provide your name on any document, including assignments and examination papers, the custom is to print your full name in the order of first name(s) followed by your family name. Since the names of some international students are often long, it may be helpful also to underline or print your family name in bold, for example, Julius **Caesar** or Julius <u>Caesar</u>. This will make sure that your records are maintained properly as it will avoid confusion in the administrative process of uploading marks.

The majority of student assignments are word-processed, and this may be a submission requirement. You should always try to use a word processor and a good quality printer, if you can, because this makes the drafting and editing phases easier and gives a more professional result. However, if handwriting your submission, make sure you leave sufficient time to copy out your draft neatly and legibly. Write on only one side of the paper – this makes it easier to read, and if you make a significant error you only have to rewrite a single sheet.

Check presentation styles carefully

There may be differences between the styles of presentation that you are used to and the ones expected in the UK. Check by reading carefully any instructions that have been given in course or module handbooks. Ask if you are unsure. For example, you might request to see a sample of work completed by a student from a previous year, to obtain an idea of the layout and standards expected.

Font

There are two main choices: serif types, with extra strokes at the end of the main strokes of each letter, and sans serif types, without these strokes (see Figure 34.2). The type to use is usually left to personal preference, but a serif font is easier to read. More likely to be specified is the point size (pt) of the font, which will probably be 11 or 12 point for ease of reading.

You should avoid using elaborate font types as generally they will not help the reader to assimilate what you have written. For the same reason, you should not use too many forms of emphasis. Choose *italics* or **bold** and stick with one only. Symbols are often used in academic work and in Microsoft Word can be added using the 'Insert > Symbol' menu.

> Serif font
> Times roman 11 pt
> Times roman 12 pt
> Times roman 14 pt
>
> Sans serif font
> Arial 11 pt
> Arial 12 pt
> Arial 14 pt

Figure 34.2 Examples of the main types of font at different point sizes

Margins

A useful convention is for left-hand margins to be 4 cm and the right-hand margins 2.5 cm. This allows space for the marker's comments and ensures that the text can be read if a left-hand binding is used.

Line spacing

It is easier to read text that is spaced at least at 1.5–2 lines apart. Some markers like to add comments as they read the text and this leaves them space to do so. The exception is where you wish to use long quotations. Normally, these should be indented and typed in single-line spacing (see **Ch 31**, p. 255).

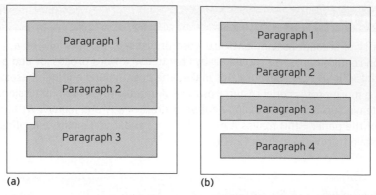

Paragraph 1		Paragraph 1	
Paragraph 2		Paragraph 2	
Paragraph 3		Paragraph 3	
		Paragraph 4	

(a)   (b)

Figure 34.3 Types of paragraph layout. (a) indented and (b) blocked. Note that in the indented model, by convention, the first paragraph in any section is *not* indented.

Paragraphs

The key thing to remember about layout is to make good use of the 'white space'. This means that you should lay out your paragraphs clearly and consistently. Some people prefer the indentation method, where the paragraph begins on the fourth character space from the left-hand margin (Figure 34.3a). Others prefer the blocked paragraph style, that is, where all paragraphs begin on the left-hand margin but are separated by a double-line space (Figure 34.3b). The space between paragraphs should be roughly equivalent to a missing line.

Sub-headings

In some disciplines use of sub-headings is acceptable or even favoured, though in others these 'signpost' strategies are discouraged. It is best to consult your tutor or course handbook about this if you are uncertain. Sub-headings are usually in bold (**Ch 29**).

Punctuation

Standard punctuation applies to all types of academic writing (see **Ch 27**).

Word count

You may be asked to work to a word count and tips for doing this are provided in **Ch 33**. If you greatly exceed this limit, this will almost certainly impact on your mark. You will also confront the reader with too much information and will probably not be writing crisply and concisely (**Ch 28**).

→ Citations and references

A citation is a mention of a source in the main body of your text – usually author surname(s) and date of publication and, in some styles, the relevant page(s). The associated reference consists of further details of the source that would, for example, allow the reader to find it in a library. Citing authors or sources is essential within your text when you refer to ideas or quotations that are not your own. This is an important academic convention that you must observe to avoid plagiarism (**Ch 32**). Providing a reference list is, therefore, standard practice and, for this reason, markers may deduct marks if you omit one.

There are several ways in which citations can be presented, and the more common methods are outlined in **Ch 31**. References are usually listed at the end of your text in a separate section, although in some systems they may be positioned at the bottom of the page where the citation occurs. You must be consistent in the referencing style you adopt, and some disciplines impose strict subject-specific conventions. If in doubt, consult your course handbook or your lecturer.

Examples

The following is an example of a citation:

According to Smith (2005), there are three reasons why aardvark tongues are long.

The following is an example of a reference:

Smith, J. V., 2005. Investigation of snout and tongue length in the African aardvark *(Orycteropus afer). Journal of Mammalian Research*, 34; 101-32.

→ Quotations and formulae

Quotations and formulae can be integrated into the text when short, but are usually presented as a 'special' type of paragraph when long (**Ch 31**). In both cases, the source and date of publication are provided after the quotation.

● **Short quotations** are integrated within the sentence and are placed within single inverted commas (Figure 34.4). Quotations within the quote are in double inverted commas.

> The cultural values identifiable in one minority group create what has been called the 'invisible clamour' (Henze, 1990) as they conflict with those of the dominant culture.

Figure 34.4 How to present a short quotation in text form in the Harvard style

● **Long quotations** are usually 40 or more words of prose (some propose 30) or more than two lines of poetry. They are indented by five character spaces from the left margin. No quotation marks are necessary unless there are quotation marks used in the text you are quoting (Figure 34.5). Usually long quotes are single-line spaced.

Some disciplines, for example, English Literature and Law, have very specific rules for the way in which quotations are to be laid out and referenced. In such cases, consult your course handbook or ask for guidance from a tutor.

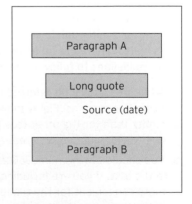

Figure 34.5 How to present a long quote, shown in outline form (see also **Ch 31**, p. 255)

Short formulae or equations can be included in text, but they are probably better presented on a separate line and indented, thus

$$\alpha + 4\beta/\eta^2\pi = 0 \hspace{6cm} \text{(Eqn. 46.1)}$$

Where a large number of formulae are included, they can be numbered for ease of cross-reference, as shown above.

→ Quoting numbers in text

Adopt the following rules:

- In general writing, spell out numbers from one to ten and use figures for 11 and above; in formal writing, spell out numbers from one to a hundred and use figures above this.
- Spell out high numbers that can be written in two words ('six hundred'). With a number like 4,200,000, you also have the choice of writing '4.2 million'.
- Always use figures for dates, times, currency or to give technical details ('5-amp fuse').
- Always spell out numbers that begin sentences, indefinite numbers ('hundreds of soldiers') or fractions ('seven-eighths').
- Hyphenate numbers and fractions appropriately.

→ Figures and tables

You may be expected to support your academic writing with visual material or data, and it is important that you do so in a fashion that best helps the reader to assimilate the information. You must also follow any specific presentational rules that apply in your subject area.

Figures

The academic convention is to include a wide range of visual material under the term 'Figure' ('Fig.' for short). This includes graphs, diagrams, charts, sketches, pictures and photographs, although in some disciplines and contexts photographs may be referred to as plates. There are quite strict rules regarding the way figures are used. Here's a set of guidelines to follow when including figures in an assignment:

- All figures should be referred to in the text. There are 'standard' formulations for doing this, such as 'Fig. 4 shows that . . .'; or '. . . results for one treatment were higher than for the other (see Fig. 2)'. Find what is appropriate from the literature or texts in your subject area.
- You should always number the figures in the order in which they are referred to in the text. If you are including the figures within the main body of text (usually more convenient for the reader) they should appear at the next suitable position in the text after the first time of mention. At the very least this will be after the paragraph that includes the first citation, but more normally will be at the top of the following page.

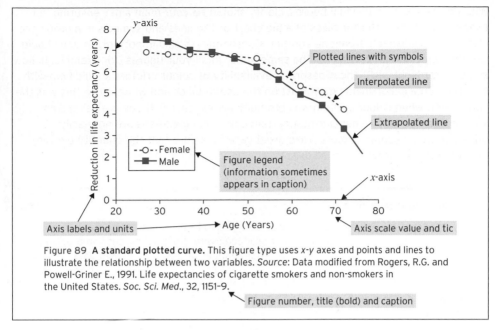

Figure 89 **A standard plotted curve.** This figure type uses *x*-*y* axes and points and lines to illustrate the relationship between two variables. *Source*: Data modified from Rogers, R.G. and Powell-Griner E., 1991. Life expectancies of cigarette smokers and non-smokers in the United States. *Soc. Sci. Med.*, 32, 1151–9.

Figure 34.6 **The basic components of a graph**

- Try to position your figures at the top or bottom of a page, rather than sandwiched between blocks of text. This looks neater and makes the text easier to read.

- Each figure should have a legend, which will include the figure number, a title and some text (often a key to the symbols and line styles used). The convention is for figure legends to appear below each figure. Your aim should be to make each figure self-contained. That is, a reader who knows the general subject area should be able to work out what your figure shows, without reference to other material. Figure 34.6 shows the basic components of a figure and their layout.

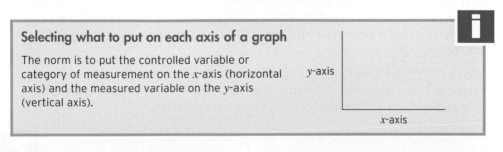

Selecting what to put on each axis of a graph

The norm is to put the controlled variable or category of measurement on the *x*-axis (horizontal axis) and the measured variable on the *y*-axis (vertical axis).

Choosing the right *type* of figure to display information is an art in itself. Although there are technical reasons why some forms of data should be presented in particular ways (for example, proportional data in a pie chart rather than a line chart), your main focus should always be on selecting a method that will best help the reader assimilate the information presented. Jones, Reed and Weyers (2003) or the 'Chart Wizard' in the Microsoft Office Excel spreadsheet program are possible starting points for exploring the range of possibilities.

When presentating individual figures, clarity should be your main aim – ensuring, for example, that the different slices of a pie chart or the lines and symbols in a graph are clearly distinguishable from one another. Consistency is also important, so you should use the same line or shading for the same entity in all your figures (for example, hollow symbols for 'controls'). The widespread availability of colour printers should help with this, but some departments may insist on the use of black and white, since this was the convention when colour printing was prohibitively expensive. If you are using colour, keep it 'tasteful' and remember that certain colour combinations are not easily differentiated by some readers. Take great care to ensure that the quantity plotted and its units are provided for all axes.

---

smart tip

Inserting figures in text

Integrated suites of office-type software allow you to insert the graphs you produced using the spreadsheet program into text produced with the word-processing program. The two programs can even be linked so that changes on the spreadsheet data automatically appear in the graph within the word-processed file. Consult the manual or 'Help' facility to find out how to do this. In MS Word, digital photographs can be inserted using the 'Insert > Picture > From File' command.

Tables

These are used to summarise large amounts of information, especially where a reader might be interested in some of the detail of the data. Tables are especially useful for qualitative information (see examples in this text, such as Table 33.2 on p. 278) but numerical data can also be presented, especially if they relate to a discontinuous qualitative variable (for example, the population sizes and occupation breakdown of various geographical regions).

Tables generally include a number of columns (vertical) and rows (horizontal). By analogy with figures, the convention is to put the controlled or measured variable on the column headers (horizontal) and to place the measured variable or categories of measurement in the rows (vertical). Do not forget to include the units of the information listed if this is relevant. Figure 34.7 shows the basic components of a table and their layout.

The rules for presenting tables are very similar to those for figures, with the important exception that a table legend should appear above the table. It is quite common to note exceptions and other information as footnotes to tables.

?

Figure or table?

In certain cases it may be possible to present the same data set as a figure or as a table. The first rule in such cases is never do both – choose the method that best suits your data and the target reader. An important criterion is to decide which will best help the reader assimilate the information. If the take-home message is best shown visually, a figure might be best; whereas, if details and numerical accuracy are important, a table might be more suitable.

TOOLKIT D   Improving your academic writing

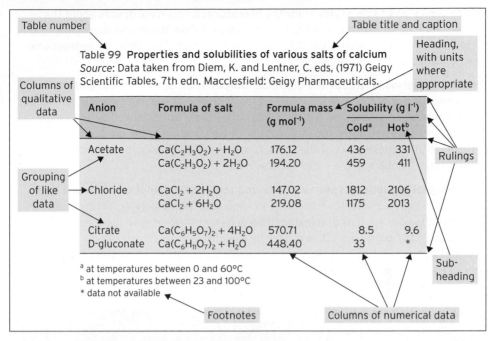

Figure 34.7 **The basic components of a table.** Note that shading is included here to emphasise the heading and data sections and would not usually be present.

✔ Practical tips for presenting your work

Don't let grammatical and stylistic errors spoil your work. It is a waste of effort to concentrate on presentation without also ensuring that you have eliminated minor errors at the review and proof-reading stages (**Ch 33**).

Adopt standard word-processing layout conventions. Adopting the following guidelines will ensure a neat, well-spaced presentation:

- one character space after the following punctuation – full stop, comma, colon, semi-colon, closing inverted commas (double and single), question mark and exclamation mark;
- no character space after apostrophes in a 'medial' position, e.g. it's, men's, monkey's;
- no indentation of paragraphs (that is, blocked style);
- one standard line space between paragraphs;
- left-justified text;
- italicised letters for foreign words and titles of books, journals and papers (**Ch 31**);
- headings in same font size as text, but bold.

Adopt figure and table styles from the literature. If you have doubts about the precise style or arrangement of figures and tables, follow the model shown in texts or journal articles from your subject area. Also, check whether relevant instructions are published in the course handbook.

Don't automatically accept the graphical output from spreadsheets and other programs. These are not always in the 'correct' style. For example, the default output for many charts produced by the Microsoft Office Excel spreadsheet includes a grey background and horizontal gridlines, neither of which is generally used. It is not difficult to alter these parts of the chart, however, and you should learn how to do this from manuals or the 'Help' facility.

In numerical disciplines, take care in laying out your calculations. Use plenty of space, working your way down the page in sequence. Don't work across the page, as this doesn't allow the flow of thinking to be apparent. Always give units, as this is a good way of trapping errors. Use a ruler for simple diagrams (for example, electrical circuits) as this will be much neater than freehand. Underline all answers and score out any rough work with a single diagonal line.

💬 Useful language for . . . asking staff about presentation of assignments

Context: these are questions you might ask a tutor or departmental/school secretary when you submit your work or in preparation for submitting it.

I've never used a cover sheet before. Have I got the details right?

Can I submit my work on a memory stick rather than on paper?

Should I put my name and matriculation number in the footer for each page?

Is there a word limit for this essay?

Context: these are questions that are specifically for your tutor.

Is this graph of the standard expected for this course?

Should I put my graphs into an Appendix?

I've forgotten what referencing system we're supposed to follow in this subject. Can you remind me where I can find out, please?

 **And now . . .**

34.1 Check for 'white' space. Look critically at your text to identify whether you have used paragraphing effectively. A useful 'trick' is to reduce the 'zoom' function on the toolbar to 25 per cent. Your written pages will then appear in multiples on the screen which will allow you to see the overall distribution of 'white' space and length of paragraphs. This may suggest some alterations to make your text more reader-friendly.

34.2 'Personalise' your work. In many institutions the convention is for students to submit written work with only their matriculation mark as an identifier. This is done in order to facilitate anonymous marking. However, if your pages become detached for some reason, it may be difficult for the marker to ensure that all your pages are actually included in the document that they mark. Thus, you should do three very basic things: firstly, staple all sheets together (paper clips fall off); secondly, using the View/header-footer function, insert your matriculation number in the footer, in a smaller font than the main text if you wish it to be less obtrusive; and, thirdly, insert page numbers in the footer also. This means that each page is identifiable as yours and will remain in sequence. If you are not in the habit of doing these things, create an assignment writing template in which you insert the matriculation/identity number and page numbers. You can then use this routinely for all future written coursework.

34.3 Check out position of tables and figures. Look back at previous assignments to identify whether you have been consistent in positioning tables and figures. There is a facility within Word (Table/Properties) that allows you to position such visual elements to the left, right or centre of a page and, depending on the nature of the content, the position can make a significant difference to the reader's perception of the information.

PERFORMING WELL IN COURSE ASSESSMENTS

35 | Assessment at university

How tests and examinations work in the UK

University assessment systems are complex and rather different from those used at school or college. This chapter explains the terminology involved and the rationale for different modes of assessment, while later chapters discuss how to tackle specific question types.

Key topics:
- → Forms of assessment
- → Marking criteria and grading schemes
- → Modules and progression
- → Degree classifications and transcripts
- → Complaints and appeals

Essential vocabulary
Aggregate mark   Class exam   Exam diet   External examiner   Finals Formative assessment   Learning objective/outcome   Marking criteria Oral exam   Peer assessment   Quiz   Summative assessment   Test Transcript

Each UK university has a legal charter entitling it to award its own degrees. These degrees are granted on the basis of performance in assessments and exams, which may vary in character depending on subject and institution. As a result, each university has its own conventions regarding style of question, format of exams and marking criteria. No two universities are the same. Therefore, it is essential that you take into account how the exam system operates in your own institution *before* you start revising.

→ Forms of assessment

Each degree programme and every unit of teaching (usually called a 'module') will have a published set of aims and learning objectives or outcomes. Your performance in relation to these goals will be tested in various ways.

- **Formative assessments** are primarily designed to give you feedback on the quality of your answers. In some cases these are known as 'class exams'; in other cases, as 'quizzes' or 'tests'. They generally do not count towards your final module assessment, although sometimes a small proportion of marks will carry forward as an incentive to perform well.

- **Summative assessments** count directly towards a module or degree assessment and are normally formal invigilated tests where you work in isolation. These may be known as degree exams and, in the honours year, in some institutions, as 'finals'. There may be several sittings or papers, perhaps covering different aspects of the course. The collective set of exams is sometimes known as an exam diet.

Formative assessment as a way of gauging your performance

As an international student, you may be apprehensive about taking exams – especially if English is not your main language. You may feel anxious because you are not familiar with the methods of assessment. In this situation, any formative assessments will be very valuable to you. These will allow you to identify your strengths and weaknesses and give you a chance to remedy any problem areas before the summative exams. Always look at feedback from formative exercises carefully and ask tutors if you do not understand the comments (**Ch 48**).

In some cases the assessment will be entirely based on in-course assignments in the form of essays, projects and problem-solving exercises (see information box below). In most cases, however, the overall mark will consist of marks from such coursework and formal invigilated exams. The latter are favoured in later years, because the possibility of collaboration, plagiarism or impersonation is limited. You are expected to perform alone under a certain amount of time pressure.

Problem-based learning (PBL)

This is a form of learning where you are asked to investigate a specific problem, usually related to a real-life professional situation, which may be open-ended in nature (that is, not necessarily having an obvious conclusion or a 'right answer'). You may be part of a small team asked to consider the problem, research the underlying theory and practice that might lead to a response, and arrive at a practical solution. Assessment of the exercise will focus on the solution you arrive at, the way in which you arrive at it and the interactions among group members. The process is often at least as important as the product. There may be group- and peer-assessment elements to your grade.

Exam papers and diets may be structured in different ways, according to discipline. The design may reflect the different aspects of learning that your tutors wish to assess (see **Ch 36-Ch 48**). For example, there may be a multiple-choice component that tests your surface knowledge across a wide range of topics, while an essay section may be included to test your deeper knowledge in fewer topics. Papers and questions may be assigned different marks that combine to form your overall mark.

Exam format

This should never come as a surprise to you as you should have checked it by consulting past papers and by confirming with lecturers that there have been no changes to the style of examination.

Various levels of choice are given to reflect the nature of the field of study. In vocational disciplines there may be a need to ensure you are knowledgeable in all areas. In other subjects a certain amount of specialisation may be acceptable. Some exam papers are divided into sections, and you will be expected to answer one or more questions from the options within each of these. This format allows a limited amount of choice while ensuring that you have covered all major areas in your studies. It is vital that you take these aspects of exam paper design into account when arriving at a strategy for revision and exam-sitting (**Ch 51, Ch 55**).

→ Marking criteria and grading schemes

Who marks your papers? How do they do it? Often students are unsure about this.

The norm is for papers to be graded by the person who delivered the lectures, tutorials or practical classes that are being assessed. However, due to large class sizes, alternative mechanisms may be employed:

- the marking may be spread out among several tutors;
- especially in multiple-choice exams, the marking may be automated;
- where teamwork is involved, peer assessment may take place (see below).

Each university, college, faculty or school will publish assessment reporting scales, usually in handbooks and/or websites. Some operate to a familiar system of banded percentages, often related to honours degree classifications, while others adopt a different form of qualitative band 'descriptors'. You should find out which system applies in your case and consult the general marking criteria used to assign work in each band. This will give you a better idea of the standard of work needed to produce a specific grade, and may help you to understand feedback from tutors (**Ch 48**).

Understand how you will be assessed

When studying marking criteria, you should note that they tend not to focus on 'correctness'. This is because in many subjects at university level in the UK there is often no such thing as a single 'right' answer. Thus, marking criteria tend to refer to, for example, 'soundness of argument'; 'logic of debate'; 'originality', and so on. Use the language in the marking criteria to help you to gain a better understanding of what is required in assessments to obtain high marks.

To maintain standards and ensure fairness, several systems operate:

- marks may be determined according to an explicit marking scheme that allocates a proportion of the total to different aspects of your answer;
- double or triple marking may take place and if the grades awarded differ, the answer may be scrutinised more closely, possibly by a external examiner;
- papers for more senior students are usually marked anonymously, so the marker does not know whose answer they are grading;
- the external marker will confirm the overall standard and may inspect some papers, particularly those falling at the division between honours grades or on the pass/fail boundary.

Peer assessment

This is where the members of a study team are asked to assign a mark to each other's performance. This might take account, for example, of the effort put in, the conduct in the assigned team role(s), and contribution to the final outcome. Clear guidance is always given about how you should assign marks. For more about team roles see **Ch 18**.

External examiners and assessors

External examiners are appointed by the university to oversee marking in specific papers and to ensure standards are maintained and that the assessment is fair. They are usually noted academics in the field, with wide experience of examining. They will be asked to comment on the exam question papers in advance and will generally consider a representative selection of written papers and project work. For finals, they may interview students in an 'oral', to ensure that spoken responses meet the standard of the written answers, and to arrive at a judgement on borderline cases. Note that where papers are borderline pass/fail, they are often double-marked before being sent to the external examiner, who recommends the final mark. Papers are dealt with anonymously until a final mark has been agreed.

Accreditation bodies in the professions may be involved in the examination process, and some answer papers may be marked by external assessors appointed by these accrediting bodies rather than the university.

→ Modules and progression

Modular systems of study at university have been developed for several reasons:

- they allow greater flexibility in subject choice;
- they can efficiently accommodate students studying different degree paths;
- they make it easier for students to transfer between courses and institutions;
- they break up studies into 'bite-sized' elements and allow exams to be spread more evenly over the academic year.

The modular system does have disadvantages, however, including the fact that it may tend to encourage students to avoid difficult subjects and to 'close the book' on a subject once it has been assessed. If you are studying in a modular system, you should be aware of these risks.

Modules may be assessed by a blend of formal exams and in-course assessment, as outlined above. If you fail the overall ('aggregated') assessment, you may be asked to return for a resit exam or resubmit new or revised coursework, while in some subjects, borderline cases are given an extra oral exam. Resit exams usually take place at the end of the summer vacation, with the result being based solely on your performance in that exam.

At the end of each academic year you will be required to fulfil certain progression criteria that allow you to pass on to the next level of study. These criteria are normally published in course handbooks. If you fail to satisfy the criteria, for example, if you failed resits, you may need to repeat the whole year or even leave the university. Possible options if repeating the year include:

- being asked to 'carry' specific modules: that is, study them again in addition to the normal quota for your next year of study;
- having a condition on your re-entry, for example, achieving a certain level of marks or passing a prescribed number of modules. This would normally be discussed with your adviser/director of studies.

→ Degree classifications and transcripts

Students with superior entry qualifications or experience may join university at different levels. There are also a range of exit awards – certificates, diplomas and ordinary degrees. However, the majority of students now enter at level 1, and study for an honours degree. This encompasses three years of study in England, Wales and Northern Ireland, and four years in Scotland.

Sometimes entry into the final honours year is competitive, based on grades in earlier years. Some universities operate a 'junior honours' year, which means you are accepted into an honours grouping at an earlier stage and may have special module options.

smart
tip

Study abroad or within placements

Credit will normally be given for years of study carried out in another country or in work placement, according to specific schemes operated by your university. This includes participation in European Community schemes such as ERASMUS (see http://ec.europa.eu/education/index_en.htm).

Nearly all UK universities follow the same system for grading honours degrees. The grades are, in descending order:

- first class (a 'first')
- upper second class (a two-one or 2:1)
- lower second class (a two-two or 2:2)
- third class (a 'third')
- unclassified or 'ordinary degree'.

However, some universities may not differentiate between the second-class divisions.

In some institutions, these classifications will take into account all grades you have obtained during your university career; sometimes only those in junior and senior honours years; and in the majority, only grades obtained in the finals. This makes the finals critical, especially as there are no resits for them.

Once your degree classification has been decided by the examination committee or board, and moderated by the external examiner, it will be passed for ratification to the university's senate or equivalent body for academic legislation. During this period you will technically be a 'graduand', until your degree is conferred at the graduation ceremony. At this time you will receive a diploma certificate and be entitled to wear a colourful degree- and institution-specific 'hood' for your gown.

Employers will usually ask to see your degree certificate (diploma) for confirmation of your degree and may contact the university to confirm your qualification and obtain a copy of your transcript (**Ch 8**). This document shows your performance in *all* assessments throughout your career at the university. There are national plans in the EU and UK to add more information to degree transcripts, such as the European Diploma Supplement or Higher Education Achievement Report (HEAR).

→ Complaints and appeals

Because of the checks and balances outlined on p. 299, the university examination system is usually robust. However, all universities have complaints and appeals procedures for situations where students feel they have been incorrectly or unfairly assessed. This will normally start with an appeal to the course leader, then the head of the school or department, and move progressively up the system if a student remains dissatisfied. Final recourse may be to an external ombudsman. Details of procedures will be published on your university's website.

Appeals against termination of studies

Your studies may be terminated for one of several reasons but most commonly failure to meet attendance or progression criteria. Occasionally, termination will be enforced due to disciplinary reasons, for example, in a case of plagiarism. In these circumstances, students will be offered a chance to appeal and will be expected to produce evidence of any extenuating circumstances, such as medical certificates, or notes from support service personnel. Such students may also wish to ask tutors to support their application where the tutor is aware of their personal situation.

✔ Practical tips for understanding how you will be assessed

Ask senior students about the exam system. They may have useful tips and advice to pass on.

Find out where essential information is recorded. This could be in a combination of handbooks and web-based resources.

If you don't understand any aspect of the assessment system, ask course administrators or tutors. Knowing how the system works is important and can affect your performance.

Notify your institution of any disability. If you have a disability, you should make the institution aware of this. You may have special concessions in exams, for example, using the services of a scribe, being allowed extra time, or having exam question papers printed in large print for you. Appropriate entitlements take time to arrange and you must ensure that arrangements are in place well before the exam date. Contact your department and disability support service for guidance.

Useful language for . . . talking about assessments

Context: you will find it helpful to learn the complex (and sometimes institution-specific) vocabulary associated with assessment. Here are some possible questions you might ask fellow students or staff.

I don't understand this learning outcome [or objective]. What does it mean? How do you think it could be examined?

From this feedback, it looks like I will need to do more work on [specify aspect]. Are there any academic support staff who could help me with this?

What proportion of the marks from our assessments during semester [term] carry forward to the main exam?

GO And now . . .

35.1 Carry out the necessary research to ensure you know how your university's exam system works for your intended degree. You should find out about:

- course and degree programme aims;
- learning objectives or outcomes;
- the format of assessments and proportion of in-course and final exam elements;
- timing of exam diets;
- assessment or marking criteria;
- the grading scheme;
- weighting of exam components;
- progression criteria.

You may wish to file this information for later reference.

35.2 Find out about in-course assessments and how they will contribute to your module or degree grade. Your course handbooks will normally include this information. Marks for in-course work can often be influenced by the amount of work you put in, so they can be a good way of ensuring you create a strong platform to perform well in degree exams.

35.3 Examine past exam papers in your subjects to investigate how they are constructed. This will allow you to see whether there are subdivisions, restrictions or other features that might influence your revision or exam strategies.

36 Multiple-choice and short-answer questions

How to tackle short-answer formats

Many university exams, especially at early stages, test your knowledge using 'objective' question types, which tend to be short and demand factual answers. This chapter explains how to adjust your revision and exam technique to suit these forms of assessment.

Key topics:
→ Tackling multiple-choice questions
→ Dealing with short-answer questions
→ Advice for other types of short-form question

Essential vocabulary
Distractor   Formative assessment   Multiple-choice question (MCQ)
Negative marking   Rubric   Short-answer question (SAQ)

A multiple-choice question (MCQ) is one in which you are presented with alternative answers and asked to select one that is correct. In some cases, you may be asked to identify several correct answers rather than one. A short-answer question (SAQ) deals with topics of limited scope and you are generally expected to produce a mini-essay, bulleted points or a diagram in response.

Both MCQs and SAQs are used as short-form alternatives to standard essay questions as a means of testing the breadth and detail of your knowledge across the whole syllabus. Generally, they are mixed with other forms of questions that are better for testing the depth of your knowledge and analytical capabilities.

Good technique and strategy with MCQs and SAQs can improve your marks and save time for answering other questions.

→ Tackling multiple-choice questions

The most common form of MCQ provides some statement or question, then offers four possible answers. One of the answers is correct and the other three are known as distractors.

- If the question simply seeks a factual answer, such as the date something happened, or the name of a person, the answers may simply present a series of alternatives to the true answer.

- Sometimes the question is devised to test your knowledge of technical terms or jargon, in which case the distractors may use similar-sounding terms to the correct answer.

- Some questions involve a quantitative problem and then give possible answers that you can only arrive at by doing the necessary calculation. The answers provided may include values that you will obtain if you carry out a faulty calculation.
- There may be a special way of identifying the answer, such as shading in a box or selecting an option with your mouse. Read the rubric carefully to make sure you do the right thing.

Example MCQ

The bone at the front of the leg below the knee is called:

A The fibula
B The tibia
C The femur
D The cruciate

B is the correct answer; A, C and D are distractors. You may know that all the potential answers are parts of a leg, but unless you know the anatomy well, you may not be able to identify the correct answer.

A good approach to **paper-based** MCQ tests is as follows:

- **First sweep.** Read through the questions fairly rapidly, noting the 'correct' answer in those you can attempt immediately, perhaps on a separate sheet. Don't fill in or submit any answers properly yet.
- **Second sweep.** Go through the paper again, checking your original answers, and thinking for a longer time about uncertain answers. This time, mark up the answer sheet properly or submit answers online. Leave questions you are still uncertain about at this stage.
- **Third sweep.** Now tackle the difficult questions and those that require longer to answer (for example, those based on numerical problems). At this stage, whether you should guess answers depends on the marking regime being used (see 'Optimising marks' in the Practical tips section on p. 308).

One reason for adopting this three-phase approach is that considering the full set of questions may prompt you to recall facts relevant to difficult questions. You can also spend more time per question on the difficult ones.

Increasingly, MCQs are presented via computers. This is usually termed computer-aided assessment (CAA) or online assessment (OA). Use of CAA means that the answers can be 'instantly' checked. Where such systems are used for formative assessments that are not part of your final assessment, the software may allow you to receive feedback on incorrect answers to help you learn more about aspects you evidently did not understand.

Alternative question formats

True/false questions, fill-in-the-missing-word and matching questions all attempt to test the same sort of knowledge as MCQs. Many of the tips given here also apply to these forms, but see also p. 307.

---

smart
tip

Getting used to software

If you are offered the option to practise CAA/OA, take it. Familiarity with the software and presentation may save you time in the real exam.

→ Dealing with short-answer questions

The various styles that can be encompassed within the SAQ format (see below) allow for more demanding questions than MCQs. For this form of question, few if any marks are given for writing style. Answers are often expected in note form or as a diagram. Think in 'bullet point' mode and list the crucial points only. The time for answering SAQ questions may be tight, so get down to work fast, starting with answers that demand remembered facts.

In SAQ papers, there is often a choice of questions. Choose carefully – it may be better to gain half marks for a correct answer to half a question than to provide a largely irrelevant answer or one that seems to cover the whole topic, but does so too superficially. Consider all sections of the question before you start answering, in case you cannot cope with secondary questions.

Time management for SAQs

Divide the allocated time up appropriately, allowing some time for choosing questions and reviewing answers. Stick to your timetable by moving on to the next question as soon as possible. Strategically, it is probably better to get part marks for the full number of questions than good marks for only a few (**Ch 55**).

Always answer the question as requested – this is true for all questions, but especially important for SAQs. If the question asks for a diagram, make sure you provide one, and label it well; if it asks for *n* aspects of a topic, try to list this number of points; if there are two or more parts, provide appropriate answers to all aspects. This may seem obvious, but many marks are lost for not following instructions. Bear in mind that markers may award marks for correct use of key phrases – so try to use the terms and subject jargon normally used in the resources, lectures and discussions. Finally, remember to check through your answers at the end. You'll be able to correct obvious mistakes and possibly add points that come to mind when rereading.

Examples of SAQs

Here are three possible ways of asking a short-answer question about the knee:

- Draw a labelled diagram of the knee.
- Briefly explain the role of the meniscus, patella and ligaments in the knee joint.
- Give five common types of injury that affect the knee, and briefly indicate how they should be treated.

- **Multiple-response questions.** These are essentially MCQs in which more than one answer can be correct – and you may or may not be told how many. Marks are usually awarded for having the correct combination of answers, so you will really have to know the topic well to score highly. Guessing is not advised, especially if you do not know how many answers might be correct.

- **Fill-in-the-missing-word questions.** These can be tough options because you are not given prompts for the correct answer. However, you may be able to obtain clues from the surrounding text or other questions. When marked by software, allowance is often made for common misspellings, but it's worth taking special care over spelling in such cases: there is no guarantee that 'your' mis-spelling will be included and there may be no human check on the wrong answers.

- **'Matching' questions.** These present you with a series of options and ask you to link these to a series of answers or matching phrases. Start with the easy matches and see which questions and options remain. If you need to guess, remember that one incorrect answer will actually result in two lost marks, because you will have ruled out the correct answer to another question.

- **'Hot-spot' and other pictorial question formats.** These mainly apply to online assessment; the question may ask that you identify part of a diagram using the cursor – perhaps by clicking, dragging an arrow or symbol, or by dragging images to the correct spot. Alternatively, you may have to provide text for a labelled item. Be especially careful to identify the exact location where markers should be placed.

- **Gobbets, précis and other specialised assessments.** Because of their subject-specific nature, it is not possible to give generalised advice on these. Consult the course handbook or lecturers to find out the recommended structure and content and the best way to approach them in exams.

Taking short-form questions as an international student

Advantages:

Multiple-choice – you will be given all the terms and simply have to make a choice.
Short-answer questions – you can keep your responses short and note-like without losing marks, hence, English language is less problematic.

Disadvantages:

Fill-in-the-missing-word – may be trickier unless you know all the specialist vocabulary well.

Short-form tests – usually organised so candidates are under time pressure, therefore, penalises students who may need a little more time to read the paper, translate the questions and compose answers.

Revise appropriately. If your paper includes MCQs or SAQs, keep this in mind as you study. Think how material might be assessed in these ways and make sure you learn potentially examinable definitions and facts. Also make sure you can draw and label relevant diagrams. You may find it useful to discuss potential questions with fellow students (**Ch 54**).

Ask for a practice opportunity. If you are unfamiliar with taking MCQ tests in English, ask the course leader/director whether it is possible to practise using questions from past exams so you can work on your technique. Some staff may be reluctant to use questions from past papers if there is a pool of questions that is reused. If this is the case, ask what alternative opportunities might be available.

Take a logical approach to MCQs. When unsure of an answer, rule out options that are clearly absurd or have obviously been placed there to distract you. Next, look at the remaining options. Can you judge between contrasting pairs with alternative answers? Logically, both cannot be correct, so try to rule out one of the pair. Watch out, however, in case *both* may be irrelevant to the answer.

Write down key information before looking at MCQ options. If you have key dates, facts or formulae to remember, write these down as soon as the exam starts. If you do this before looking at the options in the exam questions, you will be less likely to be confused or distracted by similar-sounding options.

Hints for numerical questions. If an MCQ involves a calculation, try to do this independently of the options, so you are not influenced by them. Assuming you have done the appropriate revision, and have the required knowledge and skills, numerical questions in SAQ papers can be a valuable means of accumulating marks, because it is possible to score 100 per cent in them if your answer is correct and laid out appropriately.

Optimising marks. The best way of tackling MCQs depends on the marking regime. If there is a penalty for incorrect answers in a multiple-choice test (often referred to as 'negative marking'), the best strategy is *not* to answer questions when you know your answer is a guess. Depending on the penalty, it may be beneficial to guess if you can narrow the choice down to two options, but beware false or irrelevant alternatives. If there are no such penalties, then you should provide an answer to all questions in the paper, even if this means guessing in some cases.

Guessing. If you have to do this to complete the paper (assuming negative marking doesn't apply), go with your first hunch for the answer rather than a second thought that might be influenced by the distractors. Your subconscious may have arrived at the correct answer, without your conscious mind understanding why.

Useful language for . . . talking about short-form exams

Context: these are some questions you might want to ask your tutors about this form of exam.

Are there any model answers for the SAQ component of our exam? I'm a little uncertain about what's expected in an answer as I haven't taken an exam of this type before.

Is there negative marking for the multiple-choice paper? [Assuming the answer is 'yes' . . .] How many marks are deducted for a wrong answer?

Are we allowed to take a calculator into the MCQ exam?

Can we use scrap paper for notes and working examples in MCQ exams?

 And now . . .

36.1 Compensate for any lack of past MCQ papers. Departments are usually reluctant to release past papers for MCQs, since there will often be only a limited pool of good discriminatory questions. Staff also fear that students will simply memorise answers to the questions in the pool, rather than learning the whole course. You can compensate for this by making up your own MCQs as part of your revision – this is a good way of understanding the examiner's likely frame of mind and of spotting topics to revise and facts to memorise. If studying as a group (**Ch 54**), you could all submit a specified number of questions and then answer each other's.

36.2 Seek out model answers to SAQs. These may be provided in course handbooks. They will give you an idea of the length and depth of answer required in your subject, as well as the general style of question.

36.3 Think through your exam strategy. MCQs and SAQs often form elements of composite exam papers involving several sections, each being made up of questions of a particular type. Time management in these papers can be difficult because of this complexity, so think through the order in which you will tackle the parts and how much time you should devote to each MCQ sweep and SAQ question. Because time is often limiting in SAQ papers, it is particularly important to share out time so that you don't leave any questions unanswered (**Ch 55**).

37 Numerical questions

How to approach quantitative problems

Paying close attention to mathematical aspects of your course is important because, in exam situations, if you get the answers right, it is possible to obtain very high marks. Even if you don't consider yourself particularly numerate, tackling these topics head-on can repay the effort.

Key topics:
→ Learning key mathematical skills
→ Why practice is essential
→ Tackling the problem
→ Why do examiners ask numerical questions?

Essential vocabulary
Numeracy   Part-marking   Quantitative

Some students favour questions that require a numerical or statistical approach. Others struggle where maths is involved, or suffer from a lack of preparation. Whichever category applies to you, it is worth the effort of conquering mathematical assessments, because the payback can be excellent - answering this type of question correctly is one of the few ways in which you can obtain 100 per cent in a university exam.

→ Learning key mathematical skills

You won't get very far without knowing the basic maths required for the types of problems you will encounter. This should be easy to find out by consulting the course handbook, examining past papers, reading textbooks or by speaking to lecturers or tutors.

If your course requires more advanced mathematics, it is likely that specialist modules or other forms of assistance will be available to you. In addition, most universities have academic support units that offer help with numeracy.

---

smart tip

Numerical aspects of your course

Bear in mind that these elements, while tricky for some, are often essential for understanding material encountered later in your degree programme.

When it comes to numerical problems, there is simply no substitute for practice. If you have difficulty with numerical work, practice at problem-solving or standard forms of analysis will:

● demystify the procedures involved, which, in reality, may only involve elementary mathematical operations and just appear complex on the surface;

● allow you to gain confidence, so that you don't panic when confronted with an unfamiliar or apparently complex form of problem;

● help you work faster, because the pattern of work will have become routine;

● help you to recognise the various forms a problem can take. This is useful because there are a limited number of ways lecturers can present questions and it is important to identify the relevant formulae or approach to adopt as soon as possible;

● help imprint the standard form of analysis and presentation, ensuring that you automatically adopt the correct procedure and presentation style.

---

smart tip

Have the right tools ready

Calculators greatly simplify the numerical part of problem-solving. Make sure you know how to use all relevant functions on your model.

→ **Tackling the problem**

A step-by-step approach is recommended. This may not always be the fastest method, but mistakes often occur when students miss out stages of a calculation, combine simple calculations, or do not make what they have done obvious to either themselves or the examiner. Error tracing (and, importantly, part-marking) is easier when all stages in a calculation are laid out sequentially.

Approach the problem thoughtfully

If presented as a story or scenario, you may need to 'decode' the problem to decide which equations or rules need to be applied.

● Read the problem carefully – the text may give clues as to how it should be tackled. Be certain of what is required as an answer before starting.

● Analyse what kind of problem it is. Which equation(s) or approach will be applicable? If this is not obvious, consider the dimensions/units of the information available and think how they could be fitted to a relevant formula or form of analysis. In formula-based questions, a favourite trick of examiners is to make you rearrange a familiar equation before you can work out the answer. Another is to make you use two or more equations in series. You may therefore need to revise the rules for rearranging formulae.

- Check that you have, or can derive, all the information required. It is unusual, but not unknown, for examiners to supply redundant information. So, if you decide not to use some of the information given, be confident about why you do not require it.

- Decide on the format and units in which to present the answer. This is sometimes suggested to you. If the problem requires many changes in the prefixes to units, it may be a good idea to convert all data to base units at the outset.

- If a problem appears complex, break it down into component parts.

Present your answer clearly

The way you present your answer obviously needs to fit the individual problem. In general, the final answer should be presented as a meaningful statement and any number given should carry appropriate significant figures and units. You should always show your working – most markers will only penalise a mistake once if the remaining operations are performed correctly, but they can only do this if you make those operations visible. Guidelines for presenting an answer include:

- Where appropriate, make your assumptions explicit – most mathematical models require that certain criteria are met before they can be legitimately applied, and some involve assumptions and approximations. In some cases you may be given credit for stating these clearly at the outset.

- Outline your strategy for answering briefly, perhaps explaining the applicable formula or definitions that suit the approach to be taken. Give details of what the symbols mean (and their units) at this point. If rearranging a formula, show how you have done this, using symbols first, then substituting relevant numerical values.

- Convert to the desired units step by step, that is, taking each variable in turn. Try to get into the habit of writing all numbers with their units, unless they are truly dimensionless.

Presentation tips

When you have obtained a numerical answer in the desired units, it is normally expected that you should rewrite this in meaningful English and underline the numerical part of answer. For example:

The net profit in tax year 2009 was £334,091.

Make sure you use an appropriate number of significant figures.

Check your answer

Having written out your answer, you should check it methodically.

- Is the answer of the magnitude you might reasonably expect? You should be alerted to an error if an answer is absurdly large or small. If using a calculator, beware of absurd results that could arise from faulty key-pressing or logic. Double-check any result obviously standing out from others in a series of calculations.

- Do the units make sense and match up with the answer required?
- Do you get the same answer if you recalculate using a different method?

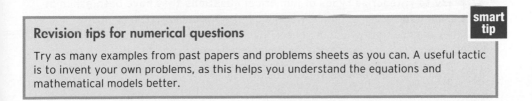

What should I do if I know my answer is incorrect?

Be prepared to say that you know your answer is wrong, but cannot identify where the error has come – you may get a small amount of credit for showing this awareness. Also, if you know what to do to obtain an answer, but not *how* to do it, you may gain some credit for giving as much detail as you can.

→ Why do examiners ask numerical questions?

Quantitative problems allow examiners to test the following:

- your numeracy, mathematical skills and problem-solving abilities;
- your capacity to recall, understand and apply theoretical models within 'real-life' scenarios;
- your ability to think clearly and work quickly under pressure;
- your ability to follow a standard format for calculation, particularly where it may be related to professional competence, as in Engineering and Accountancy;
- your ability to present a logical sequence of operations clearly, such that another person can understand what you have done.

smart tip

Part-marking in examinations

This is where the examiner will give marks for the steps of a calculation even though the final result is incorrect due to a mathematical or copying error at some early stage. Part marks can only be given if the stages in a calculation are laid out clearly. Therefore, if you know you have ended up with an incorrect answer, perhaps because the scale of it is absurd, do not immediately scribble all over your working. Move on to another question and return to the earlier one at the end of the exam; even if you can't spot the error, you may receive part marks.

smart tip

Revision tips for numerical questions

Try as many examples from past papers and problems sheets as you can. A useful tactic is to invent your own problems, as this helps you understand the equations and mathematical models better.

✔ Practical tips for approaching numerical questions in exams

Check your calculator. Before your exam date, ensure that you are allowed to use a calculator, and confirm that it is a model that is permitted for use if there are any restrictions. Make sure you understand how to carry out relevant functions. If your calculator is battery-operated, ensure a fresh battery is fitted or take a spare.

Analyse the question type. Make sure you understand which formula or formulae to use, or which approach to attempt before starting.

Work methodically and carefully. Double-check each step. Write neatly and add vital information such as units or assumptions.

Pay attention to presentation. Follow the tips given earlier in this chapter and always provide units or a written explanation with the answer.

Never give up. Even if you think you can't complete the answer, don't give up. Try to do the basics or a part answer, perhaps noting any points you can recall in a list. The part marks obtained could make the difference between grades or between a pass and a fail.

💬 Useful language for . . . talking about numeracy

Context: these questions might be used when asking for help with numerical aspects of your course.

Please can you recommend a textbook where I can find some other problems of this type, so that I can practise?

I'm having problems with the part of the course where we use [state mathematical procedure]. Is there anywhere I can get help with this?

The way this equation is presented is different from the way I learned it before. This is what we used [show version previously used]. Can you explain the difference, please?

(GO) And now . . .

37.1 When revising, create a page of formulae relevant to your subject. Note situations where each is normally applied.

37.2 Try to categorise types of numerical questions that have been asked in past exam papers. For example, work out which formulae should be applied and how they may be rearranged or linked. Thinking at this level will help you identify how to approach questions more rapidly and with more confidence.

37.3 Practise! This really is the key to success.

How to maximise your marks

You may be asked to write an essay as part of coursework or in an exam. These two situations require distinct approaches due mainly to the length of the piece of writing and the time available to produce it. This chapter considers decisions about content, organisation and production that will lead to an effective answer in either case.

Key topics:
→ What lecturers are looking for in different types of essay answer
→ Planning essay answers for coursework and exams
→ The importance of addressing the task as set
→ Reviewing your exam answers

Essential vocabulary
**Critical thinking   Formative assessment   Instruction words   Personal pronoun
Value judgement   Writer's block**

The essay is a traditional method of university assessment that is required in two very different circumstances. The first of these is in the context of coursework and the second is during an examination. In the former, the traditional essay allows you to examine critique concepts and issues in depth; in the latter you have less time and are expected to cover the topic with a sharper focus and less specific detail. This chapter will help you to adapt your approach to answering appropriately.

→ What lecturers are looking for in different types of essay answer

Coursework essays are mainly used to elicit an in-depth answer to a complex issue. They allow you to develop an argument, explain alternative views based on your understanding of the issues and evidenced by the literature you have read to research the topic. To achieve this you have a much longer period of time to spend on the research, planning, writing and proof-reading stages that are covered in **Toolkit D**. Word length limits may be imposed, but, in general, a relatively high level of detail is possible compared with an exam-style essay.

In exam contexts, there are two types of essay response required: the 'short-answer' format that requires condensed and pertinent information in a truncated style of answer; and the longer essay answer that needs to provide a clear and yet less detailed answer than a coursework essay.

'Short answer' exam questions come in several formats (**Ch 36**) and may be allocated a notional time for answering of approximately ten minutes. Those that demand an essay-style answer do require detail – but usually with a very specific focus, often indicated by the instruction word used (Table 28.2, p. 235). Each sentence has to be written quickly, but in a considered way to ensure that you are gaining the optimum value from what you write.

How much detail is required in a short-answer essay?

In many instances, it is possible to gauge the level of detail required by mapping your points against the marks allocated to the question. For example, a short-answer question worth 6 marks might be graded as one half-point against each of the 12 target pieces of information expected by the marker in a 'perfect' answer. Alternatively, a two-part question asking for a definition and then a description of what you have defined might allocate 2 marks to the definition and 4 marks to the description.

Longer essay answers in exams generally have a notional time for answering of between 30 minutes and an hour, depending on the number of questions you are asked to complete and the length of the exam. These answers often have the possibility of following the imprint of a mainstream coursework essay, but without the detailed references to source material that would be expected in coursework. The examiner is looking for a response to the question as set (**Ch 28**) and not a memorised version of an essay written as coursework on the same theme or topic. Your answer must show that you are capable of bringing together broad ideas supported by evidence with references to key sources in the literature (but only exceptionally with detailed bibliographical citation). It is important to focus on the argument or discussion rather than spend precious time and space on scene-setting description. The examiner will assume knowledge of the background and will expect you to engage immediately with the critical thinking you would have demonstrated in a coursework essay.

smart tip

Critical thinking

Longer essays are commonly used when tutors expect you to think more deeply. Often what you have to do is not framed as a question but an instruction. Typically, you will be expected to:

- **Apply** knowledge and understanding.
- **Analyse** information.
- **Synthesise** new ideas and treatments of facts.
- **Evaluate** issues, viewpoints and arguments.

Tables 21.1 and 21.2 (pp. 163–4) provide further explanation of what's expected under these headings. You should watch out for instruction words that invite these approaches, as shown in Table 21.1 (p. 163).

→ Planning essay answers for coursework and exams

Significantly, marks can be lost in essay-style assessments through poor planning and structuring of the answer. Ideally, your outline plan will lead to an obvious structure for the main body of the text, but often in exam situations a piece of writing evolves only once the writer begins to write. This is because the act of writing stimulates development of thought, potentially leading to changes in order and in content. In these cases, your initial outline plan should be seen as a flexible guideline that may change as you begin to think more deeply about the topic.

On the other hand, if the planning phase is ignored completely, and you only think about the structure while you write, then you can end up with a weakly structured and possibly rambling essay. Table 38.1 describes some of the common pitfalls that can occur when students fail to consider the structure of their writing.

Table 38.1 Common faults in the structure of essay-style answers. In these examples, attention to the planning phase would result in a better structure, and hence, better marks.

Symptom of weakness in structure	Analysis of the problem
The mystery tour. This type of answer rambles on, drifting from point to disconnected point with no real structure or direction.	The essay may contain valuable content, but marks will be lost because this is not organised and parts are not connected appropriately to create a coherent response.
A 'body' with no introduction and/or no conclusion. The main part (body) contains many useful points, but the writer fails to introduce them and fails to draw conclusions based on them.	Facts, concepts and ideas alone are not enough - evidence must be provided of deeper-level analytical thinking (Ch 21). The introduction and conclusions are important parts where this can be achieved.
The overly-detailed answer. The main body of the answer contains a wealth of information, some of which is relevant and some not. Despite the finely-grained detail, little structure is evident and there is no discrimination between the important and the unimportant.	The writer has probably been preoccupied with showing how much has been memorised, without showing how much has been understood. Relevance of the material in relation to the instruction given has not been considered at the planning stage, nor as the essay-writing progresses.
The continuous stream of ideas. Often written as if it were a conversational monologue, this lacks internal organisation, few (or too many) signposting words, no (or few) paragraphs, and little apparent logic.	Academic writing style involves structural as well as linguistic components. Both are important elements of a good answer. Hence, the writing needs to guide the reader along a logical path to enable understanding.
The waffly, irrelevant answer. Unfocused, this fails to get to grips with the question and may contain large amounts of irrelevant information, offered up seemingly without regard for the topic set.	Greater attention needs to be paid to analysis of the instruction given and converting these thoughts into a coherent answer plan. Irrelevant material should not be used as it will gain no marks.
The half-an-answer. Fails to appreciate that there were two (or more) parts to the question. Focuses solely on one part.	The essay should cover all aspects of the question as more marks may be allocated to the secondary part(s). This should be reflected in the essay plan and eventual structure.
Structure dominated by quotes. This might start with an over-used quote or be interspersed with extensive memorised quotes, with little effective use of these.	This type of structure leaves little room for evidence of original thought. Few marks are given for having a good memory - it's what is done with the information that counts.

The time limitation in exams means you will need to work quickly when planning – either use a spider diagram/mind map or linear notes to generate ideas relevant to the question (**Ch 16**). From this, decide on a structure, for example, by numbering the order in which you intend to follow in your answer. This approach will help you to think laterally as well as in a linear manner – important, so that you generate all the points relevant to your answer. As discussed in **Ch 29**, you should probably think in terms of three basic components:

- **The introduction**: states briefly what your answer will say, sets the context and gives an insight as to how you intend to approach the topic.

- **The main body**: presents the information, the argument or key points of your response.

- **The conclusion**: sums up the answer as stated, reinforces the position outlined in the introduction, and puts the whole answer into a wider context.

Can I make notes and plans in exam books?

It is perfectly acceptable practice to make notes in the exam answer booklet; however, you should always score through them before you submit the answer paper. A single diagonal line will suffice. Sometimes your plan may be used by the examiner to cross-check details of your answer (but do not count on this).

Tips for writing these elements are provided in **Ch 29**, while potential ways of organising the main body of essay-style assignments are considered in **Ch 30**. It is also important to consider the marking criteria in relation to your potential answer. It may be worth reviewing these before you start to write a coursework essay or as you prepare for exams. These criteria should be published in the module handbook. Table 38.2 provides a useful checklist in relation to presentation (**Ch 34**), structure (**Ch 30**) and content (**Chs 21**, **23** and **28**).

Approaching essay-style assessments when English is not your first language

This can be a difficult area for some international students; you may be anxious and feel under time pressure.

- **Do your preparation** – when revising, think about ways you could phrase parts of answers that include concepts, ideas or fact. Write these key phrases down and practise using them. Learn all the specialist vocabulary you expect to use.

- **Keep things simple** – use short, uncomplicated sentence structures, and build your answer from these elements. You will not lose marks for simplicity, but you will probably lose marks if you attempt lengthy complex sentences that are more likely to contain errors.

- **Focus on understanding your topic fully** – especially in exams this will allow you to answer any type of question and will prove a far better strategy than memorising a 'prepared' answer ('question spotting', p. 433) which is unlikely to be relevant to the actual question on the exam paper.

Table 38.2 Checklist for essay-style assessments in relation to typical marking criteria

Presentation	Structure	Content
Writing style: should be • objective; • formal as appropriate to academic writing; and • clear, correct, standard English with no truncated text messaging or other inappropriate abbreviations.	**Logic of writing:** your writing should be planned carefully so that it has a logical structure. Sentences and paragraphs should be constructed so that they add to the cohesion of the text. Sentence-level errors will make the text difficult to understand and may hamper your reader's understanding.	**Quality of knowledge:** writing should reflect • an understanding of the range of module/course themes and your ability to make connections across topics. This is particularly the case in exam answers; • evidence of reading from source material in addition to lecture material.
Printed submission: for coursework the norm is increasingly accepted to be word-processed and printed. Follow standard conventions of justification, spacing, spelling and punctuation. Spell and grammar check before submission.	**Logic of discussion or argument:** evidence should be organised in support of your viewpoint but expressed in ways that avoid making value judgements (p. 165, **Ch 23**).	**Relevance:** text relates to the topic defined by the task brief. If you write too much general material, especially in exam answers, and fail to tackle the deeper, more complex issues, this will have a negative impact on your grade.
Hand-written submission: in exams, you will probably have to write your answers by hand. Thus, write as clearly as possible, sometimes in larger script than you might use normally. Don't use capital letters throughout as this is difficult to read and will slow your marker down. Be sure to note the number of the question you're answering.	**Relationship to literature:** in many disciplines, the line of argument that you need to construct should relate to key words in existing literature. You will earn credit for making these connections within your text, being careful to avoid plagiarism. If you fail to make these links or to explain why you are making them, your work (and your mark) will be weakened.	**Critical thinking:** your writing must demonstrate an ability to analyse and synthesise complex ideas; and, at higher levels of study, demonstrate some ability to construct an original argument. In exams, thinking in this way spontaneously is what is being assessed and so it is worth anticipating and rehearsing some of the key arguments on key topics.
Grammar check: in word-processed documents, checking functions will highlight spelling and grammar errors. Note, some of these may not be 'errors', simply unusual uses – passive use rather than active. In exams, you will not have this function and so it is important to read over your hand-written work carefully towards the end of the exam to check for errors.	**Use of tables, diagrams, graphs or figures:** some subjects routinely require evidence to be presented in visual format. If you need to show evidence in this way, ensure that visuals are labelled appropriately and are integrated into the text in a logical manner close to the text that explains their content (see p. 288). This contributes to the cohesion of your argument and text structure.	**Use of primary sources:** in some subjects the ability to analyse and evaluate material from primary sources will set your work apart from that of others as significant and worthy of a higher grade. Hence, in exam answers you should try to incorporate some reference to such primary material for the same reasons.

Answers must be relevant. Marks can be lost is when answers do not address the question (see Table 38.1). You should:

- make sure that you consider all aspects of the question. Brainstorming techniques (**Ch 25**) are a quick way of developing an overview;

- explain what you understand by the question (perhaps the introductory paragraph, or in an exam, the introductory sentence). This will make you think about the question and may clear up any doubt about how it can be interpreted. However, make sure that you do not narrow the topic to a point that would be unreasonable;

- keep your focus on the precise task you have been asked to do (**Ch 28**). As you write, return to the question asked to ensure that you have not strayed from the key aspects of what you were asked to do.

---

smart tip

Analysing the wording of each task as set

As discussed in **Ch 28**, you need to take a broader and more in-depth look at the task in the context of the whole question. To do this, you must consider:

- **The instruction word.** In what category does that place the task? For example, have you been asked to act, describe, analyse, argue, or do something else completely (**Ch 28**, pp. 233-4)?
- **The topic.** What is the core topic about?
- **The aspect(s).** What particular aspect of the topic has to be considered?
- **Any restriction(s).** What limits have been imposed on the discussion? Your answer must encompass each element of the task to ensure that it is a logical response to the task you were set. What you write must be relevant. Superfluous material or digressions will not earn you marks.

- ensuring that your answer is planned. Creating a plan will make you think about the relevance and the logic of your argument;

- keeping to the point. Including irrelevant or repetitive content will not gain any marks and the time you spend writing it will be wasted – in the exam context, this may stop you from gaining marks on other questions. Having said that, no marks are given for 'white space': even a few general points of principle may result in enough marks to help you pass, when added to those gained in other, better, answers; and

- avoiding making unsupported value judgements including absolute statements (using words such as all, every, always). These statements impose the writer's views on the reader often using subjective language, and which fail to provide sound evidence to support the position put forward (**Ch 27**). Make sure you write objectively (p. 223) and avoid using the personal pronouns 'I', 'you', 'we' and 'one'.

Mixing topics and multi-part questions

In coursework essays it is less easy to miss the demands of a multi-part or mixed topic task; however, in exams under the pressure of time this is quite a common fault. This can arise for a number of reasons. For example, you may find that in a question that blends two topics or asks you to address two aspects, you can only respond to half of the task. In exams, it can be the result of 'question-spotting' at the revision stage (**Ch 53**). Make sure you answer all elements of multi-part assessments. These may not be worded in two or more sentences, but the use of phrases such as 'compare and contrast' and 'cause(s) and effect(s)' should alert you to this. Make sure that the weighting in marks assigned to a question is reflected in the length of the component parts of your answer.

Dealing with writer's block

If you find you tend to be unable to start an essay answer, try starting with a definition or a simple statement of fact. In coursework, you can always go back and amend this later; in exam situations, you might try using a key phrase from the question (but beware of simply restating the entire question).

✔ Practical tips for boosting your essay marks in exams

Have potential answer formats in mind as you go into an exam. Ideally, your revision and pre-exam preparation (**Ch 53, Ch 55**) will have given you a good idea of the exam format and even potential exam questions. This will ensure you do not have to start answers completely from scratch.

Balance your effort appropriately. Whereas a coursework essay introduction requires some detail, in exam answers your introduction need not be overly long. Most marks will be awarded for the main body and conclusions, so spend more time and brainpower on them.

Make sure you aren't losing marks due to poor presentation. Despite the time pressure, exam answers need to be legible and clearly laid out. If feedback indicates that tutors are having problems in reading your work, or consider it untidy, paying attention to this could be an easy way of gaining marks (**Ch 34**).

Focus on providing evidence of deeper thinking. Especially at higher levels of study, this will help you gain better grades. On the assumption that you are able to include basic information and display an understanding of it, you can gain marks for:

- supplying additional and relevant detail at the expected depth;
- providing an analytical answer rather than a descriptive one – focusing on deeper aspects of a topic, rather than merely recounting facts;
- placing the problem in context, and demonstrating your wider understanding of the topic; however, make sure you don't overdo this, or you may risk not completing the task as set – remember that you cannot be expected to give the same amount of detail in an exam answer as you would in a piece of essay-style coursework;

- giving evidence of reading around the subject, by quoting relevant papers and reviews and mentioning author names and dates of publication;
- considering all sides of a topic/debate, and arriving at a clear conclusion – you may have to take into account and explain two or more viewpoints, and possibly weigh them up, according to the question set; where appropriate, your answer should demonstrate that you realise that the issue is complex and possibly unresolved.

Useful language for . . . discussing essay questions

Context: these examples might be used when revising with fellow students and perhaps when looking over past exam papers.

How would you approach this question? I think I might start by xxxx, then include information on xxxx in the main body and the conclusion might be xxxx. What do you think?

How many questions will we have to answer in the exam? How long should we take for each one? How much time do you think we should leave for reviewing our answers?

I've looked at past papers for this exam. The essays nearly always include a factual part and an analytical part – look at these examples. I think we need to practise answering some of these, so we can get the balance right.

GO And now . . .

38.1 Focus on definitions and possible formats during revision. If you have trouble getting your answers started during exams, it can be a useful device to start with a definition; alternatively, think about stating the situation, the problem and then the potential solution. This might not be applicable to all scenarios, but if you are really stuck this will at least give you a framework for thinking and writing.

38.2 Review essay-style questions in past exam papers. Look at these particularly from the point of view of the depth of answers required. Consider both the instruction word used (**Ch 33**) and the context to gain an appreciation of the level of thinking demanded. Consult **Ch 23** if you need to review 'thinking processes'.

38.3 Use formative assessment exercises to improve your English. If you recognise that your use of language is weak, take advantage of all formative assessment exercises to help you improve. Speak with markers and tutors about how you might enhance your marks. You may find that analysing possible writing techniques can help, especially if you are aware of specific weaknesses, such as punctuation or structuring.

Tutorial assessment

How to make your contribution count

This chapter explains what is expected of you in a tutorial and what might be taken into consideration when tutors or fellow students assess your engagement with the topic or problem.

Key topics:
→ Engaging fully with the topic
→ Criteria for assessment of tutorial participation

Essential vocabulary
Assessment criteria   Marking scheme   Tutorial

The main purpose of a university tutorial is to learn interactively with others, either through discussion and debate of issues, or by considering problems you have been asked to address (**Ch 20**). Your output, such as a related essay or the answers to numerical questions, may be assessed, and, in some cases, your role as a participant may be evaluated. You need to understand exactly what is going to be considered so that you can make your contribution count.

smart tip

Presence and participation

Slipping into a lecture 10 minutes after the start may go unremarked. The same will not be true of a late arrival in a tutorial. Show courtesy to your fellow students and the tutor by being on time and engaging actively with the intensive work designed to develop your understanding of the tutorial theme.

→ Engaging fully with the topic

Preparation for tutorials was explained in broad terms in **Ch 20**. However, in the context of assessment you need to think in greater detail about how you go about tackling a set of problems or a topic. This will differ slightly depending on the type of tutorial.

Problem-solving tutorials

For problem-solving tutorials, you may be asked to work through problems beforehand or, conversely, you may be asked to review the problems in preparation for working through them as a group in the tutorial.

- Identify the area or theme being addressed.
- Read over the relevant sections in your textbook and lecture notes.

- Equip yourself with the skills to do the task. This might mean revising an area of maths or understanding relevant formulae.

- Look over the examples to see whether they are all of similar difficulty or whether they are ranged in ascending difficulty. This could, for instance, be a deliberate way of leading you through the process of developing a proof for a formula and then applying it to a more complex problem.

Improving your participation

Two extreme behaviours shown by international students unfamiliar with tutorial-based learning are either to keep quiet and only observe or to participate overly vigorously but less relevantly. Neither approach is appropriate when tutorials are being assessed and you may be marked down if you show these characteristics.

Discussion-based tutorials

For discussion-based tutorials, the topic will generally be given in advance.

- Analyse the topic in the same way that you would analyse a topic for a written assignment (**Ch 29**).

- Read over the relevant sections in your lecture notes and do the prescribed reading. Who are the key researchers or commentators on the topic? What are their perspectives on the topic?

- Make notes of key ideas and principles as appropriate, so that you can refer to these in the tutorials.

- You should be looking for aspects such as:
  - for-and-against positions;
  - cause-and-effect scenarios;
  - comparison of similar circumstances or attitudes;
  - use of specific or differing methodologies;
  - contrasting viewpoints and the evidence in support and refutation;
  - inconsistencies and flaws in argument;
  - parallels and analogies used to illustrate points.

Sometimes the tutorial discussion is designed to help you to approach an assessed exercise such as an essay. In these cases, you should bear in mind the exact phrasing of the essay topic as you listen and contribute during the tutorial, and make notes that will help you to make full use of what you learn.

---

smart tip

Student-led tutorials

Sometimes tutorials are organised so that each student is given an opportunity to lead the tutorial discussion, while the tutor observes the interplay of argument and debate. If you are required to participate in tutorials in this way, the tutorial 'characters' and the strategies to deal with them described in **Ch 20** will take on an added significance.

→ Criteria for assessment of tutorial participation

Tutorial assessment may count for between 5 and 25 per cent of your total course assessment, with part or all of that mark being for 'participation', depending on the subject. Check the course handbook for details. Several generic aspects may be taken into account:

- your attendance over the series of tutorials;
- your active participation in the discussion or problem-solving aspects of the tutorial;
- evidence of reading and/or other preparation;
- your ability to think analytically and critically about points raised during the tutorial;
- your ability to present and defend a viewpoint, and the quality of your counter-arguments;
- your ability to relate the tutorial activity to other parts of the course and to the wider subject area;
- your ability to interact considerately and constructively with others;
- marks gained for any work handed in as part of the tutorial.

smart tip

Relationships between tutorials and exams

Exams are not simply based on the lectures. They draw from the extended reading, exercises and tutorials that form part of your personal study. It is worth looking carefully at tutorial topics and the preparatory work associated with them when you are planning your revision. Be sure to include these topics as part of the work to be covered in your preparation for exam-based assessment.

✔ Practical tips for tutorial assessment

For problem-solving tutorials:

Consider how the marks awarded for each tutorial will affect your assessment. Find out how many marks you will get for each element and how this fits into the overall marking scheme. Try your best to complete the full set of examples. This will help consolidate your learning and, if you are required to submit the worked examples, could contribute to your continuous assessment marks.

For discussion-based tutorials:

Consider the question from different angles. With regard to assessment, in particular, consider your viewpoint critically and anticipate what the counter-arguments might be. Build up your response to the counter-argument. If you hold an opposing view, what would be the strengths and weaknesses of your argument?

Work out your position with regard to the topic. Reflect on what you have read and begin to evolve your personal position or viewpoint on the topic. Gather together evidence that supports your viewpoint and note down key points.

Useful language for . . . contributing in an assessed tutorial

Context: these suggestions offer you ways to be able to contribute to the discussion in a tutorial.

I got the answer xxxx. Here's how I approached the question. First, I assumed . . .

I think there are two sides to this argument . . .

I found the points made by xxxx quite persuasive. She takes the original view that . . .

Could we look at this in a different way? How about . . .?

Could I just check that I understand your point correctly? You mean that . . .

GO And now . . .

39.1 Think about the make-up and behaviour of the tutorial groups in which you participate. Look again at the 'characters' described in **Ch 20** and consider how you might need to deal with any of these types in your groups to ensure, for example, that you get the opportunity to speak in a tutorial that is often dominated by one individual. If that person dominates the discussion, it is going to affect your ability to contribute and demonstrate your engagement with the topic.

39.2 Relate your tutorial work to other forms of assessment. In the next tutorial you attend, think about the work done or the discussion that occurs and consider how this might be useful to you in terms of exam revision. Write up notes after the event or annotate any handouts you received with the conclusions you have drawn from the exercises or discussion.

39.3 Learn from other forms of meeting. Tutorials are meetings and it will help you to develop your participation style if you look at the way that other meetings you attend are conducted. You might feel that a greater or lesser degree of formality makes the dynamic work better, for example. Learn from the tactics of others by watching their processes and strategies for putting their points across, and, in particular, the timing of their contributions.

40 | Assessments of practical and laboratory work

How to improve your marks

The marks awarded to practical assessments can make up a relatively large proportion of the total for a module. Gaining better grades requires preparation beforehand, focused effort during the practical or practical exam, and care with writing up or answering.

Key topic:
→ Forms of practical assessment and how to approach them

Essential vocabulary
Continuous assessment   Spot exam   Summative assessment

Practical work is generally included in the syllabus to complement the theory covered in lectures and tutorials. Depending on your discipline, it gives you a chance to see specimens, develop skills and understand how research is conducted (**Ch 19**). However, in some courses, the theory may not have been covered at the time of the practical, so it is advisable to do a bit of background reading prior to the practical class.

The importance that lecturers attach to practical elements of the course can be seen from the proportion of your overall module grade that they assign to these aspects. This may be between 30 and 50 per cent, so you should devote a proportionate amount of study and revision time to related assessment activities.

→ Forms of practical assessment and how to approach them

Consult your course handbook at an early stage to see how your practical work will be assessed. The main methods, including tips for tackling each one, are listed below.

Continuous assessment of lab work

This is a common way of assessing practical work, where grades are awarded for workbooks or lab reports completed during the course. As these marks may be relatively straightforward to achieve, this is a good way of building up a 'bank' of good grades so that it is easier to pass or do well in the overall module assessment.

To maximise your marks for completed lab workbooks you will need to ensure that:

- your work in the lab is neat and tidy;
- you have completed all that is required of you.

Minimum attendance requirements

In some courses, you must attend all or most of the practical classes. Failure to meet this minimum may mean you will not be given permission to sit the degree examination at the end of the year.

Because lab work often seems rushed, neither of these aims may be straightforward to achieve, but both will be easier if you have prepared well (**Ch 19**). During lab sessions, check with demonstrators and staff that each part is completed to their satisfaction and take heed of their tips and suggestions (see also **Ch 34**).

When preparing a formal report from a practical, adopt the format laid out in your handbook or the lab schedule (which may differ among subjects). If no format is specified, follow that given in Table 19.1 (on p. 153). As marks are likely to be awarded for presentation, pay special attention to layout, print quality and order of sections. You may need to learn from lecturers' feedback how you can best approach writing style and the amount of detail required.

Practical exams

These 'summative' tests generally take place in laboratories during the main exam period. They usually involve:

- recall and understanding regarding specimens and techniques;
- tests of the observational and manual skills you have developed during the course;
- following procedures and using equipment;
- measurement and numerical analysis;
- interpretation or presentation of data.

Because of the 'unseen' and unpredictable nature of practical exams, there is less chance to prepare using standard revision techniques. You will need to be ready to adopt a logical approach. Make sure you read each question carefully (more than once) so you can carry out *exactly* what is required.

Past papers for practical exams are rarely available, and if they are, may make little sense in the absence of the real samples. To help your revising, you could look through the past practical schedules, highlighting parts that might be appropriate for this form of examination. Some examples of types of practical questions in the sciences are provided opposite. Spot tests and oral forms of practical exam may involve moving around a 'circuit', examining specimens, or perhaps looking at slides through a microscope, then providing quick written answers or responding with spoken answers. Key tips for this type of exam are:

- always take your time when answering;
- always take a second detailed look at the specimen to check whether your first assumptions are correct;
- consider all aspects of the question;
- start with simple points, such as a straightforward description of the specimen (the markers may use a checklist with some marks attached to these basic points); and
- if you don't know an answer, don't waste time talking unnecessarily – move on to the next question quickly, if this is allowed.

Examples of practical exam questions

The following are examples of typical question styles (imagine the precise context yourself):

Draw a fully labelled diagram of specimen A.

Graph the following data and draw conclusions.

Examine specimen N and photograph M; and describe how the specimen relates to this environment.

Construct a calibration curve for a ... test using the reagents and equipment provided. What value do you estimate for the unknown specimen X?

Comment on the syndrome evident in slide B.

Prepare a pure sample of ... using the reagents and equipment provided.

Examine table Z (or picture A) and answer the following questions ...

Given the data in Table F, calculate ...

Compare specimens A and B, explaining ...

Although you may think of the lab as an informal setting, formal practical exams will be subject to the same rules and regulations as written 'theory' exams (**Ch 35**). Some practical exams may be 'open book', where you are allowed to consult past schedules, for example, as you tackle the questions. However, don't assume this is the case unless you have been specifically informed.

Practical questions within written/online assessments

Sometimes you will find that practical elements are assessed as a component of exams that you might assume would be solely about theory. For example, there may be questions in multiple-choice and short-answer papers that relate to work done in practicals. Look at the 'small print' in your course handbook to see if this might be the case, or ask lecturers, and adjust your revision accordingly. For example, this might imply that you rehearse simple calculations and learn relevant formulae.

Know the relevant vocabulary for your subject

Practicals and lab work involve a wide range of procedures and specimens with relatively obscure names. It's worth preparing for assessment by creating a list of specialist words and memorising their meaning and grammatical use.

✓ Practical tips for sitting practical exams

Scan your practical schedules as an aid to revision. Try to see if you can predict possible question types, but avoid question-spotting (**Ch 53**). Memorise key procedures that might be tested, but remember that there may be a limited time for each question on the paper. Think about the skills you may be asked to use and go through the instructions and tips you have been given about these.

Practise labelling diagrams. If you can identify a need to provide labels on diagrams of seen and unseen specimens, you may wish to test yourself by drawing up a schematic diagram, then labelling it without reference to supporting texts or schedules. This will give you feedback on how much you already know and what you need to learn.

Practise answering numerical questions. As recommended in **Ch 37**, this is the best way to ensure you perform well on the day in these types of assessments.

Take advantage of 'open door' revision sessions. In some subjects, the lab may be opened in the period prior to exams so you can have another look at key specimens. These sessions provide an opportunity to review the material and possibly ask questions of staff in attendance – very useful if you are unsure about some aspects, or think your memory will improve if you see the samples again, closer to the exam. These sessions are also an opportunity for collaboration with fellow students, as you can ask each other questions about the specimens to test your knowledge.

State the obvious, justify your conclusions. If you find that your mind has gone blank during a practical exam, start with the basics. For example, if asked to identify a specimen, do not give up because you can't immediately do this from memory. The question-setter may be trying to see if you can adopt a logical approach to the problem, and everyone in the class may be in the same situation. Start from first principles and basic observations ('the specimen has a yellow colour, therefore I conclude . . .') and move on from there. Similarly, when you do know an answer, state why you know it. There may be marks allocated to this aspect, which you will miss out on if you simply provide a bare answer.

Review good practice in graphing and tabulating. If constructing and interpreting data in graphs and tables might be a part of your exam, it makes sense to go over the basic principles and instructions for these forms of presentation beforehand (see pp. 288–91).

Ensure that you have the correct equipment required for a practical exam. This will depend on the subject, but will be similar to the items taken to each practical (**Ch 19**). Remember to include a watch so that you can monitor time. Synchronise your watch with the clock in the exam hall so that you are working within the same time frame as invigilators and examiners. If you tend to use your mobile phone as a clock, remember that mobiles are normally not allowed to be taken into the exam room.

Useful language for . . . preparing for a practical exam

Context: these assume that you are discussing revision with a fellow student.

I've created this list of technical terms. Would you like to test me on the meaning of each one?

I think they might ask us about xxxx. Do you think it would be worthwhile going over that procedure again?

How can you tell the difference between xxxx and xxxx? I've written down three key differences. What do you think?

GO And now . . .

40.1 Consult your course handbook. Find out what proportion of marks are allocated to practical assessment and what form the assessment will take. Adjust your revision plans accordingly.

40.2 Make a list of possible questions that might come up in your practical exam. This revision exercise might best be carried out working with a fellow student so that you can share ideas (**Ch 57**). Use the learning outcomes and schedules as a source of ideas (**Ch 53**).

40.3 Make up a checklist of equipment to take to the exam. Knowing you have everything you might need ready beforehand, rather than grabbing things at the last moment, will boost your confidence.

Choosing a dissertation or project topic

How to decide on a theme and write a research proposal

Dissertations, project reports and theses are extensive exercises in writing. They contribute significantly to modules and degree classification grades, and at higher levels may be the main means of assessment. It is important to tackle them professionally. This chapter offers strategies that will help you start this process effectively.

Key topics:
→ Starting off well
→ Taking account of the options open to you
→ Deciding on your personal research interests
→ Important factors to take into account when choosing a project
→ Writing a research proposal

Essential vocabulary
Dissertation Generic Hypothesis Macro Project report Proposal Supervisor Thesis

When you look proudly at the finished version of your dissertation, project report or thesis, this will probably be one of the highlights of your university career. In most cases, its production will be the result of many months of hard work. The final document will represent the high point of your achievements at university and provide concrete evidence of your advanced academic skills.

University tutors will demonstrate the perceived importance of dissertations and reports by allocating a high proportion of marks from them towards your final grade, or in certain cases, base the assessment procedures on an oral exam focusing on your thesis.

Dissertation and project work take time and it is easy to drift aimlessly at the start of this period. However, to achieve the best possible product, it is essential to be focused from the start and disciplined in your approach.

smart tip

Taking account of the task you have been set

While there are many similarities in the production of dissertations and project reports, there are also some key differences. We have tried to provide generic material wherever possible, but also include suggestions relevant to specific outcomes for each type of document. You should select material relevant to your personal needs, your level of study and the approach required in your discipline.

To ensure you make the best possible start to your research studies, you should:

- **Make sure you understand precisely what you are being asked to produce, and how.** You can do this by reading the supporting material in the course handbook or regulations (particularly the learning objectives or outcomes), or by speaking to your supervisor or a potential supervisor.

- **Try to make the initial connection with your research or source material.** Sometimes this will appear bewildering in its breadth, obscure in its jargon or genuinely difficult to master. The only way you will overcome this is to immerse yourself in the topic, read background material and ask questions. The sooner you take this step, the better. To get an early grasp of the basic concepts, you might consider going back to a chapter from an introductory text or revisiting relevant course notes.

- **Try not to luxuriate in the comfort of having a deadline many months away.** Graduates will tell you that every part of the process took longer than they estimated, and that, if they had to do it all again, they would try to organise themselves better. The time will quickly evaporate, and the earlier you start the task, the more likely you will be to avoid stress near to the end.

- **Do something active as soon as possible.** Appropriate actions will depend on your subject, but will probably include making notes of your background reading, or creating a plan of action or timetable. In some research projects it will involve making initial observations or setting up a pilot experiment; in others on obtaining the right textbooks and references.

---

smart tip

Make the most of meetings with your tutor

In some cases you will be assigned a supervising tutor for the purpose of researching and writing your dissertation. In most instances, meetings will be arranged with that person to discuss your individual project. Make good use of these opportunities and if you are in doubt about any aspect of this work, then arrange for an additional meeting so that you can clarify your understanding.

→ **Taking account of the options open to you**

The topic you choose to research has a great influence on how well you succeed in carrying out the investigation and in writing up your work. In addition, many practical matters need to be taken into account, such as the availability of relevant literature material or equipment, or the practical feasibility of the intended investigation.

In many cases, you may find that the dissertation or project topics are prescribed or restricted. The decision is not so much one of what you would like to research, but more which topic you will choose from a list of options provided by academic staff. A variation on this closed option list is the semi-closed list, where academics provide a list of broad topics but leave the student to choose the detailed perspective that they wish to pursue.

Initially, such constraints may feel restrictive. However, the aim is to provide you with a degree of freedom within parameters controlled by the staff who will supervise and assess the finished work. They will have carefully considered the practicalities of each option and the chances of obtaining a successful outcome.

smart tip

Make your decisions with speed but not haste

If a list of dissertation or research options is presented, find out about it as quickly as possible, as there may be competition for specific topics or for particular supervisors. However, make sure you take all relevant factors into account in a deliberate decision-making process; do not choose under pressure. You should give the matter high priority. Allocate time and attention to activities that may help you make a decision, such as library or internet searches and discussions with potential supervisors.

Sometimes there is a less restricted approach to the selection of dissertation topic or research project. Here, no list is provided and you are asked to choose not only the topic but the specific research question to be addressed. In this open-choice case, you will be expected to make a selection largely on the basis of your personal interests within the discipline. These might have developed from your personal experience or from previous detailed consideration of related topics arising from your course of study, for example, from reading you did when producing coursework.

→ Deciding on your personal research interests

You should find your study area interesting and the topic should be novel and challenging. If this is the case, then your levels of motivation will be high and may sustain you through any problems you meet. If not, you will be liable to become bored or disillusioned, and this will hinder your ability to complete and write up your work. For some students, stating a primary research interest might be easy, but for many, it will be quite difficult to commit their efforts to one highly focused subject, or to decide which option on a list interests them most. There may be a range of possibilities, each with a balance of attractions and negative aspects.

Putting forward your own topic

If you have a specific topic in mind that is not on a prescribed list of dissertation or research project options, you could try approaching a potential supervisor to ask whether it might be considered. If you do this, be prepared to answer searching questions about its viability as a research theme. These may be similar to those used to assess a research proposal (p. 338). It is not advisable to choose a topic that relies solely on material in your own language because this cannot be evaluated by supervisors who do not speak their student's language.

What, then, is the best way to arrive at a decision? This may depend on your personality, the discipline and the degree of choice you have been given.

- If you have an open choice, you could brainstorm possible topics and sub-topics within your subject (**Ch 25**), then to rank these in order of your interest. You could do this in phases, moving sequentially from broader subject fields to more closely specified research areas, until a clear favourite emerges or you can narrow down the choices.

- If your choice is restricted or is from a menu of options, consider each option in turn. Do not reject any possibility out of hand until you know more about it. Obtain background information where necessary. If a reading list is offered, consult this. Rank the options according to how they interest you.

With luck, you will now have created a shortlist of potential topics. The next phase, potentially of equal importance, is to think further about the practical matters that should influence your decision.

A simple way of ranking your choices

Consider each option in turn, and award it a mark out of 10. When you have completed a scan of all the options, look again at the ones which scored highly and reject the ones that scored weakly. Try explaining the reasons for your scores to someone else. This may force you to put into words how you feel, and thereby become more confident in your decision.

→ Important factors to take into account when choosing a project

Several factors will influence your ability to complete your studies to a high standard. Again, it will be beneficial to score these aspects in relation to the specific topics in your shortlist. You may wish to take into account the following:

- **Potential research approaches.** Is it possible for you to identify the approach that might be required? What precisely is the question to be answered, problem to be solved or issue to be debated? How will you restrict the potential areas to be covered? How exactly will you go about researching your topic? You may alter the 'research angle' through time, but considering these matters might aid the decision-making process. Also, bear in mind that if you have distinct direction to your work from the start, this will greatly increase your chances of success.

- **Scope and time limitations.** In selecting a topic, it is important to guard against being over-ambitious. Ensure that you will have enough time to be able to demonstrate, through your written work, that you have completed the task required. You need to allow for:
  - the time that you will need to read, analyse or present the material;
  - any delays in obtaining approval for your work from an ethics committee, if required (see **Ch 42**).
  - the period that it may take simply to obtain the material or data you need, which can be lengthy.
  - the writing phase, which may take a lot more time than you initially think.

You should bear in mind that if you spend too much time on project work and/or writing this may adversely affect your performance in other coursework.

Improving your English language proficiency

In choosing your topic, if English is not your first language, think about the extent to which your language skills may need to be developed so that you can write up your dissertation to a level that does justice to your subject and is not limited by lack of language proficiency. You may need to factor some additional language development into your planning or, for example, taking a course on writing up research.

- **Availability of resources or experimental material.** Some dissertations or research projects run into difficulties because it is not possible to obtain the material required to carry out the work. You will need to evidence your work by reference to the literature (**Chs 23**, **25**, **27** and **31**). Access to printed material is therefore critical to the research process. You need to review the materials relevant to each potential topic that:
  - are available locally in hard copy in book and journal format within your own institution's library;
  - can be accessed electronically through your library's subscription to online journals;
  - can be obtained through inter-library loan (taking into account any cost implications); and
  - may require you to visit another library site for on-site access.

In other subjects, access to key resources such as instruments, experimental subjects and field locations may need to be taken into account.

How can I find out whether research sources will be readily available?

The best people to consult are the subject librarians in your library. They will know:

- the resources already present in your library, including stored materials;
- the main routes for obtaining information, including advanced online searches;
- alternative approaches that you may not have thought about;
- obscure resources and how to access these;
- contacts at other institutions who can help; and
- professional organisations that may have exclusive databanks that you might be able to access through your department.

- **Obtaining data.** You need to take into account the most realistic method of gathering data, recording and interpreting the findings within the time-frame that you have to do the work. If you need to analyse quantitative data, you should also consider what statistical analysis software packages you may need to master. Where your data are qualitative in nature, then you should also consider with your supervisor the most appropriate methods for gathering and interpreting the information. For example, an action research approach might require different techniques to a questionnaire-based approach (**Ch 43**).

- **Depth and novelty.** Your dissertation or research topic will need to offer sufficient depth to allow you to demonstrate your skills and it should give you scope to produce original thoughts or results. Opportunities may depend on your discipline, but might include the ability to think critically through analysis and evaluation, or the ability to design a new experiment or survey and report it professionally. Avoid choosing a well-worked area or even one that you feel is likely to provide easy results, if it will not allow you to demonstrate originality or advanced skills.

- **Extent of support and supervision.** At all levels of study, the writing of the dissertation or project report is a major task and you will not be expected to do this alone. Incorporated into the process will be a level of support provided by an assigned supervisor. However, you need to be clear at the outset about what you can expect in terms of this support. In some institutions, supervision is mapped onto the research/writing process with regular student-supervisor meetings. In others, arrangements are agreed by the partners for meetings as required. Generally, meetings with your supervisor will allow you to ask questions, seek guidance and debate some key issues. Be sure, however, that you reach an understanding with your supervisor about the extent to which you can expect them to review and provide feedback on your written work. Often this will not extend to reading the whole dissertation, nor to proof-reading the text, as this is regarded as the responsibility of the student.

How should I choose a supervisor?

If you have a choice, bear in mind that this should be a member of staff you feel comfortable talking to, who you feel will offer support and guidance, and inspire you to work hard and complete on time. Ask past students if you want a student view on different tutors, and, where appropriate, the environment where you will be expected to work.

- **Impact on your CV and career options.** Although this is rarely the primary aspect to consider, it is a factor to bear in mind. It may already be that your subject interests are very closely aligned to your ideas for your future career. You may also wish to take into account specific skills you might gain that will be of interest to an employer. If you are an undergraduate interested in further studies, your choice of topic may be valuable in giving you experience to take to a potential postgraduate supervisor.

Your relationship with your supervisor

A supervisor will typically be an academic with many other teaching, administrative and research duties. They will therefore have a limited amount of time for advising thesis or dissertation students and this time is therefore precious. It is important that you attend all meetings promptly, come well-prepared and communicate effectively. They will expect you to do the majority of the thinking and most of the work – so do not expect them to 'direct' you in anything other than general ways. Making a list beforehand of action points, issues you want to raise, or questions about the material will save time and demonstrate an organised approach. Learn to recognise when your supervisor is giving useful advice – responding appropriately to your supervisor's feedback will almost certainly improve the quality of your dissertation.

→ Writing a research proposal

A dissertation or project proposal may be required by your department before you start studying in depth or writing seriously. This may involve presenting a reasoned argument justifying the research topic and approach. This document then goes to the supervising academic or a panel of academics for consideration and approval. In some cases, your choice of topic may influence the selection or allocation of the person who will act as your supervisor. However, you should not regard your proposal solely as an administrative exercise; it will help you organise your preliminary thoughts, plan your approach and complete your work on time. You should therefore approach this task in a positive frame of mind. The benefits include:

- ensuring your research aims and objectives are achievable in the time allocated;
- compelling you to read and review some of the relevant background material to orientate your thoughts and ensure you understand key concepts and jargon;
- checking that the research methods you could and should use are realistic;
- verifying that you have considered safety and ethical issues relating to your research;
- making sure you think about resources you may require at an early stage;
- assisting you to create an outline structure for your dissertation or report;
- helping you to create a viable timetable for your work; and
- matching your interests and needs to an appropriate supervisor.

A key element that will be assessed is the 'core hypothesis' or idea underlying your dissertation or project report, so you should try to express this clearly. Essentially, this involves framing a question or topic that you will be seeking to address. The word 'address' is used deliberately here rather than 'answer', because a clear-cut right-or-wrong answer or conclusion is rarely possible, and, in fact, you will gain credit by considering the evidence from all sides of an argument or case, arriving at a clearly stated viewpoint, and giving reasons for adopting this position.

Topics that will be looked on favourably are those that are novel, take an unusual perspective on a research area, and are relevant within the research field as it stands at the time of writing. A mistake commonly made is to try to cover too 'large' a problem or area of discussion, rather than one capable of adequate analysis given the resources likely to be at hand.

Present your research proposal neatly. It should be word-processed and should stick very closely to any word limits. Regardless of any length constraints, try to write succinctly and to the point. There will be ample time to expand your thoughts when writing the real thesis, dissertation or project report. The proposal committee will be trying to arrive at a quick decision and this will be made easier if your proposal is brief. In many cases, a form may be provided for your dissertation or project proposal. This will normally include some or all of the components shown in Table 41.1.

Imagine you are assessing your own proposal

The person or group reading your proposal will be considering it from several viewpoints. They will expect to be able to answer 'yes' to the following questions. Think how you might answer them yourself when drafting your proposal.

❏ Does the student have an up-to-date and accurate view of the research field?

❏ Has the student outlined the focus of their studies (in some disciplines, the hypothesis they intend to test) in sufficient detail?

❏ Is the scope of the proposed study realistic in the time allocated?

❏ Is the proposed research study sufficiently original?

❏ Is the proposed research sufficiently challenging?

❏ Will the research allow the student to demonstrate their academic ability?

❏ Is the student planning to deal with safety and ethical issues appropriately?

❏ Will the research give the student the chance to refine their skills?

❏ Are the proposed methods appropriate and is the student aware of their limitations?

❏ Is the student likely to gain access to all the resources they need?

❏ Is the proposed structure of the dissertation or project clear?

❏ Will the proposed dissertation and the underlying scholarship meet the requirements of the department or university regulations?

❏ Has the student carried out appropriate background reading?

Finally, and in summary:

❏ Is the dissertation or project report likely to meet the required standard?

Try not to prepare your proposal in a rush – if possible, write out a near-final draft and leave it for a few days before coming back to it again with a critical mind, then make suitable modifications before your final submission.

Choosing a title

The point at which you write your proposal may be the first time you have serious thoughts about the title of your report, dissertation or thesis. Consider adopting a two-part title – an attention-grabbing statement, followed by a colon or a dash and a secondary title that defines the content more closely. Consult other thesis, dissertation and project reports completed recently to get a feel for the modern style in your discipline. Write down some options for your own work and then ask your supervisor or fellow students what they think of them. Note that the title given at the proposal stage should be seen as provisional, for the nature of the study and the outcomes may dictate a change at the end of the process.

Table 41.1 Typical components of a dissertation or project proposal. A selection of these categories will be used in individual cases. The choice of elements used in a proposal will depend on the discipline and level of study.

Component	Content and aspects to consider
Personal details	Required so that you can be identified and contacted
Details of your degree course or programme	There may be subtle differences according to your precise degree
Proposed title	This should be relatively short; a two-part title style can be useful
Description of the subject area/ Summary/Background/Brief review/ Statement of the problem or issue to be addressed	A brief outline that provides context such as: a synopsis of past work; a description of the 'gap' to be filled or new area to be explored; a summary of current ideas and, where relevant, hypotheses
Aim of research	General description of the overall purpose; a statement of intent
Objectives	Listing of specific outcomes you expect to fulfil in order to achieve the aim
Literature to be examined	Sources you intend to consult during your researches
Research methods or critical approach	How you propose to carry out your investigation
Preliminary bibliography	Details (in appropriate format) of the key sources you have already consulted
(Special) resources required	Information sources, samples, instruments, people, necessary to carry out your investigation
Outline plan of the thesis, dissertation or project report	For example, the likely section or chapter headings and subheadings
Indication of whether discussions have already been held with a nominated supervisor/indication of a potential supervisor	Valid only in cases where there is an element of choice of supervisor
Indication of whether discussions have already been held with the programme or course director in case of a project report	Valid only in cases where this is an administrative requirement
Names of possible supervisors	Your chance to influence this aspect
Timetable/plan	A realistic breakdown of the stages of your research, ideally with appropriate milestones
Statement or declaration that you understand and will comply with safety and/or ethical rules	The committee's guarantee that you have considered these; details may be required in certain cases (see **Ch 42**)

Practical tips for choosing your dissertation or research topic

Make sure that you are making an informed choice. Carry out an appropriate amount of background reading beforehand, selecting the sources carefully. You don't need to read all of the papers at the start, as this will take up too much of your study time, but you do need to gain an up-to-date awareness and basic understanding of key topics and trends in your chosen field. Choose recently published reviews of the area, especially those likely to prompt ideas about key aspects that need to be looked at in more detail. Discuss the topics with your course director or assigned supervisor so you understand fully the challenges of the topic area and avoid taking on a topic that is risky.

Speak to students who have already completed this kind of study. Postgraduates in your department might be useful contacts to ask. Discuss with them any aspects in the process that they felt were important to them when they were researching and writing their dissertations or project reports. What do they think about potential supervisors?

Look at past work. Dissertations and reports produced by students in previous years will help you gain a sense of the style and standard required. They will also enable you to look at a variety of approaches relevant to your discipline. However, don't be put off by apparently sophisticated structure and style in these completed examples. Remember that achieving this standard did not happen spontaneously. Your starting point may not be at this level, but the learning process and language development will very likely result in a similarly high standard of work.

Plan out a dissertation or report as part of the decision-making process. Sketch out the structure at the macro-level and then, later, for selected options, think about a more detailed plan. In practice, you may not stick rigidly to the plan you create, but the process of planning will help you to sort out the ideas and decide how appealing and feasible they are.

Think for yourself. When you choose your topic, try not to be influenced by other students' opinions. This is a highly personal decision. Other students may have their own reasons for liking or disliking certain topics or supervisors: distance yourself from their thoughts when you consider your own options.

Try to formulate a key hypothesis or idea to investigate. Your dissertation needs a focus and this will come from trying to answer a specific question, investigate a key issue or highlight a specific topic. Use brainstorming techniques as you read sources to help you develop your ideas and potential topics.

Remember that your proposal is only a proposal. You do not need to write the complete work at this stage. You merely need to establish, for the benefit of yourself and the reviewing group, that you have chosen a reasonable topic and are likely to succeed in producing a thesis, dissertation or project report that meets the regulations or learning outcomes of your course. The group considering your proposal will be aware that a major reason for students having problems with theses, dissertations and project choices is that they were over-ambitious at the start and you could be asked to modify your plans to ensure they can be achieved in the time-frame.

Context: discussing your options is important, whether this is with fellow students or staff. Here are some approaches you could take.

[To a fellow student] Have you thought any more about the projects on the list? Which one are you thinking about doing? Do you know whether xxxx is a helpful supervisor?

[In the library] Hello. I'm a student studying xxxx. I need to choose a project area. Could you help me to find some general reading material on the following topics . . .

[In conversation with a potential project supervisor] I've been looking at the descriptions of the different projects on offer this semester [term] and doing some background reading. I'm quite attracted by your project on xxxx. Please could you tell me a little more about what would be involved?

[In conversation with a potential thesis supervisor] I'm exploring the possibility of doing research in the areas of xxx. I would like to discuss the possibility of studying under your guidance. Would it be possible to arrange a convenient time to discuss this, please?

GO And now . . .

41.1 Set aside time to make your decision. As indicated throughout this chapter, you should consider your options very carefully and conduct the necessary research to ensure your decision is informed. This will take time, yet you must act quickly, or others may choose an option before you. Therefore, as soon as information is available, lay aside the necessary time to focus your attention on this issue.

41.2 Go back to basics. If the choices are bewildering, it may pay to revisit your old lecture notes and general texts to gain an overview of potential research areas. It may also be valuable to avoid the constraints of the booklists, if provided, and look at material that might be available online, for example, from writers and publishers in other countries. This can sometimes introduce a refreshingly different angle to a subject that might help you decide.

41.3 Imagine you are assessing your own proposal. Having completed a draft, answer all the questions in the checklist on p. 339, and for any answers that might be problematic, go back to the proposal and see if you could improve on it, or provide extra evidence to support your case.

Planning a dissertation or project

How to organise your research efforts

Efficient and effective work is the key to a successful dissertation or research project. Because of the lengthy nature of this type of study and its inbuilt complexity, careful planning is required. This chapter contains guidance on planning and time management that will assist you to work at your best. It also considers aspects of good research practice that you should take into account when setting up your project.

Key topics:
→ Creating a plan for your research
→ Making sure you research efficiently and effectively
→ Making sure you follow good research practice

Essential vocabulary
Copyright Ethics Ethics committee Gantt chart Hypothesis Informant Informed consent Milestone Perfectionism Plagiarism Schedule Timeline Writers' block

Your dissertation, project report or thesis will probably be the most extensive piece of writing you will have to complete on your course. In addition, it will require and test some demanding skills, in relation to research, English language and presentation. One essential skill you will need to demonstrate is that of planning, both in relation to project organisation and time management. This will help you avoid or counteract the following potential risks:

● underestimating the time it takes to carry out the research;

● being aimless in your initial reading;

● being inexperienced in academic writing (in English, if this is not your first language);

● having to organise large amounts of information;

● needing to keep records of research sources so you can cite them properly;

● needing to learn techniques for carrying out advanced forms of data analysis and presentation;

● underestimating the time it takes to write;

● suffering from writer's block;

● being unaware of dangers of copyright infringement and plagiarism;

● allowing time for your supervisor to give feedback and to take this into account; and

● for longer pieces of work, needing to allow time to present your work appropriately, for example, via professional typing, printing, graphics, and binding.

→ Creating a plan for your research

No single approach to planning will fit all types of research, but certain principles apply to project management in most disciplines.

Start with a plan, but regard it as flexible

The origin of your plan should be the project specification or the project proposal you have submitted (**Ch 41**). The plan should take into account several phases of work, including, for example:

1 reading around the subject to gain a solid understanding of concepts, methods and potential areas of investigation;

2 arriving at a central hypothesis or approach for your research (and discussing this with your supervisor);

3 creating a detailed and practical plan for your work, whilst regarding this as flexible in nature;

4 carrying out the research (based on, for example, observations, experiments, or readings of others' publications, depending on discipline);

5 analysing the research results, findings or ideas;

6 drafting the report, dissertation or thesis in the correct format and style (**Ch 44**); and

7 preparing and submitting the report.

---

smart tip

Managing project elements

■ Divide the total length of time available for the project into periods for each phase of work. This will allow you to monitor progress and adjust your work-rate if, for example, progress is slow in one aspect.

■ Recognise that you do not always have to schedule work in a particular sequence. To achieve the greatest efficiency, it is sometimes important to allow some aspects to proceed in parallel.

■ Sub-divide work phases if they are lengthy and there may be benefits in sub-dividing them to make the planning process more manageable (see also **Ch 41**).

Schedule your project

One relatively simple way of presenting the timeline of a project is called a Gantt chart, named after its inventor, Henry Gantt, an American management consultant. This has two axes; the horizontal one generally representing time and the vertical one showing the different tasks or elements of project activity, usually in bar chart form. Gantt charts are useful for:

● separating out the different elements required to complete a project;

● showing the interdependence of project activities; and

● indicating progress on a project as it progresses, including showing important milestones.

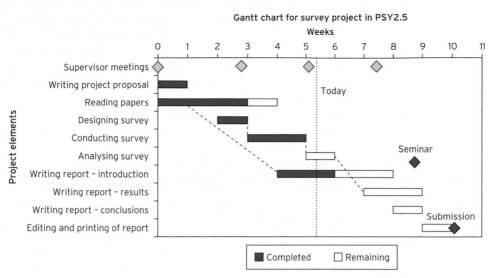

Figure 42.1 Representative Gantt Chart. This chart was created using the 'stacked bar' type of chart in Excel and illustrates progress at the start of the 6th week of a simple project based on a survey. Note how progress in each phase is shown by shading the horizontal bar for each element: this student is shown as 'behind schedule' with their reading of the literature and analysis of the survey results, but has started to write parts of the introduction to the report, so is 'ahead of schedule' on this aspect. Connections between elements are shown with a dotted line, such as the obvious need to complete the design of the survey before conducting and analysing it. Key milestones (◇) shown include meetings with the student's supervisor, a seminar to be presented in week 8 and the final report to be submitted in week 10.

Relationships between sequential activities are classified as 'end to start' and between parallel elements as 'start to start'. Aspects that must finish close together are termed 'end to end'. These connections may be shown on the chart using a dashed link line. Milestones are generally shown using a diamond symbol. Figure 42.1 shows an example of a relatively simple Gantt chart for a research project.

smart tip

Creating planning charts

Specialist computer programs are available for creating Gantt charts (such as Microsoft Project), but a generic spreadsheet such as Microsoft Excel can be used to create simple versions using the 'stacked bar' type of chart (see Figure 46.1). Be aware, however, of the danger of spending too much time producing such plans at the expense of time that should be spent on achieving the goals of the project itself.

Complete your project

Investigations into nearly all research topics could carry on indefinitely, but it is important that you recognise the need to draw your contribution to an end at a suitable point. 'Closing' a project involves making a decision about when you have enough material to write up a viable report, dissertation or thesis.

You may feel at this stage that you are not able to reach a definitive conclusion about your investigation, but in reality this is rare in research, and you will gain credit for pointing out in your discussion how the work could proceed in future. The important point is that you have enough data or ideas to demonstrate that you can follow the 'model' of a typical research report in your discipline, as it is this that will be judged. Examples could include being able to present your results in graphic form and reporting on this in the sciences; or discussing the ideas and evidence backing up a particular viewpoint in the arts.

→ Making sure you research efficiently and effectively

Efficient researching means cutting out wasteful or unproductive effort, and focusing on using your time to maximise productivity. The keys to researching efficiently are:

- thinking and planning ahead for each day or part of a day;
- understanding what you are trying to achieve during each day or part of a day;
- getting down to work as quickly as possible;
- prioritising tasks appropriately;
- avoiding distractions;
- keeping your papers and workplace well organised; and
- taking breaks when you need to rest.

Effective researching involves smart working, rather than putting in extra effort. The keys to working effectively are:

- getting started promptly;
- focusing on the end-product;
- minimising unproductive work;
- identifying things that are obstacles to progress;
- finding ways to overcome the obstacles to progress; and
- making sure you complete each component and the whole task, even if this means some loss of quality.

---

smart tip

Retaining bright ideas

As you become involved in your project you'll find that your thinking about the topic becomes a key focus in your life. Ideas will pop into your mind at the most unlikely times. Get into the habit of carrying a small notebook with you at all times so that you can note down these ideas as possible routes of research or for direct inclusion in your writing.

→ Making sure you follow good research practice

Ethics

For many research topics and methodologies, it is important to review the ethical position regarding your study. The term 'ethics' in the research context refers to the principles, rules and standards of conduct that apply to investigations. Most disciplines have self-monitoring codes of ethical practice and your institution will operate its own internal research governance policy. The types of ethical requirements vary among disciplines and your study must comply with recognised practice in your field and your institution. It is essential that you familiarise yourself with these codes and are able to bring that understanding to the initial discussion of the research project with your supervisor, who will be responsible for ensuring that your research proposal complies with ethical practice in your institution. Where necessary, your supervisor will help you prepare an application to conduct the research for submission to your institution's Ethics Committee. Note that there may be different committees and rules for clinical and non-clinical research.

Obtaining ethical approval

You should first read the guidance notes provided by your university's ethics committee or department. Once you have satisfied yourself that you have made arrangements to cover the ethical dimensions of your research project, you will be in a position to frame your proposal for ethical approval. Institutions will vary in the formats required. In general, you will need to provide information on:

- the title, purpose and duration of the project, and the location of the study;
- the methodological approach to be adopted, and information on how data will be stored securely;
- if appropriate, the way in which participants will be recruited, plus information as to age, gender and any inclusion/exclusion criteria;
- measures taken to ensure that all ethical dimensions are covered in compliance with the appropriate research code of practice in your institution, including confidentiality in reporting results; and
- if appropriate, identification of the involvement of any funding body.

In your research plan, you should make due allowance for the time taken to obtain ethical approval (your supervisor can advise on normal delays). Make sure that you carry out some relevant work, such as a literature review, while you are waiting.

Any research project involving human beings should be characterised by protection of the human rights, dignity, health and safety of participants and researchers. This is achieved by observing three fundamental tenets:

- the research should do no harm;
- consent should be voluntary; and
- confidentiality should be respected throughout.

Ethical considerations may relate to non-human as well as human research activity. Controversial areas have included the use of animals in research, cloning, human embryo research, stem cell research, *in vitro* fertilisation, and nuclear research. In the UK, experiments involving animals are subject to Home Office approval. If this is required for your work, your supervisor will guide you through the procedures. Similarly, experiments involving genetic manipulation must comply with relevant legislation and you will be guided through the necessary procedures.

Consent and confidentiality

If there are human participants in your research, they may need to be informed in writing about certain aspects of it. This is usually provided as a 'Participant Information Sheet'. Particularly in clinical research, a 'template' is often adopted to frame this explanation for participants. However, in many instances, this is often unsatisfactory because the language used, and the format and layout, are often unclear to the non-specialist. Every effort should be made to inform participants about the project as concisely as possible in 'plain' English, that is, in language that can be easily understood by participants.

Key points in a Participant Information Sheet

- Outline of the purpose of the study.
- Invitation and reason for being selected.
- Explanation of the voluntary nature of participation and of the freedom of the subject to terminate participation at any time.
- Explanation of the procedure to be followed in the research and the time commitment involved.
- Information about refunding of expenses, if applicable.
- Advantages and disadvantages of participation.
- Assurance of confidentiality and anonymity.
- Information about outcomes.
- Information about the funding source.
- Names of lead researcher and assistants.
- Information about any sponsorship or affiliation connected to the project.

If you wish people to participate in your study, then it is important that you follow this order. If you put all the information about sponsorship and the expertise of the supervising or lead researcher first, then your potential subjects may lose interest and never get to the end of the document. If English is not your first language, you should also ask a native speaker of English to appraise your Participant Information Sheet for clarity of expression. You need to take into account the potential readership, remembering that this document is not an academic paper but one that is going to be read by the general public.

In response to this information, participants are then requested to complete an 'Informed Consent Form' that requires their signature. In some instances, a debriefing form will also need to be completed once the data-gathering phase is concluded.

Human participants must be assured that their identities will be protected by the promise of anonymity. This means that the confidentiality of any representation of data, whether in aggregated forms (for example, mean value) or as qualitative material that might be obtained from individuals (for example, through questionnaires, interviews or focus groups), is protected in any printed format. It is essential that written permission to quote informants be sought from them at the time of participation in the enquiry, with the proviso that identities will be protected when findings are reported.

Data protection in the UK

The storage and use of personal information is an ethical issue. In the UK, the Data Protection Act covers procedures that must be adopted. Consult your university's web pages for information and guidance on local procedures if you plan to store information either in paper files or electronically. Legislation apart, it is simply good practice to time-limit the period in which data will remain on your records – and to inform participants how their data will be stored, and when the information will be deleted or destroyed.

Safety

It is a fundamental of research activity in the spirit of international codes of practice that the health and safety of all those involved in research activity as participants or researchers should be a priority at all times (see **Ch 41**). Your university will have a safety office and policies in place for potentially dangerous procedures or to cover risks like exposure to hazardous chemicals. Completing paper work, such as Control of Chemicals Hazardous to Health (COSHH) forms, should be regarded as an opportunity to learn about the risks associated with your work, rather than a chore.

 Practical tips for planning and organising your research

Discover how to create a Gantt chart using office spreadsheet software. The 'available chart types' help section in Microsoft Excel provides a useful tutorial on customising a stacked bar chart to produce a Gantt chart.

Keep a research diary. Take notes of what you've done each day and write down all information that might be of potential relevance to your thesis, such as interesting observations and the citation details of where you read them (**Ch 31**), or, for a lab-based project, details of equipment or procedures (**Ch 44**). You may also wish to reflect on progress in your research and make notes of points you would like to discuss with your supervisor or at a progress monitoring meeting. You should also take a note of skills events and seminars that you have attended and your thoughts on what was covered, and what you gained from attending.

Research ethical requirements for your project. Ask your supervisor in the first instance and follow any school/departmental handouts provided. Consult your university's website for up-to-date and detailed information on approaches to research ethics. In addition to the ethical policy, there may be general guidance information, discipline-specific advice, and links to useful websites.

Organise your work in parallel when you can. A good example of this is to start writing parts of your introduction while you are still in the initial phase of your research, as shown in Figure 42.1. In experimental projects, data can be analysed (and graphed) as they are produced, rather than waiting until the end of the research phase. There may also lengthy periods when you are waiting for materials or results that can be productively used: drafts of parts of the materials and methods section, or elements of the discussion and conclusion might be written at this time.

Try not to be a perfectionist. Many projects never get started, stall or fail to be completed because the people involved are aiming for perfection, when this is either impossible or impractical. Often, achieving perfection would be a waste of resources. If you identify this as a potential characteristic in yourself, try to accept that fact, and focus on minimising the larger flaws in your work and on completing the task despite any minor faults you believe are present.

When planning, set yourself an artificial deadline ahead of the submission date. This will have several benefits: it will provide potentially valuable 'slippage time' in case things go wrong; it will give you more time to let your draft text 'settle' as part of the review and editing process; and it will help you to avoid any problems with producing the final version, such as printer malfunction or unavailability.

💬 Useful language for . . . planning your research work

Context: most discussions about your research plans will be with your supervisor. Here are some possible approaches.

I've been thinking about the planning for this project and have produced a Gantt chart. Do you think I've estimated the relative times for each of the aspects correctly? How long do you think it will take me to do xxxx?

Are there any ethical [or safety] aspects I should take into account in this project?

Please can we schedule some meetings between now and the submission date?

GO And now . . .

42.1 Create a draft plan for your research project. Modify the phases shown on p. 344 to suit your own project. Estimate the time each part should take and then modify these times to suit the overall extent of the project. If you have to shorten any of the estimated times, this is a sure sign that you will be under time pressure unless you work quickly and effectively. Present your plan as a Gantt chart if you feel this will be useful.

42.2 Reflect on past performances in project work. This type of work rarely goes as predicted, especially when you are inexperienced, so previous project work might provide you with a number of lessons for your current research. It is especially important to identify occasions when your work was ineffective or slow, think about the reasons why, and decide how you can avoid problems for this project.

42.3 Familiarise yourself with the ethics guidelines that govern research activity in your specialist field. This is important to your personal development and is an aspect of your professional practice that will apply when you graduate. Often the guidelines are provided in the literature of your professional associations associated with your discipline. Look also at 'Materials and Methods' sections in relevant research papers to establish the norms for ethical behaviour in your field of work. Use a search engine to identify any major cases that have raised ethical issues in the research context.

43 Conducting research for a dissertation or project

How to investigate your topic

This chapter compares approaches for two main types of research: quantitative and qualitative investigation. It examines reasons for obtaining data of different types. It also outlines some of the main techniques used to obtain and analyse such data. In addition, it introduces the main concepts and terms commonly used.

Key topics:
→ Key features of quantitative research
→ Examples of quantitative research methods
→ Key features of qualitative research
→ Examples of qualitative research methods
→ Analysing and presenting results

Essential vocabulary

Action research Bias Case study Causality Confounding variable Control Correlation Demographic information Error Focus group Free text Hypothesis Likert scale Mean Moderator Objectivity Population Proof Qualitative Quantitative Respondent Sample Skewed Subjectivity Système International d'Unités (SI) Variable

Quantitative research methods are defined as investigative approaches resulting in numerical data. These are especially valuable when:

● obtaining measurements (for example, in Biochemistry and Physiology);

● estimating error (for example, in Physics and Engineering);

● comparing information and opinions (for example, Sociology and Psychology); or

● testing hypotheses (for example, in most investigative science disciplines).

The ideal in this type of research is for the investigator to be detached and impartial to the results of the study.

Qualitative research methods are those investigative approaches that result in descriptive textual information. The qualitative approach is especially useful when examining:

● opinions, feelings and values (for example, in Political Science, Social Policy and Philosophy);

● participant interpretations and responses (for example, in Sociology and Psychology);

● behavioural patterns (for example, in Ethnography, Anthropology and Geography);

- processes and patterns (for example, in Education, Economics and Accountancy); or
- case studies including critical incidents (for example, in Nursing and Education).

In obtaining and interpreting qualitative information, there is recognition that such information is interpreted according to a set of values belonging to the researcher.

Quantitative and qualitative research methods may be used in the same investigation. For example, mixed types of data may be obtained as in a survey inviting free text responses (qualitative data, pp. 358-9) and expressions of opinion on a Likert scale (quantitative data, see p. 354).

→ Key features of quantitative research

Quantitative research is generally 'conclusive' in nature. It is especially important in the sciences, where its aim may be to provide a reliable value for a measurement or test a particular hypothesis. Examples include:

- **Surveys and questionnaires** (for example, 'Over 45 per cent of respondents agree with this statement').
- **Measurements** (for example, 'The average insect wing length was 3.40 mm with a standard error of 0.14 mm, $n = 24$').
- **Experiments** (for example, 'Treatment A resulted in a statistically significant increase in weight gain compared with the control').

In quantitative research, your aim would usually be to base results on large unbiased samples. Large sample size is important to ensure that measurements based on the sample are representative of the population as a whole, and to improve your chances of arriving at a statistically significant conclusion.

---

i

Population and sample

Although these terms are used frequently in normal English language, they have special meanings in quantitative research.

Population means the whole group of items that might be part of a study: for example, all men in the UK; all individuals of a species of shellfish on a particular beach; all Birmingham householders who use gas as a heating fuel.

Sample means a sub-set of individuals from a specific population, for example, the 28 men whose blood sugar level was measured and compared with that of 34 who had taken drug X for five weeks beforehand; the 50 shellfish collected from Beach A, measured and compared with a similar sample from Beach B; the 45 householders selected for telephone interview about their satisfaction with the service provided by their energy supplier.

Obtaining numerical data to describe your results reduces subjectivity and allows comparisons across data sets. The inherent objectivity of quantitative research relies, however, on an unbiased approach to data collection. Bias can be defined as a partial or one-sided view or description of events. Although the aim is usually to reduce bias as far as possible, it can arise because of a subconscious decision of the experimenter. This can mean, for example, that individuals selected for observation or experiment do not represent the population, or that measurements associated with them are skewed in a particular way. Critics of the quantitative approach claim that experiments and surveys are rarely entirely free of observer bias, even if this is unintentional.

Numerical results can be analysed with statistical techniques. These allow you to compare sets of observations or treatments, to test hypotheses and to allocate levels of probability (chance) of your conclusions being right or wrong. These are powerful tools and lie at the heart of much scientific scholarship. However, just because you can measure something, or can compare data sets, this does not mean your conclusions are certain or relevant. For example, many scientists make conclusions on the basis that there is a 5 per cent chance of their being wrong, so, on average, this will be the case roughly one in twenty times. Moreover, even when a hypothesis is accepted as correct, the results may apply only to the very artificial experimental or observational environment. Statistical significance should not be confused with significance in the sense of 'importance' or 'value'.

The concept of proof

The word 'proof' in English should be used cautiously when applied to quantitative research – the term implies 100 per cent certainty, whereas this is very rarely justified owing to the ambiguity inherent in statistical analysis and experimental design. In reports and dissertations, 'hedging' language such as 'this indicates that . . .'; 'it seems that . . .' or 'this suggests that . . .' are therefore preferable to phrases such as 'this proves that . . .'

→ Examples of quantitative research methods

Surveys and questionnaires

These are valuable tools for gaining quantitative information from respondents and they can also provide qualitative data (see pp. 358, 358–9). Respondents can be a representative sample (for example, members of public chosen at random or using a sampling protocol) or a population (for example, all members of Politics Class P201). Before designing a survey, you should consider what demographic information you might need to describe the respondent(s) and associate with other responses. You should also think how you intend to report the results (see Ch 31) as this may influence the questions asked and the way you write them.

Survey questions fall into one of two categories, closed or open.

1. **Closed-answer question types:**
- **Categorical.** Here, you can only select one of the options, for example: *'Gender: M/F'* (for male/female); or *'Do you agree with the above statement? – Yes/No/Don't know (delete as appropriate)'*. Results are best expressed as percentages of responses in each category.
- **Numerical.** These request a numerical answer, for example *'What is your age in years?'* These can be summarised by appropriate statistics.

- **Multiple-choice questions (MCQs).** These are useful when there are mutually exclusive options to select. This type of question will be familiar from assessments you may have had at school and university (**Ch 36**). The answers given can be summarised easily as percentages of respondents selecting each option.
- **Multiple response questions.** These are like MCQs, only you are allowed to choose more than one answer. This type of question would be asked for a different reason than a MCQ, and the answers analysed accordingly. The answers can also be summarised as percentages selecting each option, but note that the total number of options selected may be larger than your sample size. In fact, the average number of options selected may be an interesting supplementary piece of data to report.

Examples of multiple-choice and multiple-response questions

Example of multiple choice

Which of the following assessment types is your favourite? (Tick one box)

❑ Essay long answer
❑ Short-answer questions (SAQs)
❑ Multiple-choice questions (MCQs)
❑ Calculation questions
❑ None of the above

Example of multiple response

Which of the following resources have you used in the past month? (Tick all that apply)

❑ Hard copy reference books
❑ Electronic encyclopaedia
❑ Textbooks
❑ Lecture handouts
❑ E-journals

Note the use of a non-committal answer ('none of the above') in the multiple-choice example shown.

- **Ranking (ordinal) questions.** These ask you to place possible answers in an order, for example, '*Place the items in the following list in order of preference, writing 1 for your most preferred option, 2 for the next and so on, down to 5 for your least preferred option*'. You can present the results as the most common selection at each rank or as percentages of respondents choosing each rank for a specific item (perhaps as a histogram). A 'mean rank' is another possible way of expressing the data, but this value should be interpreted cautiously.
- **Likert-scale questions.** These are named after Rensis Likert, an American psychologist who first modelled the use of a five-point survey scale in 1932. They are useful for assessing people's opinions or feelings on a scale. Typically, respondents are asked to react to a statement. An example would be:

'Smoking is dangerous for your health'. Which of the following best describes your feelings about the above statement? (Circle appropriate number.)

1 Agree strongly
2 Agree
3 Neither agree nor disagree
4 Disagree
5 Disagree strongly

Some Likert-scale designs only use four categories, missing out 'neither agree nor disagree', to force respondents to indicate a preference on one side or the other.

Responses to Likert options may be combined, as in the example 'over 57 per cent either agreed or agreed strongly with the statement . . .'.

2. Open-answer question types

Open-answer survey questions require input from the respondent and are useful when you do not know all the possible answers, or you do not wish to lead the respondent. In a student survey, an example might be 'Why did you choose module P201?' or 'Please summarise your experience in the exam'. The text responses often provide valuable quotes for a report or case study, and this use would be classified as qualitative. It is possible, however, given a reasonably large sample, to categorise the answers and present them in a quantitative fashion, for example, in the form of a pie chart showing the proportion of respondents giving each type of answer.

Measurements and error determination

A measurement is an estimate of some dimension of an object as a ratio of a standard unit. It therefore consists of both a number and the symbol for the unit, for example: 0.5 metres; 1.6 litres; 39 kg. The units chosen for most scientific studies are those of the *Systéme Internationale d'Unités* or SI, a metre-kilogram-second scheme with defined symbols for units and prefixes for small and large numbers that differ by multiples of 1000 (10^3).

All measurements contain error, which can be of two types: accuracy or precision. In practice, measurements are often assumed to be accurate and the more important thing to estimate is the precision. There are two main ways of doing this:

- **By providing a range that relates to the observer's or instrument's ability to discriminate between readings.** For example, if measuring length with a standard ruler, you might write 104 ± 0.5 mm because you were using the scale divisions on the ruler to estimate to the nearest millimetre; that is, the dividing points between adjacent values below and above 104 are at 103.5 and 104.5 mm.

- **By providing an estimated error that is based on repeated measurements of the same quantity**. For quantifying measurement error alone, this would be obtained from several independent attempts at measurement, for example, five values obtained from the same weighing machine of someone's weight (mass). In many scientific studies, this error is taken to be included in the overall sampling error obtained from measurements of several replicate items.

Accuracy and precision

Accuracy is the closeness of a measured or estimated value to its true value. Example: a balance would be said to be inaccurate if, instead of giving you a value for a standard 1 kg weight as 1 kg, it consistently gave a value of 1.02 kg. All measurements of similar weights from the instrument would thus be approximately +2 per cent wrong.

Precision is the closeness of repeated measurements to each other. For example, if you weighed a specimen several times on the same balance and got very different results each time, the instrument would be said to be imprecise. A mean of 1.000 kg might be considered to be accurate, but if the standard deviation of the measurements was 0.25 kg, this would be considered rather imprecise.

Correlation and causality

This is a way of describing the relationship between two measured variables, for example, the number of cigarettes smoked per day and life expectancy. A variable is said to be correlated with another if their values alter together, either in a positive fashion (increasing together), or in a negative fashion (moving in opposite directions). A statistic called the correlation coefficient can be used to express the strength or degree of linear correlation between two variables. This takes values between –1 and 1; the closer its value is to these extremes, the higher the cluster around the trend line, and the closer to zero, the lower. The sign indicates whether the correlation is positive or negative (inverse). The coefficient can be used in a statistical test to find out whether the correlation is significantly different from zero.

Vital to an understanding of quantitative research is an awareness that correlation does not imply causality. If A is well correlated with B, this alone is not enough evidence to state that A *causes* B. It could be something related to A, or even, due to coincidence, something unrelated to A. So, if people with high salt intake are more likely to have heart attacks, this alone does not show that high salt intake is a cause of heart attacks, although if there were no relationship between the two, you might be inclined to rule out this possibility. The only way to become more certain is to gather more evidence.

Experiments

An experiment is a contrived or designed situation where the experimenter attempts to isolate the effects of changing one variable in the system or process, and then compares the results with the condition where no change has occurred. The aim behind many experiments is to investigate causality – that is, to establish that a change in factor A causes a change in variable B. Experiments can also help elucidate in more detail how A causes B.

Experiments are at the core of the 'scientific method', in which an experiment is set up that will allow a hypothesis to be accepted or rejected. Much of the progress in the modern world has been made through scientific advances based on experiments. Nevertheless, it is useful to recognise some limitations and difficulties.

- **The situations required to allow manipulation of relevant variables are potentially artificial.** Indeed, they may be so contrived as to be unnatural, making any conclusions of dubious value.

- **It may be impossible to change one variable only in any treatment**. Inevitably, other aspects change simultaneously. These are known as confounding variables. For example, if you attempt to change air temperature, you may also change humidity. Adding 'control' treatments are the way in which experimenters attempt to rule out the effects of confounding variables.

- **Uncertainty in conclusions.** Sampling and other errors can be taken into account in statistical analysis, but the results must always be expressed with a degree of uncertainty.

- **Subjectivity or bias.** There may be an unwitting element of subjectivity or bias in the choice of treatments; the choice of conditions (sometimes selected to accentuate effects of a particular treatment); and in some cases, in the recording of results.

Concept of 'the control'

A control is an additional treatment that attempts to test the effects of changing a potentially confounding variable. Suppose it is known that Drug A is acidic in nature and that the formulation available for testing also contains an impurity, Chemical B; a suitable experimental design might include the following treatments:

1 No treatment (usually involving a placebo, or pill without any added chemicals).
2 Drug A (administered as a pill).
3 Control for effects of pH (a placebo pill with the same pH or buffering capacity as the Drug A pill).
4 Control for the effect of Chemical B (a pill containing similar amounts of Chemical B as in the Drug A pill, but without any Drug A).

If the results show an effect in treatment 2, but not in 3 and 4, the confounding variables can be ruled out; if there are also effects in either 3 or 4 or both, the confounding variables may well be important.

→ Key features of qualitative research

Qualitative research is generally exploratory in nature; it may be preceded or followed by quantitative investigations. It is especially important in the social sciences, where its aim is often to understand the complex reasons for human behaviour. Examples include:

- **Case studies.** (For example, 'Student X described her experience on her first day at university as . . .').
- **Interviews.** (For example, 'Interviewee A explained that, after seeing the video, his reaction was . . . This could be interpreted as . . .').
- **Focus groups.** (For example, 'One group member stated that her experience of peer marking was . . .').

smart
tip

Avoiding questions that lead or restrict the answers

If you conduct qualitative research appropriately, the participants providing information are less likely to be 'led' by the questions asked than they may be with the quantitative approach. For example, a free text question in a survey that neutrally asks for the participant's opinion of a political leader does not lead or restrict the respondent in the same way as a Likert-scale question (p. 354) that asks them to grade a leader on his or her response to a specific political issue. When sequencing interview questions, care needs to be taken to ensure that an early question does not place a particular idea or concept in the respondent's mind, thereby affecting their response to a later question. Therefore, you should try to move your questions or prompts from the general to the specific.

Qualitative research generally involves individuals or small samples, in contrast to the large randomly selected samples favoured in quantitative research (p. 352).

These small samples may be carefully selected, and they may not be representative of the population as a whole, but that is not necessarily an issue, because the value of qualitative research derives from the authentic and case-specific detail that it can encompass. The information obtained is potentially richer and deeper than that described in numbers and statistics, and can take advantage of the many subtle ways of using language to express opinions, experiences and feelings. On the other hand, these factors may mean that it is less easy to compare different cases and arrive at generalised conclusions.

Qualitative research, by its very nature, implies a degree of bias. However, maintaining objectivity is as important in the conduct of the research as it is in reporting findings. It is important, therefore, to recognise the tensions that can arise between objectivity and bias. This is particularly relevant when selecting cases to study, aspects to report, and language to describe observations. Observer preconceptions, value systems and cultural influences also need to be taken into account.

→ Examples of qualitative research methods

Observation and description

This category includes a wide range of approaches where the investigator will examine an artefact, person or location and describe it in words. A narrative (outline of developments through time) might also fall into this classification. Examples of suitable topics include:

- primary source material such as that found in an historical document;
- a biological habitat;
- a patient's feelings or symptoms; or
- a drawing, painting or installation.

The specific detailed features to be reported will depend on your discipline and research area. It is a good idea to discuss these with your supervisor before proceeding too far with your research.

Although description is sometimes categorised as a 'lower-level' academic thought process (**Ch 23**), the interpretations and generalisations that follow involve higher-level skills. For example, a detailed description you produce may be referred to when you are drawing conclusions about a wider topic.

Sometimes your purpose might involve comparing several sources of information. A useful technique when doing this is to create a grid or matrix where the columns represent the different sources and entries in the rows summarise the specific features of interest (modelled in Figure 25.6). In some cases, this table could be adapted for use in a report or dissertation, but it would also be useful when creating a written summary of the key features of the sources.

Surveys and questionnaires

Often both qualitative and quantitative approaches are used in surveys and questionnaires (p. 353). The main qualitative research technique is to ask an 'open' question, for example, 'What do you think about the new property valuation system?' or an instruction like 'Please provide any further comments'. These questions tend to produce a variety of free test responses from a blank response to very detailed answers. Responses to open questions can be useful to enrich a report with authentic quotes illustrating representative points of view or opposing, polarised viewpoints. In some instances, this qualitative material can be converted into quantitative information.

Interview-based case studies

Qualitative research often draws on individuals' experiences of events, processes and systems. These can be reported as case studies. In one ideal sense, such investigations might be carried out without preconception by allowing the participant to provide a completely unstructured and uninterrupted stream of thought, with conclusions drawn following examination of the information obtained. In practice, you will use a body of prior knowledge and experience to structure an interview through a series of prompting questions. If you use a similar template for each case study, comparisons will be possible, so it is important to think this through beforehand. After you have written up the interview, it is good practice to confirm the details you have recorded with the interviewee.

Action Research

i

Academic departments often encourage students to undertake studies grounded in 'local' issues. In such instances 'Action Research' approaches are popular. These are particularly common in the 'caring' disciplines such as Nursing, Social Work and Teaching. The focus is directed on the context of the researcher's practice and a problem or situation within it which requires better understanding and, possibly, identification of some change to resolve or improve that situation or practice. This requires planning of the research approach, perhaps through data collection or observation; analysis and reflection through reference to theory; and, ultimately, a recommendation for action.

Focus groups

These are small discussion groups (4-6 members is considered ideal), where participants are asked to comment on an issue or, for business purposes, a product or marketing tool. Focus groups allow you to take account of several viewpoints at a time, and to observe the outcomes of open and dynamic discussion among focus group members. Potential pitfalls include biasing any comments by leading the discussion yourself, or the tendency for focus group members to conform to a middle view if they fear exposing a minority opinion.

As focus group moderator, you would have thought through a list of discussion topics or questions related to your research interest. You would also intervene in discussion to prompt new topics or bring the discussion back to the point, because a recognised danger is that the group drifts substantially 'off message'.

It is rare that results of quantitative observations, surveys or experiments are reported without subsequent analysis. Indeed, your ability to analyse and present your results is often allocated a high proportion of credit when your dissertation or report is being assessed.

- Adequate description of your methods is vital, as one goal of quantitative research is to produce repeatable results from which general conclusions can be drawn. This normally means that a 'Materials and Methods' section contains enough information to allow a competent peer to repeat your work.

- Descriptions should use clear unambiguous language, and qualitative terms used should be defined if possible. For example, the colour of a specimen might be described with reference to a standard colour chart.

- Repetition. Simple measurements should be repeated if possible, so that a figure indicating their accuracy can be provided.

- Description. When describing results, appropriate use should be made of figures and tables.

- Analysis. The results of experiments should be analysed using statistical tests.

In analysing and presenting qualitative data, a key aim is to represent the material in a balanced and rational way. You will gain credit for this and lose marks if you do not. Do not be tempted to select only examples, answers or quotes that support your view. Consider and note the opposing evidence as well, and then arrive at a conclusion based on a careful analysis of the arguments and literature sources that have previously dealt with the topic.

A difficulty in presenting qualitative research is deciding what detail is relevant and what is not. In general, your descriptions should be 'lean' and related to the objectives of the research; however, it is not always easy to predict what details will be relevant at the outset of the research, nor which information others who read your work may wish to see recorded.

In reports, case studies are sometimes presented in a self-contained box. If these are numbered, you can refer to them in the text using the same conventions as figures and tables. Layout rules for presenting quotes from sources in an academic document should be adhered to consistently (**Ch 31**, p. 287). Consult your course handbook or supervisor if uncertain.

Practical tips for conducting research

Tips for quantitative research

When designing a survey, observe the following basic rules:

- keep your survey as short as possible. Use the minimum number of questions required to obtain the information you need and only ask a question if you have a clear idea of how you will use the information obtained.

- make sure you obtain appropriate demographic information to describe your sample and draw correlations.

- make sure your questions are unambiguous. Try out the question set with a friend or family member before using it on real subjects. This may reveal problems with the wording that you may not have appreciated.

- in deciding the order of questions, try to move from the general to the specific as there is then less chance of early questions influencing responses to later ones.

When explaining how your survey was conducted, supply appropriate details.

These should include:

- sampling methods. How were the respondents contacted or chosen? What ethical procedures were followed?

- details of respondents. You should provide a summary of demographics (gender, age, background of those responding). This information can be derived from specific questions, often placed at the start of the survey. However, observe good research practice by ensuring that the privacy and anonymity of your respondents are protected.

- questionnaire design. The principles and rationale behind the design should be discussed and a copy of the questionnaire provided in an appendix.

- procedure. How was the survey conducted?

Focus on good technique when taking measurements. Some forms of measurement may seem simple, such as length or weight measurement. However, you should take as much care as possible so that measurement error does not become a significant part of the overall error.

Consider the likely method of statistical analysis at the start, as this may influence experiment or survey design. For example, it is possible to estimate an appropriate number of replicates to use to demonstrate a certain percentage difference between two treatments if a preliminary indication of the variability among the replicates is available. Another reason for considering statistical tests beforehand is that they may require assumptions about your data, which you can ensure by, for example, a truly random sampling procedure.

Keep your experiments simple. It is better to use a design that will provide a conclusive answer to a simple question than to over-complicate matters, run into logistical problems in setting up the experiment and collecting data, and end up with inconclusive results.

Learn from 'trial runs'. These can help you work out where there will be difficulties in procedure and layout, use of instruments, and other important limitations on your experimental design. Be aware, however, that you could spend too much time working out what to do and how to do it – remember that all research involves a certain amount of compromise.

Tips for qualitative research

Gather all your sources together as soon as possible. Scan-read them or carry out a quick appraisal before embarking on a detailed description or comparative exercise. However, do not use this as an excuse for delaying the start to your work.

Always note down more information than you think you will need. You can always filter extraneous material out at a later stage, but you cannot always go back to find information you missed first time round.

Where relevant, write down full referencing details as you go along. It is essential to do this as you research since this information is easily forgotten or lost, and you may be deemed guilty of plagiarism if you do not cite your sources in a report.

Base the structure of your description on other similar studies. These may be available from the literature, or your supervisor may be able to show you past examples. Postgraduate students may be a useful source of ideas and examples.

If appropriate, use photography. This might be valuable for a field study, for example, by acting as a prompt when you start to write up. Another use could be recording notes made by a focus group on a whiteboard. By using digital imaging, you can avoid great expense.

Consult specialist texts regarding face-to-face interview-based research. This is an area where the precise approach used can influence success. Aspects to consider include: selection of interviewees; introductions; seating arrangements; the sequence of questions; and note-taking methods.

Useful language for . . . conducting out an interview or focus group

Context: this section will concentrate on some phrases you might use in face-to-face discussions with participants.

Good morning [afternoon; evening]. Thank you for coming here today. May I start by introducing myself? My name is xxxx and I am carrying out a research project on yyy. The questions I will ask you today relate to that project. I'd like to start by asking you to read this participant information sheet and sign the informed consent section at the bottom of one of the copies. You may keep the other copy.

Can I ask around the table what each of you thinks on the issue of xxxx?

That's a very interesting point. Could I ask you to expand upon it a little further?

43.1 List potential forms of bias in your research. Being aware of these will help you avoid them. Discuss your list with your supervisor to see whether you have missed anything, and to explore methods of avoiding the most important sources of bias in your work.

43.2 Find out about the statistical tests that can be carried out using the specific software available to you. Will you be able to accomplish your aims using tests within a spreadsheet program like Excel, or will you need more sophisticated software? What 'learning curve' is required to understand and master these tests? To help overcome potential difficulties, try out the software functions using dummy values, before using them with real data.

43.3 Seek out and try to learn from 'model' approaches to your topic. Whether you are conducting a focus group or carrying out an experiment, you should be able to find, perhaps with the help of your supervisor, a published study carried out in a similar way. Examine the approach and methods used in order to see if you can apply similar approaches to your own investigation. Look at the ways the results have been presented to see if these might be suitable to express your own findings.

44 | Report writing

How to select and shape your content appropriately

Writing reports of one kind or another is a part of many degree courses. These often have discipline-specific formats and it is important to follow these and select the correct information to put into the different sub-sections. This chapter considers common formats which may be suitable for the literature survey, the scientific report and the business report.

Key topics:
→ Common features of report writing
→ Representative formats for reports

Essential vocabulary
Business report   Literature survey   Scholarship   Scientific report   Scoping

---

The purpose of any report is to convey information, usually on a well-defined topic. Conventions have evolved for the structure, style and content of reports in different subjects, and, while the scholarship underlying the report will always be foremost in markers' assessments, presentational aspects are also judged as important, so you should follow the appropriate format very carefully. You can find out about aspects of the research that precedes the writing of experimental and business reports in **Ch 19**, **Chs 21-23** and **Chs 41-43**. Methods of conducting literature reviews are covered in **Ch 45**. Presentation is covered in **Ch 34**.

? Why are you asked to write reports at university?

Report writing is regarded as important because it:

- compels you to complete your work and present it in a neatly organised form for assessment;
- helps you to develop important professional skills;
- provides a record for replication or development of results for future research.

→ Common features of report writing

Writing a report is often a lengthy task and may follow a long period of research in the library, on the internet or in the laboratory. However, you should not consider the research and writing phases as separate. Your research must take into account the style and format of the report, while elements of writing up your work and/or ideas can and should be carried out as you continue to explore your topic.

Keep your focus tight

Students often fall into the trap of being over-ambitious in their goals. In general, it is better to cover a limited topic well than to write a shallow report covering a wide area.

The following stages are likely to be involved in most exercises culminating in a report:

1 **'Scoping'.** Here, you will be deciding on a topic or a specific aspect of a subject on which to concentrate. Sometimes the topic is decided for you, but in other cases it may emerge as you research (see **Ch 41**). Even in the second situation, having a notional goal when you start is important: this will give you impetus, even though you may change the precise focus later.

2 **Research.** This consists of finding and selecting relevant information. Research may be experimental, as in many science subjects (see **Ch 43**), or it may be desk-based, analysing and evaluating reports, texts and other sources (**Chs 22–23**, **Ch 45**).

3 **Writing.** This involves communicating your work using appropriate language. It's important that your writing provides evidence that you have been thinking at the appropriate level (see information box below and **Ch 21**).

4 **Presentation.** You will be expected to present your work to a high professional standard and some marks will normally be awarded for this aspect.

Aspects of report writing

Description: reporting your experiments or summarising facts you have gathered.

Visual summaries: making diagrams, flow charts, graphs or tables to demonstrate your points more clearly.

Analysis: looking at results or facts and possibly working out descriptive or hypothesis-testing statistics.

Discussion: weighing up different aspects of a position.

Solution(s): explaining different options to solve an issue or problem being addressed.

Evaluation: deciding what's important and why.

Recommendation: identifying the best solution and giving evidence to support that choice.

Arriving at a conclusion: stating a position on the basis of your research.

→ Representative formats for reports

Table 44.1 summarises the general components of reports and what they should contain. Reports for different purposes and in different subjects follow different designs and include various components, not always in the same order. Table 44.2 provides some examples, but you should follow closely the guidelines published by your faculty, school or department.

Table 44.1 Typical components of reports, and notes on the expected content of each part. These are arranged *alphabetically* and would not appear in this order in any report. For representative examples of report formats, see Table 44.2. *Always adopt the precise format specified in your course handbook.*

Section or part	Expected content
Abbreviations	A list of any abbreviations for technical terms used within the text (for example, 'DNA: deoxyribonucleic acid'). These are also given within the text at the first point of use, for example 'deoxyribonucleic acid (DNA)'.
Abstract	A brief summary of the aims of the experiment or series of observations, the main outcomes (in words) and conclusions. This should allow someone to understand your main findings and what you think they mean. This is normally written last, but is usually positioned at the beginning of the report.
Acknowledgements	A list of people who helped you, sometimes with a brief description of how.
Appendix (pl. appendices)	Includes tabular information, usually, that only an expert would want or need to consult; a section where you can put items such as a questionnaire template, and data or results that would otherwise disrupt the flow of the report or make the results section too lengthy.
Bibliography/ references/ literature cited	An alphabetical list of sources cited in the text, following one of the standard formats (**Ch 31**). Note that in some disciplines, the bibliography lists all the sources you have read.

Discussion (or conclusions)	• **Scientific-style reports.** A commentary on the results and an outline of the main conclusions. This could include any or all of the following:
	  - comments on the methods used;
	  - mention of sources of errors;
	  - conclusions from any statistical analysis;
	  - comparison with other findings or the 'ideal' results;
	  - what the results mean;
	  - how you might improve the experiments;
	  - how you might implement the findings;
	  - where you would go from here, given more time and resources.
	Sometimes you might combine the results and discussions sections to allow a narrative to develop - to explain, for example, why one result led to the next experiment or approach. Bear in mind that a large proportion of marks may be given for your original thoughts in this section.
	• **Non-scientific-style reports.** In this section you might restate the problem or issue to be addressed, outline the key 'solutions' or responses to the problem, and then explain the reason for favouring one solution over another by providing evidence to support that choice. In some, but not all, instances, a set of recommendations might be appropriate and an indication of how they could be implemented.

Executive summary	Takes the place of an abstract in a business report. Gives the key points of the report, usually no more than one A4 page long. It should start with a brief statement of the aims of the report, provide a summary of the main findings and/or conclusions, perhaps given as bullet points, and then give a summary of the main conclusions and/or recommendations. You would normally write this part last.
Experimental	A description of apparatus and method, similar to materials and methods.
Glossary	A list of terms that might be unfamiliar to the reader, with definitions.

Table 44.1 (cont'd)

Section or part	Expected content
Introduction	• **Scientific-style reports.** An outline of the background to the experiments, the aims of the experiments and brief discussion of the techniques to be used. Your goal is to orientate the reader and explain what you have done and why. • **Non-scientific-style reports.** The context of the study and an outline of the problem or issue to be addressed, in other words, the aim of the report. This may require reference to the literature or other resource material to be used.
Main body of text	Your appraisal of the topic. It should systematically address solutions or issues in response to the report's purpose and provide an analysis of all pertinent matters. It may be sub-divided into sections reflecting different aspects (**Ch 30**). In a scientific literature review, the approach is often to give a chronological account of developments in the field, quoting key authors, their ideas and findings. This section may include tables comparing different approaches or results in different studies. Figures tend to be rare, but may be used to summarise concepts or illustrate key findings.
Materials and methods	A description of what was done. You should provide sufficient detail to allow a competent person to repeat the work.
Results	A description of the experiments carried out and the results obtained, usually presented in either tabular or graphic form (never both for the same data). You should point out meaningful aspects of the data, which need not be presented in the same order in which the work was done.
Table of contents	Effectively an index to allow the reader to find parts in which they are interested. May also include a table of diagrams. More likely to be included in a lengthy report.
Title page	The full names of the author or authors, the module title or code and the date. In a business report this may also include the company logo, client details and classification (for example, 'confidential'). • **Scientific-style reports.** A descriptive title that indicates what was done, indicates any restrictions, and sometimes describes the 'headline' finding. • **Non-scientific-style reports.** A concise but comprehensive title that defines the topic.

Literature surveys

These follow the relatively uncomplicated format shown in Table 44.2(a). Two important formatting aspects to consider are citation of literature references and presenting quotes from your sources (**Ch 31**). Aspects of finding and analysing the literature are discussed in **Ch 45**.

Scientific reports

Representative formats are shown in Table 44.2(b), (c) and (d). These tend to mirror the format of journal articles in the primary literature for each subject area (**Ch 23**). Aspects you should bear in mind are:

● Anyone reading your report should be able to assimilate your findings quickly, and should be able to find relevant information in the expected place.

● Your text should be objective and balanced, considering all possible interpretations of your results.

Table 44.2 Designs of different sorts of report. The literature review (a) has a simple structure. The main body is the largest part, and may be sub-divided into sections. The general scientific report (b) has a focus on materials and methods, but in some disciplines the components may be presented in a different order, as shown in the model for the report in chemistry (c). An undergraduate lab report (d) will probably be a stripped-down and shorter version of (b). A non-scientific style of report (e) would not focus on materials and methods, but might have a main body of text dealing with the topic being considered. A typical business report (f) includes the conclusions or recommendations as part of the main body and provides an executive summary for quick reading. It often has appendices and a glossary for the non-specialist. See Table 44.1 for details of content for each section. Note that formats may vary according to institution, discipline and supervisor.

(a) Literature review	(b) General scientific report	(c) Scientific report in chemistry	(d) Laboratory report in the sciences	(e) Non-scientific report	(f) Typical business report
Title page	Title page	Title page	Title page	Title page	Title page
Abstract	Abstract	Abstract	Introduction	Introduction	Executive summary
Introduction	Abbreviations	Abbreviations	Materials and methods	Main body of text	Acknowledgements
Main body of text	Introduction	Introduction	Results (brief)	Conclusion	Table of contents
Conclusions	Materials and methods	Results	Discussion/conclusions		Main body of text
References or literature cited	Results	Discussion			Bibliography/references
	Discussion	Materials and methods/Experimental			Appendices
	Acknowledgements	Acknowledgements			
	References	References			Glossary

- Appropriate statistical analysis should be included.
- You should provide enough information to allow another competent scientist to understand and repeat your work.

Reports for non-scientific subjects

Increasingly report writing is becoming a feature in non-scientific subjects. A report-style response could be required for a case study, project or group problem-solving exercise, for example. Table 44.2(e) shows a representative structure. A good approach for the main body of text in these report-style tasks is to follow the situation – problem – solution – evaluation + (optional) recommendation (SPSER) model (**Ch 31**). This provides a basic skeleton. You may wish to tailor the headings and sub-headings to fit the context of the topic or problem that you are addressing, but the essence of the SPSER model remains intact 'below the surface' of these headings.

Business-style reports

The main aim of a business report is to provide information that helps decision-making. These reports differ greatly in their style and formality and the chief factor to consider is your audience. Table 44.2(f) illustrates one possible format. Possible variations might include:

- a report aimed solely at a shop-floor manager: relatively short and informal, focusing on production statistics and limitations;
- a business plan aimed at an investor or bank manager: fairly brief, focusing on financial projections given in charts and tables; and
- an academic analysis of a business sector: relatively lengthy and formal, quoting many sources and views.

Structurally, a business report is unlike an essay in that you should use headings and sub-headings so that your reader can find relevant information quickly.

Language of reports

The 'academic' English used in report writing is a specialised sub-set of the normal language which may be unfamiliar from your earlier learning (p. 223). Even UK students struggle with the specific phrasing required – for example, the expectation is that:

- impersonal language is used to indicate objectivity, such as avoiding personal pronouns (I, me, one, you, we, us) and using passive rather than active voice (for example, 'pressure was applied' rather than 'we applied pressure').
- tense of verbs is chosen carefully: for example, past tense when describing events ('Jones (2005) commented that . . .'), but present tense when this is appropriate ('Figure 3 shows . . .).
- the specialist vocabulary is used: such jargon has arisen in most disciplines to convey an exact meaning. Vague and slang terms should never be used.
- 'absolutes' are avoided, to demonstrate even-handedness: you should be cautious about using terms like always, never, most, all, least and none – only use these words if you are certain of the facts. 'Hedging' language is generally preferred, such as 'suggests that', 'appears that', 'may' and 'might'.

Find a model for the layout you need to adopt. This might be given in your course handbook or could be adopted from an example that you feel is well-organised. If this is dissimilar to the models shown in Table 44.2, you may wish to map the expected content to the sections in a similar fashion using Table 44.1.

Be ruthless in rejecting irrelevant information. You must keep your report as short and to the point as you can. Especially if you have spent a long time obtaining information or conducting an analysis, you may be tempted to include it for this reason alone. Don't. Relevance must be your sole criterion.

Consider your writing style. Reports can be dense and difficult to read. Try to keep your sentences relatively simple and your paragraphs short. In reports you can use sub-headings and bullet points to break up the text. All these devices can make the content easier for your reader to read and understand. Use academic English at all times (see **Ch 27**).

Choose appropriate chart types. If you wish to present diagrams and graphs, keep these simple and use the title and legend to explain what you want to show in each case. Use a variety of types of chart if you can.

Think about your likely conclusions from an early stage. This may shape both the research you do and the content. However, make sure you keep an open mind if the evidence points you in another direction.

💬 **Useful language for . . . writing a report**

Context: the following examples include language forms common in academic English.

These results suggest that there has been a recent decline in herring stocks in the North Sea (note use of 'suggest' to show that you acknowledge other conclusions are technically possible).

Although Johnson et al. (2009) reported that xxxx, Figure 3 demonstrates that xxxx (this sentence is designed to contrast past results with the author's present findings, hence the different use of tense – 'reported' is past tense and 'shows' is present tense).

A review of publications using this method indicates that . . . (note impersonal 'academic' phrasing – although we know the author carried out the review, he/she does not write 'I carried out a review of publications and found . . .').

GO And now . . .

44.1 Compare Tables a–f in Table 44.2 with the model you have been asked to adopt. You will see similarities and differences that reflect the purpose of each type of report. How does this relate to the specific format you have been asked to adopt?

44.2 Research types of graph. To add variety and impact to scientific and business reports, you should select the right type of chart – and you can only do this if you know about the different formats available. The Help function in your software package will explain how to upload data into a spreadsheet and obtain the corresponding graph possibilities. This can help you to achieve an indication of what potential graph types would look like.

44.3 Focus on higher-level academic thinking skills. In most forms of report, you will be assessed on the analysis and evaluation you make, based on a thorough summary of the topic. If you aren't 100 per cent certain of what is involved in these skills, consult **Ch 21** and read examples from your subject area with this in mind.

45 | Literature surveys

How to research and shape a survey of facts and viewpoints

A review of literature is a specialised form of academic writing that requires a specific research approach and writing style. This chapter outlines ways of finding and selecting relevant literature and writing about the work of others in an appropriate way.

Key topics:
→ Selecting a topic
→ How to find the literature on your subject
→ Keeping track of references and their relevance

Essential vocabulary
Article Citation Dissertation Literature survey Primary (literature) source
Review School of thought

Conducting a literature survey is similar in many ways to writing a dissertation (**Ch 44**) in that it involves reading about a topic and summarising what different authors have said about it. You may wish to compare and contrast different viewpoints or research themes, or describe the development of an academic field through time. However, the product should be more than that, as the alternative name – the literature review – implies: you will need to carry out an *analysis* and *evaluation* of the literature, rather than merely describing what others have written (see **Ch 21** for an explanation of these terms).

Definition: literature survey ℹ️

A literature survey reviews comprehensively all the available publications related to a specific academic topic. It documents this literature; identifies the schools of thought within it; categorises viewpoints; explores the origins and development of authors' opinions; analyses and evaluates the relevance and meaning of the facts and viewpoints encountered.

→ Selecting a topic

The first stage in a literature survey is choosing a specific area to research. If you are allowed a choice, you may be asked to choose from a list, or you may be expected to find a topic yourself within a broad area (see **Ch 41**). In either case, you will find it useful to do a little reading before selecting.

Possible criteria for selecting a subject include:

- a topic that you find interesting;
- a research field with a reasonable amount of literature to discuss – not too small, with only a few papers available, nor too large, with too many;
- a subject where the literature is accessible – for example, published in English, or in journals available from your library;
- a field where there are different views or approaches that you can compare;
- a controversial area, or a topical subject;
- a field where a recent breakthrough has been made.

Narrow down your topic if you can and choose a working title. The wording of this is important, because readers' and markers' expectations of content will be influenced by your title. You should be prepared to alter the title or add a secondary element to it as your research develops and you decide on the precise approach or viewpoint you will adopt.

→ How to find the literature on your subject

Your review will take into account information provided by various forms of written source:

- **Textbooks:** good for gaining an overview of a field.
- **Monographs:** books on a single, often narrow, subject.
- **Reviews:** analysis of a research area, often detailed and more up to date than books.
- **Reference works:** useful for obtaining facts and definitions, and a concise overview of a subject.
- **Research papers:** very detailed articles published in hard-copy or online journals, covering specific subject areas.
- **Websites:** not always wholly reliable as sources, but may be useful for comparing viewpoints and sourcing other information.

See also **Ch 22** regarding library resources and how to access them.

---

smart tip

Consulting different types of resource

Be an open-minded researcher: there is little to be gained from reading several textbooks each covering broadly similar content, when other relevant material may be found in different formats, such as journals, that may provide more detailed analysis or fresh approaches.

If your work is supervised, your supervisor may be able to provide some articles to start you off, or some references may be given in handouts supporting the exercise. The majority of the papers you will consult will be primary sources (p. 179), and when you start will seem to be written in exclusive specialist language that may be difficult to understand. However, as you become familiar with the terms of your subject, this will become less of a problem.

If you are unfamiliar with library research methods, it is a good idea to consult a subject librarian. Not only will they be able to teach you basic techniques, but they can also show you how to access databases and other tools to search for relevant material. Your library's website may also carry useful tips and online access routes to databases and e-journals (**Ch 22**).

There is a constant stream of academic work feeding into the primary literature. So long as you have one paper as a starting point, you can work *backwards* in the literature relatively easily by looking for other relevant references in the text, especially within the introduction and discussion of the paper. Use the context and article title as a guide to relevance. Each paper you then read will refer to others, and before long you will accumulate a body of references and have a feel for the important papers in your field.

Working *forwards* in the literature from a relevant paper is a little less easy. In some fields there are citation index journals that indicate which papers have been cited by others. This can let you see where a chosen reference has been mentioned recently – and sometimes the citing article will be of interest to you. Another approach is to put key words or authors into a database or search engine and see what appears. You can also scan current journals for related material, though this is much less likely to turn up relevant material.

→ Keeping track of references and their relevance

As you read each article and review, you should be taking notes of key points (**Ch 27**), either in a notebook, or on index cards (see below). The matrix format of note-taking (Figure 25.6 on p. 206) is a valuable way of summarising different aspects of sources and lets you see the whole picture more easily.

You may also wish to file papers so that you can find them when required. The simplest method is alphabetically by author, and then by date, as in a bibliography. An alternative, which is valuable if you expect to gather many papers, is to give each paper a sequential number and note this on your index system or database. Papers are then filed in numerical order. This avoids the need to reorganise papers if your files become full.

One thing you will have to do is cite your sources in your text and prepare a bibliography or reference list. This is standard academic practice and helps avoid accusations of plagiarism (**Ch 32**). You will need to follow departmental guidance notes for the precise format or take an example from the discipline literature. **Ch 31** provides further information about methods of citing and quoting, and the main styles of referencing.

Despite the availability of computer programs such as *Endnote* for organising references, some people like to keep the reference details of their sources on index cards, along with any notes they make about them. This serves two purposes:

- When writing up, you can put the cards into piles representing different topics or viewpoints and then organise these appropriately, for example, by date. This makes it easier to include every reference in its 'right' place.

- The cards can be organised alphabetically to create your bibliography/reference list. If your review involves many papers, however, you may wish to spread the task of typing these by entering them into a word-processor file as you go along.

Writing in a balanced, objective style and arriving at a conclusion

Although you may have, or develop, strong views about your topic and the issues and controversies that you discuss, it is vital that you write in a balanced way that gives a fair summary of the reasons for opposing viewpoints. This is one reason why an impersonal, passive style is usually favoured in academic writing. However, it is important that you try to arrive at a conclusion (see **Ch 29**). In doing so, you should give reasons why you have arrived at a particular viewpoint. Do not be afraid of being critical, so long as you can back up your position with supporting evidence.

✓ Practical tips for writing a literature survey

Try not to read aimlessly and passively when reading material related to your topic. Making notes is one way you can avoid this. Just as in revising, it will help you memorise key points. See **Ch 25** for advice and tips.

Start writing as soon as you can. Word processors allow text fragments to be moved around with ease. This means that you can write up some parts of your survey (especially descriptive parts) as you go along, and reorganise these when you have a better picture of the whole subject.

Discuss drafts with your supervisor or a friend. Your supervisor may not ask to see your drafts, but you will probably gain valuable advice if you can persuade them to comment. A friend, even one who doesn't know your subject, will also be able to point out where your explanations are obscure or your view seems biased.

Organise your references from an early stage. It can be very time-consuming searching for details and writing your bibliography or reference list and it is best not to do this at the last moment, when you should be focusing on higher-level aspects.

Review and edit what you have written. If at all possible, aim to finish your writing a week or so ahead of the submission date. Then, leave your work for a day to two and return to it, reading it in one sweep. This will help you take a more critical look at what you have written (**Ch 33**).

Useful language for . . . writing a literature review

Context: to give an idea of the style normally adopted, the following might be examples of expressions found in a literature review.

The first publication in this area was the seminal work by [author1], who identified xxxx, and suggested the following classification of terms: xxxx. Later, [author2] refined this hierarchy, by introducing xxxx.

The literature on this topic represents two schools of thought: those like [name(s) of key author(s)], who believe xxxx; while others, such as [name(s) of key author(s)] have concluded that xxxx.

In conclusion, this review has summarised evidence in favour of xxxx, but has shown that there is also a possibility that xxxx. It is clear that further research should be carried out to determine whether xxxx.

GO And now . . .

45.1 Consult your subject librarian. Visit the library or its website to find contact details and make an appointment. This meeting will be more productive for both parties if you prepare a short list of questions about your research needs.

45.2 Set up appropriate filing systems and databases. As suggested above, you can use index cards to store details of your references, or create a simple database using a word processor or spreadsheet. There are commercial products for storing details of references (for example, Endnote), but, especially for a short writing project, you will need to balance the effort, time and cost you invest in these systems against the benefits. In addition, you will probably need to set up a file storage system to keep your papers tidy and well-organised.

45.3 Read a selection of literature reviews and surveys in your subject area. This will give you an idea of the writing style you should be adopting and the depth of analysis for which you should be striving.

How to display your work effectively

In certain disciplines you may be asked to prepare a poster to summarise research you have done, often as part of a teamwork exercise. The main aim is to develop your communication skills, including how you select and present the content and are able to discuss your work with others.

Key topics:
→ Researching and deciding on content
→ Designing your poster
→ Constructing and setting up a poster
→ Defending your poster

Essential vocabulary
**Abstract   Peer   Peer assessment   Point size   Poster defence
Rhetorical question   White space   Yellow Pages**

The idea behind a poster display is to present a summary of research or scholarship in an easily assimilated format. Poster sessions are common at academic conferences, particularly in the sciences - they allow many participants to report findings or ideas within a single session and help people with similar interests to meet and discuss detailed information.

The concept has been adapted for undergraduate and postgraduate work for several reasons.

- It allows you to present the results of your work to tutors and fellow students.
- It provides a good end point for teamwork (**Ch 18**).
- It makes you focus on the essence of the topic.
- It develops your presentational skills.
- It allows tutors to observe and assess your verbal communication skills.

Any or all of these aspects may be assessed as part of the exercise. Find out how the marks are divided before you start so that you can allocate your efforts appropriately. If peer assessment is involved, you may wish to discuss this openly at an initial team meeting (see **Ch 18**).

> **Definition: peer assessment**
>
> This is where members of a class assess each other's work. For a poster presentation, members of a group may assess each other's contribution as part of the team, and/or members of the class may judge each other's posters.

The advice presented here will assume that your poster is part of a team exercise where you have been asked to look into a specific aspect of the subject you are studying. The same principles will apply if it is a solo effort, for example if you are reporting the results of a research project.

→ Researching and deciding on content

It might be a good idea for your team first to do a little independent study, so that everyone can gain a general picture of the whole topic. At some point you will want to meet up to decide on the exact focus of your poster, and perhaps allocate specific research tasks for each member. At this stage you should only be thinking about the wider aspects of the topic you feel you need to cover, rather than specifics and precise wording. Even seemingly narrow subjects will have scope for different approaches. Although an impressive 'take-home message' is important, you should also bear in mind the need for visual impact in your poster when making your choices. There are certain components included in most posters, however, as detailed below.

You will normally be allocated a space to set up your poster (typically 1.5 metres wide by 1 metre high) and, although this may initially seem a large area to cover, you will probably have to select carefully what to include. This is because your poster will need to be legible from a distance of 1 metre or so, and the large font size required for this inevitably means fewer words than you might otherwise prefer. When thinking about content, therefore, it is best to assume that space will be limited.

---

smart tip

Typical components of a poster

- ❏ **Title:** phrased in a way that will attract readers' attention
- ❏ **Author information:** names, and in the formal academic type of poster, their affiliation
- ❏ **Abstract or summary:** stating the approach taken and the main conclusions
- ❏ **Introduction:** providing brief background information essential for understanding the poster
- ❏ **Materials and methods:** describing experimental or field research, background theory or historical overview
- ❏ **Results:** key findings or examples
- ❏ **Conclusion:** giving the 'take-home messages' of your study or project
- ❏ **Acknowledgements:** stating who has helped you
- ❏ **References and sources**

→ Designing your poster

The key design principle for your poster is to generate visual impact. It needs to stand out among the others in the session and provide a visual 'hook' to draw a spectator towards the more academic content. This can be achieved in several ways:

- a striking overall design concept related to the topic;
- effective use of colour or a prominent colour contrast between the background and the poster elements;
- a large image, either attractive or horrific, at the centre of the poster;
- an amusing or punning title;
- some form of visual aid attached to the poster, such as a large model related to the topic.

Examples of imaginative poster design

- A poster about forest ecology where the text elements are presented as 'leaves' on a model tree.
- A study of urban geography where the poster has the appearance of a street map with aspects written within each building.
- A physiology poster where an organ like the liver is drawn at the centre, with elements attached to it via arteries and veins.

For convenience, most undergraduate posters are composed of A4 or A3 sheets, or shapes derived from them. These 'panels' will be attached to the main poster board, usually by drawing pins or Velcro pads, and their size or shape may place a constraint on your overall design – check the overall dimensions as soon as you can, to work out your options for arranging these sheets.

The next important aspect to decide is how your readers will work their way through the material you present. Each panel will be read left to right in the usual way, but the route through the panels may not follow this rule. Various options are shown in Figure 46.1. Whichever you choose, it is important to let your readers know which path to take, either by prominent numbering or by incorporating arrows or guidelines into the design.

The ideal text size for your poster title will be about 25–40 mm high (100–170 point size) for the title, 15–25 mm for subtitles (60–100 point) and 5–10 mm (25–40 point) for the main material. If you only have an A4 printer at your disposal, remember that you can enlarge to A3 on most photocopiers, although this may restrict you to black-and-white text. Linear dimensions will increase by 1.41 times (that is, 141 per cent) if you do this. Once point size and panel dimensions are known, you can work out a rough word limit for each component. When members of the team are working on the content, they will need to adhere to this limit. Besides being succinct, your writing style should make it easy to assimilate the material, for example, by using bullet points and sub-headings.

---

smart tip

Group style

We all have our own styles of writing and it is important that take this into account when composing the text, and ensure that differences in writing style among team members can be eliminated so that the overall style is consistent.

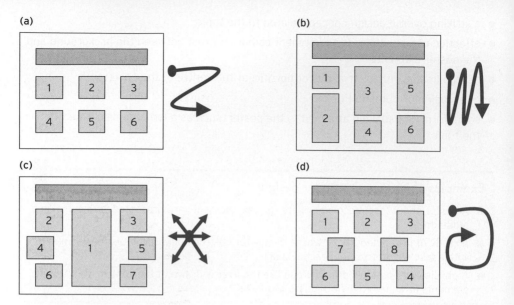

Figure 46.1 Options for laying out a poster. The numbers and arrows indicate the route taken by the reader, while the deeper-coloured bar at the top would contain the title and author details.

→ Constructing and setting up a poster

At an early stage, you should draw a diagram of your poster, mapping out the main components to scale. You may also wish to create a mock poster to the exact dimensions to gain a better idea of what the final version will look like.

Each part will need to be printed or copied according to your design brief. Using panels as shown in Figure 46.1 makes it easier to construct the poster as a series of independent components and to bring these to the poster session for final assembly. They can be attached to your board directly or pasted on to card first. You may also wish to laminate each component, or cover it in clear plastic film. A photocopying specialist (see *Yellow Pages* under 'Copying and duplicating services') may be able to carry this out for a charge.

→ Defending your poster

The poster 'defence' for undergraduate work imitates the poster session at a conference where delegate researchers mill around the posters, quizzing the authors about their work. These sessions can be very stimulating for all involved, and collaborations and job offers may result.

If your poster exercise involves an element of defence, it will probably take the form of a 5-10-minute question-and-answer session with your tutors. Expect probing questions to find out how much knowledge and understanding lies behind your presentation, not just what you have selected to display.

Practising for a poster defence

If English is not your first language, then you may feel timid about 'defending' your poster. Practice can improve your confidence. Ask a friend to ask you questions, listen to your answers and suggest improvements to your phrasing. Here is a list of typical questions about posters that you should be ready to answer.

- Why did you select this topic?
- Who did which part of the research?
- Who thought of the design?
- Who made up the components?
- Can you give me further information on ... ?
- How does this finding relate to ... ?
- What does this graph or image mean?
- Where next for this topic or research area?
- How might you improve your poster?

✔ Practical tips for creating better posters

Use the poster title effectively. A two-part title can be used to draw the reader in – the first part being a 'hook' and the second giving more detail. The chapter titles in this book are examples of this approach, but there will be scope for more humour in your poster title, perhaps through a pun on the subject material.

Check out the font sizes you plan to use. Print out a specimen sheet and stand 1–1.5 metres away. You should be able to read the material easily from this distance. Copy some random text (for example, from a website) on to a sheet at the same font size and carry out a word count to gain an idea of what your word limit will be for each component.

Make sure that your poster is able to 'travel well'. You should think about how you take it from the point of construction to the display venue. The components should be portable and packaged in a weather-proof way.

Remember that 'white space' is important in design. An overly fussy presentation with many elements covering the entire area will be difficult to assimilate. In this case, 'less can be more' if it helps you to get your central message across.

Consider colour combinations carefully. Certain colours are difficult to see against others and some pairings may be difficult to distinguish for those who are colour-blind (for example, red and green). Bold, primary colours will attract the eye.

Use imaginative materials. A visit to a craft shop or a do-it-yourself store might give you some ideas. For example, you might see a piece of fabric or single roll of wallpaper at a cheap price that could provide an interesting background.

Use language to draw the reader in. For example, if the titles and sub-headings are given as a series of rhetorical questions, a casual viewer will naturally want to read the text to find out the answer.

Don't provide too much detail. Keep the wording sparse, and be prepared to talk further about matters raised in the text during the poster defence.

Use a handout if you have too much detail to cover. If you've done lots of research but have to cut some interesting parts out of the final design because of space constraints, consider giving readers a short handout to cover these aspects. This should contain the poster title, author names and contact details.

State your 'take-home message' clearly. Leave your reader in no doubt about your conclusions. You could, for example, list them as a series of bullet points at the end.

Work as a team when answering questions. Be ready to support each other, filling in if someone is unable to answer. However, all members should know the fundamentals of the topic, as any group member may be expected to respond.

💬 Useful language for . . . discussing a poster

Context: these might be the sorts of thing you would say when 'defending' a poster.

I was delegated the task of finding out about xxx. I did a literature survey in the library and read a number of the original papers. I drafted the section shown here, then the team members worked together to edit it.

The original concept design was xxxx's idea. However, I came up with the idea of xxxxxxx.

I think we worked really well as a team on this exercise. After our first meeting, we each took on specific tasks. When we came back together, it was easy to work on the various writing and presentation styles so that we could assemble the parts into the poster you see here.

GO And now . . .

46.1 Find out the dimensions of your poster space and draw this out to scale. If you copy this sheet your team can use it to sketch out possible designs that will work better.

46.2 Have a critical look at research posters in your department. These are often displayed after they have been used at a conference. You will probably find them well-presented, but some may be rather detailed and formal in appearance. Learn from good and bad aspects of what you see.

46.3 Ensure your team works collectively to achieve the best grade. If your poster is produced as a group exercise, spend some time at the start discussing team roles and how you should work together as a team to maximise your marks. Read **Ch 18** to find out more about team interactions and use the terms introduced there to inform your discussion.

Spoken presentations

How to give a talk or seminar with confidence

Giving a presentation can be a rewarding experience. By following simple guidelines, you can prepare yourself well, gain in confidence and communicate your message effectively.

Key topics:
→ Planning and preparing your script
→ Effective speaking
→ Using presentation software such as *PowerPoint*
→ Answering questions

Essential vocabulary

AV aids   Diction   Lay people   Overhead transparency   *PowerPoint*   Prompt
Rhetorical question   Seminar

You may be asked to give a spoken presentation in several situations – from a brief summary at a tutorial to a lengthy seminar on a research project. Your talk may be relatively casual or it may be supported by high-tech visual aids. This chapter will focus on more formal types of presentation, although similar principles apply elsewhere.

→ Planning and preparing your script

Whatever the occasion, it is important to be well-prepared. Having a well considered plan, good supporting material and a clear picture of your main conclusions will boost your confidence and improve your audience's experience. However, over-rehearsal can lead to a dull and monotonous delivery and you should try to avoid this.

Experienced speakers know that being slightly nervous is important, because this creates energy and sparkle when delivering the material. Their view is that if the adrenalin isn't flowing, their presentation will probably lack vitality. Turn any anxiety you may have to your advantage by thinking of it as something that will work for you rather than against you.

smart tip

Keep your introduction positive

Never start a talk by being apologetic or being defensive about your language or work. For example, you may be tempted to say that you are unprepared or lack expertise. This will lower your audience's expectations, probably unnecessarily, and get you off to a weak start.

Start your presentation with the basics

Don't forget to begin with the seemingly obvious, such as definitions of key terms. Not all your audience may have the same background in the subject as you. If they aren't on the same wavelength, or don't understand key terms, you may lose them at the very beginning.

Structure

Every substantive presentation should have a beginning, a middle and an end. The old maxim 'say what you are going to say, say it, and then say what you have said' conforms directly to this structure and you need search no further for an outline plan.

- **Introduction.** Your task here is to introduce yourself, state the aim of your presentation, say how you intend to approach the topic and provide relevant background information.

- **Main content.** This will depend on the nature of the talk. For a talk about a project in the Sciences or Engineering, you might start with methods, and then move on to results, perhaps displayed as a series of graphs that you will lead your audience through. For a seminar in the Arts, you might discuss various aspects of your topic, giving examples or quotes as you go.

- **Conclusions.** Here your aim is to draw the talk together, explaining how all your points fit together and giving ideas of where things might develop in the future – for example, suggestions for further research or different angles to approach the subject. Finally, you should recap your whole talk in a series of 'take-home statements' and then thank your audience for their attention.

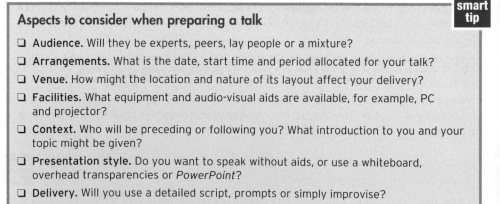

Aspects to consider when preparing a talk

- ❑ **Audience.** Will they be experts, peers, lay people or a mixture?
- ❑ **Arrangements.** What is the date, start time and period allocated for your talk?
- ❑ **Venue.** How might the location and nature of its layout affect your delivery?
- ❑ **Facilities.** What equipment and audio-visual aids are available, for example, PC and projector?
- ❑ **Context.** Who will be preceding or following you? What introduction to you and your topic might be given?
- ❑ **Presentation style.** Do you want to speak without aids, or use a whiteboard, overhead transparencies or *PowerPoint*?
- ❑ **Delivery.** Will you use a detailed script, prompts or simply improvise?
- ❑ **Requirements.** What might you need to bring? What equipment might you need to practise with?
- ❑ **Liaison.** Who should you contact to confirm details or make special requests?

Creating a script to provide a series of prompts

Presentations begin as pieces of writing that evolve through several phases:

1 creating a brainstorm or concept map of what you need to cover;

2 laying out themes or headings with brief explanatory notes;

3 producing a script - more or less the full text of your talk with 'stage directions' and an indication of timing; and

4 reducing the script to a set of key words and bullet points - your prompts.

As you become more experienced, you will find you can move directly from phase 2 to phase 4, perhaps thinking through appropriate wording in your head rather than writing the exact words down.

Working from prompts, sometimes called 'cues', is recommended, whether they are produced as headings on cards or as bullet points in a *PowerPoint* slideshow (or similar). These basic headings provide the structure of your talk, so that you don't ramble or lose your place. They also help to promote an air of informality that will involve your audience. All you need to remember is roughly what you intend to say around each point. If you practise on this basis,

● you will become become more confident in the material;

● you can identify any complex parts that you cannot easily put into words, and practise these independently;

● you can find out whether your presentation will fit the allotted time;

● you can make the presentation to a friend and ask them to comment on your pronunciation, audibility and clarity, presentation style (including gestures) and use of visual aids.

---

smart tip

Reading your talk from a written script is probably a bad idea, even though you may feel more confident if you know in advance every word you are going to say. This kind of delivery always seems dry; not only because it results in an unnatural way of speaking, but also because you will be so busy looking at your script that you will almost certainly fail to make eye contact with your audience.

For similar reasons, you should probably not memorise your presentation, as this will take a lot of effort and may result in the same flat or stilted delivery as if you had scripted it word for word.

→ Effective speaking

This is more than speaking loudly enough to be heard and pronouncing your words clearly so that the audience can make them out. These skills are fundamental - although you will already realise that many speakers fail to do this. Ask a friend to check and comment on your diction to make sure you meet these basic criteria.

Good speaking not only ensures that information is transmitted, but also engages the audience. You can do this in two main ways - through your actions and body language, and through the approach you take.

Developing a speaking style

If English is not your first language, then you may find it difficult to develop a natural speaking style. This will come with practice, but initially you may need to rely on extensive prompts or script certain parts. Try to learn from other speakers you hear, such as newsreaders on TV, or your lecturers. Adopt language techniques and phrases that you feel are helpful in getting the message across, and try to work these into your own personal style.

First, don't just stand still and speak in a monotone. Aim for an element of variety to keep interest levels high:

- Move around a little – but make sure you face the audience so that you will be heard, and do not pace up and down excessively.
- Use moderate hand gestures to emphasise your points – but don't wave your hands around excessively.
- Ensure you make eye contact with the audience – but don't stare at one person or area all the time.
- Liven your talk by shifting between modes of presentation, for example, by drawing a diagram on the board or presenting a visual aid – but don't overdo this or the audience may be distracted from your theme.

Second, try to involve your audience. Use rhetorical questions to make them think, even though you will be supplying the answers. Ask them direct questions, such as 'How many of you have read this article?' then follow up with '. . . for the benefit of those who haven't, I'll just recap on the main points'. If it would be relevant, ask them to do an activity as part of the presentation. This takes confidence to handle, but it can work well and is especially valuable to break up a longer talk where attention may wander.

smart tip

Pace your talk

When you practise your talk, check the clock and note down marker timing points during it. When it comes to the real thing, check how you are doing in relation to the marker points and speed up or slow down as necessary. In some cases, the real talk will take longer than you anticipated. This will either be because the initial business of getting set up has eaten up some of your allotted time, or because you have relaxed during the presentation and said more than you thought you would. In other cases, you may find that slight nervousness means you have spoken faster than intended.

→ Using presentation software such as *PowerPoint*

The standard methods of supporting a presentation with images and information used to be either overhead slides or 35 mm photographic slides. Overhead transparencies have the advantage over simple spoken presentations of letting you see the same thing as your audience, while still facing them, but if filled with text they can seem dull. Slides are valuable where ultra-high-quality images are required, but an important disadvantage is that they require complex equipment and procedures to produce.

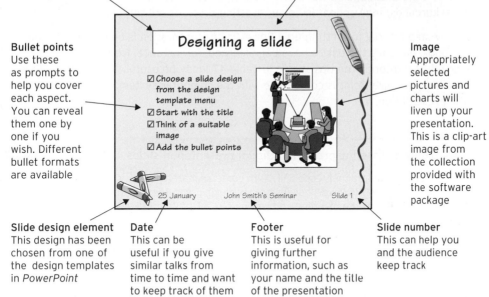

Slide title
You can use this to help your audience keep track of the topics you are covering

Slide background
You can alter this and the colour of text if you wish, even when using one of the design templates

Bullet points
Use these as prompts to help you cover each aspect. You can reveal them one by one if you wish. Different bullet formats are available

Image
Appropriately selected pictures and charts will liven up your presentation. This is a clip-art image from the collection provided with the software package

Designing a slide

☑ Choose a slide design from the design template menu
☑ Start with the title
☑ Think of a suitable image
☑ Add the bullet points

25 January   John Smith's Seminar   Slide 1

Slide design element
This design has been chosen from one of the design templates in *PowerPoint*

Date
This can be useful if you give similar talks from time to time and want to keep track of them

Footer
This is useful for giving further information, such as your name and the title of the presentation

Slide number
This can help you and the audience keep track

Figure 47.1 Elements of a typical *PowerPoint* slide. Similar features are available using other software.

Nowadays, both these media have largely been replaced with digital 'slides' produced via software such as Microsoft *PowerPoint*. These systems provide flexibility and allow you to incorporate digital images with ease. A significant disadvantage is that a computer and (expensive) digital projector is required to show them. If you are planning to use this type of software, check whether appropriate facilities will be available in the room or can be borrowed or booked.

You can select from a variety of designs for each *PowerPoint* slide, most of which help you to structure your talk around a series of bullet points and to mix text with images or graphs (see Figure 47.1). This may help you to organise your prompts, but you should make sure you don't simply read them word for word from the slide. Few things are more boring than a speaker reading out what you can already see on a screen.

If you doubt your ability to speak freely around the bullet points, you can use the notes facility within *PowerPoint* to write down information you might not remember. You can then print out each slide and associated notes together on a single A4 page to act as a support during the presentation. Use the 'Print > Print What: > Notes Pages' command, but select 'Pure Black and White' under 'Color/grayscale' or your printout (including slide backgrounds) may appear in colour, wasting precious printer ink.

A step-by-step tutorial for setting up a *PowerPoint* presentation is beyond the scope of this book, but once the basics have been learned, for instance, from a handbook or online self-help tutorial, the tips shown in Table 47.1 may be useful. Always check that your version of *PowerPoint* is compatible with the computer system you will be using for the presentation.

---

smart tip

Allow plenty of time for preparing digital presentation slides

The technology is helpful but, especially with complex material, each slide can take a lot of effort to set up. However, because of the flexibility of this system, you can save some time by merging the planning and writing phases of your talk into one session. For instance, once *PowerPoint* slides are constructed, it is relatively easy to change their order or to alter formatting.

→ Answering questions

This is a part of a talk that many people worry about, as they have no control over what may be asked, and feel they might look stupid if they don't know an answer. You can deal with this element in several ways.

- **Prepare for likely questions.** Try to anticipate what people might ask and have an answer ready.

- **Ask for clarification if you don't understand a question fully.** You could also ask the questioner or chair to repeat the question if a part of it was indistinct or didn't seem to make sense to you.

- **Repeat the question for the benefit of those who might not have heard it.** The questioner will be facing you, not the audience, and their voice may be indistinct. This will also buy you some time for composing an answer.

- **Think before you answer.** Rather than blurting out the first thing that comes to mind, take time to weigh up the different aspects. You may feel the necessary pause is long, but this will not be how the audience perceives it.

- **If you don't know an answer, say so.** Everyone will see through a speaker who is trying to hide their lack of knowledge. Try saying 'I don't know the answer at the moment, but I'll find out and get back to you' if you want to say something rather than leaving a pause.

Table 47.1 Tips for constructing slides with digital presentation software such as *PowerPoint*

Aspect	Comment
Background and text colouring	Choose a background or slide design template with care. A lighter background with dark text will attract attention, but may be hard to concentrate on over the long term, whereas a darker background with light writing may be more restful on the eye.
Slide design	The standard *PowerPoint* designs are tried and tested, and are especially useful if you have little time to prepare for a talk, but many of your audience will have seen them before. You can easily be more original, for instance, by incorporating an image into the background, but be aware that this will take time to set up.
Text size and font	Standard *PowerPoint* text size defaults to values that mean that it is difficult to get much information on each slide. You can override this feature, but there is a good reason for it: too much on each slide is bad practice. A point size of 28 is probably the lowest text size you should use. Sans serif fonts, such as Arial, are said to be easiest to read on-screen.
Use of images	If you can, try to include an image in at least half of your slides. Even if these are only partially relevant, they help to maintain audience interest. A text-only presentation consisting of nothing more than bullet points will seem very dry. Use clip-art or images from copyright-free web resources if you don't have any images of your own.
Revealing your points one by one	Use the 'animation' feature to build up your slide line by line as you wish. This will help you pace your talk and ensure that the audience is listening to you, rather than reading ahead on the slide. To keep the audience on track, you may find it advantageous to use a slide giving sub-headings and reintroduce this as you move on to each new sub-topic on your list.
Use of special features	You can use special features for introducing each new slide and, within each slide, you can make text enter from different directions in different ways and even accompanied with noises. You can also link to websites (if your computer is appropriately connected) and run digital video clips. Resist the temptation to go overboard with these 'bells and whistles', because although such features can make a talk livelier, they tend to distract from your main message. More features mean that more can go wrong.
Handouts	Think about providing your audience with a handout of the slides. In *PowerPoint* you can use the 'File > Print > Print What: > Handouts > 6 slides per page' option to do this. When printing, it is best to select 'Pure Black and White' from the 'Color/grayscale' options, or all of the slides may print in colour, including the background. Numbering your slides (see Figure 47.1) will help your audience keep track with the handout.

✓ **Practical tips for delivering a presentation**

Dress appropriately for the occasion. You should look smart, but should feel comfortable in what you wear. Turning up in informal clothes may be interpreted as showing a lack of respect to your audience and may lead to the expectation of a sloppy presentation.

To reduce tension, take deep breaths. This can be done both before you address the audience and during pauses in your presentation.

Make sure you can be heard. At the start of your talk, ask the audience if they can hear at the back. Alternatively, when practising, try to use the room where the presentation will take place and ask a friend if they can hear you. If you know someone in the audience, you could ask them to signal to you if you are talking too quietly (or too loudly). Remember that a full room creates different acoustics from an empty one.

Make sure your audio-visual aids can be seen. If you are using some kind of projection system, make sure that you – or your shadow – don't block out the projected image. It's a good idea to ask your audience if they can see clearly before you start.

Engage the audience. Speak directly to the audience, not to the floor, your notes, the screen or a distant wall. Look at their faces and take cues from their reactions. If they don't seem to understand what you've said, repeat it in a different way. If they look bored, speed up, or ask a rhetorical question to engage their thoughts. Imagine the members of the audience are your friends – speak to them with enthusiasm, warmth and genuine feeling. They will respond in kind.

Don't speak too quickly. This is a common response to nerves. Make a determined effort to slow yourself down and speak clearly.

Check pronunciation. If you are uncertain of the correct way to say words in your presentation then check them out with a native English-speaking fellow student.

Have a 'plan B' if your talk overruns or the projection system fails. Plan things so that you can miss something out from the main section of the talk if you are under time pressure (for example, by skipping over a few *PowerPoint* slides). This is preferable to being unable to complete your conclusions – people may be more interested in those than in the detail of your presentation, and they can always ask about the skipped material at the end. Print out the *PowerPoint* slides, perhaps in handout or note form, so that you can still use these if the projection system fails.

Try to enjoy the occasion. If you seem to be taking pleasure from speaking, your audience will also enjoy the session. Conversely, if you don't seem to be interested, why should they be?

Useful language for . . . delivering a presentation

Context: these are expressions that can be useful for spoken presentations.

Good afternoon [morning/evening]. The title of my presentation today is xxxx. This slide shows the structure of my talk. Firstly, I'm going to introduce xxxx, then . . .

This figure illustrates the main evidence why it is thought that xxxx . . . As you can see, xxxx does xxxx, meaning that xxxx.

That's a very interesting question, and one that is hard to answer. My feeling is that xxxx . . .

47.1 Learn how to use presentational software in advance. Even if you have no talk to give in the near future, time spent learning how to use *PowerPoint* or similar software will make it much easier, should you choose to use this form of visual aid.

47.2 If you feel shy, take small opportunities to practise speaking so that you can build up confidence. These might include making a comment at a meeting or asking questions at other talks - anything that gets you used to hearing your own voice speaking in a formal situation.

47.3 Learn from other speakers. Starting with your lecturers, think about what makes the good ones good and the bad ones bad (see also Table 15.1 on pp. 123-4). Try to model your own style and presentation technique on someone whose approach you admire.

48 | Exploiting feedback

How to understand and learn from what lecturers write on your work and exam scripts

When you receive back assessed work and exam scripts, these are usually annotated by the marker. It is essential that you learn from these comments if you want to improve, but sometimes they can be difficult to understand. This chapter outlines some common annotations and describes how you should react to them.

Key topics:
→ Types of feedback
→ Examples of feedback comments and what they mean

Essential vocabulary
Feedback   Formative assessment   Pointer   Proofing   Summative assessment

There are two principal types of assessment at university: formative and summative. Formative assessments are those in which the grade received does not contribute to your end-of-module mark, or contributes relatively little, but which gives you an indication of the standard of your work. It is often accompanied by a feedback sheet or comments written on the script. Summative assessments contribute directly to your final module mark and include end-of-term/semester exams, project reports or essay submissions.

→ Types of feedback

The simplest pointer you will receive from any type of assessment is the grade you receive; if good, you know that you have reached the expected standard; if poor, you know that you should try to improve.

If you feel unsure about the grading system or what standard is expected at each grading level, your course or faculty handbooks will probably include a description of marking or assessment criteria that explain this (see **Ch 53**, pp. 430-1).

---

smart tip

Obtaining informal (preliminary) feedback

Your fellow students or family members can help by reading through your work and commenting. Even though they may lack subject knowledge, they will be able to comment on the clarity of your writing or the logic of your argument.

How well are you performing?

The answer, of course, depends on your goals and expectations, but also on your understanding of degree classifications and their significance. Even in early levels of study, it may be worth relating percentage marks or other forms of grades (descriptors) to the standard degree classes – first, upper second, lower second, third and unclassified. Certain career and advanced degree opportunities will only be open to those with higher-level qualifications, and you should try to gain an understanding of how this operates in your field of study and likely career destination.

Written feedback may be provided on your scripts and other work. This will often take the form of handwritten comments over your text, and a summary commenting on your work or justifying why it received the mark it did. Sometimes the feedback will be provided separately from your script so that other markers are not influenced by it.

Always read your feedback

The comments in your feedback should give you constructive direction for later efforts and are designed to help you to develop the structure and style of your work, as well as encourage you to develop a deeper understanding of the topic. Ensure that you collect the hard copy of your marked work so that you can study the feedback. Where students ignore points, especially those about presentation or structure, then they may find themselves heavily penalised in later submissions.

→ Examples of feedback comments and what they mean

Different lecturers use different terms to express similar meanings, and because they mark quickly, their handwritten comments are sometimes untidy and may be difficult to interpret. This means that you may need help in deciphering their meaning. Table 48.1 illustrates feedback comments that are frequently made and explains how you should react to obtain better grades in future. This should be viewed with Table 33.3 (p. 279) which explains some proof-reading symbols that lecturers may use. If a particular comment or mark does not make sense to you after reading these tables, you may wish to approach the marker for an explanation.

Dealing with feedback

Some feedback may be verbal and informal, for example a demonstrator's comment given as you work in a practical, or a comment on your contribution during a tutorial. If you feel uncertain about why your work has received the grade it did, or why a particular comment was provided, you may be able to arrange a meeting with the person who marked your work. Normally they will be happy to provide further verbal explanations. However, do not attempt to debate your marks, other than to point out politely if part of your work does not appear to have been marked at all, or part marks appear to have been added up wrongly.

Table 48.1 Common types of feedback annotation and how to respond. Comments in the margin may be accompanied by underlining of word(s), circling of phrases, sentences or paragraphs. Relevant chapters to consult are noted in brackets in the right-hand column.

Types of comment and typical examples	Meaning and potential remedial action
Regarding content	
Relevance *Relevance?* *Importance?* *Value of example?* *So?*	An example or quotation may not be apt, or you may not have explained its relevance. Think about the logic of your narrative or argument and whether there is a mismatch as implied, or whether you could add further explanation; choose a more appropriate example or quote. **[Ch 28]**
Detail *Give more information* *Example?* *Too much detail/waffle/padding*	You are expected to flesh out your answer with more detail or an example to illustrate your point; or, conversely, you may have provided too much information. It may be that your work lacks substance and you appear to have compensated by putting in too much description rather than analysis. **[Ch 21, Ch 28]**
Specific factual comment or comment on your approach *You could have included . . .* *What about . . . ?* *Why didn't you . . . ?*	Depends on context, but it should be obvious what is required to accommodate the comment.
Expressions of approval *Good!* *Excellent!* ✓ *(may be repeated)*	You got this right or chose a good example. Keep up the good work!
Expressions of disapproval *Poor* *Weak* *No!* ✗ *(may be repeated)*	Sometimes obvious, but may not be clear. The implication is that your examples, logic or expression could be improved.
Regarding structure	
Fault in logic or argument *Logic?* *Non sequitur (does not follow)*	Your argument or line of logic is faulty. This may require quite radical changes to your approach to the topic. **[Ch 29, Ch 30]**
Failure to introduce topic clearly *Where are you going with this?* *Unclear*	What is your understanding of the task? What parameters will confine your response? How do you intend to tackle the subject? **[Ch 29]**
Failure to construct a logical discussion *Imbalanced discussion* *Weak on pros and cons*	When you have to compare and contrast in any way, then it is important that you give each element in your discussion similar coverage. **[Ch 30]**
Failure to conclude essay clearly *So what?* *Conclusion?*	You have to leave a 'take-home message' that sums up the most salient features of your writing and should not include new material in this section. This is to demonstrate your ability to think critically and define the key aspects. **[Ch 29]**

Table 48.1 (cont'd)

Types of comment and typical examples	Meaning and potential remedial action
Regarding structure (continued)	
Heavy dependency on quotations *Watch out for over-quotation* *Too many quotations*	There is a real danger of plagiarism if you include too many direct quotations from text. You have to demonstrate that you can synthesise the information from sources as evidence of your understanding. However, in a subject like English literature or law, quotation may be a key characteristic of writing. In this case, quotation is permitted, provided that it is supported by critical comment. **[Ch 31]**
Move text *Loops and arrows*	Suggestion for changing order of text, usually to enhance the flow or logic. **[Ch 27]**
Regarding presentation	
Minor proofing errors *sp. (usually in margin – spelling)* *⋏ (insert material here)* *⌐ (break paragraph here)* *❓ (delete this material)* *P (punctuation error)*	A (minor) correction is required. Table 33.3 provides more detail of likely proof-reading symbols. **[Ch 33]**
Citations *Reference required* *Ref?* *Reference (or bibliography)* *list omitted*	You have not supported evidence, argument or quotation with a reference to the original source. This is important in academic work and if you fail to do it, you may be considered guilty of plagiarism (**Ch 32**). If you omit to attach a reference list, this will lose you marks as it implies a totally unsourced piece of writing, that is, you have done no specialist reading. **[Ch 31]**
Tidiness *Illegible!* *Untidy* *Can't read*	Your handwriting may be difficult to decipher. Allocate more time to writing out your work neatly, or use a word processor if allowed. **[Ch 34]**
Failure to follow recommended format *Please follow departmental* *template for reports* *Order!*	If the department or school provides a template for the submission of reports, you must follow it. There are good reasons, such as the need to follow professional conventions, especially in sciences; you must conform. If you don't, you may lose marks. **[Ch 19, Ch 40]**

---

smart tip

Applying feedback to exam performance

Look at the comments and advice given on written coursework and identify ways in which you can use the feedback constructively in the answers you give in exams. For example, if structure is identified as a weakness, then practise speed-planning answers so that your answers become focused and succinct.

✔ Practical tips for dealing with feedback

Be mentally prepared to learn from the views of your tutors. You may initially feel that feedback is unfair, harsh or that it misunderstands the approach you were trying to take to the question. A natural reaction might be to dismiss many of the comments. However, you should recognise that tutors probably have a much deeper understanding of the topic than you, and concede that if you want to do well in a subject then you need to gain a better understanding of what makes a good answer from the academic's point of view.

Always make sure you understand the feedback. Check with fellow students or with the lecturers involved if you cannot read the comment or do not understand why it has been made.

Respond to feedback. Make a note of common or repeated errors, even in peripheral topics, so that you can avoid them in later assignments.

💬 Useful language for . . . asking about feedback

Context: expressions you might use when discussing feedback comments with a lecturer.

Excuse me. I wonder whether it would be possible to arrange an appointment to go over your feedback on my essay. There are some points I don't understand.

I'm afraid I couldn't read your handwriting here. Could you explain please?

I don't understand what you mean here. I thought what I had written covered that issue, but you seem to want more. What other points could I have made?

(GO) And now . . .

48.1 Check out the marking criteria for your department, school or faculty. As explained above, these may help you interpret feedback and understand how to reach the standard you want to achieve.

48.2 Decide what to do about feedback comments you frequently receive. For instance, do lecturers always comment about your spelling or grammar; or suggest you should use more examples; or ask for more citations to be included? If so, look at suitable English grammar textbooks or relevant chapters in this book, to see if you can adjust appropriately.

48.3 Learn to criticise drafts of your own work. This is equivalent to giving feedback to yourself and is an essential academic skill. Annotate drafts of your own work – this is an important way to refine it and improve its quality. Stages you can adopt when reviewing your written work are discussed in **Ch 33**.

Physical and mental preparation

How to prepare for exams

To achieve your full potential in assessments and exams, your brain needs to be operating at its best. This also means that the rest of your body will need to be in good physical condition, as the health of body and mind are linked closely. This chapter explains how you can ensure that you are in the best possible shape in the run-up to exams.

Key topics:
→ Well-being, health and nutrition
→ The role of physical exercise
→ Mental exercise, relaxation and sleep
→ Preparing the ground
→ Thinking positively

Essential vocabulary
Aerobic exercise   Caffeine   Micronutrients   Vitamins   Well-being

Good academic performance depends on your mind operating at or near to its peak ability, but we're all aware that our intellectual powers vary according to a range of influences, and are not always at their best. Having a better understanding of factors that influence your brain's function will help you prepare better for your forthcoming assessments or exams.

→ Well-being, health and nutrition

Most experts agree that that a healthy mind thrives in a healthy body. However, we don't always take care of our bodies or minds in the best possible way. For students, this condition may result from any of a number of factors related to university life. If you wish to take a professional approach to your exams, you may need to look for ways in which you can adapt your lifestyle to ensure that you are in the best possible physical and mental shape to face your exams. Table 49.1 provides a checklist of things to do, and things not to do, as you approach your exams. You may wish to focus on some of the following:

● **Regulating your sleep pattern.** Try to ensure that you have enough sleep and make sure that your pattern of waking coincides with the general working day, and in particular with your exam times.

● **Avoiding or cutting down chemical influences likely to interfere with your mental capacity.** The chief of these is likely to be alcohol, a known depressant. Others include nicotine, certain prescription drugs and most non-prescription drugs.

Table 49.1 A quick checklist of things to do and things not to do to improve your preparation for exams

Positives (try to do these)	Negatives (try not to do these)
❏ Gain mental agility (puzzles, quizzes, sums, examples, reading)	❏ Abuse alcohol or other drugs that may impair your mental capacity
❏ Improve mental stamina (work for longer periods)	❏ Be distracted by less important things (e.g. TV programmes, socialising)
❏ Become fitter (a healthy mind in a healthy body)	❏ Study so much you do not sleep enough or distort your waking rhythm
❏ Eat well	❏ Avoid key topics that you dislike
❏ Get your body clock in tune with 'exam time'	❏ Read your notes rather than carry out appropriate active revision methods
❏ Clean away clutter and start with a clear desk	❏ Carry out unfocused revision that fails to take account of learning objectives
❏ Sleep well (make sure you are physically as well as mentally tired)	
❏ Carry out active revision that takes account of your learning style	

- **Avoiding overuse of stimulants.** Taking chemicals like caffeine (present in tea, coffee, 'Red Bull' and Coke-like drinks) may provide a temporary boost, but there is an inevitable downside after this, and your sleep pattern may be disrupted.

- **Keeping well hydrated.** Your water intake or lack of it has known effects on the ability to concentrate and learn.

- **Knowing how and when to relax.** Exercise has an important role to play here, as does escapism, such as watching a film or playing games. Near to exams, these leisure and rest activities should not take up too much time, but they should remain a part of your timetable.

You should try to eat well when studying as your brain requires a good supply of energy and essential nutrients. A good breakfast is a good idea to kick-start your day, followed by light snacks to keep your energy levels up. Small, frequent snacks are best because after you eat large meals there are known hormonal responses that slow down metabolism and mental activity, leading to drowsiness and lethargy. If this effect is familiar to you, avoid fatty foods and note that more complex carbohydrates like starch provide a more slowly released supply of sugars.

Vitamins and micronutrients are known to enhance health and mental activity. Anyone who eats healthily should not be deficient in these dietary factors, but you may wish to consult a health professional if in doubt over the use of vitamin supplements.

If you feel unwell in the period prior to exams, you should visit your doctor or university health service, not only in hope of a diagnosis and treatment, but also to obtain necessary documentation that might explain a weak performance.

Key facts about your brain

Your brain takes up only about 2 per cent of your body's mass, yet it receives some 15 per cent of your blood circulation. It consumes about a fifth of your total oxygen intake, and metabolises roughly a quarter of your body's glucose. Your brain absorbs approximately 50 per cent of the oxygen and 10 per cent of glucose circulating in your arterial bloodstream.

(Source: Magistretti et al., 2000)

→ The role of physical exercise

Aerobic exercise is an excellent way to relax mentally, reduce stress and improve sleep patterns. Carried out regularly over a long period, exercise improves your stamina, a valuable commodity for extended exam schedules, which can be physically exhausting as well as mentally draining. Non-aerobic and meditation workouts such as yoga, Pilates and Tai Chi also have potential to help you in the run-up to exams by helping you to relax.

Exercise is also important in the short term because it stimulates brain activity by improving the blood supply to your brain, an organ that requires a surprising amount of oxygen and energy to function well. You should try to do some physical activity, even if it is as simple as a walk or swim, on most revision days. This basic exercise is probably the best quick fix to remove feelings of mental lethargy.

→ Mental exercise, relaxation and sleep

As an organ, your brain responds to being exercised. In a similar fashion to your muscles, the more it works, the better prepared it is for future effort. Unsurprisingly, revision itself is an excellent mental preparation for exams. This 'exercise' factor is independent from memorisation carried out during your revision; as you move through your revision timetable, your brain will become used to its daily mental workout and will be better prepared for the challenge of the exams.

---

smart tip

Some ideas for exercising and relaxing your mind

Exercise:

- doing puzzles like crosswords and sudoku;
- playing computer games (not in excess);
- taking part in TV and pub quizzes;
- reading for leisure (in short bursts).

Relaxing:

- shutting your eyes and breathing slowly and deeply for 2–3 minutes;
- watching films or TV soap operas;
- taking a brief walk or swim;
- having a bath, jacuzzi or sauna.

These activities should be brief, relaxing and should not impinge on timetabled periods of study. Ideally, they should be incorporated into your revision timetable (**Ch 50**).

Equally, there will be times when your mind needs to relax. This can be accomplished by focusing your thoughts on a completely different matter. Physical activities and games can have this useful effect. A good sleep pattern is vital to rest your brain between intensive study sessions and before exams. Unfortunately, the anxiety many people feel immediately prior to exams is not conducive to sleep. If you have this as a persistent problem, you may wish to adopt some of the following tips, suggested by McKenna (2006):

- get up earlier, consistently – this has the effect of making you more tired at the end of the day;
- keep a consistent waking routine (even at weekends) – you can control this element, but not when you feel tired;
- go to bed only when you feel ready to sleep;
- keep bed for sleep – if you want to read, watch TV or eat, relax in a living space to do this;
- if you generally feel that afternoons are not your best time for studying, exercising in the afternoon can be helpful as a way of freshening you up for a study stint when you are more alert later in the day;
- eat and drink (especially stimulants like caffeine and depressants like alcohol) well ahead of the time that you plan to go to bed;
- rather than toss and turn when you cannot sleep, get up and do something useful until you feel tired;
- drift off to sleep thinking about positives, rather than negatives; and
- tell yourself a story, preferably a boring one, as you attempt to fall asleep.

smart tip

Maintaining a regular and appropriate sleep pattern

Your aim should be to align your waking times to the times of your exams. Some people like to rise early and others to rise late. Some people find that napping during the day is helpful as a means of renewing their energy, while others find that this puts them off regular sleep patterns. Whichever type you are, remember that exams mostly fit into the working day and you must make sure that your regime has not turned night into day.

→ Preparing the ground

If you wish to revise effectively, it is crucial that you know what you are trying to accomplish. One way of gaining this understanding is to divide the revision and exam-sitting process into components and look at what you need to achieve at each stage. The process is essentially about managing information – the facts and understanding gained during your course – and can be separated into three main elements:

- information-gathering;
- information-processing; and
- information-retrieval and delivery.

If you do the right things in each of these phases, you will greatly increase your chances of achieving excellent grades.

In the information-gathering phase, your aim is to ensure that you have copies of all that you require close to hand, and to make sure that it is well organised so that you can consult what you need, quickly.

❑ Check that you have all the lecture notes and make arrangements to download or copy them, if you do not have these things in place.

❑ File your notes in sequence.

❑ Buy or borrow the textbooks that support your course (check the reading list in the course handbook). Alternatively, look these up in your library catalogue and place reservations on them if they are available only on limited access.

❑ Gather together all other materials that might be relevant, such as completed coursework with feedback.

❑ Bookmark any online resources that you might be expected to consult.

❑ Obtain copies of past papers and model answers, if available.

❑ Find out where the learning objectives or outcomes are published (for example, in the course handbook), and make a copy of them.

❑ Look in your course handbook for any special guidance notes on the exam and its format.

smart
tip

Managing time for information-gathering

You must not let the information-gathering phase take up too much of your revision time – recognise that it can be a displacement activity and limit the time you allocate to it within your revision timetable (**Ch 50**).

The information-processing phase involves analysing and manipulating the material you have gathered, with the learning objectives and past exam papers in mind. The principle is not to study passively, for example, by reading through the written material, but to try to do something active, to help you to memorise it (**Ch 51** and **Ch 52**).

smart
tip

Successful information-processing

As part of an approach based on active revision, you will probably wish to reduce or 'distil' the notes you have made (**Ch 57**). This can only be done effectively with a clear idea of the sorts of question that will be asked and an indication of the depth at which you will be expected to deal with the material. In part, this information can be obtained by studying the learning objectives or outcomes and past exam papers.

Thinking about thinking

It is important to recognise that university teaching is not solely about information transfer. You should not just accumulate information and memorise a series of facts from lectures and other source material; you must be able to *use* information. In short, you must develop skills in critical thinking. The facts are still required, but it is what you do with them in response to the exam or assessment instruction that is important

(**Ch 55**). When you analyse the instructions used in exam questions, you should take into account what type of thinking process the examiner has asked you to perform (**Ch 28**, **Ch38**), and try your best to reach the required level.

Thinking about learning

To study successfully in the UK, you may find it useful to consider or reconsider the ways in which you learn best. This is a personal matter: people differ greatly in their preferences for processing and retrieving information. For some students, developing an understanding of this aspect of their character makes a huge difference to their levels of attainment. In **Ch 13** we discuss various types of learning personality, different methods of diagnosing your learning style, and the best ways of approaching study and revision once you know where your learning preferences lie.

Understanding the UK university exam system

As an international student, you should take steps to understand the assessment system at your university, which may differ in several respects from your past experience.

Your department or school will provide plenty of helpful information about assessment. You can find it in course or programme handbooks, printed or online. Accessing this material will help you process the course material and your notes appropriately. You should look for:

■ learning outcomes/objectives;

■ design of exam papers, type of exam, style of questions and weighting of marks;

■ marking criteria.

Chs 53 and **55** discuss these sources of information in greater detail.

Beware of changes to the syllabus or to the construction of exam papers

smart tip

Courses may change over time, as can the staff teaching them. These changes can have a considerable impact on content and the course structure. If you see a mismatch between the syllabus as taught and the learning objectives or question papers you should discuss this with your course leader or departmental administrator. The same applies to checking whether you can assume that this year's exam papers will be constructed in the same way as in previous years.

Information retrieval and delivery

The information retrieval and delivery phase will occur in the exam hall as you answer the specific questions as set. **Chs 55-57** provide tips for maximising your performance during this phase.

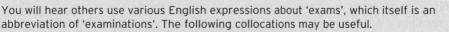

'Exam speak'

You will hear others use various English expressions about 'exams', which itself is an abbreviation of 'examinations'. The following collocations may be useful.

✓ People **sit exams** = **do exams** = **take exams** = **have exams**

✗ Common error: students make/made exams (meaning to sit exams, but incorrect)

✓ People **pass exams with flying colours** (idiom) (or 'pass with distinction')

✓ Some people just **pass exams** by the 'skin of their teeth' (idiom, meaning very near failure)

✓ Sadly, some people **fail exams** (or flunk exams – slang)

✓ Such people have to **resit or retake exams**

→ Thinking positively

A key aspect of mental preparation for exams is to think positively. These tips will help you adopt a positive frame of mind when revising:

● Get started on your studies, somehow. Don't put off this crucial moment. Once you become engaged with the material, your natural curiosity and interest in the subject will take over. Even if the topics have not seemed interesting in the past, once you begin to understand them in depth they may become more so.

● Adopt an approach of breaking large topics into smaller sections. That way each time you complete a section you will feel you have made progress.

● Make sure you mark off what you have completed in your revision timetable (**Ch 50**) as you cover the material. After a few sessions, this visual summary should give you a feeling of having made real progress.

● Link up with someone else studying the same subject and make a pact to try to encourage each other (**Ch 54**). Quizzing each other or working together on areas of the course that you both find difficult can help both parties feel more in control of the subject matter and, if you continue to have difficulty, you can go together to speak with your lecturer or tutor about your queries.

● Focus on the main goal (your degree, and the type of job you hope will come after it) and reflect on how each small study session is one small step on this important journey in your life.

● Recall positive experiences from your past exam-sitting history, focusing on how your hard work paid dividends in the end, despite any lack of confidence you may have felt at the time.

In the vital period just before you enter the exam hall, it is important to be completely focused and positive. Although there are benefits from meeting up with fellow students and sharing feelings and ideas about potential exam questions, these exchanges will almost certainly make you more nervous. If this is likely to be the case, find a spot nearby where you can gather your thoughts in peace and then time your entry to the exam hall to avoid meeting your friends. Things to concentrate on during this period are:

- your exam strategy – how you plan to tackle this particular paper (**Ch 55**);
- your approach to the questions – how you plan to structure your answers;
- key facts or formulae (you are unlikely to memorise them at this stage, but running over them may keep them fresh in your mind if you have already learnt them by heart: **Ch 52**);
- your determination to succeed and how you aim to squeeze every mark possible out of your brain in response to the instructions on the exam paper;
- how you plan to ensure your answers are relevant;
- how you need to be working quickly and effectively for every second of the exam; and
- what you plan to do when all your exams are finished and how quickly this particular exam will be over.

✔ Practical tips to help prepare yourself for exams

Ensure you eat healthily. This should include eating the right amount of calories (neither too many, nor too few) and plenty of fruit and vegetables.

Give 'you' some time. Studying without any let-up won't necessarily mean that you will do more. Taking some time out for you – listening to music, reading a novel, playing a game, pampering yourself with a favourite activity – will make you feel good about yourself and contribute to your sense of confidence and well-being. It will also help create a sense of revitalised motivation.

Go for a short walk. If you are feeling drowsy or lacking in concentration or focus when revising, go outside for a quick walk. A brisk ten-minute walk around the block will be sufficient to wake you up. You might use the route you take as one of your memory 'journeys' so that you could 'revise as you walk' (**Ch 52**).

💬 Useful language for . . . preparing for assessments

Context: you might use these expressions in discussions with your fellow students.

I've done a lot of revision yesterday and today and I'm thinking of going to the gym [swimming pool, cinema etc] this afternoon [evening] to relax. Would you like to join me?

I've been checking through my notes for subject xxxx. I'm missing notes for one of the lectures. Do you remember I had to go to the doctor last semester? I think it must have been that day. Do you think I could borrow your notes to copy them so I have a complete set?

Have you checked out the learning objectives for this module? I was looking at this one and wondering what sort of exam question they could ask to test it. Do you have any ideas yourself?

49.1 Build up your language bank. For all students and even if English is your first language, you can work constructively on identifying and learning useful key words, structures and specialist expressions that relate to each of your subjects. This will mean that your won't waste valuable time in the exam trying to find the best form of words to explain your ideas.

49.2 Try to become more aware of time. Challenge yourself to estimate time-spans. Is what you imagine to be 10 minutes more like 20? If you are widely out in your estimation, this might be a factor in your time management on the exam day.

49.3 Practise writing against the clock. Calculate the exact time that you'd have in the exam to respond to one question and write a practice answer within that time allocation. This will give you a better idea of how much you can write in the time and alert you to strategies for giving the best answer you can; for example, by limiting the length of your introduction so that you have more time to devote to constructing the analysis or argument that the examiner wants to read.

50 Creating a revision timetable

How to get yourself organised for exam study

Organising your activities in the run-up to exams is vital to ensure that you make the best use of the limited time available. Creating a revision timetable not only improves your time management but also helps you to balance your efforts among subjects and topics.

Key topics:
→ Setting up and using a revision timetable
→ Using your time effectively when revising

Essential vocabulary
Active learning   Cramming   Revision timetable

If your use of time is generally haphazard, a revision timetable will help to keep you on track with your studies. In addition, a timetable can help motivate you and provide confidence as you complete each topic. Used well, it can prevent you spending too much time on your favourite topics at the expense of others, and it can also ensure that you include relaxation activities to boost your energy and ability to concentrate.

→ Setting up and using a revision timetable

- Create a blank timetable. This will allow you to create an 'action plan' that gives details of the specific topics you intend to work on at any given time. The example illustrated in Table 50.1 and provided in blank form on p. 461 is based on six subdivisions of the day, with two potential study periods in each morning, afternoon and evening. If you prefer to use shorter or longer units of work, modify the format appropriately, using a word processor or spreadsheet.

- Now fix your start and end dates: these are the points at which you wish to begin revising and the precise dates when your exams are to be held. Print or photocopy enough copies of the blank timetable to cover this period and write in these key dates.

- Start to fill in the timetable by noting your *essential* non-study commitments, such as employment, shopping, cooking, travelling, team sporting activities and important social or family duties. If at all possible, these responsibilities should be minimised when you are revising, especially as the exams draw closer. Contact employers and others as far as possible in advance so you can warn them of your needs.

50 Creating a revision timetable

Table 50.1 Sample revision plan for a student studying Environmental Sciences

Week: 12

Personal revision timetable — Umar Banerjee

Key to subjects/topics: Geography | Biomes + Diversity | Environmental Chemistry

	Monday	Tuesday	Wednesday	Thursday	Friday	Saturday	Sunday
Morning	Geog Lectures 1 & 2	Env Chem Topic B	Biomes + Div Week 3	Env Chem Topic C	Geog Lecture 8 & 9	WORK	Lie in
	Env Chem Topic A	Geog Lectures 3 & 4	Biomes + Div Week 4	Env Chem Topic C	Study buddy meeting Geog	WORK	Laundry
Lunch							
Afternoon	Env Chem Topic A	Geog tutorial	Geog Lectures 5 & 6	Biomes + Div Practicals	Env Chem Topic D	WORK	Biomes + Div Practicals
	Prep for last Geog tutorial	Break	HOCKEY	Biomes + Div Practicals	SPARE	WORK	Mock exam with Ajit
Evening meal							
Evening	Biomes + Div Week 1	Env Chem Topic B	EVENING OFF!	Library – look out past papers	SPARE (go out to union if up to speed)	Shanti's birthday bash	Evening meal with Dilip and Mihir
	Biomes + Div Week 2	SPARE	EVENING OFF!	Geog Lecture 7 (difficult)	SPARE	Shanti's birthday bash	

Avoid over-elaborating your timetable

Don't be tempted to procrastinate by taking too long pondering over your timetable or making it overly neat – it does not need to be a work of art.

- Decide on the ideal number of 'sessions' you wish to study in each day and week, or are able to allocate due to your other commitments. Work out the total number of study sessions during the whole revision period and decide when they will be. For example, if you work best early in the day, you may wish to bias your studies to the morning slots that are available.

- The next stage is to allocate these revision sessions to the different subjects or topics you need to cover. You may wish to carry out this process in two stages – roughly allocate the total time among three modules, then more specifically divide each module's allocated time among the individual topics that were covered. Be flexible – you may wish to spend a whole day on one topic to get deeper into the material, or break another day up to create variety. In allocating time slots for revision, work your way backwards from the exam date, as this will ensure that you cover each subject adequately just before the relevant paper.

  Try to balance the time appropriately among topics or subjects. Your aim should be to give more time to 'difficult' topics than to 'easier' ones, remembering that difficult or uninteresting material sometimes yields 'easy' marks when you have mastered it. As an incentive, you may wish to follow subjects you dislike with those you prefer.

  If you aren't happy with the time available to study each topic when this process is complete, you may need to increase the total time you have allocated and reconfigure the sheets.

- In allocating time, recognise that you cannot work continuously if you want to study effectively. If you spend lengthy hours revising without any rest you may retain little because you aren't concentrating. Lack of focus and concentration will become worse if you tire yourself out.

  Break up your work with relaxation, preferably involving physical activity. You may wish to set up 'rewards' (for example, watching TV or meeting friends) – but only take these if you achieve your goals; if you do not, use these periods to catch up.

- Include some empty slots in your timetable to allow for unforeseen problems or changes in your plans. Your timetable should be flexible – if you lose time somewhere due to unforeseen circumstances, you should try to make it up later using these slots or switching slots from recreation to study.

- If at all possible, try to ease back on your revision load near the exam. You should plan your revision to avoid last-minute cramming and fatigue.

What's the ideal length of time for a study session?

Too long and you risk getting bored with the subject and losing concentration; too short and you won't be able to make progress. Table 50.1 proposes sessions of about $1^{1}/_{2}$ hours in length, but you may prefer to sub-divide or combine these.

Monitoring your efforts

When there's a lot to be done, marking off the studying you have completed on your timetable, perhaps with a brightly coloured highlighter, can provide a visual indication of how much you've covered and hence boost your confidence and morale.

→ Using your time effectively when revising

Studying effectively is not simply a matter of allocating lots of time to the task: you must organise your activities well and use appropriate techniques to help you retain the material covered.

- Early in the revision period, focus on ensuring you have all the necessary materials to hand and that these are well-organised – especially lecture notes and textbook information (see p. 403). Ask a friend for copies of their notes if you missed a lecture, or download copies of summaries, overheads or slideshows. Pay special attention to these topics when revising, as you will not have the same feel for the subject if you did not attend the lecture. Look out your textbooks or visit the library as early as possible to ensure that you can reserve the books required. Avoid spending too long on this phase as a diversion from any real revision.

- Give your timetable the highest priority if conflicting demands are placed on you. If this means being a little selfish, explain to others why you need to focus on your studies. On the other hand, don't be a slave to your timetable. Be prepared to be flexible. If you feel you are really making progress with a topic, stick with it rather than changing topic. Make sure, however, that you make up the displaced work at a later point.

Consider your specific revision needs in advance

As an international student, you may feel you have specific requirements as part of your revision – such as a need to revise technical terms or language, or understand references lecturers have made to unfamiliar UK-based examples. It's a good idea to identify these needs in advance, perhaps in collaboration with another student from your country, so you can programme any extra revision you may need to do.

- Recognise when your concentration powers are dwindling – take a short break when this happens and return to work refreshed and ready to learn. Remember that 20 minutes is often quoted as a typical limit to full concentration effort.

- Remember to have several short (5-minute) breaks during each hour of revision and a longer break every few hours. In any day, try to work for a maximum of three-quarters of the time.

- Use active learning techniques (**Ch 51**) so that your revision is as interesting as possible: *the least productive approach is simply to read and reread your lecture notes.*

Are you a morning, afternoon or evening person?

Identify the best time of day for you to study (**Ch 9**). Focus your revision periods in these slots, and your routine tasks and recreation when you will feel less able to concentrate.

Practical tips for keeping your revision focused

Make good use of your course handbook. This will help you find out about the structure of your exam and the content that will be covered. If learning objectives are published, refer to these to gain an insight into what lecturers will be expecting of you in the exam (**Ch 53**).

Use past papers as a guide. Past papers will give you an indication of the style of questions asked. Try to modify your revision to accommodate the question style (**Chs 35–40**). Note carefully the structure of the exam and, especially if it has sections, whether each part will require a different approach to revision, such as memorising particular facts or a requirement to synthesise answers from several sources.

Work out, as best you can, how the exam will be weighted towards different topics. Bias your revision time accordingly.

Use lists to keep track of progress. As you revise, make an inventory of topics you need to cover, definitions you need to learn, for example. Crossing out the jobs you have completed will give you a sense of accomplishment and, from this, a feeling of confidence.

Test yourself continuously. The only way you will know whether you have absorbed and memorised something is to test yourself, for example by trying to write what you think you have learned on a blank sheet of paper (see p. 427). If you leave it until the exam to find out, it may be too late to do anything about it.

Try to keep your mind working. If you find you 'drift away' after a period studying the same topic, try adopting the notion that 'a change is as good as a rest': you may find you can keep your attention up by shifting between subjects at appropriate intervals.

Context: these expressions may be useful when discussing revision with other students.

When are you planning to do most of your studying? I'm a morning and evening person, so I'm planning to get up early and go to the library, then come home for lunch and cook something, then go back to the library in the evenings.

How are you planning to revise [topic]? I was thinking of getting hold of a past exam paper and going through the questions one by one. Would you like to do that with me?

Here's my draft revision timetable. I've left some slots open for meetings with you to discuss how we're getting on. Is that OK? Will you be free at these times?

GO And now . . .

50.1 Create your own study timetable. The next time exams loom, copy the blank revision timetable in the Appendix (p. 461) and use this to organise your studies as indicated within this chapter. The copyright for personal use of this table is waived, so you can photocopy it several times to cover as many weeks of study as you have allocated.

50.2 Compare study timetables with a 'study buddy'. If you can team up with a partner studying the same subjects (**Ch 54**), it might be valuable to compare your approaches to revision. When you have completed your draft revision timetables, discuss how they differ and why.

50.3 Focus your work by sitting mock questions. As you finish each section of revision, use questions from past papers to gain feedback about your recall and depth of understanding. You don't have to provide a complete answer to a question to do this – an outline plan of an essay-style answer would be sufficient, for instance. Alternatively, if you can answer a complete question, you could pass this on to a fellow student or staff member for comment and learn from what they have to say.

How to use your revision time effectively

Active learning is the key to understanding and remembering course material for recall during exams. It involves thinking through concepts, ideas and processes, as well as techniques for effective memorising.

Key topics:
→ Basic active learning approaches
→ Preparing to learn and memorise

Essential vocabulary
Active learning   Chunking   Cramming   Distilling   Learning objective/outcome   Mnemonic   Rote learning   Swotting

Unless you are lucky enough to have a photographic memory, simply reading course material is a poor method for remembering and understanding it. Experience, backed up by research, indicates that you will remember things much better if you *do* something centred on the material (that is, 'actively' learn it). Moreover, this way of revising sometimes reveals flaws in your understanding that you may not appreciate when simply reading the material. There are many possible approaches to active learning and you should choose those that suit your learning preference (p. 111) and your circumstances.

→ Basic active learning approaches

You should probably use both the techniques outlined below for every exam.

'Distilling' or 'chunking' lecture notes

This involves taking your 'raw' lecture notes and reducing them to a series of headings and key points. This can be done in several 'sweeps', gradually reducing pages and pages of notes to just a few headings. An alternative approach to distilling is to reorganise your notes in grid format, as shown in Figure 51.1. The 'aspects' should be chosen to be relevant to likely exam questions. By creating this type of table you will force yourself to analyse the information you have been taught and hence understand it better.

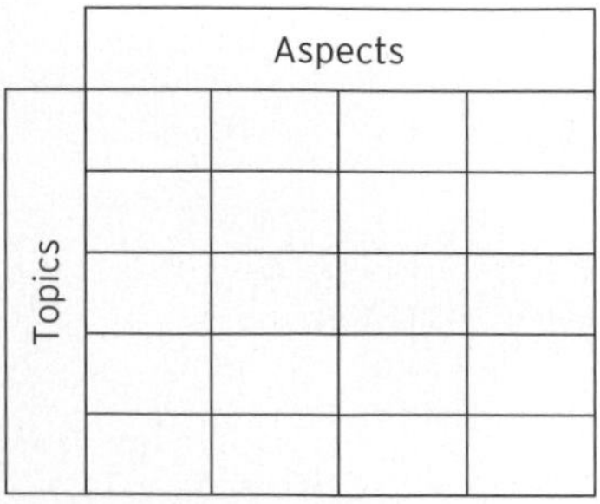

The act of writing out the material when distilling or chunking your notes seems to help place it in a 'map' within your brain and aids recall. Another valuable

Figure 51.1 A grid for reorganising notes

aspect of these approaches is that they allow you to gain an overview of the topic – you can then appreciate where each aspect slots into the bigger picture. This may help you to memorise facts and place them in context within your exam answers. Finally, these methods are better than simply rewriting the material, because you need to *think* about the material as you transcribe into the new structure.

Alternative words and phrases for 'revision'

A number of slang terms are used by UK students to describe the act of revision:

- **swotting** (also *to swot up* on something and *swot*, meaning someone who spends a lot of time revising rather than socialising)
- **cramming** (also *to cram*) (American English)
- **boning up** (also *to bone up*)
- **mugging up** (also *to mug up*)

You may also hear fellow students talk about 'burning the midnight oil' or doing an 'all-nighter' to revise or to finish an assessment on time.

Answering past papers and problems

Looking at past exam papers is important to let you see both the type and scope of questions normally asked. The depth of answer required may not be so obvious, and if this is in doubt, consult subject tutors. You can then take a variety of active approaches, from thinking through an answer in your head (weak); writing out an answer plan rather than a full answer (good); and setting yourself a mock exam or timed exam question based on a particular paper (excellent). If possible, discuss your answers or plans with subject tutors and fellow students.

Particularly for subjects requiring numeracy, problem-solving and doing examples are acknowledged ways of testing understanding and reinforcing what you have learned. Try to recognise patterns in the types of calculations and problems usually asked. Consult with subject tutors if you do not understand how to answer any questions.

smart tip

Benefits of mock exams

These help you practise writing against the clock. Although time-consuming, this gives you an idea of how quickly you will have to work and how much you will need to condense ideas to fit the time allowed. They also give you practice in writing quickly and neatly by hand, which is useful because this is a skill that may have eroded if you regularly use a keyboard and word processor rather than write by hand.

→ Preparing to learn and memorise

Understanding concepts and committing facts to memory can be hard, especially when you find a subject difficult or unattractive, or there is lots of obscure jargon to learn. To give yourself the best chance to absorb the material, you'll need to ensure that you have prepared mentally, and that your working environment is configured appropriately. The following principles might help:

- **You need to be ready to learn.** Make sure you are not preoccupied by thoughts of anything else.

- **Make sure your desk space allows you to focus on the work in hand.** Declutter your desk. If necessary, take your papers to a library or a similar place, where there is plenty of space in which to lay them out.

- **Make sure you pace yourself.** You can only study effectively in short bursts, so take frequent breaks to keep your concentration at a peak.

- **You need to be determined to learn.** Avoid aimlessly reading material in the hope that it will 'sink in'. Convince yourself that you really want to learn. If you intensively focus on the material, fully intending and expecting to learn, you will.

- **Gain an overview of what you have to learn.** Knowing the context helps you absorb and remember facts. If you see the bigger picture, it's easier to fit the component parts into it.

- **Limit the amount you have to learn.** Condense the material into lists or smaller chunks. Split large groups of information into smaller parts.

- **'Visualise' and 'associate' to learn.** At its simplest, this means knowing how many items you need to remember. It could also include recalling a doodle on the page of your notes beside the text. More complex methods include associating facts with a familiar journey or location (see **Ch 52**).

- **Check your recall.** Don't trust to chance that you have learned the material – test yourself continuously (p. 427).

Further information about some of these tips is provided in **Ch 52**; which includes a range of other methods to aid recall.

Make your notes memorable. Use coloured pens and highlighters, but beware of overuse of emphasis and 'absent-minded' or purposeless highlighting, that is, when you highlight almost everything or don't really think why you have highlighted something.

Use concept or mind maps. These help to condense your knowledge of a particular topic. If you include drawings you may find that such image-based notes make recall easier.

Test your recall of diagram labels. Draw up important diagrams without labels, copy these, and then use them to test yourself from time to time.

Try recitation as an alternative to written recall. Talk about your topic to another person, preferably someone in your class. Talk to yourself if necessary. Explaining something aloud is a good test of understanding.

Prepare a series of 'revision sheets'. Note details for each particular topic on a single piece of paper, perhaps arranged as a numbered checklist. If you have the room, make your sheets into a set of wall posters. Pinning these up on a wall may help you visualise the overall subject area. Some people like to use sticky notes for this purpose.

Share ideas and discuss topics with other students. The act of explaining can help imprint the knowledge in your brain, and it has the useful side effect of revealing things you don't really know, even if you thought you did (see **Ch 54** for further discussion).

Make up your own exam paper. Putting yourself in the examiner's mindset is very valuable. Inventing your own questions and thinking about how you would answer them requires a good understanding of the material.

Seek out model answers. If they are not provided in course documentation, ask your lecturer if there are any model answers available so that you can review them. They will help you to achieve a better understanding of what will be expected in terms of approach, style, standard and format of responses.

Memorise definitions. These can be a useful starting point for many exam answers. Make up lists of key phrases and facts (for example, dates and events) associated with particular topics. Test yourself repeatedly on these, or get a friend to do this.

Adapt your revision methods to your preferred learning style, using information gained from Ch 13. For example, if you feel you are a 'visual learner' (Table 13.4), consider using diagrams and mind maps to summarise your notes.

Useful language for . . . talking about revision techniques

Context: these examples may be useful when discussing revision with other students.

Have you got any ideas for swotting up all that stuff from [module/topic]? I'm struggling with all the new terms that [the lecturer] introduced . . .

You know those diagrams we have to learn for [topic]? I've made up some blank ones with arrows to the key features. Would you like a copy?

Would you like to set up a mock exam for Sunday night? We could make up a paper based on questions from past papers and discuss each other's answers afterwards . . .

GO And now . . .

51.1 Try out a new learning technique. Next time you have a 'low-stakes' exam or test (one that does not count too much towards an end-of-module mark), pick one of the tips listed above, and see whether it works for you.

51.2 Find a study buddy. Compare lecture notes and ideas for possible questions in the forthcoming exams. Together, assess and try out any of the tips in this chapter, especially if they might work better with two people being involved.

51.3 Think about the suitability of where you usually study. How might you improve the existing location? Is it working well for you? Should you consider trying somewhere else? What other places might be available to you?

Memory tips and techniques

How to develop tools and strategies for remembering information and ideas

Knowing key facts is critical if you wish to approach exams with confidence. You will then be able to demonstrate higher-level skills in your answers, because you can focus on gathering and analysing your knowledge, rather than struggling to recall details of your subject. This chapter outlines some ways in which you can train your memory to work for you in exams and in other situations.

Key topics:
→ Where memory begins in learning
→ Strategies for organising notes into memorable formats
→ Tricks for recalling facts and cues

Essential vocabulary
Acronym   Flash cards   Johari window   Mnemonic   SWOT analysis

Being in a position to recall information under exam pressure is important, both in relation to the 'building blocks' of your answers – the essential facts and knowledge of your discipline – and in relation to the deeper thinking you have done about the subject. Moreover, in many cases the exam 'questions' will ask you to apply your knowledge in an unpredicted way. If you lack the crucial facts and theoretical framework to be able to do this, your marks will inevitably suffer. In some cases, being unable to recall details can lead to a feeling of panic in the exam that makes things even worse.

Few of us have natural 'photographic' memories and some struggle to retain information and ideas, especially in topics that we lack interest in or have difficulty understanding. Sometimes, also, it is the volume of material that has to be covered that makes remembering it difficult. However, you can gain in confidence and also perform better under exam conditions if you learn some elementary memory 'tricks' that can help you to recall information more easily in the exam hall.

A warning about rote learning

In some educational systems, memorising complete answers, sometimes called 'rote learning' or 'learning by rote', is expected and rewarded. In UK higher education, this will not be the case. You must not only learn relevant information, but also *use* the facts, ideas, concepts and theories you have learnt to support your exploration of topics that might be examined. It will not be sufficient simply to repeat information; you will also need to analyse it.

→ Where memory begins in learning

While this chapter is about the memory tricks you can use in exams, it is important to recognise that the act of memorising begins at a much earlier stage in your revision – in essence, you need to be able to understand what it is that you need to remember before you can adopt and adapt tricks to pull this information out in the exam. This involves the information-gathering and information-processing phases discussed in **Ch 51**.

The first step is to identify the content of your course, the key concepts of the subject within the themes that have been covered in lectures, tutorials, practicals and seminars as well as the topics that have been covered in assignments (information gathering). From this material, you then begin to synthesise organised revision notes that provide you with the facts and deeper understanding of the topics (information processing). For many people, this is an important preliminary stage to learning in that it provides a degree of reassurance that they have all the material required in a manageable form, but they would probably not yet claim 'ownership' of that knowledge. This point marks the transfer to the next stage of revision where you embark on active learning strategies (**Ch 51**) to embed this understanding into your knowledge-base, so that you are able to retrieve and deliver the information in an exam situation.

---

smart tip

Memory and learning styles

Appropriate memory techniques are closely linked to your personal learning style (**Ch 13**). For example:

- **Visual learners** - normally have a preference for practical approaches involving the use of images (for example diagrams and concept maps)
- **Aural learners** - generally prefer to discuss topics, or to recall lectures
- **Read-write learners** - usually opt for text-based approaches, such as writing and rewriting notes and bullet points
- **Kinesthetic learners** - tend to prefer to learn by physical activity such as manipulating materials

Each of the different approaches outlined in this chapter may suit one type of learner more than another, so it may be useful to analyse your preferred learning style as part of your revision.

→ Strategies for organising notes into memorable formats

For all students preparing for exams, there is a need to learn a considerable volume of facts – for example, dates of legislation, permutations of chemicals, stages in a procedure or sequences of events. However, it is important to recognise that university exams are not simply about information transfer from lecturer to student and then back to the lecturer. Thus, facts in themselves are not sufficient for most university exam formats. Instead, in your answers you need to demonstrate the understanding and analysis that distinguishes your ability to think critically (see **Ch 21**). A measured answer responding to the task is required, rather than one simply listing facts or providing a disorganised jumble of information on every aspect of the topic. This means that you need to create memorable revision notes that reflect your understanding of the way that the course – and hence the subject – fits together.

Ways in which you can format your notes include the following:

Creating lists

This is the most basic technique of all. The idea is to distil your notes into a series of headings (see **Ch 51**). Doing this in several phases helps to imprint the knowledge and the end result provides an overview of your subject that allows you to place knowledge in its context. This method is particularly suited to those with verbal-linguistic or read-write learning preferences. Numbering your lists can be a useful memorising device (p. 426).

Organising complex information in grids

Tables and grids are good devices for helping to analyse systematically complex information that has been presented in a seemingly haphazard way, or that can be simplified by categorising the component parts. These grids or matrices can be particularly helpful in organising and remembering content for questions that require comparative and contrastive analysis. Figure 52.1 provides an example.

Creating 'contrast grids'

This technique adapts the 'Johari Windows' method developed by Joe Luft and Harry Ingham (Luft and Ingham, 1955), and called after the first letters of their forenames. The method looks at pairs of contrasting aspects of an issue or situation and organises information or viewpoints within a two-by-two grid. Originally designed to aid self-assessment of personality, the technique can be used for other contexts (see Figure 52.2).

Sketching concept maps (mind maps)

Another form of organisational diagram (Figure 52.3) is variously called a concept map, scatter diagram, spray diagram or mind map. In their most refined form, these are extremely visual, relying on colour and shape to produce an image that is both memorable and attractive. Some practitioners are able to use concept maps to encapsulate an hour-long lecture or public speech. For practical purposes, in exam revision and in the exam itself, the use of concept mapping has to be quick, legible and coherent. If you are happy with the strategy, the concept map can be a useful revision device as well as providing an outline plan of a response to an exam question.

Making time lines

You can use a time line (Figure 52.4) to plot the progress of events, a procedure or a development. Time lines can be drawn as vertical or horizontal. You might find these especially useful where a significant series of events have been referred to at different points in a lecture series.

	Viewpoint of individual employees	Viewpoint of Trades Unions	Viewpoint of industrial companies	Viewpoint of Government
Reduction in hours of statutory working week	• • • •	• • • •	• • • •	• • • •
Corresponding reduction in pension entitlement	• • • •	• • • •	• • • •	• • • •
Reduction in holiday entitlement	• • • •	• • •	• • • •	• • • •
Reduction in number of days per annum as sick leave	• • • • •	• • •	• • • •	• • • •

Figure 52.1 Example of a grid used to analyse viewpoints on an issue. In this case, the lattice of the grid allows the learner to note, in the relevant box, key points held by different stakeholders (listed along the top) on various aspects of a proposed policy (listed on the left).

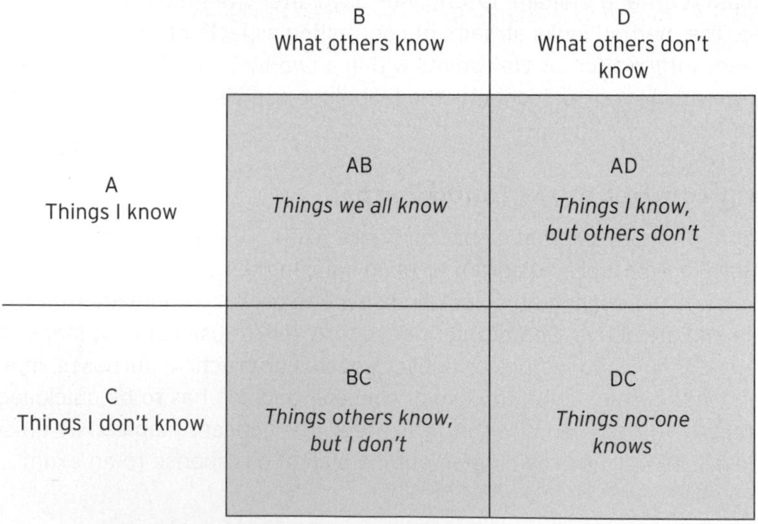

	B What others know	D What others don't know
A Things I know	AB *Things we all know*	AD *Things I know, but others don't*
C Things I don't know	BC *Things others know, but I don't*	DC *Things no-one knows*

Figure 52.2 A 'contrast grid' used to analyse different viewpoints. This example could describe a student reflecting on their own learning in relation to others in a group. Note the letter coding to show how each combination is arrived at.

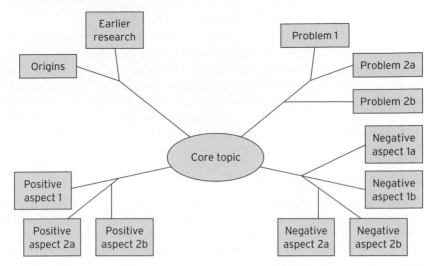

Figure 52.3 Example of a concept map. Adding colour and other visual links can help you to memorise the components.

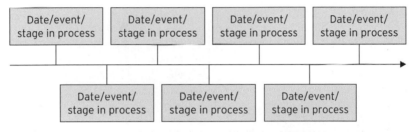

Figure 52.4 Example of a time line

Drawing diagrams

Diagrams can be created to show hierarchies, processes or relationships, as illustrated in Figure 52.5. They can provide you with an outline for a potential answer. They can be formal representations that might be used within your answer. Diagrams are extremely useful to those with a visual or visual-spatial type of learning preference. However, take care when your diagrams are simply personalised sketches that are meaningful to you but possibly not to others. Although they can be a memory aid to give you cues in writing your exam answer, they may not add significant value to the content.

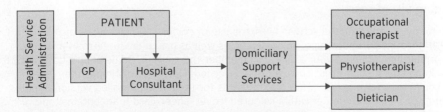

Figure 52.5 Example of the use of a diagram. This describes the organisation of health support.

Setting up posters or 'Post-it®' notes

This approach is useful for those who find that it helps their recall if they subliminally absorb information. It is a technique that particularly suits kinesthetic learners. The strategy is to construct a zone made up of posters or sticky 'Post-it®' notes on a wall in your hallway, bedroom, kitchen or bathroom to help embed the information into your memory, as part of your normal world. Thus, should your mind go blank in the exam, then you will be able to recall the missing information more easily simply by thinking back to the pattern of the notes in the context in which you have positioned them. This strategy relates to the 'pegging' of rooms described on p. 426.

Carrying out SWOT analyses

A **SWOT** analysis helps to analyse a situation, for example, as part of an appraisal of a case study or for a topic where a particular standpoint might be taken. It requires you to list aspects of the situation under one of four headings – **S**trengths, **W**eaknesses, **O**pportunities and **T**hreats. This analytical activity is an active learning technique that makes you think about the material more deeply. Noting bulleted points in a grid format, as shown in Figure 52.6, can be a useful memory aid that suits those with good visual recall.

Strengths	Weaknesses
• point 1	• point 1
• point 2	• point 2
• etc.	• etc.
•	•
•	•
•	•
• point 1	• point 1
• point 2	• point 2
• etc.	• etc.
•	•
•	•
•	•
Opportunities	Threats

Figure 52.6 Example layout of a SWOT analysis. Each quadrant contains a series of bulleted points.

Using visual cues

In many of the models described here, the use of colour, different types of writing/printing, underlining, emboldening as well as use of layout, arrows and other symbols can influence your ability to remember the content. Some people go as far as to keep notes on different colours of paper or index cards to distinguish the level of their notes – for example, white sheets/cards for the longer, detailed version of notes on a topic pinned together with a coloured 'cover' sheet/card that contains topic headings and sub-headings for 'flash card' revision. In all of these strategies the aim is to capitalise on your visual memory as an aid to recall of concepts or written information.

The final stage of revision is to ensure you memorise the material ready for information retrieval and processing. Some of these strategies for organising information will contribute to your ability to recall knowledge under examination conditions. However, there are some additional memorising techniques that you might find useful. Some need a significant amount of practice beforehand to ensure that you can apply the strategy under the potentially stressful environment of the examination hall.

'Mnemonic' relates to the Greek word meaning 'of remembering'. This term encompasses a range of strategies that work on the principle of remembering by association. Some examples are provided below.

Nonsense words

Typical ways of using mnemonics are to create 'words' that are made up of the initial letters of lists of items you need to remember. These are called acronyms. Thus, some people find it easier to remember the first line of the Periodic Table as the acronym **HHeLiBeBCNOF**, whereas others can remember this more readily as: **H**ealthy **He**rbert **Li**ves **Be**side **B**oring **C**ountryside **N**ear **O**pen **F**ields (hydrogen, helium, lithium, beryllium, boron, carbon, nitrogen, oxygen and fluorine). Another nonsense word acronym describes the purpose of research: **SCADAC**: **S**ystematic **C**ollection and **A**nalysis of **D**ata for **A**ction and **C**hange.

Rhymes

From UK folklore, there are many established rhymes that can be used to aid recall. For example: 'Thirty days hath September, April, June and November . . .'. However, it is possible to make up your own rhymes either as a kind of doggerel verse or sung to some common 'nursery rhyme' type of tune. You will have similar examples from your own country.

Spelling tricks

Clearly, it does not represent your abilities very well if you misspell words that are key to your study. Therefore, it is important to devise strategies to help ensure that you use the correct form in your written work. For example, architects and designers might need to distinguish between the 'storeys' (levels of a building) or 'stories' (tales). It may be easier to remember the one that they usually want is 'storeys' because it contains the word 'store' and a store usually has different levels. Similarly, students of accounting might find it difficult to remember how to spell 'debt' and 'debit' and they might find it helpful to remember that 'debit' rhymes with 'credit'. You can design your own spelling tips if you keep a note of any rhymes or features that you encounter.

Journey 'pegs'

In this approach you have to think of a fairly long journey with which you are reasonably familiar. The preliminary work that has to be done is to identify staging posts on the journey corresponding to the number of points that you need to remember. The strategy is then to 'map' the facts by relating each memory point to a staging post on the journey. This works from the principle of association where the different elements to be remembered are 'pegged' onto the known journey.

Special place 'pegs'

This is another strategy that relies on pegging the unfamiliar onto the familiar. You need to imagine a room, a picture or a view that is familiar to you and you select key items of furniture or features in the picture or view to associate with the factual elements that you need to recall. In the exam, you simply visualise the situation and then recall the items that you 'pegged' to them. A further refinement is to create a story around the image so, for example, you go into the room and switch on the lamp (West Germany), move over to the television (France) and switch that on also. You put your mug (Italy) onto the coffee table (Belgium) and place a cushion (Netherlands) on the sofa (Luxembourg) before you sit down. This 'story' could help you recall the six members of the original European Economic Community.

Story 'pegs'

Some people find that they can take the journey and special place pegs to a further level by creating a longer story that relates the events to the recall items. Here, people can base their story on a familiar tale, for example, 'The three little pigs' to remember Napoleon's path to taking over large tracts of mainland Europe – the house of straw (Iberian Peninsula), the house of wood (Italy) and the house of bricks (Russia). Alternatively, stories can be created by the individual and can be as innovative, ridiculous, violent or colourful as you wish. The object is to create a sequence of events that is meaningful to you and can easily be recalled along with the related associations.

Is the effort in 'pegging' worthwhile? **?**

Some argue that the effort put into creating these scenarios might be better spent on just learning the material 'parrot fashion' and it is also suggested that these pegging strategies introduce an additional series of stages in the memorisation process. However, the technique responds to the learning styles of some people – if it works for you, it is worth the time and effort, especially where more conventional memorising techniques have failed you in the past.

Numbered lists

Listing is a basic revision tool (p. 131) and for people who like to learn in a linear fashion the use of numbered lists can be especially helpful. This is most valuable where there is a sequence inherent in the facts, and when knowing the total for the list can be useful in identifying whether you have recalled all the facts you originally collated. Breaking up larger lists into main points and sub-sections can be useful, particularly if the layout of the page 'staggers' the information by indentation and numbering of sub-sets. This can assist you to recall the image of the page and the list layout.

Logic rituals

For most of us, there are key things that we simply find difficult to remember time after time. However, if you can identify some ritual of logic that you can apply each time, you do have a way of unblocking that elusive piece of information. For example, the chemistry student who cannot remember how to calculate the density of liquid, can recall the units of density, grams (mass) per millilitre (volume), which helps in remembering that density is calculated as mass over volume.

✔ Practical tips for memorising for exams

Practise, practise, practise. There is simply no substitute for going over the material and/or your memory aids again and again.

Practise mnemonics. You should be able to rattle them off without difficulty – but of course you must be able to recollect what the mnemonic represents.

Practise using memory journey, special place and personal story 'peg' strategies. If these appeal, give yourself some practice in using this strategy before you go into the exam.

Practise recalling and writing quickly. As students increasingly type their assignments and work from pre-printed handouts in lectures, there are fewer opportunities to practise remembering and writing at speed, skills that are critical to answering questions against the clock in an exam. By rapidly scribbling down your memory cues, you can also work on developing the skill of writing quickly as part of your revision.

Review what you have learned. If anything is the key to memorising, this is it. Don't just rely on the vague hope that you will be able to recall something – check that you can, and check frequently. If these 'self-tests' indicate that you can't recall everything, go back and start again. This repeated activity works to imprint the knowledge – and if it works, you will *know* that you know the material. Here's a possible method to try:

1 Read the material and, as you do this, write it out in list form, focusing fully on each point, trying hard to remember it. Note the number of items on the list.

2 Turn over the list and remove all clues about it (for example, close your textbook).

3 Immediately, rewrite the list. If you can't remember everything, go back to point (1) and start again until you can rewrite the list completely.

4 Do something else for 5 minutes, then rewrite the list without clues. If you can't remember everything, go back to point (1) again.

5 Do something else for an hour, then rewrite the list. If you can't remember everything, go back to point (1) again.

6 After 24 hours, again try to rewrite the list. If you can't remember everything, go back to point (1) again.

This method also works well with diagrams.

◉ Useful language for . . . talking about memorisation

Context: these phrases may be useful when discussing how to remember key facts.

Do you want to hear the mnemonic I've made up for [topic]?

You should see my room right now. I've covered it with post-its about [topic]. I'm a kinesthetic learner. I've found it helps me to visualise moving about the room and seeing the different bit of information in different places.

I don't like using a highlighter on my notes or underlining words. I find after a while it becomes an automatic action and doesn't help me to remember anything.

(GO) And now . . .

52.1 Revisit your notes with memory tricks and strategies in mind. Go back through your revision notes and identify where you could devise an acronym, or use another memory strategy to help you learn and recall information.

52.2 Challenge a fellow student. Ask them to race you in noting down the key points of a particular response within a fixed time period. This will give you both the chance to practise creating a quick answer outline based on your memorising strategies and also give practice in writing quickly.

52.3 Swap memorisation strategies with friends. You could learn from each other and someone may have developed a strategy that is particularly valuable to your own subject, course or situation.

How to make full use of learning outcomes, past papers and other assessment information

You can gain a deeper understanding of how you will be assessed from a range of sources. Studying these can help you to focus your revision and to enter the exam room better prepared.

Key topics:
→ Using learning outcomes or objectives
→ What marking criteria can tell you
→ Exploiting past papers
→ Learning from model answers
→ Setting your own questions and exams

Essential vocabulary
Benchmark   Learning objective   Learning outcome   Marking criteria
Mock exam   Model answer   Question-spotting

Universities publish a great deal of useful information that can help you to improve your exam performance. The most important sources are likely to be: module learning outcomes or objectives, marking or assessment criteria, past exam papers and model answers. As part of your revision, you should find out what exists and make full use of it.

→ Using learning outcomes or objectives

You will normally find the learning outcomes in the module handbook alongside the detailed description of the curriculum (they are sometimes called learning objectives). These statements represent the 'take-home messages' of the teaching and they state what you are expected to accomplish in your learning. This is then tested in exams and other forms of assessment. Despite the obvious importance of learning outcomes, many students fail to look at them when studying.

The UK approach to learning outcomes

As part of the approach to quality assurance in the UK (and EU) higher educational systems, universities and hence organisers of degree programmes and modules, are asked to be very specific about what students should be expected to know and understand following each element of teaching. These 'learning outcomes' are outlined in the programme and module specifications, and should be made available to students in course handbooks.

Some schools departments lay out learning outcomes as a series of bullet points relating to individual lectures (for example, 'Following this lecture, you should be able to . . .'). In other cases, the outcome(s) may be framed in more general terms. Departments may also publish aims and goals for the entire module and it is also worth looking at these to place the course elements in context.

The relationship between exam questions and learning outcomes is generally easy to see if you look at past papers and match up the exam questions with the relevant learning outcomes and course material. However, you should be aware that the learning outcomes may have changed through time – ask the module organiser if in doubt.

If you do not feel able to achieve a particular learning outcome, it is worth checking with teaching staff. Perhaps you may have misunderstood the topic or the intention behind the outcome, in which case they may be able to provide you with further explanations. Also, a specific outcome might be redundant because a lecturer was unavailable or made a late modification to their teaching – check!

Compatibility between content and assessment

In an ideal world, there should be an alignment between the learning outcomes, the syllabus and the assessment methods. In other words, you should not be examined on a topic that was not covered in the course.

→ What marking criteria can tell you

Marking or grading criteria provide an indication of what sort of answer would gain a particular percentage mark or grade in relation to a university's marking scheme. You'll probably find marking criteria in faculty, school or departmental handbooks or websites, because they tend to apply across many modules. However, they may also be published in each module handbook.

Typical marking criteria include the following elements:

- **Content:** covering the range of ideas or information discussed and their relevance to the question actually set.
- **Depth:** referring to such aspects as complexity, detail, intellectual insight and originality of argument.
- **Writing style:** relating to, for example, the logic, clarity and the quality of the English.
- **Presentation:** referring to the neatness and possibly also to the structure of your work.
- **Use of examples:** taking account of the relevance, accuracy and detail of those you quote.
- **Evidence of reading:** accounting for any reading around the subject you may be expected to do: this may come from the examples and sources you quote (not just those given in lectures).

- **Originality:** involving independent thinking (backed by supporting evidence and argument) or a new synthesis of ideas: these are dimensions that are highly valued, especially in later years of study.
- **Analysis:** including interpretation of raw data or information found in original (primary) sources.

Have a close look at your department's marking criteria. If you wish to gain high marks, these will tell you what standard your answers must be. Note, however, that although marking criteria provide a 'benchmark', the exact mark given will always depend on the topic and question and is a matter for the professional judgement of the academic and the external examiner.

Example of marking criteria

These are the marking criteria for a first-class answer (70-100 per cent) in a science subject at honours level:

- Contains all the information required with either no or very few errors.
- Shows evidence of having read relevant literature and uses this effectively in the answer.
- Addresses the question correctly, understanding all its nuances.
- Little or no irrelevant material.
- Demonstrates full understanding of the topic within a wider context.
- Shows good critical and analytical abilities.
- Contains evidence of sound independent thinking.
- Ideas expressed clearly and concisely.
- Written logically and with appropriate structure. Standard of English very high.
- Diagrams detailed and relevant.

→ Exploiting past papers

Past papers or sample questions are a vital resource. They may be published electronically on websites or virtual learning environments, or in paper form within the library. If you can't find them in these locations, ask staff or senior students for help.

---

smart tip

Linking past papers and learning outcomes to enhance your revision

A possible approach is to photocopy past papers and then cut and paste all the questions into separate pages for each topic in the lecture course. By comparing the resulting groups of questions with the learning outcomes and the material as taught, you can gain a much better picture of how you will be assessed, what types of question might turn up, and what type of revision needs to be done.

Firstly, use past papers to understand the structure of your exam papers, including:

- the format of answers expected (for example, essay, short-answer questions, multiple-choice questions);
- the number of questions you will be required to answer of each type;
- what the mark allocation is among sections or question types;
- the time allowed for answering;
- whether there is any choice allowed;
- whether the arrangement of sections forces you to answer on specific topics.

Secondly, use past papers or sample questions to understand the style being used. When looking at each paper, ask yourself the following questions:

- How much and what type of factual knowledge is required?
- How deep an understanding of the topic is required?
- How much extra reading might be required?
- How much or how little freedom will you have to express your opinion or understanding?
- Do lecturers have consistent styles of questions?

Use your answers to create both your revision and exam strategies and the content of your answers (**Ch 50**, **Ch 55**).

→ Learning from model answers

If model answers are provided, allow time in your revision to read them carefully.

Consider each question thoroughly *before* you read the model answer. Jot down a few thoughts about the way you would tackle it. Identify the relevant learning outcomes that apply and think about the methods the lecturers are using to assess these.

Now read the model answer. This should be helpful in several ways, depending on how detailed it is.

- You should be able to grasp the language and style expected – for example, the type of introduction required, the use of headings and diagrams, what sort of things are in the conclusion.
- You should be able to evaluate the depth expected – for example, the balance between *description* and *analysis* that is present, the level of detail in any examples given, including use of dates, terminology and citation of authorities and authors. Especially at higher levels, university exams are more about using information to support a reasoned answer than simply repeating facts (**Ch 21**).
- You should be able to see how the different facets of the question have been addressed. Examine each part of the answer and identify what aspect it deals with, and how.

Learning from poor answers

If your lecturers also provide a 'bad' model answer, see what you can learn by comparing this with the good answer. Are you guilty of any of the errors highlighted by the comparison?

→ Setting your own questions and exams

After you have revised each section or topic, take the time to write out a few potential questions in the style of those seen in past papers. How would you set about answering your own questions? Write down plans as you would with an essay plan during the exam. This process helps you prepare mentally for sitting the exam. Consider it a bonus if any of the questions you predict come up in the real paper, but do not be tempted into question-spotting (see tip box).

Avoid question-spotting

At worst, this involves predicting (guessing) a limited number of exam questions in the hope that they come up and revising that material only. This risky strategy is rarely successful:

- Most examiners pre-empt it by making sure that questions are not repeated between exam diets and that patterns do not occur among papers. The chances of 'your' question coming up are very low.

- If your predictions are false, you will probably be unable to answer on other topics because you have not prepared for them.

- If there are subtle elements to the wording of the question, you may be tempted to provide the answer to your predicted question, rather than the precise one asked. You will then lose marks due to lack of relevance.

A 'mock exam', where you attempt to answer questions or a paper under realistic exam conditions, can help you in the following important ways:

- testing your subject knowledge – and giving you early feedback about what you do and do not know;

- helping you get into exam-answering mode and 'voice' – so that you can get rid of your rustiness before the proper exams start, can get going quickly in the actual exam and can start writing quickly and appropriately;

- timing your answers appropriately – so that you optimise marks and don't make the cardinal mistake of missing out questions through lack of time;

- practising planning and laying out an answer quickly – so that you get used to the process of thinking rapidly through your answer before starting to write and, where appropriate, can check that you know the appropriate layout of your answer; and

- reducing the effect of nerves – rehearsing can help you perform better on the day. You should be less anxious if you are familiar with the act of answering.

Practical tips for focusing your revision

Keep the exam paper format in mind as you revise. Assess the style of questions at an early point and choose study methods appropriate to the style of questions you will encounter (**Chs 35-40, Ch 51**).

Use the learning outcomes to check your progress. Your revision should include reading the learning outcomes for each topic and ticking each off when you feel you know enough to be able to accomplish them.

Dealing with a lack of past papers. Your tutors may be reluctant to release past papers in cases where there is a limited pool of 'good' questions for them to use, as this might reward students who simply memorise answers. This is often the case where the paper is made up of multiple-choice questions. One way round this is to set your own questions, perhaps as part of a study group, and use these to test each other.

Useful language for . . . talking about assessment information

Context: these examples may be helpful when talking to staff or fellow students.

I'm not sure what this learning outcome means. Can you explain it to me?

[In the library] Can you tell me whether there are past papers for [module] on file?

Can you provide a model answer for this sort of question, please? I'm really not sure how to tackle it and it would be really useful to see what you are expecting.

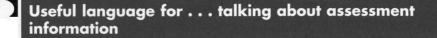 And now . . .

53.1 Make links between marking criteria, thinking processes and your study technique. Look at your department's marking criteria or the aspects noted on p. 431. Compare these with the levels of thought processes outlined in Table 21.2 on p. 164. This will help you appreciate the depth of learning required in your subject and level of study, and influence your revision and exam answers.

53.2 Set up a mock exam as part of your revision. You may wish to 'buddy up' with someone else doing your subject.

● Choose a paper that you haven't studied closely (in fact, you may wish to hold one back for this specific purpose).

● Find a place to work that closely replicates the exam experience, such as a quiet library area.

● Sit selected questions or only one question as you see fit.

- If it seems appropriate, give a full answer to a question for which you have prepared. Alternatively, lay out your answers as plans rather than whole essays.

- If answering a full question or paper, allocate yourself an appropriate amount of time for answering – this should be as realistic as possible so that you can get a 'feel' for the speed at which you need to work.

- Afterwards, you could ask for a study buddy's or subject tutor's opinion on your answer. This feedback could be very useful. If you can't find anyone to do the checking for you, critically compare what you have written with your notes.

53.3 Assemble the important information about your next exam. Before revising for any exam, and certainly before entering the exam room, you should use published material to gain a clear understanding of:

- what the examiners might ask you;
- the format of the paper and questions;
- the depth expected;
- the length of the exam and its component parts;
- how your answers will be marked.

How to work with fellow students to improve the revision experience

Teaming up with others as part of your revision effort is recognised as beneficial in many respects. It is particularly valuable for international students as a way of learning alongside others. It also helps to develop your language skills. This chapter explores some aspects of this 'study buddy' revision approach.

Key topics:
→ What is study buddying?
→ The advantages of study buddying

Essential vocabulary
Extrovert   Introvert   Study buddy

Revising for examinations is a positive experience in lots of ways. It heightens your understanding of your subject and allows you to make connections between different elements of the course. It needn't be a solitary activity and many people find that it improves their learning to work on revision with another person studying the same subject.

→ What is study buddying?

The study buddy concept is based on a mutual arrangement between two or more students studying the same or similar subjects, who agree to support each other in their learning by conducting joint study sessions within their revision timetable (**Ch 53**). Examples of suitable revision activities include:

● meeting together to work through tutorial questions, comparing answers and analysing the correct approach;

● studying a topic as individuals and then meeting at an agreed time to test each other on the topic;

● speaking to each other about a specific topic (even giving a 'mini lecture');

● sharing resources, such as missed lecture notes, handouts, website and textbook information;

● sharing advice about modules that one person may have passed but the other(s) have not;

● working together on formulating answers to questions on past papers;

● providing psychological support when one of you needs motivating or prompting to study.

How can you find a buddy?

The obvious starting points are friends from your class, members of a tutorial group or lab partners. You could also simply ask around before or after lectures or put up a request on an online discussion board. A lecturer might be willing to make an announcement on your behalf, asking anyone interested in forming a study group to come forward at the end of the lecture. You'll be surprised how many others will be interested in this activity.

This technique probably suits some learning types better than others (see p. 420). You'll need to decide for yourself whether it will be appropriate for you and, crucially, you'll need to find someone else who thinks the same way.

Study buddying across cultures

You may find that exchanging different approaches and ideas with someone from a different cultural and educational background provides insights into the learning and revision processes that could prove valuable to both parties. In study buddying, everyone has a contribution to make and so you have to be sure that you are able to make as strong a contribution as others in the group. For instance, if English is not your first language, then you may feel that your English is too weak to participate fully. However, if you have other skills that are stronger, such as mathematical understanding, then that will add to the group's skill and knowledge base.

→ The advantages of study buddying

The study buddy approach works very much on the principle that two or more heads are better than one. The process of working together to tackle problems, key issues or difficult areas can assist all those involved to learn more effectively.

- You can help with areas where you are stronger; and you can receive help from others to strengthen your weaker areas.
- Discussing the topic will help you understand and remember the content. It will also help you to rehearse the vocabulary and language structures you will need for your written answers.
- Explaining your understanding to someone else can help to clarify the issues, process or technique in your own mind. It can also help the other person, who may learn better when things are explained by a peer, because the language is less formal. Each person may also feel more comfortable about asking questions and seeking clarification or become less anxious about making mistakes.
- The pair or group dynamic can have a fun or competitive element that motivates some people; it can also generate confidence knowing that others feel the same.
- Arranging to meet with someone else to revise means you are more likely to do the necessary preparatory work.

Useful advice:

- Don't neglect yourself by spending too much time supporting others.
- Make sure you and your study buddies focus on studying rather than chat.
- Don't assume that study buddying is an easy option to avoid the hard grind of studying alone – solo study may, in practice, be a part of the study buddy process.

smart tip

Some practical ideas for buddy activities

Partnerships work in different ways; here are some strategies students have found useful.

- Partners work on problems individually for a set amount of time and then reconvene to compare method and answers.
- Student A uses a white-board or flipchart to explain a process to partner, Student B. Student B asks for further clarification. Then they reverse roles for another topic.
- Partners make up a 'bank' of short-answer topics by writing the question on one side of an index card and the answer on the other side. They test each other on random cards drawn from the pile.

Practical tips for working with colleagues to improve your revision

Arranging meetings. Pick a mutually acceptable time and find a location that will allow you to sit and discuss your work without disturbing others. Ensure that you turn up with all the relevant notes, calculators, worked examples, resources and dictionaries as appropriate. Aim for a neutral venue. Groupwork areas may be available in your library or you may find study rooms in the library, department, hall of residence or student association. You might be able to take over tutorial or small lecture rooms (check the booking system first): these may have the advantage of having whiteboards, which you can use to note down points or give explanations to each other. Ask your tutors or the departmental secretary if you can't find anywhere suitable – they may be able to help.

Ground rules. Agree some basic rules, for example, start and stop times, and limit breaks to no longer than 15 minutes. Stick to what you all agreed. Make sure that it's clear that if anyone feels the strategy is not working for them, they can walk away from it without fear of offending the others.

Tackling the revision. Compile a 'wish list' of aims/topics at the beginning of each session and cross them off as you complete them.

Seeking help. If, between you, an answer is not found, seek some guidance. Teaching staff are usually delighted when students show their interest in their topics by asking questions, so you shouldn't feel nervous about asking for help. You may find that it is less embarrassing or daunting to do this as a pair or a group. A lecturer who might seem unapproachable or remote in a lecture may be easy to talk to and responsive when dealing with individual or small group questions. Email first to make an appointment.

Short or long sessions? Working intensively for a shorter time is often better than a prolonged session where people end up chatting about other things. Keep focused.

Context: these examples are suitable for discussions between potential or actual buddies.

Hi. You're studying the same module as me, aren't you? - [mention module name] - How are you getting on with your studying? I was wondering if you'd like to meet a couple of times to discuss possible exam questions and the way we would approach them . . . What do you think?

For our next meeting let's each think of three or four possible exam questions, then meet back here and discuss whether we think these topics or formats are likely to come up and, if so, how we would approach them.

Context: this example is suitable for discussions between buddies and staff.

[To a lecturer] xxxx and I have been revising together and we have a number of questions we'd like to ask you about [topic]. Would it be possible for us to arrange a meeting with you to discuss them?

And now . . .

54.1 Think about how you can set up a study buddy group. Who might you approach? What subjects would the pair/group cover? Where could you meet? How much time do you have to work in this mutually supportive way?

54.2 Decide which of your revision topics or exam formats would best suit the study buddy approach. It may be more appropriate to learn some material by yourself, and tackle other topics within a group.

54.3 Think about extending buddy activities beyond the revision period. These forms of working relationships could apply at any time in your studies, not just before exams.

55 | Exam strategies

How to ensure you have the appropriate tactics

Assuming your revision has gone well, the main pressure point in an exam is time. Effective use of this resource through an appropriate strategy is vital to ensure the best possible performance.

Key topics:
→ Key information required for a strategy
→ Producing a strategy
→ What to do during the exam
→ Arriving well prepared

Essential vocabulary
**Invigilator   Law of diminishing returns   Multiple-choice question   Rubric
Short-answer question**

An exam strategy is effectively a plan for managing your time and effort during an exam. This is vital to optimise your marks, because rushing answers or failing to complete the paper are reasons why many students perform poorly (**Ch 57**). Having a clear strategy will also mean that you will be more confident going into the exam room and will address the questions in a more focused way.

→ Key information required for a strategy

Each exam will probably require a different strategy. For each one, you will need to do some research beforehand, by finding the answers to the following questions:

● How long is the exam?

● How is the paper subdivided into sections and questions?

● What is the nature of the questions?

● What proportion of the marks is allocated to each section/answer?

● What restrictions on answering are there?

You can find out these details from course handbooks or staff. Past papers are another source of information, but the rules may change, so it is worth confirming that the format is still the same.

Example: choosing a strategy

A common type of restriction in exam papers forces you to cover the full range of the syllabus by stating that you must answer one question from each of a number of sections, each covering a different subject area. As well as influencing your exam strategy, this type of restriction should also affect the way you revise (**Ch 53**).

Exam strategies do not need to be complex, but they do need to be planned with care, and ideally in advance as part of your revision effort. Table 55.1 illustrates some ways in which a strategic approach can help you avoid problems with exams.

→ Producing a strategy

The following is a straightforward method for an exam with a set of similar-length essay or short-answer questions:

- Translate the exam's total length into minutes.
- Allocate some time (say 5 per cent) to consider which questions to answer and in which order. Allocate another 5 per cent as a 'flexibility buffer'. Subtract these amounts (10 per cent) from the total time.
- Share the remainder of the time among the questions to arrive at an 'ideal' time for each answer.
- Think about how you intend to divide the time for each answer into planning, writing and review phases (see information box below).
- Try to memorise roughly how long you intend to allocate to each section, question and phase, before going into the exam.

You might prefer a slightly different model where you would review all your answers towards the end of the exam, rather than reviewing each immediately after you have written it. If this would suit you better, you will need to deduct a further 5–10 per cent from the total before allocating planning and writing time to each answer.

Papers with mixtures of question types require more complex strategies. Much will depend on your estimate of the time each type of answer should take: base your estimate on previous experience (for example, in mid-term/semester exams) if you can, and take into account the proportion of marks allocated to each type of question or section. You may also need to decide on the order in which you do the different types of questions.

Example: exam timing

You have a 2-hour exam (120 minutes), in which you have to answer 10 short-answer questions from a list of 20. You might allocate 5 per cent of the time (6 minutes) to reading the paper, choosing questions and reviewing answers. That leaves 114 minutes, which means each question should be allocated 11 minutes, giving you 4 extra minutes for flexibility.

Table 55.1 Weak approaches to exams and how to avoid similar problems

Approach	Experience	How to avoid this problem
The disorganised person	Dora has lost the scrap of paper that she used to note when and where her exam was. She plans to arrive at the time and place she vaguely remembers and see if she recognises anyone in the queue. Her bus is late however, and everyone has already gone in. She arrives breathless at her seat, only to find she's forgotten her pen and it's an Atomic Physics paper rather than European history . . .	Dora could: • have checked the details the night before; • have planned to take the earlier bus to allow for delays; • have used a checklist (Table 55.2) to make sure she has everything needed; • speak to the invigilator, who can give her correct information; • be allowed to sit part of the proper exam, if she can still get to the right place in time.
The nervous exam-sitter	Nadeem is totally consumed by nerves on the day of his big exam. He needs to visit the toilet immediately beforehand and then feels nauseous. In the exam, the words on the exam paper swim before his eyes and he can't make sense of the first question, nor any of the rest. The questions don't seem to relate to any of his course work. He rushes out of the exam hall, frustrated and anxious . . .	Nadeem could: • reflect ahead of time on his view of exams – why he feels nervous – and try not to allow a spiral of anxiety to develop; • try to exploit his energy rush positively, for example, by brainstorming key points as soon as he goes into the hall, thus giving him confidence; • use relaxation techniques within the exam hall.
The 'get-me-outa-here!' student	Gregori would rather be anywhere else than in an exam hall. He rushes through his answers, then hands in his paper 30 minutes before the end and rushes to the union bar to wait for his friends to come out. During post-exam discussions, he realises that one of his answers is incomplete and he hasn't even attempted section B . . .	Gregori could: • familiarise himself with the format of the paper before the date; • plan his time in the exam so that he uses all of it profitably; • use spare time for checking answers to ensure he has done as instructed.
The perfectionist	Lin has spent ages revising and knows the topics inside out. When she turns over the exam paper, she is delighted to find her ideal question and knows she can produce a brilliant answer. One-and-a-half hours later, it's nearly finished. Only problem is, she now has another two answers to complete in 30 minutes . . .	Lin could: • do much the same as Gregori, but also recognise that she will gain a better mark for doing reasonably well in all the questions, rather than extremely well in just one; • practise writing answers against the clock to improve her technique.
The mind-blocked writer	Mike has prepared for the exam well, but when he looks at the question paper, his mind has gone a complete blank. He can't remember anything to do with the subject material and feels like leaving the exam straight away . . .	Mike could: • begin by brainstorming a topic he knows well, from a nucleus of information that he can add to, and relate this to the questions asked; • ask a departmental representative for a clue; a note will be taken of this, but it's better than writing nothing and it will get him started.
The laid-back dreamer	Patsy can't really be bothered with all the stress of exams and the need for all that stress. At the start, she takes ages to choose a question and more time to think over her answer. In the middle, she finds herself dreaming of the summer vacation. Suddenly the exam is over, and she's only half way through her first answer . . .	Patsy could: • focus on the exam and why it's important to her; • make a conscious decision to concentrate on the exam paper; • consider how much vacation time she will need to spend on revision if she fails.

For example, in the case of a paper with a multiple-choice component and an essay section, you may wish to do a sweep of the multiple-choice part first, then the essays, then return to complete the harder multiple-choice questions.

Your strategy should be flexible, in case things don't turn out the way you planned them – but only make changes during the exam if you are certain of what you are doing, and why.

What if the exam paper is differently arranged from your expectation?

You will have to rethink your strategy quickly. It will still be worth doing this, as the implications of running out of time could be serious.

→ What to do during the exam

- Quickly check the rubric at the top of the paper and that the questions are arranged as you expected.

- Look carefully at all the questions on the paper. You may wish to mark off the ones you feel you can answer well, or adopt some form of scoring system (for example, marks out of ten) for how well you think you can answer them.

- Thinking about your strategy, and the 'ideal' time for each question, decide which answers, if any, might require more time, or might provide a good return in marks for a little extra time invested, and which questions might require less time. A potentially good answer should be allocated only slightly more time than one you don't feel so happy about. If you concentrate too much on any one answer, the law of diminishing returns means that you will take time from other answers without gaining compensatory credit (see Figure 55.1).

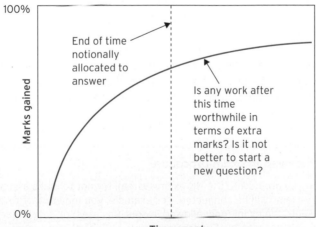

Figure 55.1 Why it does not pay to spend too long on any one exam answer. The marks you gain tail off the longer you carry on writing. The extra return will simply not repay the investment of time. Ensure that you start answers to all questions to gain the 'easily obtained' marks, rather than wasting time perfecting one answer.

- Answer questions in a sensible order, which does *not* have to be the order they appear in the question paper. For example:
  - Some people prefer to answer 'fact-based' questions first, before they forget details memorised just before the exam.
  - Some people prefer to answer their 'best' question first, to get a good start to the paper. Others would prefer to do this second or even later, when they feel 'warmed up'.
  - Most people would agree that you should leave a question you feel unhappy about until the end: during the rest of the exam, ideas may come to you about it - note them down as you go along.

Example: benefits of answering all questions

Suppose you had a paper with four questions but only answered two, trying to do your very best in them. You might score, say, 75 per cent in each, but your total percentage mark would be (75 + 75 + 0 + 0) divided by 4, or 37.5 per cent (usually a fail).

On the other hand, if you answered all four questions, but perhaps less well, you might score 55 per cent in two and 45 per cent in the other two. Your overall percentage mark would be (55 + 55 + 45 + 45) divided by 4, or 50 per cent (usually a pass).

→ Arriving well prepared

The most important aspect of preparation is revision. No amount of exam technique will substitute for this. However, by ensuring that you also have the logistical aspects of exam-sitting under control, you can reduce the chance of making damaging mistakes and help to calm your nerves in advance of the event.

You may need to register and, in some cases, pay for certain exams - check this at an early stage. You should also confirm the date of the exam, where it will take place, when it will start and how long it will last. This information may be given in the course handbook, posted on noticeboards, published on a website or within a virtual learning environment module, or may also be provided by the exam office/registry by post. However, it is *your* duty to ensure that you arrive at the right place at the right time. Write down the information. Double-check, perhaps by asking a member of the class who has found out independently.

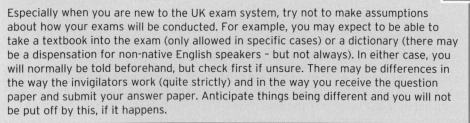

Anticipate differences in exam procedure

Especially when you are new to the UK exam system, try not to make assumptions about how your exams will be conducted. For example, you may expect to be able to take a textbook into the exam (only allowed in specific cases) or a dictionary (there may be a dispensation for non-native English speakers - but not always). In either case, you will normally be told beforehand, but check first if unsure. There may be differences in the way the invigilators work (quite strictly) and in the way you receive the question paper and submit your answer paper. Anticipate things being different and you will not be put off by this, if it happens.

Table 55.2 Checklist of items to bring with you to written exams

✓ Item
❑ Writing equipment: pens and pencils (plus replacements), ruler, rubber, highlighter(s), correction fluid
❑ Student matriculation (ID) card (staff will use this to check your identity)
❑ Special equipment: calculators, protractor, compass, Walkman or similar for aural exams (check beforehand that you can use these aids properly), spare batteries
❑ Texts, where allowed for 'open book' exams
❑ Dictionary, if allowed (Note this must be arranged beforehand with your department)
❑ Sweets and a drink, if allowed
❑ Clock or watch for timekeeping
❑ Mascot (good luck toy or charm)

On the day, plan carefully so that you can arrive in good time – this will allow for unanticipated circumstances and will help to reduce the anxiety element at the start of the exam (**Ch 56**). Going over a checklist of items to bring to the exam (Table 55.2) may also calm you.

In the exam room always double-check on the rubric at the top of the paper. It is not unknown for students to sit the wrong exam by mistake.

✔ Practical tips for time saving in exams

Don't over-elaborate your answer plans. Use simple forms of diagrams or mind maps to brainstorm and plan your answer (**Ch 16**).

Use diagrams and tables in your answer. This saves time otherwise spent making difficult and lengthy explanations, but make sure they are worthwhile and that you refer to them in the text.

Use standard abbreviations. This will save time repeating text. Always explain the abbreviations at the first point of use. However, this is not necessary for 'standard' abbreviations such as e.g. (for example), i.e. (that is) and etc. (et cetera – and so forth).

Always watch the time. There is no point in having a strategy if you forget to stick to it. You may find it helps to take off your watch and put it where it can be easily seen on the desk. Some students find it helpful to work out the end times for each question beforehand as an aid to timekeeping. As the allotted period for each answer draws to a close, make sure your mind is on finishing your answer.

Consider speed of writing and neatness. Might you be wasting time by trying to write too neatly or using a type of pen that slows you down? Ballpoint and liquid gel pens are probably the fastest. Conversely, are you writing too quickly and making your script difficult to interpret? You can only gain marks if the examiner can read your script.

Don't be irrelevant in your answer. Remember that time taken to write irrelevant material is time lost from another question. Don't waste time including irrelevant facts just because you memorised them during revision. This may do you more harm than good (**Ch 57**).

Keep your answer simple and to the point. It should have clear explanations of your reasoning. Even when working quickly, keep your mind on the task. You must answer the specific question that has been set (**Ch 57**).

 Useful language for . . . talking about an exam strategy

Context: these expressions might be appropriate when discussing your strategy with a fellow student.

[For a specific paper] Because I write slowly, I'm going to allow more time for the essay part of the paper and try to get through the multiple choice part more quickly.

How much time are you going to allow for going over your answers at the end of the paper?

Last exam I spent so much time on one question that I missed out half of the paper. This time I'm going to plan out my time better, so that I put down something for each question.

GO And now . . .

55.1 Prepare at an early stage. Even before your thoughts turn to revision, look through the course handbook and other information to make sure you have a good idea of how the material presented will be assessed (**Ch 53**). This will help keep your note-making and reading strategies in line with your exam strategy.

55.2 Create a strategy for each of your exams. Discuss your strategy with someone else on the course to see what they think of it and how they intend to handle the exam.

55.3 Ask a tutor's advice. If you are in doubt about any of the assumptions that may lie behind your strategy, ask a tutor.

How to reduce anxiety and perform well under pressure

Turn exam anxiety to your advantage. Recognise that 'nerves' are your body's way of preparing you to perform at a higher level. Boost your confidence by having a 'game plan' ready.

Key topics:
→ Panic due to lack of preparation
→ Perfectionism as a source of anxiety
→ Performing under pressure

Essential vocabulary
Adrenaline Game plan Invigilator Mind-set Negativity Perfectionism

Many people worry about exams, even the most able students, so if you are particularly anxious you are not unusual. Nerves are best overcome through confidence generated by thorough preparation. Even if you've studied hard, it isn't possible to know 100 per cent of the coursework, or to anticipate what exactly will be examined – and apprehension about the consequences of this is perfectly natural. Instead of worrying about it, turn it to your advantage by recognising that being nervous helps provide both the motivation to study harder and a surge of adrenalin that is the body's way of helping you raise your game on the day.

> **smart tip**
>
> **Always try to think positively about your exams**
>
> Time spent worrying is time wasted – instead, use it to your advantage by tackling the work. It's vitally important to believe that you can achieve something – and this carries through right to the very end of the exam. The last fact you learn and the last point you put down on paper might be the one that ensures you pass or takes you into a higher grade band.

→ Panic due to lack of preparation

Feeling ill-prepared is probably the most common reason for being nervous about exams. Many a student has experienced the sensation of panic that comes when they realise that they have probably not done enough studying during the year – and that the time remaining for cramming has become very short. If this applies to you, make a resolution to space out your workload next time round, then determinedly try to maximise your return on the time remaining. If you apply yourself to the task with a positive attitude, and are willing to work hard, you will be able to achieve quite a lot in a short time. The following tips may help.

- When time is limited, effective use of it is vital. Quickly create a revision timetable that helps you optimise your activities (**Ch 50**). Stick to it rigidly. Reduce all sporting and social events to a bare minimum and cut down on any employment you have taken on.

- Over brief periods, you can stretch your working hours – for example, setting an early alarm isn't something you might normally think of doing, but this can easily add an hour or two to each day.

- Spend some time with others in your class to exchange ideas about what's worth studying and to obtain quick answers to minor problems with coursework.

- Be strategic in your work and approach to the exam by following these steps:
  - Without taking 'question spotting' to extremes (see p. 433), study so that you maximise the return on the time put in. Use a highlighter to mark critical learning objectives from the course handbook.
  - Now make sure you have the framework and basic understanding to begin an answer on each of these topics.
  - Next, focus on the key facts you must remember.
  - Finally, and only if you have time, get into the detail and examples.

- Exploit the time remaining as much as possible, by adopting active revision techniques (**Ch 51**) and using normally 'redundant' time effectively. For example, try to do small chunks of revision when commuting or in the time between lectures – this all accumulates.

---

smart tip

Speed reading and skimming

The tips presented in **Ch 24** can help you lift the essence from a text or set of notes in the minimum time.

→ Perfectionism as a source of anxiety

Exams, with their tight time limits and tough marking criteria, are especially stressful for perfectionists. To counteract this tendency, focus on the following points before, during and after the exam:

- Don't go into an exam expecting to produce a perfect series of answers – recognise that this simply won't be possible in the limited time available.

- Don't spend too long planning your answer – for example, as soon as you have an outline essay plan, get started.

- Don't spend too much time on the initial parts of an answer, especially the first sentence, at the expense of the main message.

- Concentrate first on getting all the basics across – markers are looking for the main points first, before allocating extra marks for the detail. You may wish to present these at the start of your answer as insurance against running out of time.

- Don't be obsessed with neatness, either in handwriting or in the diagrams you draw – but make sure your answers are legible.

- Don't worry if you've forgotten a particular fact. You can't be expected to know everything. The detail required for essays or reports in coursework cannot be replicated in the time available for an exam answer, and the markers understand this.

- After each exam in a series, avoid prolonged analyses with other students over the 'ideal' answers to the questions; after all, it is too late to change anything at this stage. Put all your mental energy into preparing for the next exam, so that you are ready to face that challenge with confidence.

Mind gone a complete blank?

We all face this from time to time and also realise that the key to remembering a fact, date or name is often to think of something else. So, leave a blank space in your answer paper and come back to it later. Alternatively, if you can't see any way to answer a whole question, try one of the following:

- Brainstorm connections from things you *do* know about the subject.
- Work from basics, such as natural subdivisions of the topic (for example, hierarchical levels, such as parts of the body).
- As yourself 'Who? What? When? Where? Why? How?' in relation to the key subject matter (**Ch 28** on p. 237).
- Think diagrammatically: base your brainstorm on doodles and images – this may open up different thought patterns.
- Search for associations: read through the other questions in the paper – they may trigger your memory.
- Get on with other questions if you can – the subject material might trigger your memory on others that are proving to be stumbling blocks.

→ Performing under pressure

First, recognise that exams are to some extent a test of your ability to perform under pressure, and accept the challenge laid down by the system. To do this, you need to be well prepared and particularly to have practised. If you've done well in the past, draw confidence from this. Self-tests and mock exams (**Ch 51**, **Ch 57**) are a good way of getting into the right frame of mind. They'll teach you much about the format and timing of the exam, and help you develop good habits.

Exams represent artificial situations contrived to ensure that large numbers of candidates can be assessed together with little risk of cheating. There is a lot to be said for treating them like a game. If you understand the rationale behind them, and adapt to their conventions and rules, this will aid your performance.

One positive approach is to think about all the exams that you have taken in order to achieve the standard to gain entry to your UK university. You will have learnt how to tackle these exams and succeed; in the UK context, work out what is to be expected and you will build on this success. Check out the content of the exam paper, the breadth of revision you need to do, what happens on the day and how your work will be assessed. In this way you'll build up the strategic knowledge to help you resolve any anxiety about the unknown. Speak with someone who has taken exams in the UK before and ask them to 'talk you through' the procedures in the exam hall. In this way, you will know what to expect from the moment that you arrive at the exam hall to the moment that the invigilator tells you to put your pen down.

Performing under pressure as an international student

International students are often under additional pressures relating to their sponsors' expectations; if this is the case for you, try to focus your energy on working towards the exam rather than on worrying about failing. All students – home and international – need to keep a sense of perspective. The logic goes:

Negative mind-set: energy spent worrying about exam failure → reduces time spent on revision → causes more worry about lack of revision → results in lower potential for achievement → poor marks;

Positive mind-set: take the same energy and direct it to finding out about the exam itself and the procedure of exams → leads to confidence building → provides more energy for revision → improves confidence → builds an upward spiral of confidence thus building further confidence (and reducing nerves) → better marks.

✔ Practical tips for combating the symptoms of exam anxiety

Sleeplessness. This is commonplace and does little harm in the short term. Get up, have a snack, do some light reading or other work, then return to bed. Avoid caffeine (for example tea, coffee and cola) for several hours before going to bed.

Lack of appetite/upset tummy. Again, these symptoms are common. Eat what you can, but take sugary sweets into the exam (and/or drinks, if allowed) to keep your energy levels up. If allowed, take some water to avoid dehydration.

Fear of the unknown. Confirm dates and times of exams. Go through your pre-exam checklist (**Ch 55**). Check any paperwork you have been given regarding the format and timing of the exam. Take a mascot or lucky charm with you if this helps. In extreme cases, it might be a good idea to visit the exam room, so you can become familiar with the location.

Worries about timekeeping. Get a reliable alarm clock or a new battery for an old one. Arrange for an alarm phone call. Ask a friend or relative to make sure you are awake on time. Make reliable travel arrangements, so that you arrive early.

Blind panic during an exam. To reduce the symptoms, try doing some relaxation exercises (see below) and then return to your paper. If you still feel bad, explain how you feel to an invigilator. Ask to go for a supervised walk outside if this might help. If you have problems with the wording of a specific question, ask to speak to the departmental representative at the exam (if they have left the room, they can be phoned).

Feeling tense. Shut your eyes, take several deep breaths, do some stretching and relaxing muscle movements. During exams, it may be a good idea to do this between questions, and possibly to have a complete rest for a few seconds or so. Prior to exams, try some exercise activity, or escape temporarily from your worries by watching a movie.

Running out of time. Try not to panic when the invigilator says 'Five minutes left'. It is amazing how much you can write in that amount of time. Write note-style answers or state the areas you would have covered: you may get some credit. Keep writing until the invigilators insist that you stop.

Needing a toilet break. Don't become anxious or embarrassed about the need for a toilet break. Put up your hand and ask to go out. Your concentration will improve afterwards and the walk there and back will allow you to refocus your thoughts.

Think positively. You can do this!

💬 Useful language for . . . talking about exam nerves

Context: you might use these sentences when chatting to a fellow student.

You always seem so calm before exams. What's your trick?

I've never been to the hall where we're having our exam. Would you like to walk over there after our lecture to see where it is and what it's like?

I'm off to the gym! There's only so much studying I can do at a single sitting, so I'm going to try to work off some of my adrenaline, then come back later on.

(GO) And now . . .

56.1 Begin your revision early. Good preparation breeds confidence, which counteracts nerves.

56.2 Discuss how you feel about your exams with someone else. It always helps to realise you are not alone. However, try not to dwell on your mutual anxiety – try to gain a boost from friendship in adversity and focus on the celebration you will have when the exams are over.

56.3 Complete the exam checklist (p. 445). Knowing you have everything you need will boost your confidence.

Improving your exam performance

How to avoid common mistakes and enhance your grades

Why aren't you doing as well as you'd like to in your exams and tests? This chapter focuses on the main reasons why exam answers receive low marks and provides a framework for assessing how you could improve.

Key topics:
→ Identifying reasons for weak performance and areas for improvement
→ How to ensure you answer the question
→ Reviewing your answers to gain marks

Essential vocabulary
Brainstorm   Question-spotting   Value judgement

Poor exam performance is a relative term that depends on your expectations. There will probably be occasions when you can easily diagnose the reasons for weak marks. Lack of preparation, poor performance in the exam room, or revising the 'wrong' topics are common examples. In these instances, your expectations after the exam were probably low and you can accept that you deserved a low grade.

At other times, you may feel your marks were not as good as you thought they were going to be. You may have misunderstood the topic or failed to understand fully the implications of the question. Here, there is a gap between your expectation and the results of your efforts – one that is vitally important to understand if you wish to do better in future.

→ Identifying reasons for weak performance and areas for improvement

Where might you have gone wrong in the past, and how might you improve? To find out, you will need to:

● **reflect carefully on past exams.** Look back and think about how things went, and whether you might have been guilty of any of faults shown in Table 57.1. You may find it beneficial to look at the original question papers. Also, refer to any feedback on coursework or comments on exam scripts if these are available to you. If you don't understand any of the comments, try to meet with the marker and ask for an explanation. Such discussions can often be very valuable, so you should try to arrange this.

Table 57.1 Checklist of possible reasons for poor exam marks. Use the list to identify where you may have been at fault, and find possible routes for improving your performance.

Reason	Relevant for you?	Possible cure(s)
Not answering the exact question as set: • failing to recognise the specialist terms used in the question • failing to follow the precise instruction in a question • failing to address all aspects of the question	❑	A range of solutions - discussed in detail within this chapter
Poor time management: • failing to match the extent of the answer(s) to the time allocated • spending too long on one question and not enough on the others	❑	A better exam strategy is required (**Ch 55**)
Failing to weight parts of the answer appropriately: not recognising that one aspect (perhaps involving more complex ideas) may carry more marks than another	❑	A better essay plan may be required (**Ch 30**)
Failing to provide evidence to support an answer: not including examples or not stating the 'obvious' - like basic facts or definitions	❑	Recognise that this material is required to gain marks; a better essay plan may be required (**Ch 30**)
Failing to illustrate an answer appropriately: • not including a relevant diagram • providing a diagram that does not aid communication/omits labels	❑	Need to understand how diagrams should be used to support writing (**Ch 34**)
Incomplete or weak answers: • failing to answer appropriately due to lack of knowledge • not considering the topic in sufficient depth	❑	Need a better revision plan (**Ch 50**), a better revision technique (**Ch 51**) or a better understanding of the thinking process demanded at university (**Ch 21**)
Providing irrelevant evidence to support an answer: writing only to fill space	❑	See material on answering the question (**Ch 38**, p. 320)
Illegible handwriting: if it can't be read, it can't be marked	❑	May need to consider type of pen being used, slow down writing speed or change writing style
Poor English: facts and ideas are not expressed clearly	❑	Need to address academic writing skills (see chapters in **Toolkit D**)
Lack of logic or structure to the answer	❑	Need to plan your writing better (**Ch 30**)
Factual errors	❑	Poor note-taking (**Ch 16**), learning (**Ch 13**), revision (**Ch 51**, **Ch 53**) or recall
Failing to correct obvious mistakes	❑	Need to review and proof-read answers (p. 455 and **Ch 33**)

- **Try to do something about the faults you have identified.** Many of the causes of poor exam performance are simple to correct, once you have identified which might apply to you. If, after reading through this 'self-help' chapter, you still do not understand where you went wrong or what corrective action to take, you should ask to meet with your tutor(s) to seek their advice.

Avoiding poor performance

If 'nerves' affected your performance, then you might consider different methods of preparation or ways of settling yourself at the start of the exam (**Ch 55**).

If you ran out of time and some of your answers were incomplete, you probably need a better strategy for using time in your exams (**Ch 55**). This is a simple fault to rectify.

If you feel that your vocabulary is weak or your English style inappropriate, you might need a longer-term approach that would involve creating a glossary (Table Z.2, p. 460) or reading about text structuring or punctuation.

If feedback indicates faults in the way you structure your writing in terms of the logic of the argument (**Ch 48**, pp. 394-5), then you should arrange to meet with a tutor or lecturer to examine the way that you order your points. This may give you some guidance about different approaches to constructing an argument since sometimes these vary from one language and cultural community to another.

→ How to ensure you answer the question

Most lecturers agree that the number-one reason for a well-prepared student losing marks is because their answers *do not address the question*. This is especially true for essay-style questions (**Ch 38**) but also true for short-answer questions (**Ch 36**) and other assignments.

The main tips for answering questions directly and purposefully are covered in **Ch 38** and include:

- Making sure you consider all aspects of the question.
- Ensuring your work is well planned.
- Explaining what *you* understand by the question.
- Focusing on the precise task you have been asked to do.
- Keeping to the point.
- Making sure you answer all elements in multi-part questions.
- Avoiding making value judgements (**Ch 27**).

Include basic material in your answer, such as key terms and their definitions, and critical dates and names. Especially if a strict marking scheme is being used, tutors will unable to award you marks if you do not provide this information. Draw on your understanding of the whole topic when creating an essay plan. Don't just focus on key phrases of the question in isolation, but consider their context. Be aware of the risk, if you have decided to 'question-spot' (**Ch 53**), of answering your own pre-prepared question, rather than the one that has actually been set.

Dangers of relying on rote learning

Some international students use a strategy of memorising lengthy information that they think will be needed in the exam, even to the extent of memorising complete answers. This is sometimes called 'rote learning' (p. 419) and leads to answers that may be factually correct, presented in good English and cover the material within the topic, but to write it, the student will have used their powers of recall, not their powers of critical thinking (**Ch 21**). In addition, their response may have only partial reference to the question or task as presented on the examination paper. Be wary of rote learning because examiners often create questions that 'trap' this approach. For example, they might bring together two unexpected topics in one question. In that event the memorised answer is unlikely to be relevant to both dimensions.

smart tip

Reasons for loss of marks at advanced levels

The following are reasons why you might be marked down at higher levels of study:

- Not providing enough in-depth information.
- Providing a descriptive rather than an analytical answer – focusing on facts, rather than deeper aspects of a topic.
- Not setting a problem in context, or not demonstrating a wider understanding of the topic. However, make sure you don't overdo this, or you may risk not answering the question set.
- Not giving enough evidence of reading around the subject. This can be corrected by quoting relevant papers and reviews.
- Not considering both sides of a topic/debate, or not arriving at a conclusion if you have done so.

→ Reviewing your answers to gain marks

Many students want to get out of the exam room as soon as possible, but you should not do this unless you are convinced you have squeezed every last mark out of the paper. Your exam strategy (**Ch 55**) should always include an allocation of time for reviewing. Correcting simple errors could mean the difference between a pass or a fail or between degree classifications. These are some of the things you could look for when reviewing your work (see also **Ch 33**):

- **Basics.** Make sure you have numbered your answers, answered the right number of questions.
- **Spelling, grammar and sense.** Read through the answer critically (try to imagine it has been written by someone else) and correct any obvious errors that strike you. Does the text make sense? Do the sentences and paragraphs flow smoothly?
- **Structure and relevance.** Once again, ask yourself whether you have really answered the question that was set. Have you followed precisely the instruction(s) in the title? Is anything missed out? Are the different parts linked together well? Look for inconsistencies in argument. Add new material if necessary.

If required, 'small-scale' corrections like spelling errors and changes to punctuation marks can be made directly in your text using standard proof-reading symbols (**Ch 33**). If you want to add text because you find you have missed something out, place an insert mark (Λ or ⋏) in the text and/or margin, with the annotation 'see additional paragraph x'; then write this paragraph, clearly identified, at the end of the answer. You will not lose any marks for having to do this.

> ### Try to help staff to help you
>
> It's important to realise that the person who marks your work is not an adversary. Most lecturers are disappointed when giving students a poor grade, but they approach the marking process professionally and with strict objectivity. Tutors are often very frustrated when they see that simple changes in approach might have led to a better mark, and they cannot assume that you know things that you do not put down on paper.

✔ Practical tips for improving your exam performance

Go in well prepared. There is no substitute for effective revision. However, being well-prepared means more than memorising facts and concepts. To do well you also need to arrive at the exam room in a good mental state, with a plan and a positive attitude and the determination to get down to work quickly and effectively.

Convert your brainstorm into a plan as quickly as possible. You can do this very quickly simply by numbering the headings in the brainstorm in the order you intend to write about them.

Have relevance as your rule. As you create your answer plan, keep asking yourself the following questions. Am I really answering the question? Have I covered all the necessary material? Is all that I have included relevant to the question? Use these questions as a mental checklist before you finalise your plan and continue to refer to it as you construct your response to the task you have been set.

Useful language for . . . talking about exam performance

Context: this language might be helpful when speaking with a tutor or lecturer about your exam performance.

I'm having a lot of trouble writing my answers in English. Do you have any tips you could give me to help me to speed up?

I think I don't interpret the instruction words in questions correctly. Could we go through these three examples to look at differences between what I thought you wanted and what you actually wanted?

Could we go through my past exam paper together, please, to find out where I lost marks?

GO **And now . . .**

57.1 Analyse your past exam performances. Work through the points in Table 57.1 and make a resolution to improve at least one aspect of your revision or exam technique.

57.2 Rethink your timetable for revision. Review the nature of your revision for previous exams. You may need to consider whether you are spending too much time on memorising facts rather than on understanding concepts. Reconfigure your revision timetable with this in mind so that you achieve a balance between learning factual information and broader understanding. Using both types of knowledge to support your answers will contribute to good marks in exams.

57.3 Think more deeply. If feedback suggests that the depth of your answers is too shallow, but you don't fully understand how you could improve, have a look at the material on thinking processes (Table 21.1 on p. 163) to see whether this might make things clearer. If after reading this material, you feel you would like to have more concrete examples relevant to your subject or a specific exam question and answer, ask for a meeting with a tutor or lecturer to discuss this further.

Appendix: student resources

The following pages have blank versions of tables for your own personal use. These are all copyright free, so you can photocopy them and use them as many times as you require.

Table Z.1 A budget for student expenditure. Depending on the item, it may be more convenient to fill in a yearly, monthly or weekly total and add a figure to the other columns by multiplying or dividing appropriately.

Budget period: [   ]

Predicted income Source	Yearly total (£)	Monthly total (£)	Weekly total (£)
Parental allowance/family income			
Term-time employment			
Child benefit/tax credits/other state benefits			
From savings (interest or capital)			
Scholarships and grants			
Loan			
Loan			
Other			
Other			
Total predicted income			

Predicted Expenditure Source	Yearly total (£)	Monthly total (£)	Weekly total (£)
Tuition fees			
Accommodation (rent, mortgage)			
Food			
Leisure and entertainment			
Annual memberships and fees (e.g. sports clubs, societies)			
Books and other course equipment and supplies			
Home and contents insurance			
Utilities (e.g. electricity, gas)			
Phone (mobile and landline)			
TV licence and satellite/cable fees			
Travel costs including insurance			
Clothing and laundry			
Childcare			
Health (including optician, dentist, prescriptions)			
Credit-card/loan repayments			
Miscellaneous (e.g. haircuts)			
Presents			
Holidays			
Allowance for contingencies (e.g. unexpected car bill)			
Other			
Total predicted expenditure			

Predicted income minus predicted expenditure	

Table Z.2 Quick personal glossary.

A	B	C	D	E	F
G	H	I	J	K	L
M	N	O	P	Q	R
S	T	U	V	W	X Y Z

Table Z.3 Personal revision timetable.

Week:

Key to subjects/topics:

	Monday	Tuesday	Wednesday	Thursday	Friday	Saturday	Sunday
Morning							
Lunch							
Afternoon							
Evening meal							
Evening							

References and further reading

BBC English Dictionary, 1992. London: BBC Worldwide Publishing.

Belbin Associates, 2006. *Belbin Team Roles* [online]. Available from:
www.belbin.com/belbin-team-roles.htm

Bloom, B. S., Englehart, M. D., Furst, E. J., Hill, W. H. and Krathwohl, D. R., 1956.
Taxonomy of Educational Objectives: Cognitive Domain. New York: McKay.

Briggs Myers, I. and Myers, P. B., 1995. *Gifts Differing: Understanding Personality Types*.
Palo Alto, California: Davis-Black Publishers.

Chambers Dictionary (2003). Edinburgh: Chambers Harrap Publishers Ltd.

Chicago Manual of Style, 15th edn, 2003. Chicago: University of Chicago Press.

Foley, M. and Hall, D., 2003. *Longman Advanced Learner's Grammar*. Harlow: Longman.

Fowler, H. and Winchester, S., 2002. *Fowler's Modern English Usage*. Oxford: Oxford
University Press.

Graham, B., 2006. *The Role of Minerals and Vitamins in Mental Health*. Available at
www.nutritional-healing.com.au (Last accessed 16 January 2007).

Information Literacy Group, 2009. *Information literacy*. Chartered Institute of Library
and Information Professionals (CILIP). Available at: **www.informationliteracy.org.uk**
(Last accessed 14 January 2009).

Intellectual Property Office, 2009. Copyright. Available from:
www.ipo.gov.uk/types/copy.htm

Jones, A. M., Reed, R. and Weyers, J. D. B., 2003. *Practical Skills in Biology*, 3rd edn.
London: Pearson Education.

Krueger, R. A. and Casey, M. A., 2000. *Focus Groups: A Practical Guide for Applied
Research*, 3rd edn. Thousand Oaks, California: Sage Publications.

Longman Dictionary of Contemporary English, 2003. Harlow: Longman.

Luft, J. and Ingham, H., 1955. 'The Johari window, a graphic model of interpersonal
awareness', *Proceedings of the Western Training Laboratory in Group Development*.
Los Angeles: University of California, LA.

Magistretti, P. J., Pellerin, L. and Martin J.-L., 2000. 'Brain energy metabolism:
an integrated cellular perspective', *Psychopharmacology: The Fourth Generation
of Progress*. American Society of Neuropsychopharmocology. Available at:
www.acnp.org/Default.aspx?Page=4thGenerationChapters (Last accessed 14 May 2007).

McKenna, P., 2006. *Make a New You with Paul McKenna: Sleep*. Available at:
www.timesonline.co.uk/article/0,,32769-2540709,00.htm
(Last accessed 16 January 2007).

Morris, D., 2002. *Peoplewatching: The Desmond Morris Guide to Body Language*. Vintage: London.

Patents Office, 2005. *Basic Facts about Copyright* [online]. Available from: **www.patent.gov.uk/copy/indetail/basicfacts.htm**

Penguin A-Z Thesaurus, 1986. Harmondsworth: Penguin Books.

Ritter, R. M., 2005. *New Hart's Rules: The Handbook of Style for Writers and Editors*. Oxford: Oxford University Press.

Rutherford, D., 2002. *Vitamins: What Do They Do?* Available at: **www2.netdoctor.co.uk/health_advice/facts/vitamins_which.htm** (Last accessed 16 January 2007).

Sana, L., 2002. *Textbook of Research Ethics: Theory and Practice*. New York: Kluwer Academic.

SCONUL, 2009. Society of College, National and University Libraries: The Seven Pillars of Information Literacy model. Available at: **www.sconul.ac.uk/groups/information_literacy/sp/model.html** (Last accessed 14 January 2009).

Shamoo, A. E. and Resnik, D. B., 2003. *Responsible Conduct of Research*. Oxford: Oxford University Press.

Trask, R. L., 2004. *Penguin Guide to Punctuation*. London: Penguin Books.

University of Dundee, 2005. *Code of Practice on Plagiarism and Academic Dishonesty* [online]. Available from: **www.somis.dundee.ac.uk/academic/Plagiarism.htm**

Glossary of key terms

Terms are defined as used in the higher education context; many will have other meanings elsewhere. A term in **colour** denotes a cross-reference within this list.

Abbreviations:

abbr. = abbreviation

gram. = grammatical term

Latin = a word or phrase expressed in the Latin language, but not 'adopted' into English

pl. = plural

sing. = singular

vb = verb

Abstract A summary of the content of a piece of written work that appears at the start, allowing readers to understand what the document contains.

Academics University professors and lecturers.

Accent The tone or inflection in the pronunciation of language.

Acculturation Adopting some features of the host culture and continuing to observe the values and practices of a person's home culture.

Acronym (gram.) An abbreviation formed from the first letter of words to form a word in itself, e.g. radar, NATO.

Action research This mode of research involves the practitioner identifying a problem within their work, study or social situation and then setting out to plan and execute a fact-finding study for evaluation. The aim is to find solutions to practical problems.

Active learning Knowledge and understanding gained from doing an activity focused on the module content, which involves thinking allied to some physical action, such as distilling notes and drawing mind maps.

Adrenaline A hormone produced in stressful situations that causes a range of physiological responses that assist an individual to overcome the perceived threat or danger.

Aerobic exercise Vigorous exercise that causes a distinctly raised heart rate, stronger, faster breathing (higher oxygen use) and possibly sweating.

Aggregate mark Sum of all the marks for a given course. Some elements may be given different weightings (i.e. count for more or less) than others.

Alumni **(pl., Latin)** The graduates of an institution. Also, as singular, *alumnus* (male) and *alumna* (female): a graduate or former student.

Ambiguous Describes a sentence, phrase or word that could be interpreted in more than one way.

Analogy A comparison; a similar case from which parallels can be drawn.

Analyse To look at all sides of an issue, break a topic down into parts and explain how these components fit together.

Analysis Using words to explain the essential characteristics of something, breaking down its component elements to allow, for example, study of its nature, function or meaning.

Ancient universities A group of seven or eight older UK universities, created in the twelfth to sixteenth centuries.

Anecdotal Idea or 'fact' spread by word of mouth, which may therefore be unreliable.

Annex See Appendix.

Annotate To expand on given notes or text, e.g. to write extra notes on a printout of a *PowerPoint* presentation or a photocopied section of a book.

Antonym A word opposite in meaning to another.

Appendix (pl. appendices) Additional material gathered in a section at the end of a piece of text (sometimes called annex/annexes).

Argue To make statements or introduce facts to establish or refute a proposition; to discuss and reason.

Argument Discussion in which different views may be expressed on a topic; one's own view of a topic, usually supported by evidence.

Article A report in an academic journal.

Articulation A formal credit-rating and transfer agreement between two educational institutions, one of which agrees to recognise and grant specific credit and advanced standing to an applicant from the other who satisfies specified criteria.

Arts subjects Subjects that focus on culture and expression and provide knowledge and intellectual skills rather than occupational or professional skills. Examples include the humanities (for example, languages, literature, history and philosophy) as well as law and some branches of psychology and geography.

Assertive The quality of putting your own views or feelings forward, not necessarily in an aggressive way, but confidently, so you make sure that they are heard or taken into account.

Assessment criteria The factors that will be taken into account in assigning a grade. See also **marking criteria**.

Assignment Coursework, usually completed in own (i.e. non-contact) time.

Assimilation (in relation to **culture shift**) Adjusting to a different culture by integrating as fully as possible in the new culture.

Asterisk A symbol (*) that is used to mark a significant point in text.

Aural Pertaining to the ear; that which is heard. In the context of learning styles, preferring to receive, learn and transmit information in spoken form.

AV aids Audio-visual equipment used, shown or demonstrated during a presentation.

Back-up A second copy of work; in computing, an independent copy of a digital file.

Banter (idiom) Informal, joking conversation (usually between friends).

Benchmark An action or example used as a standard which becomes a measure against which other things should be judged (also vb, to benchmark).

Bias A view or description of evidence that is not balanced, promoting one conclusion or viewpoint.

Bibliography A list of all the resources used in preparing for a piece of written work. The bibliography is usually placed at the end of a document. Compare with **Reference list**.

Blurb A piece of writing used as publicity, typically for a book, and appearing on the jacket or cover.

Brainstorm An intensive search for ideas, often carried out and recorded in a free-form or diagrammatic way.

Browser Software program used for accessing, viewing and interacting with websites, e.g. Microsoft Internet Explorer.

Budget A scheme, often tabulated, for predicting and organising income and expenditure over a defined period.

Building society A UK financial institution, with origins as a society offering saving packages and loans to its members, especially mortgages for buying a house. More recently, building societies have offered many of the services associated with banks, and many are owned by shareholders rather than members.

Business report A report produced to provide information that helps decision making in a commercial context. It often follows a formulaic or 'house' style.

Caffeine A stimulant alkaloid drug found in tea, coffee, many soft and energy drinks, and in 'keep-awake' tablets. Can disturb sleep patterns if taken late in the day and has diuretic properties.

Campus The area in a town or city that is occupied by university buildings. Some universities have more than one campus.

Case study This is an in-depth examination of specific social groups, events, a process, individuals or institutions. Such studies can be quantitative or qualitative.

Causality The notion that one event causes another to occur. A high degree of **correlation** does not imply causality.

Chaplaincy On university campuses, the focal point or centre for all faith communities.

Chronological Arranged sequentially, in order of time.

Chunking Breaking a topic down into more manageable bits.

Citation (1) The act of making reference to another source in one's own writing. (2) A passage or a quotation from another source provided word for word within a text. See **References**.

Citing Giving details of a reference. See **Citation**.

Class exam The exam at the end of each term or module. Traditionally, class exams were formative in nature. See **Formative assessment**.

Clique An exclusive group.

Code of conduct Set of rules for using a facility, such as a library.

College A collection of academic units that teach, research and administer in related disciplines. See also **Faculty** and **School**.

Commentary Text that explains the meaning or background of something that may be complex to understand, for example, a set of longer detailed documents or a sequence of events or procedures.

Concept map See mind map.

Confounding variable An uncontrolled source of error that varies in step or opposition with some other controlled variable. This can give a 'spurious correlation' between the controlled variable and the measured variable, and hence can lead to erroneous conclusions. See also **Control**.

Conjecture An opinion formed on incomplete evidence.

Contingency Something put in place in case of emergency or to cover unforeseen circumstances (e.g. a sum of money reserved for use, depending on circumstances).

Continuous assessment Assessment throughout the academic year. Also known as in-course assessment.

Control In experiments, a treatment included to check whether a potential **confounding variable** appears to have an effect. For example, if examining the effects of an acidic drug on a response, it might be decided to check for the effects of pH on the response, to demonstrate that effects were due to the drug itself and not its effects on the acidity of the medium.

Copyright A legally enforceable restriction of the copying and publishing of original works, allowing the author(s) or assignee(s) or their agents alone to sell copies.

Correlation The strength and the direction of the relationship between two independent **variables**.

COSHH (abbr.) Control of Substances Hazardous to Health: UK regulations controlling the use and disposal of harmful substances.

Counselling Service provided by the institution to support students, giving guidance or advice, especially at times of personal stress or difficulty.

Cramming Revising intensively.

Creative person In teamwork, someone who is good at coming up with ideas, designs or can do the craftwork associated with presentation.

Critic In teamwork, someone who reviews what is being planned or done and comments on good and bad aspects as they see things.

Critical thinking The examination of facts, concepts and ideas in an objective manner. The ability to evaluate opinion and information systematically, clearly and with purpose.

Culture shift Adjustments that people make when they move from one culture to another.

Curriculum vitae (Latin) A standard document for assisting a possible employer to find out who you are and what experience, skills and qualities you have to offer.

CV (abbr.) The abbreviated form of curriculum vitae.

Delegate (vb) To ask another to take responsibility for or to carry out a specific task, or act on one's behalf or a team's behalf (e.g. a fellow team member).

Demographic information Data that relate to changes in population characteristics.

Demonstrator A person, often a postgraduate research student, assigned to help undergraduate students during lab or field work.

Department An academic division within a university structure, usually dealing with a particular discipline or subject similar to School.

Describe To state how something looks, happens or works.

Description Using words to explain what something is, or looks like.

Devil's advocate (idiom) In debate, someone who puts forward a view without necessarily believing it, in order to stimulate discussion or argument.

Dewey decimal system A library catalogue system that gives each book a numerical code. Compare with Library of Congress system.

Dialect Language items - words and phrases - that are particular to a region or place.

Dichotomy A division into two.

Diction Manner of speaking; in the context of spoken presentations, good diction implies clarity and enunciation (clear pronunciation).

Discipline In the university context, a field of study.

Displacement activity An activity that takes the place of another, higher-priority one; e.g. tidying your room instead of studying.

Dissertation A formal written study of a specialised subject, usually submitted as part of the assessment for a university degree.

Distilling To extract the important points. In note-making, focusing on the main points, headings and examples, minimising detail.

Distractor An incorrect option in a multiple-choice question. Ideally, distractors should not be easily identified unless the respondent knows the topic well.

Drone (vb) To speak using a single dull tone. Sometimes used idiomatically as a noun to describe someone who speaks in that way.

Drop-in facility Term applied to services where you do not need an appointment. A staff member allocates times when he or she will be available.

Ebrary Commercial software used to distribute and access electronic documents, such as e-books and e-journals.

Egotist Someone who thinks chiefly of himself (herself), and usually highly.

E-learning A range of online (generally web-based) methods of delivering materials and resources for learning. See also **Virtual learning environment**.

Ellipsis (gram.) The replacement of words deliberately omitted from the text by three dots, e.g. 'A range of online . . . methods of delivering materials and resources for learning'.

Employability That blend of subject knowledge, subject-specific, generic and career-management skills, personal qualities, values and motivations that will help a student gain suitable employment and perform effectively throughout their career. See also **Graduateness**.

English for Academic Purposes (EAP) A term used to describe the teaching and learning of English language relevant to studying at university level.

Error Degree of deviation from a true value, which can be of two types, accuracy or precision. In practice, measurements are often assumed to be accurate (having a mean value close to the true value), and the more important thing to estimate is the precision (how much scatter there is among replicate values).

Ethical Describes an approach to study that ensures that the study is conducted in an honest and principled way that does no harm.

Ethics The term 'ethics' in the research context refers to the moral principles, rules and standards of conduct that apply to investigations.

Ethics committee Panel of university staff which considers research proposals in the light of the institution's rules for clinical and non-clinical research. There may be at least one committee for each of these types of research.

Etiquette A set of rules, often unspoken or unwritten, governing behaviour.

EU (abbr.) European Union (see also **European Economic Area**).

Euphemism Avoiding unpleasantness by substituting an inoffensive expression that normally does not refer directly to the matter.

European Economic Area (EEA) The countries of the **EU** plus Norway, Iceland and Liechtenstein (Note: this does not include Switzerland).

Exam diet A block of exams; the period when exams are held.

Exemplification – giving an example.

Exemplify To provide an example of something.

Expression A way of saying or writing something.

External examiner An examiner from outside the institution whose role is to ensure that standards of examination are maintained.

Extra-curricular Something carried out while at university that is not, strictly, a part of the academic content of the course (the curriculum).

Extrovert A person whose focus is on the external rather than themselves. Generally, a person who is outgoing, sociable and unreserved.

Facilitate To assist. In education, applied to actions that help someone understand something, or carry out a learning task.

Faculty A collection of academic units whose members teach, research and administer in related disciplines or support these activities. US sources may use this term to refer to the collective academic staff of a university or university subdivision. See also College and School.

Fallacy A logically erroneous argument used in reasoning or debate.

Feedback This term is used in at least two senses in higher education. One meaning refers to staff providing formative feedback on your work, giving you tips and hints on how you can improve. Another meaning refers to the evaluative feedback you will be asked to give about your course.

Fidget Someone with irritating mannerisms involving hand or body movements.

Finals The summative exams at the end of degree or a year. See **Summative assessment**.

Finger tracing The act of running your finger immediately below the line of text being read to follow your eyes' path across a page, starting and stopping a word or two from either side.

Fishbone (plan) Following a branching pattern like the bones of a fish.

Flash cards Used as a memory aid, these cards have a cue word/date/formula on one side and a meaning/significant event or development/proof on the other side. Students may opt to use them as a tool in revision.

Flow chart A type of diagram showing the organisation of key processes or a hierarchy, such as a social structure.

Focus group Small discussion group (4-6 members is considered ideal), where participants, often people who share a common experience, are asked to comment on an issue or, for business purposes, a product or marketing tool.

Formative assessment An assessment or exercise with the primary aim of providing feedback on performance, not just from the grade given, but also from comments provided by the examiner. Strictly, a formative assessment does not count towards a module or degree grade, although some marks are often allocated as an inducement to perform well. See **Summative assessment**.

Frame of reference A structure of concepts and experience that allows someone to understand or evaluate new ideas or behaviour.

Freelance Someone who is not formally attached to an organisation (for example, a university) and who carries out work, and is paid for it, on a task-to-task basis.

Free text When describing a question/answer in a survey or questionnaire, the option to comment on an issue in your own words.

Fresher A new student, especially during their first days and weeks of study. US sources may refer to 'freshman'. In the UK, freshers and the activities for this group are directed at *all* generally new students including postgraduates.

Further education (FE) college A post-school educational institution that teaches a range of qualifications below university degree standard.

Gambit A manoeuvre or ploy designed to produce an outcome favoured by the user.

Game plan Any long-term strategy to put in place to fulfil an objective (idiom, from sporting contexts).

Gantt chart A graphic representation of the elements of a project, used to show different subsidiary activities, their start and endpoints and interrelationships.

Generic That which is general, or applies in many cases.

Gist The essence of something, e.g. a summary or a list of key ideas from a piece of writing or a talk.

Glossary A list of words (like this) with an explanation of their meaning (in this case within the context of the UK higher educational system).

Graduate attributes Skills and personal qualities that have been developed in a student by the end of their period of study.

Graduateness A term that summarises the skills and personal characteristics expected of someone who possesses a university degree. The concept goes beyond the possession of **transferable skills**, and may involve having subject-related knowledge; the capability to manage tasks and solve problems; being able to communicate well; the ability to work with others; and having self-awareness. See also Employability.

Group dynamic The working personality of a group; the ways in which members of a group interact and their relationships change through time.

Guidance Help or assistance.

Hall of residence University accommodation, principally for first-year students.

Headword The main entry for a word listed in a dictionary.

HEAR The Higher Education Achievement Record that may be provided by your university to record your achievements (this may be called a progress file).

Hierarchical The quality of having a set classification structure with strict guidelines of position.

Higher education University-level education (UK term).

Hypothesis A testable theory (pl. hypotheses).

ibid. (abbr., Latin) Short for *ibidem*, meaning 'in the same place'; especially used in some referencing systems, e.g. Chicago method, when referring to the immediately previous source mentioned.

Idiom (gram.) A form of language used in everyday speech and understood by native speakers, but whose meaning is not immediately apparent from the actual words used, e.g. to 'pull someone's leg' (make them believe something that is not true).

Indentation In text layout, the positioning of text (usually three to five character spaces in) from the margin to indicate a new paragraph.

Informant In research, this term is taken to mean a person who participates in the research activity by providing data in response to the enquiry method adopted by the researcher.

Informed consent Consent given based on the sound understanding of the research being undertaken.

Instruction words The words indicating what should be done; in an exam question or instruction, the verbs and associated words that define what the examiner expects of the person answering.

Introvert A person whose focus is on the internal self rather than the external. Generally, a person who is shy, withdrawn and reserved.

Invigilator A person who supervises an exam and ensures that university regulations are followed during the exam.

Jargon Words or phrases used in a specific context. These may be obscure (little used) or technical (having a special meaning in a given situation).

Johari window Developed by Joe Luft and Harry Ingham, and called after the first letters of their forenames, the Johari window method looks at pairs of contrasting aspects of an issue or situation and organises information or viewpoints within a two-by-two grid. The original Johari technique was designed to aid self-assessment of personality, but the grid technique can be used for other contexts.

Justification In printing, this is the term that describes the positioning of the print in relation to the left and right margins. Some academic staff or schools/departments prefer full-justification, that is, where the print on both left and right sides of the sheet are lined up against the margin; others prefer only the left margin to be aligned in this way.

Key skill A skill or competence (ability to accomplish a task) learned in one situation, such as a university module, that can be applied in another context, such as an occupation. Often referred to in the plural, especially in contexts of **employability** or **graduateness**.

Keyword A word or short phrase that is associated with other aspects of a topic and that can stand for the topic or aspect in, for example, lecture notes.

Kinesthetic Regarding learning personality, someone who learns best from physical activity, by using their senses, or by recalling events in which they were involved.

Lab (abbr.) Shortened form of 'laboratory'.

Landscape orientation The positioning of paper so that the 'long' side is horizontal. See also **Portrait orientation**.

Law of diminishing returns A principle that states that there is a point in a process when little outcome is gained for extra effort put in. In the context of exams, the point beyond which few marks will result from continuing with a particular answer and where applying effort to other questions might be more productive.

Lay people Those who are not experts but have an interest in a subject.

Leader In team work, a person who takes control of group activities and delegates tasks to others.

Learning objective What students should be able to accomplish having participated in a course or one of its elements, such as a lecture, and having carried out any other activities, such as further reading, that are specified. Often closely related to what students should be able to demonstrate under examination.

Learning outcome Similar to a learning objective, often focusing on some product that a student should be able to demonstrate, possibly under examination.

Learning personality A type of person who tends to a specific learning style.

Learning style The way an individual takes in information, processes it, remembers it and expresses it (also known as a learning preference).

Legend The key to a diagram, chart or graph, e.g. showing which lines and symbols refer to which quantities.

Library of Congress system A library catalogue system that gives each book an alphanumeric code. Compare with **Dewey decimal system**.

Likert scale Usually a 5-point scale on which respondents are invited to place their view. A typical set of options would include: i. Strongly disagree; ii. Disagree; iii. Neither agree nor disagree; iv Agree; v. Strongly agree.

Linear Progressing in a sequential fashion, for example, following the order of topics mentioned in linear lecture notes.

Literature survey A report on the literature on a defined area, usually specified in the title. May include the author's independent conclusions based on the sources consulted.

'Lose the thread' (idiom) To speak without following a clear train of thought or logic.

Macro Generally, a higher, less detailed level (as opposed to 'micro').

Manipulative Being devious in order to achieve one's own aims.

Marking criteria A set of 'descriptors' that explain the qualities of answers falling within the differing grade bands used in assessment; used by markers to assign grades, especially where there may be more than one marker, and to allow students to see what level of answer is required to attain specific grades.

Marking scheme An indication of the marks allocated to different components of an assessment, sometimes with the rationale explained.

Glossary of key terms

Matriculation The annual process of registration or enrolment for a course.

Matrix A two-dimensional representation, often using rows to dignify one variable and columns another (as in matrix notes).

Mean In statistics, a measure of location of a **sample** or **population** calculated as the sum of all the data values divided by the number of values.

Micronutrients Also known as trace elements, are dietary elements (cf. **Vitamins**) required in small quantities that are essential for efficient metabolism and physiological function.

Milestone A significant event in a project, such as a meeting or submission date for a preliminary report.

Mind map A term, coined by Tony Buzan, that describes a visual form of taking notes which starts with a note of the topic in the centre of the page and uses successive branches and short text descriptions to indicate themes and subsidiary topics (sometimes also called a concept map). It is said to be more easily understood and memorised if small meaningful diagrams are incorporated into the map.

Mindset An attitude towards an issue, usually implying a fixed or rigid approach.

Mnemonic An aid to memory involving a sequence of letters or associations, e.g. 'Richard of York goes battling in vain', to remember the colours of the rainbow: red, orange, yellow, green, blue, indigo, violet.

Mock exam A practice exam, e.g. using a past exam paper and conducted with similar timing to the real exam.

Model answer An example answer provided by a tutor or examiner to an exam question, or potential exam question, sometimes indicating where marks will be allocated and why.

Moderator Acts as a facilitator in a **focus group** by instigating the discussion and ensuring that the conversation is maintained and remains on task.

Monologue A speech or talk delivered by one person.

Multifaceted Having many features.

Multiple-choice question (MCQ) A type of question where several possible answers are given and the candidate must identify the correct answer.

National Insurance number (NI No.) A unique number assigned to all UK workers, required for paid employment and to receive certain state benefits.

Navigation Method of finding your way to a place or, in this book's context, to relevant information.

Negative marking A form of marking used especially in **multiple-choice questions** where a mark or marks are deducted for giving an incorrect answer. This acts to reduce any incentive to guess answers.

Negativity A feeling that things are not going well or may not go well. Expecting an outcome that is not positive to you.

Network (1) A group of computers linked together. (2) Your personal contacts, e.g. friends, family, fellow class members, study buddies, team members, etc.

Nightline A charitable organisation run by students of London universities, providing emotional support for students and an information service (www.nightline.niss.ac.uk).

Numeracy The ability to use numbers, understand mathematical concepts and carry out standard mathematical operations.

Objective(s) Goals outlined in specific terms and tending to relate to individual, achievable outcomes that are required to achieve the ultimate aim. Ideally objectives will state 'what', 'how', 'where' and 'when' (as appropriate). Some people favour SMART objectives that are Specific, Measureable, Achievable, Realistic and Tangible.

Objectivity Having a view or approach based on a balanced consideration of the facts.

Online Connected to the internet.

***op. cit.* (abbr., Latin)** Short for *opus citatum*, meaning 'in the place cited'. In some forms of citation this term is used to refer to a previous citation of the same text or article.

Opinion A personal view or judgement on a topic.

Oral exam An exam carried out by discussion with the examiner(s).

Organiser In teamwork, someone who is good at planning activities and placing others in work groups, or is good at obtaining resources.

Overdraft A facility agreed with a bank or building society whereby you can hold a negative balance in an account. If not agreed with the bank, or exceeding the agreed limit, an overdraft usually attracts a fee or high interest rate.

Overhead transparency Transparent slide (roughly A4 in size) used for projecting notes during lectures. Also known as an 'acetate'.

Painstaking Conscientious and thorough in completing tasks.

Paraphrasing Restating text, giving the sense, idea or meaning, but in other words.

Part-marking A type of assessment, where marks are awarded to the component parts of an answer. This often includes allocating marks for adopting the correct process to arrive at an answer and for the presentation of the working and answer, and not solely for stating the correct answer at the end.

Peer Fellow student, equal.

Peer assessment An assessment where grading, or part of it, is provided by fellow students.

Peer pressure A social influence on a person's behaviour due to opinions, attitudes and behaviours of one's friends or colleagues or those of a similar age or social grouping.

Pejorative Critical, derogatory, negative.

Perfectionism The personal quality of wanting to produce the best possible product or outcome, sometimes regardless of other factors involved.

Personal development plan (PDP) A reflective analysis of who you are, what you've done and what you plan to do.

Personal pronoun (gram.) Word referring to people. Can be first person (e.g. I), second person (e.g. she) or third person (e.g. they); subjective, objective and possessive. Additionally, applicable to words such as 'ship', which are referred to as 'she'.

Pharmacy Where medicines are dispensed (sometimes called a 'chemist').

Phrasal verb (gram.) An idiomatic verbal phrase consisting of a verb and adverb or a verb and preposition. See Idiom.

Plagiarism Copying the work of others and passing it off as one's own, without acknowledgement.

Planner A diary that has sections designed to help you to manage your time and plan for lengthy pieces of work, such as written assignments.

Pointer When giving feedback, a piece of advice (that points you in the right direction).

Point size The size of a font when printed. A measure of the size of text letters, numbers and symbols. The unit is imperial, each point being $1/72$ of an inch high.

Polytechnic Shorthand for polytechnic college or polytechnical college, post-school educational institutions in England and Wales whose curriculum focused on technical subjects rather than the arts. See also Post-'92 universities.

Population In statistics, the whole group of items that might be part of the study.

Portrait orientation The positioning of paper positioned so that the 'short' side is horizontal. See also Landscape orientation.

Poster defence A session during which the authors of a poster may be questioned about its content, perhaps by a peer, a tutor or a conference delegate.

Post-'92 universities A group of universities formed following a 1992 Government initiative to increase the status of polytechnic colleges.

PowerPoint Microsoft software used for giving presentations. Allows the user to produce digital slides with text, images and other elements that can then be projected for viewing.

Practical A laboratory-based course component. Sometimes also used to refer to a field visit.

Practical tip A hint or suggestion designed to help you with carrying out a task.

Premise/premiss A statement or assertion that forms the basis for a position in thought, debate or argument.

Preservation (in relation to culture shift) Maintaining all the conventions and values of the home culture to the exclusion of the host culture.

Primary school A school teaching pupils between the ages of four and eleven or twelve. Many pupils will attend nursery school before this and all pupils will attend secondary school or equivalent after this.

Primary (literature) source The source in which ideas and data are first communicated.

Principal The head of a university, especially in Scotland. See Vice chancellor.

Prioritising Ranking tasks in precedence, taking into account their urgency and importance.

Procrastination The act of delaying an action or task until later.

Progress file A summary of academic progress that includes a personal development plan and a transcript.

Project report A written report or thesis (qv) on a specific piece of research work, usually presented in a discipline-specific format.

Prompt A reminder in a presentation that tells the speaker where they are within the presentation and what should be said next.

Pronoun (gram.) A word that may replace a noun: I, you, he, she, it, we, they. For example, 'Traffic lights are red, green and amber. *They* light in a particular sequence.'

Proof In science, evidence that indicates a hypothesis is true. The word 'proof' should be used cautiously when applied to quantitative research – the term implies 100 per cent certainty, whereas this is very rarely justified owing to the ambiguity inherent in statistical analysis and experimental design.

Proofing The process of looking at a draft (typically a printed copy) and checking for errors. This used to apply to mistakes in transferring handwritten or typed text into metal print, but now tends to refer to authoring or transcription mistakes.

Propaganda Skewed or biased reporting of the facts to favour a particular outcome or point of view.

Proposal For a dissertation or research project, a document outlining the scope and methods of the research you intend to carry out and, in some cases, indicating how you plan to organise your writing.

Prospectus A document providing information about university courses aimed at potential applicants.

Provenance Regarding a source of information, who and where it originated from, and why.

Qualitative Data (information) that cannot be expressed in numbers, e.g. the colour of the lecturer's tie or the quality of life of elderly patients.

Quantitative Data (information) that can be expressed in numbers, e.g. the width of the lecturer's tie or the number of elderly patients included in a survey.

Question-spotting Guessing which specific topics will be asked about in an exam, and how the questions will be phrased.

Quiz Written, online or oral question session, often relatively informal.

Quotation Words directly lifted from a source, e.g. a journal article or book, usually placed between inverted commas (quotation marks), i.e. '...' or '...'.

Quoting The lifting of text word for word from another work for inclusion in your own – signified by the use of quotation marks and a reference to the original. Style guides may require quoted material to be indented or italicised and indented.

Reality check An appraisal or audit of a situation that allows people to face facts.

Reciprocal arrangement An arrangement where two or more bodies (for example, two libraries) agree to share facilities with each other or with each other's clients.

Red-brick universities A group of six universities based in the old industrial towns of England, so-called because many of their buildings were brick-built.

Reference list A list of sources referred to in a piece of writing, usually provided at the end of the document. Compare with Bibliography.

References The journal articles, books and other sources used in research for a written piece of work. See Citation.

Reflect In the academic context, to look back over past events; to analyse how you have learned and developed as a person and your feelings about this; and to re-evaluate your experience on the basis of these thoughts.

Regulations A set of fixed rules for behaviour, for example in an exam, in the library or when using IT facilities. Not observing the relevant regulations can result in punishment of various types, depending on the severity of the offence.

Representation The act of representing your fellow students, for example, on a staff–student liaison committee or as an elected sabbatical student union officer.

Research postgraduate Students who are usually studying for doctoral qualification based on a proposal for a unique research study which is examined by submission of thesis and an oral examination (*viva voce*).

Respondent An individual providing answers to a questionnaire or survey.

Restriction The limits or bounds set on a task.

Review In the academic context, a text that summarises research, findings and knowledge on a specific topic.

Revision timetable A schedule for study that sub-divides the time available among the topics that need to be revised.

Rhetorical question A question asked as part of a talk or written work where an answer from the audience or reader is not required or expected, and indeed where the answer is usually subsequently provided by the speaker or author. Used as a device to direct the attention and thoughts of the audience or reader, e.g. 'Why is this important? I'll tell you why . . .'

Rote learning Learning by memorising, where knowledge is acquired but not necessarily with comprehension.

Rubric In the context of exams, the wording at the top of the exam paper, concerning timing, numbers of types of questions that must be answered, and candidate details that must be supplied on the answer paper.

Russell Group universities A group of 20 UK research-intensive universities which formed a coalition in 1994 to represent their collective interests to Government.

Samaritans A charitable organisation providing emotional support for people who are experiencing feelings of distress or despair, including those that may lead to suicide (www.samaritans.org.uk).

Sample In statistics, a sub-set of individuals from a specific **population**.

Scam Dishonestly obtaining information from someone for criminal purposes.

Scepticism A doubting state of mind.

Schedule A plan for a series of events, such as the elements of a project; for laboratory or field work, a document that outlines the background and series of steps necessary to achieve the objective of the session.

Scholarship The knowledge, work or methods involved in serious studying.

School In higher education, an academic division within a university structure, usually covering a particular discipline or subject (similar to **Department**). See also **College** and **Faculty**.

School of thought A group of people sharing a particular perspective on a subject or topic.

Science subjects Subjects that involve studying the physical and biological world and where knowledge is gained using the scientific method of hypothesis testing. There is a focus on occupational and professional skills. Examples include physics, chemistry, maths, engineering, biology and medicine, as well as some branches of psychology and geography.

Scientific method The scientific approach to a problem, involving the creation of a **hypothesis** and testing it using evidence obtained in experiments or by observation.

Scientific report A report on a piece of scientific observation or experiment that follows a generic format, with subdivisions (e.g. abstract, introduction, materials and methods, etc.) in a particular order.

Scoping Exploring a topic to identify what it might involve or include, for example, when defining the focus for a research study.

Seasonal Affective Disorder (SAD) A condition that is related to the short number of daylight hours in the UK winter months.

Secondary school A school teaching pupils roughly between the ages of 11 and 18. All pupils will attend a primary school before this. After age 16, the compulsory element of education ends and pupils elect to attend (this may be at a sixth form college).

Secondary source A source that quotes, adapts, interprets, translates, develops or otherwise uses information drawn from **primary sources**.

Seminar A small group meeting to discuss an academic topic; similar to a **tutorial**, but generally with an extended period where one speaker addresses the group.

Services When applied to housing, inputs to daily life such as cleaning, heating, lighting, electricity and/or gas, telephone, internet connection and rubbish collection (see also **Utilities**).

Short-answer question (SAQ) A type of question where only a few sentences and paragraphs are required in answer, or perhaps the drawing or labelling of a diagram.

Signpost word A word or phrase that indicates transitions between phases in speech or in written text.

Skewed When data are non-symmetrical in distribution around their mean.

Skimping Doing something with the least possible effort or investment of time or money.

Smokescreen (idiom) Something that hides the real meaning.

Sports union A section of the students' union or student association that represents and administers university sports clubs.

Spot exam Type of exam where candidates move round different 'stations' carrying out an exercise at each. Often used in subjects like anatomy, where stations might include specimens or microscope slides.

'Straw man' (idiom) A weak or imaginary opposition that can be easily refuted in debate.

Stress A response to some form of external pressure, resulting in mental or emotional strain or suspense, typified by worrying, fretting and agonising.

Structural model In relation to the planning of writing, a specific approach to organising the material.

Student Association The student-run organisation that provides support services and social events for the student body. Sometimes called the students' union.

Students' Union See Student Association.

Study buddy A mutual arrangement between two or more students studying the same or similar subjects, who agree to support each other in their learning by conducting joint study sessions.

Subconscious That part of your brain which can make you act without thinking about making the action.

Sub-heading A type of heading used to organise different topics within a piece of text. These are acceptable in some subjects, but not in others – ask a staff member in the relevant department or school.

Subjectivity Having a view or approach based on a personal opinion, not necessarily taking a balanced account of all the facts.

Summarising The act of creating a broad overview of an original piece of text, briefly stating the main points from the original but expressing ideas using your own words (other than for technical words with precise meanings).

Summative assessment An exam or course assessment exercise that counts towards the final module or degree mark. Generally, no formal feedback is provided. See **Formative assessment**.

Superscript Text, including numerals, above the line of normal text, usually in a smaller font, e.g. ^{2}. Contrast with subscript, which is text or numerals below the line, thus $_a$.

Supervisor The academic who takes overall responsibility for a student as they conduct their research according to the agreed proposal outline.

Swot, Swotting (vb) slang term for studying, especially revision for exams. Sometimes called 'cramming' in American English. The verb 'to swot' should not be confused with SWOT analysis.

SWOT analysis This is a framework that presents a style of analytical assessment. The student lists aspects of the situation under scrutiny in the context of four headings - Strengths, Weaknesses, Opportunities and Threats.

Synonym (gram.) A word with the same meaning as another.

Syntax (gram.) The way words are used (in their appropriate grammatical forms), especially with respect to their connection and relationships within sentences.

Système International d'Unités (SI) An internationally agreed form of the metre-kilogramme-second system of measurement. It is widely adopted in the sciences.

Take-home message (idiom) The essence of a lecture or piece of text. The aspect you should remember above all else when revising, completing an assignment, or answering an exam question.

Taught postgraduate Students who are usually studying for a Master's degree through a taught programme of study with a final assessment in the form of examination and submission of a dissertation. This level of study can last between 9 and 12 months.

Team role The role of a team member within a team situation, e.g. leader, worker, creative person.

Tenet A guiding principle.

Terminator paragraph (gram.) The paragraph that brings a piece or section of writing to an ending or conclusion.

Test Relatively informal examination often used to help students evaluate their own performance as a course progresses.

Thesaurus (pl. thesauri) Collections of words that are similar in meaning (synonyms). Useful for finding alternative words when writing.

Thesis (1) A written piece of work discussing a piece of research and submitted for assessment as part of a degree, often bound. (2) An intellectual proposition; a theory, concept or idea.

Timeline a linear representation of a series of events, or a project, often including key dates; type of diagram showing events in their sequence of occurrence, as in timeline lecture notes.

Time management The act of planning your use of time carefully, to achieve your desired balance of study, work, rest, social and other activities.

Glossary of key terms 481

Topic An area within a study; the focus of a title in a written assignment.

Topic paragraph The paragraph, usually the first, that indicates or points to the topic of a section or piece of writing and how it can be expected to develop.

Topic sentence The sentence, usually the first, that indicates or points to the topic of a paragraph and how it can be expected to develop.

Trait A personal characteristic, inherited rather than learned, although not absolutely so.

Transcript The certified details of a student's academic record, e.g. modules taken, performance in exams and modules, as recorded by a university.

Transferable skill Skills and attributes that can be applied in different situations.

Tutor A person who conducts (leads) university teaching, especially tutorials; usually a member of academic staff, but also sometimes a postgraduate or associate member of staff.

Tutorial A small-group meeting to discuss an academic topic, led by a tutor.

Typo (abbr.) Short for typographical error – a typing mistake or, less commonly, a typesetting error.

Unambiguous Having a single meaning; not capable of uncertainty in interpretation.

Utilities These are essential services such as water, gas, electricity for which there may be a 'standing' or set charge made for each payment period. Sometimes these charges are made monthly, sometimes quarterly. Note that not all properties in the UK have a gas supply; all will have an electricity supply.

Value judgement A statement that reflects the views and values of the speaker or writer rather than the objective reality of what is being assessed or considered.

Values Beliefs that reflect our sense of what is moral or ethical; customs, ideals, principles, qualities and standards that one feels are important.

Variable A mathematical quantity that can take different values in different cases.

Verbatim From Latin, meaning word for word, e.g. verbatim notes are word-for-word copies (transcriptions) of a lecture or text.

Vice Chancellor The head of a university, especially in England, Wales, Northern Ireland. See **Principal**.

Virtual learning environment (VLE) Web or internet-based software that assists students to learn, by providing coordinated and organised access to, for example, course content, communication tools, links or assessments from a single 'portal'. In some cases of distance learning nearly all the teaching is delivered in this way, but the norm is for VLE activities to be 'blended' with traditional methods, such as lectures, tutorials and practicals.

Vitamins Organic dietary compounds (cf. **Micronutrients**) required in small quantities, that are essential for efficient metabolism and physiological functioning.

Well-being The status of your mental and physical health, usually used in a positive sense as indicating that you are 'feeling good about life'.

White space An area of a page with no text written on it. Depending on design, thought to make presentations more attractive to the eye and easier to read by focusing readers' attention on the key points made elsewhere.

WiFi (abbr.) This stands for <u>Wi</u>reless <u>Fi</u>delity and is commonly used to denote availability of wireless internet connection.

Work-life balance Keeping a sensible perspective on your studies and the other aspects of your life.

Worker In teamwork, someone who is happy to carry out the necessary tasks to achieve the team outcome, and has the skills to do so.

Writer's block The inability to structure thoughts; in particular, the inability to start the act of writing when this is required.

Yellow Pages A book supplied to most households (available in libraries) which lists telephone numbers and addresses for local businesses and services (also available via www.yell.com).

Index

presentation of work (*cont'd*)
qualitative/quantitative research 360
quotations 287
reports 365
reviewing 277, 278, 281
tables 290-1, 292, 293
useful language 292
presentations
poster 377-82
spoken 383-91
stress related to 71
see also PowerPoint presentations
'preservation model' 33
primary schools 9-11
primary sources 179, 182, 183, 185, 319, 373-4
prioritising tasks 73-4, 77, 78, 99, 346
problem-based learning (PBL) 298
problem-solving skills 66
problem-solving tutorials 323-4, 325
procrastination 75-7, 109
project reports 332-42
choosing a project 335-7, 341
consent and confidentiality 348-9
ethical issues 346-9, 350
Gantt charts 344-5
impact on CV 337
matrix approach 358
options available 333-4
planning 343-50
practical tips 341, 349-50
proposals 338-40, 341, 344, 347
qualitative research 351-2, 357-9, 360, 362
quantitative research 351, 352-7, 360, 361-2
research interests 334-5
resources and materials 336
safety issues 349
starting off well 333
typical components 340
useful language 342, 350
see also reports
pronouns 223, 224, 369
pronunciation 228
proof 353
proof-reading 275-82
feedback 395
symbols 276, 279, 282, 456
propaganda 165, 166, 183
proposals 57, 338-40, 341, 344, 347
prospectuses 20, 23, 25
provenance 180
punctuality 58, 75, 114
punctuation 194, 198, 226-7, 286

presentation of work 291
reviewing work 277, 278
see also grammar

qualifications 12, 13, 23, 301-2, 393
qualitative research 351-2, 357-9
analysis and presentation 360
confidentiality 348
data collection 336
focus groups 359, 362
interview-based case studies 359, 362
key features 357-8
observation and description 358
practical tips 362
surveys and questionnaires 355, 358-9
tables 290
useful language 362
Quality Assurance Agency for Higher Education
69
quantitative research 351, 352-7
analysis and presentation 360
correlation and causality 356
data collection 336
experiments 356-7, 361-2
key features 352-3
measurements 355, 361
practical tips 361-2
surveys and questionnaires 353-5, 361
see also numerical data
questionnaires
confidentiality 348
dissertations/project reports 336
qualitative research 358-9
quantitative research 352, 353-5, 361
questions
asking 56, 109
assignments 251, 252
closed-answer 353
failure to answer 453, 454
fill-in-the-missing-word 307
'hot-spot' 307
Likert-scale 354-5, 357
'matching' 307
model answers 432
multi-part 321, 454
multiple-choice 298, 304-6, 307, 308, 309,
329, 354, 443
multiple-response 307, 354
numerical 305, 310-14, 330
order of 444
past exam papers 430, 431-2
poster presentations 380-1